American Audiences
on Movies and Moviegoing

American Audiences

on

Movies and Moviegoing

Tom Stempel

THE UNIVERSITY PRESS OF KENTUCKY

Publication of this volume was made possible in part
by a grant from the National Endowment for the Humanities.

Published by The University Press of Kentucky
Scholarly publisher for the Commonwealth,
serving Bellarmine College, Berea College, Centre
College of Kentucky, Eastern Kentucky University,
The Filson Club Historical Society, Georgetown College,
Kentucky Historical Society, Kentucky State University,
Morehead State University, Transylvania University,
University of Kentucky, University of Louisville,
and Western Kentucky University.

Editorial and Sales Offices: The University Press of Kentucky
663 South Limestone Street, Lexington, Kentucky 40508–4008

05 04 03 02 01   5 4 3 2 1

Library of Congress Cataloging-in-Publication Data
Stempel, Tom, 1941–
    American audiences on movies and moviegoing / by Tom Stempel.
    p.   cm.
    Includes bibliographical references.
    ISBN 0–8131–2183–3 (cloth : alk. paper)
        1. Motion picture audiences—United States. 2. Motion pictures—Evaluation.
    3. Motion picture industry—United States—Finance—Statistics. I. Title.
    PN1995.9.A8 S73 2000
    791.43'01'3–dc21 00–036335

This book is printed on acid-free recycled paper meeting
the requirements of the American National Standard
for Permanence in Paper for Printed Library Materials.

Manufactured in the United States of America.

For Audrey
Finally, a book of her own
I know it's not a pony, but still . . .

Contents

Acknowledgments

There are, as usual, people and institutions to thank:

First, there are film and cultural historians David Bordwell, Kristin Thompson, Janet Staiger, Michael Medved, and Neal Gabler. I have never met any of them, and I disagree with all of them at some points in this book. But I have to thank them because my disagreeing with their writings has made me think longer and harder than writing by many others with whom I agree.

In a similar vein, there is Evander Lomke, an editor at the Continuum Publishing Company. Evander worked on the two books of mine that Continuum published, and he encouraged me in this book and helped me focus the concept, even though Continuum eventually passed on the project.

Nancy Lathrop, a former student of mine (now Nancy Lathrop Rutherford) graciously agreed to be a guinea pig and let me try out on her the first version of the questionnaire for this book. If she had not told me some wonderful stories, the project would have stopped right there.

Ally Acker talked me into reading the manuscript for her 1991 *Reel Women: Pioneers of the Cinema, 1896 to the Present* (New York: Continuum), and while doing notes on the manuscript for her I got into the process of comparing film rentals that you will see used in this book. So thanks for the start, Ally.

My late friend Tovah Hollander put out the questionnaire on the Internet back in 1993, before the Net was the monolith it was to become, so we did not get the volume of responses I would have liked, but the quality was good. Unfortunately, Tovah died at much too early an age before she could answer the questionnaire herself.

Thanks also to my friend Mary Ann Watson, a professor at Eastern Michigan University, who passed out the questionnaire to her students.

Thanks to Ned Comstock at the Doheny Library at the University of Southern California for suggesting several sources of information. And thanks, as always, to the staff at the Margaret Herrick Library of the Academy of Motion Picture Arts and Sciences, without whom anybody writing about film would be lost. In particular, Scott Curtis of the Herrick staff made several interesting suggestions.

Leonard Maltin's annual *Movie & Video Guides* were essential in dating films, and while Maltin is the gold standard in these matters, the Internet Movie Database is beginning to overcome its early reputation for inaccuracies. The IMDB is particularly good for *really* obscure movies that Maltin is too classy to list.

Without my wife, not only would I be without a movie-going partner, but I also would not have an on-call-twenty-four-hours-a-day computer specialist to keep me from deleting the entire book. Without my daughter Audrey, her husband Daniel, and their daughter Ilana, I would not have been in position to have certain insights that show up in the first and last chapters. When my brother John went to the University of Kentucky in the late eighties, he discovered that the University Press of Kentucky published several film books per year, which made his Christmas shopping for me very easy. In turn, it convinced me that this book might have a home at the University Press.

Maria Elena de las Carreras, Virginia Van B. Keene, and Erik Bauer read the first draft of the manuscript and all of them gave me helpful feedback on it, as did the anonymous readers of the second draft for the University Press of Kentucky. Alix Parson not only took the author photograph, but helped us find the photograph for the cover of the book.

And finally, of course, thanks to all those who responded to the questionnaire for this book. I think nearly everybody got quoted at least once, so I will not list everybody's name here. Without them there would be no book.

Introduction

Moviegoing in America is a blood sport.

Not that you would know that from most academic writing about it. Bruce Austin's *The Film Audience: An International Bibliography of Research* shows that what little research has been done on movie audiences is mostly sociological and/or economic.[1] These approaches tend to be quantitative research, with the results expressed in a variety of numerical ways. As valuable as it is, the social science approach is inclined to drain the life out of the moviegoing process. After all, I used the term "moviegoing" in the title of the book, not just "moviewatching," since the latter suggests passivity. Watching movies is an emotional if not physical activity.

Numbers do not get at how personal moviegoing is. I wanted to address moviegoing from a qualitative rather than quantitative point of view, if only to restore the human side of it. There have been very few books that have gone into the territory I want to explore.[2] David Rosenberg's *The Movie That Changed My Life* is a collection of essays by famous writers about movies, but writers being as narcissistic as they are, the essays tell us more about the writers than they do about the movies and the moviegoing experience.[3] Janet Staiger's *Interpreting Films: Studies in the Historical Reception of American Cinema* is an attempt by one of America's leading film scholars to apply reception theory (a theoretical look, often with psychological research, at how people perceive films) to a group of American films.[4] What Staiger does is review what has been written about the films and how they were received, depending on "tutored" sources, that is, what the official cultural custodians and commentators had to say. In the epilogue to her book, Staiger admits, "Only indirectly has this study asserted claims about people who have traditionally had no access to public and printed records of communication. Such an unspoken mass deserves as much attention as does the popular press—if not more." I would say "more," given how often the popular press is wrong, as numerous examples in this book demonstrate.[5] But Staiger adds, "How to do this for historical readers in a responsible scholarly way, however, is a very real problem."[6]

So here I am, a fool rushing in where Staiger fears to tread. Her question is quite legitimate: how do you do research what audiences think and feel about their relationships to the movies? While my approaches may come close to some conventional social science methods, I am a film historian by trade and have no desire to write a dry sociological tract. I used three approaches to gather information for this book. The first was personal observations of audiences. I have been looking at and, perhaps more importantly, listening to movie audiences since I was a kid. This is one reason the book begins with the year 1948, since I started going to movies the year before. I still keep one ear on the film and one on the audience. The obvious limitation to this is that while I have seen a lot of films with a lot of audiences, I have not seen every film with every audience.

The second approach I utilized was to look at the box office results. For consistency I used the annual year-end listings and the lists of all-time box office champions that are published in weekly *Variety* each January. Although the term "box office" is often used, as it is by me, these figures are generally the domestic rentals, that is the money returned by the theatre owners to the distributors, not the actual money taken in at the box office. While one might question some of *Variety*'s figures, as I did in a few cases, the trade paper is the most consistently reliable source I have found. In many cases I have given the figure for film rentals, but often I have just made a comparison of a film with others in the same year, to give you a sense of how the film performed in relation to other films. This may irritate you, by the way, when you learn that a favorite, high-class film of yours was outgrossed by a film you either have never heard of or thought was beneath contempt. Every year I am appalled that some films I think are awful are among the top grossers and some I like do not do as well. The audiences may not always be *right*, but they are the audiences.

What this film rental information can tell us is what the box office response was to a film or type of film at the time of its release. What films did the audiences turn out in greater or lesser numbers to see at that time? This is different from what historians or critics may have told us. If someone asked you what genre of films in the fifties had five films—more than any other genre—in the top fifteen grossing films of the decade, you would probably guess wrong (as did everyone I asked that question while working on this book). The answer is in chapter 2.

Of course, there are limitations to looking at the box office results for films. They are quantitative, and as you have suspected, I have reservations about purely quantitative research in this area. Just because many people turned out to see a film does not necessarily mean they uniformly liked it, as will be seen with one of the highest grossing films of all time in chapter 12. Large numbers may have turned out for a film because of the promotion for a film, the star or the genre being "hot," or the word of mouth at the time being great. Box office results generally do not tell us about the change in attitudes people have about movies over time, although sometimes the grosses of reissues can give an indication. Films that are much beloved at a given time fall off in popularity, as you will see with one of the most popular—at the time—Oscar winners for Best Picture in chapter 2. And the reverse happens, too: a picture that was only a moderate hit in its time, or even officially a flop, such as *The Wizard of Oz* (1939) or *Citizen Kane* (1941), can gain in popularity over the years. Very often, as with *Oz*, the change comes from showings on television. In several places, I have included material on viewing movies on television, since more people see movies on television and video than they do in theatres.

The third approach to finding out what audiences think and feel was the simplest: I asked them. The major source of information for this book, and the heart of the book, comes from responses to a questionnaire I designed (see appendix) for this book. (Another reason for starting at 1948 was so that I was not spending all my time in retirement communities getting responses.) If you insist on statistics, I received responses from 158 people. Only seven came from a friend of mine who posted the questionnaire on the Internet back in 1993,[7] fourteen responses came from friends and friends of friends, and five came from a class at Eastern Michigan University taught by Mary Ann Watson. A total of 132 responses came from my students at Los Angeles City College (LACC). Before you complain about this only being a bunch of college-age students, I should tell you that both the youngest (in her late teens) and the oldest (in her seventies I think) respondents came from this group. One of the advantages of teaching at LACC is we have students of all ages; from all over the country; as well as from every continent except Antarctica (which is why I have included material on watching American films overseas); members of every race; and representatives of all five major sexual orientations and several minor ones. I was quite frankly less interested in getting a statistical spread, although it looks as though I did, as I was in getting people who could articulate their feelings and attitudes. Everyone who replied succeeded in doing that, some better than others.

I organized the material from the questionnaires in a roughly, but not absolutely, historical way. The flow of the book is not in a straight line, which means elements constantly connect with and counterpoint each other. What I found from the material in the questionnaires, and what is the major controlling thesis for the book, is that the relationships (that's plural) between the movies (obviously plural) and their audiences (also plural) are much richer and infinitely more complex than we have even begun to imagine. This book begins to imagine the complexity of those relationships.

The research in this book shows, for example, that audiences have a greater variety of responses to a film than we tend to assume. Generally audience response has been written about as "the audience loved it" or "the audience hated it," but for example early in the book there is a wide range of responses to *The Ten Commandments* (1956). In that same section, different people respond to different elements of that same film, which is also true later of the responses to *The Godfather* (1972). You will see that audiences also vary in the intensity of their responses to films such as *Psycho* (1960) and *Doctor Zhivago* (1965). Like several of the early readers of the manuscript, you may want to pause in your reading to watch a movie being discussed, if only to reaffirm your own feeling that *that* person could not *possibly* be right about *that* film. Do come back to finish reading the book, however, unless you find you just *cannot stand* what the audiences are telling you about the films. A few early readers of the manuscript felt this way, since they were horrified to learn that other people do not feel about movies and moviegoing the way *they* do. Some of the film directors mentioned in the book may not like what the audiences have to say about them and their films. As may those academics who will be appalled that I have been talking to ordinary moviegoers rather than elite ones such as themselves. However, this is not a book about, or for, elitists. It is a little too earthy for that.

One result that surprised me in reading the responses was how much moviegoing in America is connected with family. You will find evidence of this at the beginning of the book and popping up, sometimes when you least expect it, throughout. You may be particularly surprised at the comments about how much drive-in theatres were associated in people's minds with going to the movie with families.[8] What I have often suspected, and the evidence in the book supports it, is that peoples' responses to given films change over time, as with *Dr. Strangelove or: How I Learned to Stop Worrying and Love the Bomb* (1964) and *Top Gun* (1986), for example. I will leave other results of the research to surprise you, but be assured there is of course material about race (as Ken Burns found in doing his documentaries about the Civil War and baseball, if you are discussing American history, you are dealing with race), sex (*you* try writing about American film history and *not* dealing with sex) and violence (as American as cherry pie, as H. Rap Brown put it, years before Littleton and *Natural Born Killers* [1994]).

I left the respondents' replies much as they wrote them, but I have cleaned up their obvious misspellings and adjusted their grammar to clarify what they are saying. I hope you will still get the full flavor and variety of the people and their comments, without the aggravation of wanting to correct their obvious mistakes. I did, however, leave in lapses of memory, including my own, because of what they reveal about the way our memories handle the moviegoing experience.

As you may have begun to understand, this book is very much a view of American moviegoing since 1948 from the audiences' points of view. You will probably find some of what the respondents say funny. I cannot guarantee you a laugh on every page, but you may smile a lot. You may find some things they say appalling. You may find some moving. You may find some bizarre. You may find some fascinating. You may even find some boring, in which case you have my permission to skim. But watch out: that bit you skimmed will probably connect with something else in some way you had not expected.

After all, I have not abandoned my responsibilities as a film historian. As freewheeling as I want the discussion to be, this is not just an Internet chat room. My job as a film historian is to provide, in the way I structure the flow of the material, connections. Or, as Yale history professor William "Wild Bill" Emerson once put it, historians are to do "like the cavalry did in an earlier time, add tone to what might otherwise be merely a vulgar brawl."[9]

Childhoods

In the first week of May 1948, the United States Supreme Court ruled in the Paramount case that the distribution and exhibition practices of the major studios of the American motion picture industry were a violation of U.S. antitrust laws. This decision, which led to the major studios having to sell off their theatre chains, was the beginning of the end of the major studio system of motion picture production. At the time, few people in Hollywood realized the enormous implications of the decision for American filmmaking. I certainly did not, but then I was not living in Los Angeles then, and I was not yet a professional film historian. I had only just gotten into heavy moviegoing the year before. And I was only six years old.

I was living in Bloomington, Indiana, where I was born and brought up. If you have seen the 1979 movie *Breaking Away*, that is my hometown, although when I was growing up there in the forties and fifties, absolutely no young men rode around on bicycles singing Italian opera as they do in the movie. However, a year after *Breaking Away* came out, I was back in Bloomington and saw several guys riding bicycles and singing Italian opera. Maybe movies do influence behavior.

They certainly influenced mine at the age of five. I had become hooked on movies in 1947 when I went to see what was a revival screening of Twentieth Century-Fox's 1939 Western *Jesse James*. I am sure I had seen movies before, but this is the first specific film I remember seeing. It grabbed my imagination with its color and its setting, since the Missouri locations looked like the country around Bloomington. The action—riding, shooting, a train robbery, a bank robbery—helped, too.

Action is always one of the ways movies capture children, especially boys. Some twenty-five years after I got hooked on movies, Alejandro Munoz, one of the people who filled out the questionnaire on moviegoing for this book, got hooked by a different kind of action. He was living in Huntington Park, California, in the seventies and was taken to see martial arts movies starring Bruce Lee and Chuck Norris. His reaction was "quite simple: I was left flabbergasted.

I had been an avid comic book collector at the time, but nothing I could have read prepared me for the cinematic experience. It is difficult to describe, but my reaction to movies left me feeling that this was a fantasy. Seeing larger-than-life images on a big screen left me remembering details and scenes from a movie long after I had viewed it. In particular, I remember coming out of those martial arts movies, kicking and jumping around, trying my best to imitate the big screen heroes."

We did not have martial arts in the forties, so like many of my generation, I played cowboy. And hoped that Jesse James would come back. He did. Shortly after I had seen *Jesse James*, the Harris Grande theatre, one of two in Bloomington running Saturday matinee Westerns, announced two other Westerns and *Jesse James Rides Again* (1947). I went. I was disappointed at first. It was in black and white, not color. And then twenty minutes into the picture, Jesse was trapped in a burning barn, and words on the screen announced that the story would be continued next week. It was a Republic Pictures serial. Naturally, I had to go back the next week to find out what happened. And the next. And the next. By the end of thirteen chapters, I was a confirmed movie addict.

At least that is the way I remember it: Jesse trapped in a burning barn. The image stayed with me for almost fifty years. In 1993, *Jesse James Rides Again* finally showed up on videotape. I bought it, made a batch of popcorn, watched it, and discovered that at the end of the first chapter, Jesse and the girl (I didn't remember any girl!) are caught in a steamboat that is about to explode. The barn does not show up until the end of Chapter Eight, and then it is not on fire but just blows up.

Memory can play tricks, as many of the people answering the questionnaire either showed indirectly or admitted. "Arnold Quinlan" (Certain people responding to the questionnaire have preferred to have me use pseudonyms for them; their names are put in quotation marks the first time they are mentioned. In some cases, such as Quinlan, you can understand why they might want to use pseudonyms.) remembers at least some of his first experience, which happened on a rainy Saturday.

> My father (at least at that age, I was pretty sure he was my father) had left us on the muddy curb. He handed me a sawbuck. Enough money for me, my half-brother's ticket (later his "halfness" would fall under question), my half-sister (her "halfness" is a close call), three sodas, and a jumbo popcorn. The remaining change would have to be guarded with my twelve full years of existence. Of course, I never thought twice. Why should I? I was armed to the gills with two devastating "black belt theatre" moves. I played football and had three paper routes. How was I to know my pocket

had a hole in it? How was I to know? Anyway, on that particular Saturday—that "the details seem fuzzy as I look back" Saturday—we would
experience the likes of Buster Keaton (the one with the rock-dodging
avalanche), the Keystone Cops and a Laurel and Hardy classic (I'm not
sure which one). All I can think about is that damn hole and his damn
precious money. "You're tearing me apart! You say one thing, he says another and back again!" Needless to say, it would be a while before I would
go to the theatre again. [1]

Al Gonzalez, an actor and would-be filmmaker, tries to remember his first
movie from the late sixties:

To the best of my recollection, my first moviegoing experience was either
the Disney-type films or the Japanese Godzilla films. *Chitty Chitty Bang
Bang* (1968) and *Destroy All Monsters* (1968) come to mind. Regardless
of which came first, I remember them both as being very exciting for
someone at age five. The sight of Dick Van Dyke getting that old car to fly
was as much fun as seeing space dinosaurs beating the hell out of each
other on Planet X. For that matter, seeing space dinosaurs beating the
hell out of Dick Van Dyke would have been great, too.

I was not the only kid of my generation to get caught up in serials like *Jesse
James Rides Again*. They were a standard part of the children's Saturday matinee, and it often took some wheeling and dealing for kids to get to the theatres.
Judith Amory, who was growing up watching movies first in New York and
then in Houston at the same time I was a kid in Bloomington, had a particular
problem:

Since my father was a rabbi, it took a lot of negotiating to get permission
to go to [the Saturday matinees], but I finally did. I could go if I went to
synagogue on the Friday night, and alternated weeks on Saturday morning—one week movies, one week synagogue. This did not work out too
well, since the movies were primarily serials, and missing every other one
led to complete bewilderment. The kids sat in the first few rows and bed-
lam prevailed. The serials—Westerns, cops and robbers, science fiction,
horror—always ended on a cliffhanger. There were often yo-yo contests,
raffles, and so forth, as well as movies.

Slightly younger than Judith Amory, Sam Frank remembers how the Garfield
theatre in Alhambra, California, would have three-hour kiddie matinees in the

fifties, but he recalls, "They would always advertise 'loads of cartoons,' but instead of an hour-long orgy of these Technicolor pleasures, we would only get three. I was one of many kids who felt cheated by the misleading ads in the local paper and the misleading poster in front of the theatre." Not surprisingly, Frank grew up to become a film critic.

Both little boys and little girls enjoyed Saturday matinees. Peggy Dilley also remembers children's matinees in the fifties. "The theatre was packed, nearly every seat filled with noisy, bratty kids eating sweets and popcorn and spilling them and sticky sodas on the floor, with hardly any adult supervision. It was a blast! We were in our element, our world, where we were king! I guess I noticed it more than most because I was one of the oldest. I was at the beginning of the baby boom, born in 1948, and I took care of most of the others, except for a couple of teenage boy bullies."

Jill Mitchell recalls Saturday matinees in Eau Claire, Wisconsin, in the seventies:

All us kids would line up around the block to see the 10 A.M. showing of something along the lines of *Herbie the Love Bug* [The actual title is just *The Love Bug* (1969); Herbie does not show up in the titles until the sequel] or *Pippi Longstocking* [1970]. Susie Johnson's mother would make us popcorn to bring to the show. *My* mother never did anything like that; besides, it seemed to be sort of against the law or something. Her mom made us hide it to sneak it in. At first it seemed like a bad thing to do, but once we got it in, I felt like we got away with something and we were pretty cool. There was this old, unkempt ladies' room at the top of these steep, smelly, carpeted stairs. It had this neat vanity mirror with fluorescent lights right over the top. The ladies' room in the movie theatre must be one of the first entrees to womanhood for a little girl. You can go in with your girlfriend and stand in front of the mirror with all the other grownup women and do your best at primping, all the while watching and listening to how real women do it. It was always such a disappointment afterwards to have to walk into the theatre and have your peers screaming riotously and throwing popcorn everywhere. The world of adulthood seemed like forever away.

There were two theatres in Bloomington that played Saturday matinees for kids. The Harris Grande, a former vaudeville house, was the classier of the two and had the kinds of activities Amory remembers. The other theatre for B Westerns on Saturday was the Roxy, which was a little more primitive than the Harris Grande. The Roxy was long and narrow, which caused it to go out of business after wide-screen movies appeared in the mid-fifties, simply because there was no room in the theatre for a wide screen. It was also reputed to have fleas and maybe even rats, although I never felt the former or saw the latter. Sunday through Friday the Roxy played second- and third-run studio features, but Saturday morning, beginning at 9:15 A.M. it showed a complete program consisting of one or more cartoons and two B Westerns. The advantage to going to the first show was that it let out by noon and we could play cowboys on the way home, which took us through the central campus area of Indiana University, a wooded area of several acres that was the perfect place to play, especially cowboys.

Boys of my generation had their particular favorite cowboy stars. Mine was the Republic star Allan "Rocky" Lane. Years later, I saw several of his films again on television and he seemed rather bland. Jim Binkley, my best friend in those days, had a particular fondness for Lash LaRue, one of the more bizarre Western stars. James Horwitz, remembering his days as the self-styled "Front Row Kid," describes Lash: "He had a certain something. You could not quite put your finger on it. He made the 'Front Row Kids' a little uncomfortable in their seats. The black gear. The whip. The sharp nasally voice. The droopy eyes. The vague resemblance to Humphrey Bogart. Lash LaRue seemed to hint at things the 'Front Row Kids' did not yet know anything about."[2] Lash LaRue's life after B Westerns lived up to his image. He turned to preaching, was arrested in Georgia on charges of drunkenness, and appeared in an X-rated movie called *Hard on the Trail* (1971).[3]

Boys were not the only ones who enjoyed the B Westerns. My brother's wife, Susan, grew up in Kentucky in the fifties and liked Westerns, especially Lash LaRue. When I expressed astonishment that a well-brought-up southern lady would like Lash, she smiled and reminded me that southern ladies have their dark sides, too.

My brother, who is three years older than me, probably took me to most of those Saturday matinees. Most of us begin our moviegoing with the family, and some of us start very early. Dorian Wood, a nineteen-year-old operator of the *Back to the Future* Ride at Universal Studios, writes, "My mother told me a few years back about the time she went to see *The Omen* (1976) while pregnant with yours truly. She actually swore that the idea that she would give birth to the spawn of Satan crossed her mind and that she had nightmares about it for weeks. Anyway, when I finally came into this world, my parents dragged me along to the movies every other night."

Even for people who grow to be movie fans, the first experience can be terrifying. The first movies Wendi Cole remembers seeing "are all scary. My mother took me to a double feature. One was about bugs that set fire to people and the other was about dogs that were killing people. I remember burying my face in her lap and crying. I could still hear the sounds of people screaming though. It was awful. It was my absolute worst moviegoing experience. Today I am deathly afraid of most bugs (especially roaches); however, I *love* dogs."

Lam Yun Wah, whose parents took him to see movies in Hong Kong when he was just three or four years old, recalls, "It was a knight-killing-monster-saving-princess-type of cartoon film. My memory was that I was frightened by this movie. I didn't understand anything about the film, and I was horrified by the darkness of the theatre and by the huge images with sharp, bright colors. A few years after, I had to watch *The Jaw* [He may mean *Jaws* (1975)] with my family. I turned away from the screen most of the time and watched the light coming from the projection room. I thought then that people must have been crazy to pay and go through all these torments."

Sometimes the scariness had an opposite effect. Carlos Aguilar's first experience was seeing a revival of *Snow White and the Seven Dwarfs* (1937) with his parents. "It was the scariest time I had ever experienced up to that day. I remember feeling good about having companionship in whoever it was that took me to see it. I knew I would survive it, but it did not feel like a day at the park. That affair taught me to love movies. After that, I knew that I could feel alive in a dark movie house."

Most moviegoers' early experiences were more pleasant. Ervin Riggs, a mechanic in his twenties, can't recall his exact age at the time but definitely enjoyed his first movie experience. "[My] feet were too short to touch the ground while sitting in the movies chair. The movie was about a bunch of Muppets. I can still remember the curtains opening and the Dolby sound beating against my heart while I'm trying to stretch my eyes open to see the big movie screen. It scared me at first, but as the movie continued I seemed to get more relaxed. After the movie was over, I turned towards my mom and said, 'Turn the big TV back on.' My mom just laughed and shook her head."

Lam Yun Wah's mother also helped him get over his earlier frights when she took him to see *Gone With the Wind* (1939) at the age of ten.

> It was then shown in an art house quite far from my home. To go there one had to take a bus to a pier, take a ferry, and then a bus again. My mother secretly longed to watch the film and relive her youth; I longed to watch it to experience the glamour of the Hollywood classics. This film became a little secret between us. She bought the tickets days before, and on that day we had a quick early lunch, spent two hours going to the cinema. My heart throbbed with excitement. We watched this four-hour-long movie, and then spent another two hours to go home. Once home, my mother hurried to prepare dinner for us. I was about to tell my brother and sister about this film we saw, but I stole a look at my mother and, even with my ignorant heart of a ten-year-old, I felt mother looked guilty.

She is always a traditional Chinese housewoman, and she'd never come home so late. And she did it because she'd gone to a movie! Now my father would be back any time, and she still hadn't prepared us dinner. I shut up and felt as guilty as my mother did. I've seen that film many, many times now, and every time I remembered those eight hours with my mother when I was ten. My mother is sixty-five now, and sometimes I wonder whether she remembers that special film of ours.

It is not only the movie itself that people remember from their first experiences. Javier Rodriguez, a California telephone operator, recollects "going to the concession stand to buy sodas and popcorn with my family. And I remember fighting with my brother over the sodas and who gets to hold the tub of popcorn my mother had just bought for us to share between us. . . . It was a family get-together and a nice evening out."

Angela West's recollection of her first moviegoing experience, at the age of five, also involved food.

My father took me and my sisters to see *The Apple Dumpling Gang* (1975) at a drive-in movie theatre in North Carolina. I remember my father laughing so hard at Don Knotts that he almost cried. I'd never seen my father more happy and less worried about responsibility than he was at that moment. I realized the power that movies can have over all of us. The ability to reach the poor, the rich, the father that had to work three jobs to support a family. It was almost like a miracle worker. Of course, I was more involved in the caramel-covered apples than anything else.

Many of us first went to the movies with our mothers. In my family my mother, a former newspaperwoman, was the movie fan. The year before I was born, she had taken a trip with friends to California and had actually seen Gary Cooper on the street. My father, the head of the journalism department at Indiana University, seldom went to movies and tended to sleep through them.

Virginia Van B. Keene's most memorable early movie experience was seeing *Fantasia* (1940) with her mother in one of its late forties or early fifties rereleases. For her it is still

as vivid as yesterday. Mother and I went alone to a quiet weekday matinee. Being alone with Mother was a special occasion in itself, and she'd selected my first movie with care. I already knew "The Nutcracker Suite" by heart. We didn't have a TV and I had never seen one, so I'd never seen a moving image on a screen. The wonder I felt when the lights went down and the movie began pretty much sums up the essence of my relationship with the movies. It was breathtaking magic! Mother thinks that I was four or five. She was unsure that I'd be able to sit through the whole film, but I remember that I hardly moved and pleaded with her to see it again.

Anthony Thompson's experience seeing *Fantasia* with his mom was less pleasant. "I wanted to see it at first, until the movie started rolling, and there was nothing but a gay sound track and absolutely no dialogue. I squirmed in my seat for at least thirty minutes and then began to have an all-out temper tantrum. My mother could only take so much, and she slapped the shit out of me. I ran out of the theatre and waited for her, sitting on the lobby carpet picking at somebody's ground-in chewing gum."

Seeing a film with your mother at a young age can be helpful, as Scott Hemmann found out. He and his mother had gone to a comedy that included a shot of a blonde in a convertible. "It was as if she was talking, but her mouth wasn't moving! I remember thinking that maybe God was talking. That was my first recollection of a voice-over. My mom explained that this represented the woman's thoughts to the audience." Jill Mitchell, a film student in her late twenties, also learned about film and other things from the movies her mother took her to.

> My mother used to be a film nut, especially for Woody Allen films. I was my mother's constant companion, so I saw a lot of films—even very mature films for a little girl. I was three or four years old when my mother started to take me to the movies. She loves to say to this day that I understood Allen's humor as a little girl and that I would often laugh at a particular line before the rest of the audience. My mom gave me a lot of approval for being a sophisticated moviegoer. I am sure this constant exposure to and encouragement in the movie theatres was an enormous influence in the way I saw things growing up.

Monica Dunlap, a filmmaker in her forties, also learned from an early excursion with her mother. They saw a short film about the grooming-exercise routines of two women—one who did it wrong and one who did it right. Dunlap says she was "determined upon seeing that film to use Sunday [the one who did it right] as my life's role model, and when we got home, I rigged an outfit using my father's dress socks, etc. to imitate Sunday's outfit. As you see, from the very beginning, I already relied upon the movies to tell me how to live."

Going to the movies with mothers could also be educational in the strictest sense. Julio Carmona remembers, "My mother and the rest of my family didn't really know English, so we usually went to a theatre on Sunset Boulevard that had Spanish subtitles. Most of my first movie experiences were either in Spanish or with subtitles. It really didn't matter to me whether they were in Spanish or English; what mattered to me was that I was watching a movie." Other children saw going to the movies as a way to get away from their mothers. For Mario Franco and his brother, the movies were a "place to escape from our mother's supervision. As I grew older and started junior high school, my mother would give me my bus fare, but instead I used the money to go to the movies after school. I preferred to walk five minutes to school and then back so I could see my movie."

Brothers like mine could also be counted on to take their siblings to the movies but without the helpful motives that mothers may have had. Laura Rivas's first moviegoing experience was at age five.

> I remember my brother asked me if I wanted to go with him to see *The Night of the Living Dead* (1968), so I went. I was so happy, I did not ask him what the movie was about. So we were watching. I was sitting next to the wall, and he was sitting next to me. The movie started, and everything was OK until I saw this monster coming out from the ground. It was bleeding and saying he wanted a brain, so I screamed. I was scared through the whole movie. I was imagining things like the monster was going to come from under the floor. I just put my feet on top of the front chair. I was crying, so my brother took me home. We didn't finish watching the movie. He was so embarrassed. Everybody was looking at us. I didn't want to go to sleep that night, because I was afraid.

Coni Constantine's brother took her to see *The Exorcist* (1973) when she was seven without telling her what the movie was about. She was "just terribly grateful that my brother was including me in his plans. Needless to say, the movie scared me to death and I had nightmares for months. However, I didn't find the sensation of being scared out of my wits too undesirable, because this film triggered a fascination with horror films that continues to this day."

On the other hand, when David Bromley went with his brothers and sisters, the problem was not on the screen. His mother would give him a dollar for the ticket and some candy. "My brothers would always try to scam some of my money by offering me a great big nickel for that small dime! Tragically, it worked until my older sister caught on and smacked the crap out of them. Ahh, to be the youngest!"

When Lawrence Dotson was five or six years old, his brother took him to see a kung fu movie. What Dotson remembered most about the film "was that there was a rape scene and that it was the first time I had a seen a naked woman on the big screen. Sure, I had seen plenty in my dad's *Playboy* collection, but this one was live and thirty feet wide."

Marci Kozin conspired with her older brother to persuade their mother to let her go to see *Porky's* (1981), because it was

> about a bunch of high school kids who keep running into trouble, fall in love, you know they were just like the Archie gang. Well, she agreed and allowed her fourteen-year-old son and eleven-year-old daughter to see the movie, but she wanted to see it too. The three of us sat down in the theatre, the previews came on and the movie started, and I got to see all the way to where a girls asks some guy, "Why do they call you meat?" That was it, I was dragged up the aisleway, and my brother was left in the theatre by himself to finish watching the rest. It took five or six years before I ever saw the rest.

I can understand why my brother would go with me to the Saturday matinees, but until I became a grandparent myself, I could never figure out why my grandmother, one of the first women to teach at the university level at Indiana University, would be willing to sit through some of the dreck I wanted to see as a kid. Now that I am a grandparent, I know: grandparents will do anything to be with their grandchildren. Now in her fifties, Peggy Dilley remembers one such outing as her most significant early moviegoing experience.

> My grandmother took me to see *Cleopatra* (1963) when it first opened in a big fancy theatre in Detroit. It was just [the two of us], like girlfriends. It was the strangest thing. I don't know why she took me. It was one of the nicest experiences, maybe the nicest experience I ever had with my grandmother. It was like some kind of religious ritual initiation that set up a special bond between my grandmother and me, as if she were bringing me into a new, secret world where special knowledge and power would be passed on from her to me. I was the oldest of fifteen grandchildren and always had been her favorite, and she was, in her quiet way, the head of the family—even in some ways the head of a community, the head of a church. And she was the shyest person, who hardly ever spoke to anyone, but she opened up to me as if we were back in 1910–1920, when she was a kid, and I was her childhood best friend. The really strangest thing about the whole experience was that it was the only movie I know of that my grandmother ever went to see, and she went with me.

Grandparents can also help children get around their parents. Laurel Jo Martin's father had the same view of movie theatres that Russian political leader Vladimir Lenin had of religion, so she did not see her first film until she was fourteen, when her father allowed her to go with her grandfather to see *Fiddler on the Roof* (1971) because she had been reading the Sholem Aleichem stories the movie was based on.

For young women especially, going to the movies with their fathers can be a special event. Kasey Arnold-Ince remembers "an exciting 'date' out with my dad, seeing a Technicolor marvel called (I think) *The Magic Sword* (1962). Knights, beautiful girls who turn into grotesque witches, bubbling sulfuric streams that eat the flesh off hapless people who fall in, oafish monsters, rearing horses, and the indiscriminate use of purple velour highlight this memory." Robin Magee's father took her to see the R-rated *Blazing Saddles* (1974) when she was in junior high school, and she thought it was hilarious but did not get all the sexual jokes until later.

Going with your father could also be scary. The mother of "Teddi Lawrence" (an actress who used a pseudonym on her reply; she hopes to eat lunch in this town again) made Teddi's father take his daughter to see *On Golden Pond* (1981) when she was eleven. Teddi writes, "Because of the complete fear I had of my father, I cried (with my face to the window) all the way to the theatre, all through the movie, and all the way home. My dad didn't talk much at the time and didn't notice. My mother forced me to spend that time with my father. It was a father-daughter movie, no less. No wonder I've always had a distaste for Jane Fonda."

Anthony Thompson's parents got divorced, and he only saw his father at Christmas. When Thompson was young, his father took him and his brother to see *Pee Wee's Big Adventure* (1985). "My father took us to Westwood and we ate at Hamburger Hamlet. The movie was incredibly funny. My father was mad he had to sit through such garbage. Plus I threw up from eating too much hot fudge cake."

Moviewatching can also help the father-son relationship, as Peter Albers remembers.

The most important early memories of film for me are with my father. We were not baseball fans, or rather we were Red Sox fans. So, as I said, we were not really baseball fans. What we *did* share was a love for film comics. Along with Charlie [Chaplin] and Laurel and Hardy, we adored Bugs Bunny and W.C. Fields, Jaques Tati, Danny Kaye, Terry Thomas, Tom and Jerry, Droopy Dawg, and our favorites were the Roadrunner and the Marx Brothers. I recently saw Bob Costas interviewed, saying that fathers often don't have much to talk about or much in common with their sons, but they can share baseball together. Well, these films were what we shared, and I'll tell you something: Baseball is a wonderful thing, but side-splitting laughter, to the point where you are quite literally rolling on the floor, with tears pouring down your cheeks, that takes days to recover from *after* you finally stop roaring, is something really wonderful to share between a father and son. And as we pounded the arms of chairs, screaming, and my mother would run in and say, "*What* is going on?" I have to say I felt like I had a lot in common with my Dad.

Sometimes the nature of the family can mean a dysfunctional set of filmgoing experiences, as in the case of film student Kulani Jackson, whose godfather took him to a Ray Harryhausen festival at the Strand Theatre in San Francisco. "We watched eight films in one day. I was taken to a *Planet of the Apes* (1968–1973) festival by my mother's boyfriend . . . (who was later thrown out of the house for molesting me!), also at a downtown theatre. In addition, according to family folklore, I was taken along for a ride to porn theatres on Market Street from age three to seven. I also saw *A Clockwork Orange* [which had an X rating in 1971] at age nine (again with my godfather). As I write this, I suddenly understand why I'm so jaded and perfect for Hollywood."

Sometimes a family introduction to movies is not necessarily crucial in developing a movie fan. James Ford's parents were "not huge moviegoing people. I do recall seeing things like *One Hundred and One Dalmatians* (1961), *Lady and the Tramp* (1955) and other Disney movies, but they didn't have a significant impact. I really didn't go for singing dwarves or animated spaghetti-eating dogs. I've always been a little odd."

Peter Albers's love of the silent comedies he used to watch on television with his father began some years earlier with summer screenings in a library of old Chaplin and Laurel and Hardy shorts. Albers is not the only viewer to get caught early by older films. Ted Cantu went to a silent film festival at the age of eight and saw films of Chaplin and Laurel and Hardy as well. He writes, "My aunt had fallen asleep, but I stayed awake like a greedy demon. It was a brand new experience; it changed me. I began building makeshift movie projectors at home. They didn't work, of course, but I was transformed."

I fell in love with the silent comedies before I ever saw any. The September 3, 1949, issue of *Life* magazine ran an essay by James Agee about silent comedy called "Comedy's Greatest Era."[4] I was enchanted by it, as were other readers, whose collective response in letters to the magazine was one of the greatest in the magazine's history.[5] I clipped the article and kept it for years, even after I began to see some of the films and realized that as beautifully poetic as Agee's writing was, his memory for the details of the films he was writing about was as faulty as mine later proved to be about *Jesse James Rides Again*. The still pictures with the article were particularly intriguing, since I had not seen—and would not see for many years—the films they came from. One of Buster Keaton alone in an empty church haunted me for years, at least partially because it never showed up in the Keaton films that were generally available at the time, such as *The General* (1927). It was more than twenty years later when I finally stumbled onto the film it came from.

The year after the Agee article, I saved my pennies and bought my first book on film history—Deems Taylor's *A Pictorial History of the Movies*, which had just come out in a revised edition.[6] However, it was virtually impossible to see the films mentioned in the articles and books. We did not have a television set until 1950, and then the local station showed hardly any old movies. Occasionally, though, there were revivals of earlier films in movie theatres, as there had been with *Jesse James*. I saw *Gone With the Wind* in the early fifties, along with *The Wizard of Oz* and the 1935 version of *Mutiny on the Bounty*. None of them particularly impressed me the first time around. The burning of Atlanta was spectacular enough, but the love stories in *Gone With the Wind* did not then appeal to me as they did to girls.

Judith Amory saw the film for the first time in the early fifties as well, when she was nine or ten.

My parents had seen it the night before, and to find out if I would like it, I asked, "Are there any children in it?"

"Well, yes, one for a very short time," my mother answered. I went, nevertheless, by myself, and enjoyed the funny parts, the exciting parts, and the scenery, although I don't suppose I understood it much. At fifteen, I had read the book backwards and forwards several times and saw the movie again, this time hanging on every moment. I could have wished nothing different except more fidelity to the plot (for example, inclusion of Scarlett's two other children). I saw it a third time, at eighteen, in England.

And then! A few weeks ago it was on cable television, and I watched it, appalled. How could I possibly—determined integrationist that I was, veteran of many a fight in my Southern high school, defender of equal rights for all human beings—have seen this movie three times, loved it, and not be offended by the vicious racism? I still don't understand how someone could consciously hold the principles I did and not react violently. Of course, I saw it in the 1950s, when the concept of sensitivity had not arisen, and one could hold strong principles without seeing offense in everyday language, entertainment, etc. But I would not have thought the gulf between then and now as deep as that (even though I'm irritated by political correctness)!

So I don't think it can ever be watched again without shame, which is a pity because of the several excellent performances . . . the humor, the marvelous set pieces, and yes, the romanticism that still lingers to some extent in my memory.

I saw *Gone With the Wind* again in the early sixties and now enjoyed the melodrama of it. Offense at the racism of the film did not begin to bother me seriously until I saw the film in the late sixties.

The revivals of such films as *Gone With the Wind* were generally at one of the three first-run theatres in Bloomington. The Indiana had been built in 1923, before concession stands in theatres were common,[7] and there was a candy store next door, where you could stock up on popcorn before the show. The decor was pre-Disney fairy tale castles, which sometimes fit the films but mostly did not. The Princess was more Art Deco and rather plainer. The Indiana generally played the films from Metro-Goldwyn-Mayer, Warner Brothers, Universal, and any A pictures released by Republic. The Princess played the films of Twentieth Century-Fox, Paramount, Columbia, and United Artists. The third first-run theatre, the Von Lee, started in the late forties as an art cinema to show the foreign films, but it also occasionally showed older American films. It was there in the mid-fifties that I finally saw *Citizen Kane* for the first time. It struck me then as a rather dark and depressing movie.

The frequency of revival screenings in Bloomington, as elsewhere in the country in the late forties and early fifties, was low. However, with my growing interest in movies, both new as well as old, I need not have worried. The Supreme Court, with its 1948 ruling in the Paramount case, was going to help me out.

It is easy now to look back and see the influence of that Court decision on the motion picture business. The major studios sold off the theatres they owned to show that the companies' monopolistic practices would not be repeated. And if there was no guaranteed market of studio-owned theatres, then there was not much point in keeping under contract all those people who made the pictures with which each studio filled up its theatres. From a business standpoint, selling theatres and firing employees made some sense, although it reflects a degree to which the old moguls who had dominated American filmmaking since the early twenties were simply tired and unable to change how they thought about their business.

The creative people in Hollywood, however, were reacting to the changes in the business by making films that examined movies and the industry, both present and past. And the studios were beginning to remake their previous successes. Hollywood was starting to be haunted by its own past.

Hollywood's Fifties

Unlike earlier films about Hollywood, such as *Hollywood Cavalcade* (1939) and *The Perils of Pauline* (1947), which merely looked at Hollywood's past with light nostalgia, *Sunset Boulevard* (1950) viewed the connection between Hollywood's past and present more harshly. *Sunset Boulevard* was first conceived as a lighthearted comedy on that theme, but turned darker as Billy Wilder, Charles Brackett and D.M. Marshman Jr. worked on the script.[1] When the completed film was shown to the industry, the elder statesmen of the business were furious, with Louis B. Mayer telling Wilder he should be tarred and feathered and run out of town. The film was not only a commercial success, but it also obviously worked for most of the rest of the Hollywood establishment. Subsequently nominated for eleven Academy Awards, it won only three.

There are people in the civilian audience who pick up on the Hollywood details of *Sunset Boulevard*, particularly if they are studying film. Nancy Lathrop, seeing it for the first time as a film student in the seventies, "liked it because it was all the film history stuff I'd been reading about, and filled with all the little clichés, the mystique of old Hollywood." It convinced her that movies made after 1945 might actually be good. Her first reactions to the film, like most viewers, were to the characters, especially Norma Desmond. The character and especially Swanson's performance are what people tend to remember about the film, more than the historical connections.

Kurt Knecht, however, got more from the film. At the time he saw *Sunset Boulevard*, he was performing chores at the house of an older woman in exchange for room and board. She wanted him to travel with her, but "I did not want to sell myself out to her. I was really confused. A friend of mine suggested that I watch *Sunset Boulevard*. This film was motive force that got me out of that terrible situation."

Shortly before *Sunset Boulevard* was released, Betty Comden and Adolph Green arrived at MGM to write a new musical. Comden and Green decided to set the film in the transition to sound films, since "We both knew the period intimately and were amateur authorities on silent films and early talkies."[2] Their film *Singin' in the Rain* (1952) was an immediate hit both with Hollywood and with the general audience. The same producer's *An American in Paris* (1951), a more self-consciously arty musical, won the Academy Award for Best Picture the year before. It originally grossed almost half a million dollars more than *Singin' in the Rain*,[3] but *Singin'* has stayed more vividly in people's memories and is revived more often than the earlier film.

As with *Sunset Boulevard*, what people remember about *Singin' in the Rain* are the performances—especially Gene Kelly's. Lisa Evans says of the first time she saw the film, "All I remember is Gene Kelly dancing, but that's enough. I love dancing movies, and I personally love to dance myself." When she saw it at a later age, she "thought the movie itself was corny, but Gene Kelly's choreography enthralled me." She later choreographed stage musicals and has used Kelly as an inspiration.

As a film history professor, I have occasionally used *Singin' in the Rain* in class to show the introduction of sound, since it is a reasonably accurate portrayal of the period. Even in class what students still respond to are Kelly and the other performers, although as we get further away from the traditional film musical as a living genre, there are actually a few people (very few) who do not like it. "John Slipstone," a thirty-year old student of mine, referred to it as an "old-lady movie. My mother loves it. I can leave it," But recently I had a student who liked it not only for the nostalgia about the twenties, but for the nostalgia it gave him for fifties' musicals.

John Houseman came to work at MGM as a producer about the same time Comden and Green did, and he was also aware of the change in the business. He later wrote about the early fifties, "Now the industry was in its decline: that made it the right time to make a picture about the Great Days,"[4] which he did with *The Bad and the Beautiful* (1952). Like *Singin' in the Rain*, Houseman's film took advantage of all the skills available in the traditional major studio in order to make a comment on the heyday of the studios. *The Bad and the Beautiful* has a high MGM gloss to it, which along with its wit, turned it into a hit, although Houseman and his writer Charles Schnee's view of Hollywood is darker than that of *Singin'* and closer to Wilder's. That darkness also surfaces in many of the other "Hollywood" films of the fifties, such as *The Star* (1952), *The Barefoot Contessa* (1954), *The Big Knife* (1955), and even *A Star is Born*, the 1954 musical remake of the 1937 film. With the exception of *A Star is Born*, which had not only musical numbers but Judy Garland to sing them, those other darker views of Hollywood were not generally successful commercially.

Hollywood began to focus on its past in another way. From its earliest days, Hollywood had believed in remaking its hits, on the grounds that if it was successful once, it should be again. The fifties overflowed with remakes. To take one from each year from 1951 to 1959: *Folies Bergere* (1935) was remade as *On the Riviera* (1951); *A Slight Case of Murder* (1938) as *Stop, You're Killing Me* (1952); *Mystery of the Wax Museum* (1933) as *House of Wax* (1953); *House of Strangers* (1949) as *Broken Lance* (1954); *High Sierra* (1941) as *I Died a Thousand Times* (1955); *It Happened One Night* (1934) as *You Can't Run Away From It* (1956); *Love Affair* (1939) as *An Affair to Remember* (1957); *Sentimental Journey* (1946) as *The Gift of Love* (1958); and *Imitation of Life* (1934) was remade under its original title in 1959.[5]

Some of the remakes were successful, either artistically, or commercially, or both. I remember the collective sob of the Indiana University coeds watching the Saturday night showing of *An Affair to Remember,* as Cary Grant learns why Deborah Kerr did not make their date on the Empire State Building. Many contemporary critics thought the film was inferior to the original, but it worked for audiences at the time. And when Nora Ephron, David S. Ward, and Jeff Arch, who were of an age to have been affected by the 1957 version, wrote *Sleepless in Seattle* (1993), it is *An Affair to Remember* and not *Love Affair* to which all the references are made. *A Place in the Sun* (1951), a remake of the 1931 *An American Tragedy*, was so involving that fans swooned at the close-ups of Elizabeth Taylor and Montgomery Clift, to which the film's director George Stevens is reported to have said, "They'll fall for anything."[6]

Even though these remakes were commercially successful, most of them were inferior to the originals. I was particularly taken with *High Society*, the hit 1956 musical remake of *The Philadelphia Story* (1940), when it was first released. I could not understand why several critics insisted that all the wit of the original was missing. Many years later I saw *The Philadelphia Story* and learned that the critics were absolutely right. *High Society* seems to diminish as the years go by, while *The Philadelphia Story* gets stronger.

As a fan of the original *Jesse James*, I was predictably looking forward to Fox's 1957 remake, *The True Story of Jesse James*. It was passable but disappointing. I was surprised many years later when it showed up on television, and I realized that while I could recall many details of the original film, I could remember virtually nothing of the remake. So I watched it again, and my amnesia became clear: all the texture of small-town midwestern American life that was part of the original had been squeezed out of the remake. Its director, Nicholas Ray, was good at more urban subjects but did not have the same feel for the subject that Henry King, the director of the 1939 version, did.

Ray had previously directed *Rebel Without a Cause*, a film that certainly struck a chord with the younger portion of the audience in 1955. He was obviously trying to fit Jesse James into the *Rebel* mold, but it did not work. The 1939 film had cost $1.165 million and brought in domestic theatrical rentals (money paid by the theatres to the distributors) of $3 million. The 1957 version cost $1.585 million and brought in rentals of $1.5 million.[7] Not all remakes were catching the movie audience of the fifties.

By the middle of the fifties, movie audiences were rapidly diminishing. Movie attendance in America had reached an all-time high of ninety million admissions per week in 1946, but by 1954, attendance was down to forty-six million per week.[8] The reason given for this in most film histories is the arrival of television in the late forties, but film historian Douglas Gomery has noted that the decline began considerably *before* television began to make an impact. At the beginning of the fifties, Gomery notes that only one million television sets were in use in the country. He credits the decline in movie attendance to the move to the suburbs by returning veterans and their families, and the start of the baby boom, which kept more people at home, away from the movies. Television's arrival simply intensified the process.[9]

Some gimmicks with which Hollywood tried in the fifties to regain its audiences were changes in screen size, shape, and dimension. Hollywood had toyed with three-dimension movies as early as the 1920s, but without any sustained success.[10] In December 1952, the first 3–D feature, the independently produced *Bwana Devil*, opened in Los Angeles and was an immediate hit. Major studios jumped into production of 3–D films throughout 1953, and by the end of 1954, the first craze was over. What the 3–D films promised and what they delivered to audiences were two different things.

The idea of the 3–D movies is that since the human brain can combine what two eyes see into the perception of depth—a film technique that can let each eye see the slightly different view of that eye can recreate that perception of depth. The Natural Vision system did this by having two cameras in synchronization shoot two pieces of film, one for each eye. The films were then projected by two projectors, and audiences wearing Polaroid glasses, which allowed only the appropriate images for each eye to be seen, would get the sense that the action on the screen extended behind the screen, and in the most-used peculiarity of the system, in front of the screen. *Bwana Devil*, a jungle movie, promised the audience "a lion in your lap" and more or less delivered it. *House of Wax* had a rubber ball on a ping-pong paddle bouncing out over the head of the audience. In one of the most infamous 3–D scenes, a character in *The Charge at Feather River* (1953), trying to scare off a snake, spits at the audience. Some 3–D movies used the system creatively, such as *Inferno* (1953)—in its 3–D views of the expanse of the southwestern desert in which the hero has been abandoned—or *The Creature From the Black Lagoon* (1954)— in its underwater sequences.

Audiences turned off 3–D rather quickly—not just to avoid all the things being thrown at them, but because the systems were riddled with technical problems. Since they used two separate reels of film, a theatre had to have four projectors to run the film without an intermission: two to run the first large reel, two to change to for the second reel.[11] For proper presentation, both projectors not only had to be in synchronization, but with the films in vertical alignment as well, and with equal illumination from the projection bulbs. That simply did not happen enough.

There were also the glasses. They were made from cheap cardboard and often smelled of chemicals, and sometimes the theatres ran out of glasses. The glasses worked fine if you kept sitting up straight for the entire film, but they lost their effectiveness if you tilted your head. And they did not fit easily over normal glasses. The combined problems of projection[12] and bad movies killed off the first 3–D boom in the fifties.

There have been occasional attempts at reviving 3–D movies, with some of the technical problems solved. In 1971, a soft-core porno film called *The Stewardesses* was a box office success; you can easily imagine what it put in the audience's faces. The one inventive use of 3–D, involving a pool cue, seemed almost accidental. There was another revival of 3–D in the early eighties, but without even the brief success of the fifties. There were still the technical problems. One of Steven Krul's worst filmgoing experiences was at the 1982 3–D film *Parasite*. "Besides the movie just generally sucking all around, the theatre I saw it in was having trouble with the 3–D. The first quarter of the film was in 3–D. Then it stopped and worked intermittently afterwards. It was the first movie I had been to where the audience just got up while the movie was still going on and walked out demanding a refund, which the theatre reluctantly obliged."

The glasses were still the ultimate stumbling block for watching feature films, although they were less of a problem for short films. Virginia Keene had been dragged by her father, who was interested in film technology, to see the first 3–D movies in theatres in the fifties, but she says, "The process never did a thing for me except give me a headache," until she saw the *Captain Eo* (1986) short in the eighties:

Seeing that little film at Disney World ranks high among my "best ever" film experiences. I have always had double vision and therefore a total lack of depth perception. Everything I see looks like a photograph. I depend upon shadows and image size to determine depth. Since I've never known what depth perception looked like, I've adjusted to the handicap and never missed it—until Captain Eo slapped me in the face! What an utterly astonishing experience. I guess a good analogy would be always being color blind and suddenly having the color turned on—if only for a moment, to understand the possibility. Amazing. I was completely unprepared for the experience and so it took my breath away. I was moved to tears and unable to convey my feelings to anyone else. Something about the technology makes it work even for me—movie magic at its pinnacle!

In the nineties, the large-format IMAX system showed several films made in 3–D. As a veteran of the fifties 3–D craze, I felt I owed it to myself to see a couple. In 1996, I saw *Across the Sea of Time* (1995), which used turn-of-the-century stereopticon slides along with modern 3–D footage of New York. The glasses had been replaced by headsets with stereo sound speakers, there were none of the visual ghost images of the earlier systems, but I still had eyestrain after the forty-minute film was over. In early 1999, I saw another one—*Encounter in the 3rd Dimension* (1998)—but I cannot tell you if the headache I got was from the 3–D or from the fact that, to paraphrase Steven Krul from above, the film generally sucked. Having cast Elvira in the film, the filmmakers never thought about what two things the audiences expected to be thrown in their faces.

The most sustaining technological gimmick introduced in the fifties was the increase in the size of the theatre screen, designed to give the audience a picture much bigger, brighter, and sharper than they could get on television. Opening a few months before *Bwana Devil* was the first of the big-screen processes, Cinerama. Originally developed in 1939 by Fred Waller, its 1952 version used three cameras to photograph in three segments a total arc of 146 degrees. Three projectors in the theatres projected the film on a large curved screen, and the sound was provided by multispeaker stereophonic sound.[13] The width of the image filled almost the complete range of human vision.

This is Cinerama (1952) was the first film in the process and was an instantaneous hit. The film was primarily a travelogue but began with a ride on the Atom Smasher roller coaster at Rockaways Playland, photographed from the front of the first car. The breadth of the image pulled the audience into the picture, making several people ill with motion sickness. The film continued with conventional travelogue sequences, ending with an aerial flight over the United States. *This is Cinerama* brought in film rentals of $12.5 million and was the eighth highest-grossing film of the fifties. *Cinerama Holiday* (1955), the second film in the process, also a travelogue, grossed $10 million and was the sixteenth highest-grossing film of the decade. *Seven Wonders of the World* (1956) grossed $9.3 million.[14] Then the grosses declined even more sharply.

From a viewer's perspective, Cinerama had several flaws. The most obvious was the presence of "lines" that divided the three panels of the image. Careful composition of the shots could hide the lines sometimes, but even then the division was often noticeable as the horizon line seemed to turn at an angle at the line. In one of the two story films shot in the three-camera Cinerama system, *How the West Was Won* (1962), James Stewart's hair seems to have a mind of its own as it is caught in slightly different angles right at the dividing lines in an early scene. The system was limited to only 27mm lenses (a relatively wide-angle lens), so there was a constant distortion, particularly in shots where the camera moved. And when the system broke down, it was spectacular. When I saw *The Wonderful World of the Brothers Grimm* (1962) in 1962 in Indianapolis, one of the three projectors got out of synch with the other two, and characters walking across the screen would disappear in thin air, only to reappear seconds later in the panel on the right side of the screen. It made the film more surreal than its makers intended.

Cinerama was replaced by several one-camera wide-screen systems such as Todd-AO, which was used for the 1956 Oscar-winner of the Best Picture award, *Around the World in 80 Days*. The process had been used the year before in *Oklahoma!*, but *80 Days*, helped by producer Mike Todd's relentless publicity campaign for it, was an enormously popular hit. The wide-screen system was especially effective in the sequence where Phileas Fogg (David Niven) and Passepartout (Cantinflas) take a hot air balloon over the Alps. At $22 million, the film was the third highest-grossing film of the fifties, but its popularity faded quickly. It has never had a major successful revival, and it looks very bad on video. Its charm evaporated, and for all its travelogue elements, many of its sequences were obviously shot on the back lots of the Hollywood. Film historian Aubrey Solomon has seen it over the years and says, "In 1956, it was a totally involving experience. The scope of the production, Todd-AO, and stereo all added to the fun. I saw [*80 Days*] again in 70mm at the Academy [of Motion Picture Arts and Sciences] two years ago and couldn't sit through it. I tried once again last year at a 35mm screening and found it very heavy-handed. This one definitely doesn't hold up."

The most financially successful genre in American movies in the fifties was not, as you might have guessed, Westerns or musicals. Instead, five of the top fifteen grossing movies of the decade were biblical films.[15] They represented many of the trends of movies in that decade. By 1950, neither Cecil B. De Mille nor anybody else in Hollywood had made a biblical picture since De Mille's 1932 film *Sign of the Cross*. De Mille returned to the biblical picture in 1949–1950 with *Samson and Delilah*. Like most of De Mille's films, it is rather turgid, but the story provided the kind of spectacle De Mille was noted for. The climax of the film is Samson pulling down the temple, a dazzling bit of special effects.[16] (Rick Mitchell, a film editor and historian, had the odd experience of seeing *Samson and Delilah* in downtown Los Angeles, where the audiences are primarily Latino, shortly after the 1971 earthquake, and the destruction of the temple was accompanied by an aftershock. Mitchell was "less afraid of the theatre falling in than of being trampled by the Latino families running for the exits.") The picture grossed $11.5 million, and by the end of the fifties, it was still the twelfth highest-grossing film of the decade. The most famous reaction to the film was from someone who did not see it. Groucho Marx, thinking of the relative physiques of the stars, Victor Mature (robust) and Hedy Lamarr (delicate), refused to see any picture in which the leading man's breasts were larger than the leading lady's.

Samson and Delilah was not a remake, but most of the biblical films that followed in its success were. MGM had already begun to prepare a film based on the novel *Quo Vadis?*, about Christians in early Rome, when De Mille's film opened. The novel had been filmed twice before in Italy, in 1912 and in 1924. MGM's version came to the screen in 1951 and grossed $10.5 million.

Quo Vadis? was one of the first movies I went all the way to Indianapolis to see. In the early fifties, the general distribution pattern of films was to play them first in the largest cities, and then after a "clearance" period, they would play the smaller towns. Indianapolis, an hour or so north of Bloomington, often played films months before they appeared in Bloomington, so until I got my driver's license in 1958, I had to talk my mother into taking me. We made at least a couple of trips a year to Indianapolis and the old movie palaces in the downtown area. Inevitably these were for "event" movies, and the biblical pictures fit into that category, even before they were shown in reserved-seat engagements later in the decade. Even as a nine-year-old, I was impressed by Peter Ustinov's bravura performance as Nero and with the film's images of the burning of Rome. The rather genteel orgy scene went right past me, although Patricia Laffan as Poppea seemed like fun. I did not realize exactly how stolid Robert Taylor was in the lead until I saw the film again years later on television.

Twentieth Century-Fox entered the wide-screen race with CinemaScope in 1953 with *The Robe*. CinemaScope had been around in different forms since the twenties, but Fox, impressed with impact of Cinerama, saw that the system of lenses could be "a poor man's Cinerama," in John Belton's phrase.[17] The anamorphic lenses "squeezed" a wide-screen picture onto normal 35mm film, and an equivalent lens on the projector "unsqueezed" the image into a picture roughly two and a half times wide as it was high (the previous normal ratio was four [width] to three [height]). While theatres had to undergo extensive remodeling to accommodate the three projection booths required by Cinerama, CinemaScope could fit into most theatres, the narrow ones like the Roxy in Bloomington being the exceptions.

Like *Quo Vadis?*, *The Robe* had been in preparation for some time, and the decision to shoot it in CinemaScope was made at the last minute. By 1952, the film rights to the 1942 best-seller were held by producer Frank Ross. The head of production at Fox, Darryl F. Zanuck, bought the project once he had made sure one of his top screenwriters, Philip Dunne, was available to do a rewrite to put the script Ross had "into English."[18] Zanuck wanted Dunne because of Dunne's literate screenplay for Fox's 1950 biblical picture *David and Bathsheba*. That film had been a big success, grossing $7.1 million in the United States. Zanuck felt it did not do as well as it might have overseas because of all the talking in the film, so he encouraged Dunne not to have too much dialogue in *The Robe*. Zanuck was delighted when Dunne managed to work in "three or four good violent action scenes."[19]

One reason Zanuck wanted a good script on the film was that he was concerned that audiences might laugh at it, always a potential problem with biblical pictures and one that De Mille's films never entirely avoided.[20] So in addition to the action scenes, Dunne brought a more sophisticated view of Roman history than what normally showed up in Hollywood biblical films. Zanuck and Dunne were relieved that audiences did not laugh. *The Robe* brought in $17.5 million, making it the fourth highest-grossing film of the fifties and establishing the impact of CinemaScope.

Even though Zanuck had concerns about the audience acceptance of *The Robe*, he approved the development of a sequel to it before the first film was released. Dunne also wrote the screenplay for the sequel, *Demetrius and the Gladiators* (1954), as he wrote, "using bits and pieces left over from the original: those actors we hadn't killed off, plus the expensive sets, wardrobe, and props which had embellished our reconstruction of Caligula's Rome. It was a harebrained venture, but somehow it worked. . . . All in all, we came up with a good adventure yarn and, at least in my opinion, a far better pure movie than *The Robe*."[21] *Demetrius and the Gladiators* cost $1.99 million (compared to *The Robe*'s $4.1 million[22]) and grossed $4.25 million.

The highest-grossing biblical film of the fifties at the time, as well as the highest-grossing film of the decade, was *Ben-Hur* (1959), also a remake. MGM had had a horrifying experience with their production of the 1926 version, losing over a million dollars on it,[23] but the success of *Quo Vadis?* inspired them to try again. Sam Zimbalist, the producer of *Quo Vadis?*, was assigned to produce it, and the director was William Wyler, better known for his sensitive dramas. The cost of the silent version was $4 million, but the 1959 version cost $15 million.[24]

The 1959 version of *Ben-Hur* managed to combine the flash of De Mille (in the naval battle and the chariot race) with the literacy of the Dunne-Zanuck approach (poet Christopher Fry and playwrights Maxwell Anderson, S. N. Behrman, and Gore Vidal were some of the writers who worked on the script). The combination of solemnity and size impressed audiences, especially in its reserved-seat engagements. It was definitely a film worth going to Indianapolis to see, which our whole family did. The movie's domestic rentals were $38 million, and Hollywood was equally impressed, giving it a record eleven Academy Awards.[25]

The biblical spectacle continued as a genre into the sixties, although with diminishing results, being killed off altogether by George Stevens's monumental 1965 flop *The Greatest Story Ever Told*. Stevens was wrong; "they" would not fall for "anything." Since then, the biblical film has never returned to Hollywood filmmaking with any degree of success. The 1985 *King David* fell into all the traps that Dunne and Zanuck had avoided in *David and Bathsheba*. (Dunne had figured out that you can only have time to tell one of David's three main stories in a film, while the 1985 film tried to squeeze all of them in; Dunne had Gregory Peck to read his lines, Andrew Birkin and James Costigan had Richard Gere.) Martin Scorsese's 1988 debacle *The Last Temptation of Christ* managed to eke out some positive critical comments, although some came from critics who did not want to give any ammunition to the Christian Right attacking the film.[26]

Although *Ben-Hur* made more money at the time, the one biblical film from the fifties that everybody remembers is Cecil B. De Mille's 1956 remake of his 1923 film *The Ten Commandments*. It cost $14 million[27] to make and was the second highest-grossing film of the fifties, with rentals of $34.2 million at the end of the decade. Its subsequent reissues over the years have raised its rentals above *Ben-Hur*'s to $43 million.[28] Its impact over the years has been more pervasive than *Ben-Hur*'s. *The Ten Commandments* is not as good a movie as *Ben-Hur*, but it is more fun. It also appeals to audiences in more different ways than almost any other movie. Angela West was only seven when she saw the movie and liked it because it was "such a collection of different genres: romance, adventure, suspense, drama. I felt as if I was on a roller coaster. I also learned a lot in an educational sense about the Bible and the history of the people." Martin Scorsese also responded to the variety of elements in the film, "I like De Mille, his images, his theatricality. I've seen the film forty or fifty times. Forget the script—you've got to concentrate on the special effects, the texture, the color. The Angel of Death killing the firstborn children in green smoke. The Red Sea, the lamb's blood of the Passover, the parting of the waters. De Mille presented a fantasy, dreamlike quality on film that was so real, it excited me as a child and stuck with me for life."[29]

Donna Crisci also saw it as a child. "I thought it was great fun. Yul Brynner, who had already made me cry in *The King and I* (1956), was my idea of handsome, and I fell for every cliché and heartwrenching moment in the thing." She and her friends went around playing "Hebrew slave" afterwards. (Crisci seems susceptible to that sort of thing: several years later she and her friends saw

Cleopatra and went home and put sequins on her eyelids.) Monica Dunlap also saw the film as a child, but only remembers "a jumble of chariots."

Lam Yun Wah saw the film first as a child, then saw it again in a theatre when he was fifteen. To keep himself from going crazy after examinations in school, he went to a film every day. When he got to the theatre for *The Ten Commandments*, it was so full he had to sit in the front row. He had forgotten the film runs nearly four hours and that in this theatre, it ran without an intermission. "The images were so big, the music was so loud . . . I almost broke my back" sitting in the front row.

Although the film was certainly imposing, some viewers had concerns about its religious accuracy. Jon Conrad was also taken to see it when he was a kid and was "very involved and impressed, although even then I wondered about all the additions to the Bible narrative." Jack Hollander, the son of a rabbi, watched it a lot as a child, but "I have seen it too many times, and I have no compulsion to rehash this ridiculous plot (I'm referring to the trash that was NOT in the Bible—why couldn't the filmmakers stick to the *original* screenwriter!)."

Others were more impressed with the religious aspects of it. Olufemi Samuel says, "Believe it or not, it moved me closer to the Lord! This movie really revealed the power of the Almighty Lord, and I was very moved." Douglas Choe's view of the film is not quite so effusive: "God is a big, mean guy." And Dennis Wilkes was only temporarily affected by the film's religious aspects. It "instilled the fear of God in me. Fortunately I grew out of it." Alejandro Munoz says he has "the most profound relationship [with the film] than any other movie I have ever seen. Primarily because this is a movie that deals with Christ [wrong Testament—Jesus does not even make a cameo appearance] and I am a devout Catholic. This is the only movie I ever recall viewing as an entire family, and this act was repeated almost every year during my adolescence. . . . In short, this film is tied to me more spiritually than cinematically."

Munoz's comments mention an element of the film that has helped to sustain its popularity. Whereas many successful films have been shown often on television, *The Ten Commandments* has been shown on a regular basis for many years, usually on a Sunday near Easter and Passover. T. Taylor, an actress, thinks the film "had a pretty big influence on the shaping of my religious views. Yes, our society does need moral structure. Today my views are a little different. I'm glad I grew up with this film rather than *Pulp Fiction* (1994) and MTV."

Peggy Dilley,[30] who introduced herself in the first line of her reply to the questionnaire as someone who had been diagnosed as schizophrenic, also remembers the family ritual of watching. "*The Ten Commandments* was a big event in my religiously oriented, Baptist, some turned to Jehovah's Witnesses, family. I think I saw it on some holiday, probably Easter. We either gathered around the TV; my mom, my three brothers and me, in our apartment in the basement of my grandparents; or else we all watched it upstairs in my grandparents' cozy living room with a fire going. Maybe it was Christmas. Make it up any way you like. Memory is never factual, you know. Maybe I'm making this all up, and I was an orphan."

Wajeeh Khursheed first saw it on videotape in Nigeria in the early eighties. "We passed this tape around among all our friends just so that we could watch the famous parting of the sea." Kalani Mondoy saw the film on television every Easter with his family, but has never seen it on the big screen in a theatre, although he would like to, to see all the "great miracles." D'Arcy West thinks she may have seen it on television, although she admits she may be thinking of some other Technicolor biblical epic. She adds, "It was fairly engrossing, though. I would choose that movie over MTV."

The family viewings brought a variety of reactions. Skylaire Alfvegren was forced through many viewings of *The Ten Commandments* and resents the film. "I thought it was corny. I didn't like the topic. Biblical themes brought to film are just a horrible combination. I do remember thinking Charlton Heston was really, really grand, though. That flowing white hair, that self-confident stance, that godly voice, such a commanding presence." H. Peter Albers saw the film on television as a kid and "Back then I thought Charlton Heston was a good actor." Valerie Hornig, like Donna Crisci, was impressed more with Yul Brynner, and she was also impressed with Yvonne De Carlo (who played Sephora, Moses's wife), saying those two actors gave "very passionate performances with a tried-and-true story line."

Because it is a film seen by many people many times over a period of years, attitudes about *The Ten Commandments* change. Donna Crisci, who was impressed with it in the theatres, now watches it and "laughs at the campy acting, (especially [Anne] Baxter's 'Oh, Moses, Moses.' 'Who is this fair young god, come into Pharaoh's court?' But then, who *could* say those lines?) but can enjoy it through the hoot." As a kid, Al Gonzalez liked the parting of the Red Sea, and "when God wrote with fire, I thought his movie ranked as high up on my list as all those Godzilla movies. Well, I grew up and caught a few minutes of it on TV recently. I still think it's great. It makes me laugh more than most comedies made today can. And I still rank it with the Godzilla movies." Alex Kuyumjian saw *The Ten Commandments* many times over the years and "seemed to have liked it better the last time I saw it. The effects of the water parting were really done quite well for how old the film was. The actors in this film were at their best as well." Shaun Hill-Kret says, "As a kid, this movie blew me away with all the special effects and large crowd scenes. I found it breathtaking. Now, fifteen years later when I watch it, I find it cheesy." Kulani Jackson saw it *then* and was "most excited by the parting sea" and seeing it *now* "laughed at C. Heston." "Michael Thomas" thinks films like *The Ten Commandments* "lost a lot of their power because they no longer have any spiritual impact on my life." Aubrey Solomon saw the film in its first-run engagements and was impressed: "The plagues were very exciting at age eight," and "To this day, it's still a marvel of moviemaking, although its windy preachiness gets to me. I almost wish Yul Brynner would win for a change."

As evidenced by some of the comments above, the moviemaking skills involved in *The Ten Commandments*—particularly the special effects—were what have dazzled the audiences of the film for forty years. Dorian Wood has a reason for remembering the deliverance of the commandments. "The strange thing was that when the Mount Sinai-burning bush sequence [actually, they are two different sequences] would come on, my parents would always nearly shove my face into the screen, asking me to pay close attention to the commandments being dictated by God, in the form of a swirling flame. So whenever I'd go to Sunday School, the nun would go over the Ten Commandments, I'd always be reminded of the rising flame, and I'd get really scared."

The effect that most people remember is the parting of the Red Sea. Rick Mitchell saw it in its original road show engagement, and it became "the film that really triggered my interest in special effects, which I had previously taken for granted in science fiction films I'd seen. Like most kids of the time, I was attracted by that long trailer which built up to, then teasingly dissolved out of, the opening to the Red Sea. I initially sat through the first three hours of the film waiting for it rather than paying too much attention to the film."

Javier Rodriguez saw the film for the first time in a theatre and says, "I was amazed at the special effects. The one at the Red Sea was so powerful. But what I liked was how the sea parted. I mean it looked so real and almost natural on the screen." Nancy Lathrop had heard about the Red Sea parting for years before she saw it, and when she finally saw it, she said, "That looks fake."

I was not entirely persuaded when I saw the film in its first-run theatrical engagements. The water looked like it was too many different colors in too many places. Although the film did win an Academy Award for special effects, even the people who worked on the film knew the parting of the Red Sea was not as good as it could have been. The special effects work got rushed in the final days of postproduction work, and De Mille ended up approving shots that really should have been taken through another pass or two in the printing stage.[31] Sometime in the late eighties or early nineties, without any publicity, Paramount made adjustments to the videotape of the film. The parting of the Red Sea looked more convincing on videotape than it did in the original film, which was appropriate, since more people see the film on television than they do in the theatres. There was an announcement by Paramount in 1997 that it had restored the film digitally, since "original elements and sequences had deteriorated in parts of the movie."[32] The company did not mention if the parting of the Red Sea was one of those parts.

There was another sequence of *The Ten Commandments* that people often responded to. The one scene that has stayed with Eva Mahgrefthe is "the drunken revelry and fashioning of the Golden Calf when Moses left to receive the commandments. I enjoyed the carnival-like atmosphere, all the while nervous knowing they would shortly feel Moses's wrath." Others found it memorable as well. Albert Nazaryan was only seven and had only recently come to the United States when he first saw *The Ten Commandments* on television. "All I can recall were the slave girls and the Golden Calf sequence and how it got me excited. My parents must have been pleased for my enthusiasm for the Bible."

De Mille had provided everything for the middle-class American audience: action, adventure, history, the Bible, special effects, an enormous and detailed physical production, and of course, as De Mille's 1940s stablemate at Paramount Preston Sturges put it in *Sullivan's Travels* (1941), "a little sex."

Sex and Seriousness

I hit the first stages of puberty in the summer of 1953, when I was eleven years old, and I began to develop a serious addiction to movie starlets. For reasons that baffle me to this day, I was particularly susceptible to the charms of several contract actresses at Twentieth Century-Fox. In theory, at that time it should have meant Marilyn Monroe. For me personally, it certainly should have meant Monroe. In late 1951 or early 1952, my uncle Bud, my mother's brother, gave me a calendar with a beautiful naked blonde woman lying on a red sheet. (My mother was surprisingly liberal about this and the Playboy magazines my brother and I brought home later in the fifties, much to the astonishment and delight of the other boys in the neighborhood.) I was a little underdeveloped to completely appreciate the calendar at the time, although I liked the idea of it. I liked it even more when the news story broke in early March 1952 that the girl on the calendar was Fox starlet Marilyn Monroe. My bedroom became a shrine the local boys made pilgrimages to.

Still, Monroe—then and throughout the fifties—just didn't seem my type. There was certainly both a carnal and a comic appeal, but I was much more taken with her partner in the 1953 film *Gentlemen Prefer Blondes*, Jane Russell, and not particularly because of Russell's famous superstructure. Russell not only seemed a little more grown-up than Monroe, but she seemed smarter. Smart, older women have always appealed to me.

Having revealed my preference, I can easily explain my crush on Paramount's Audrey Hepburn, but how can I explain being infatuated with Fox's Terry Moore? Well, she was perky and very wet in movies like *Beneath the Twelve-Mile Reef* (1954). But then I also have to admit to a crush on Debra Paget, another Fox starlet at the time, and one of the blandest young actresses ever to appear in films. I suppose we all have past crushes on movie stars (and people in real life as well) that we feel embarrassed about now.

In theory, to be politically correct, I should be embarrassed to admit to a crush on the Rita Moreno who was a Fox starlet in the fifties, while admiring the Moreno who has done much better work later: winning an Academy Award for *West Side Story* (1961), and winning Emmies and Grammies for television and recording work. Moreno has spoken out often since the fifties about how she felt humiliated to have to play the stereotype of the "barefoot spitfire" Latina in movies like *Garden of Evil* (1954),[1] while wanting to play more conventional parts. But in the fifties, she was not generally allowed to show the range of her talent, and I was reacting to what I saw. And what I saw was someone totally different from anybody I knew in Bloomington, Indiana. We may have had barefoot "poor white trash," but we did not have any barefoot Latina spitfires that I knew of, and I had not been around to see any of the earlier women of that type on the screen, such as Lupe Velez. Moreno was exotic, very appealing because she was different, and showed more passion on the screen than most of the conventional white heroines in films. The fact that she was consistently barefoot may have been the beginning of the minor foot fetish I have to this day. And just to make the issue of political correctness even more complicated, I do admire all the efforts Moreno has made to overcome the stereotypes and the way she has run her career. Lust—adolescent or otherwise—can evolve into affection, amusement, and nostalgia.

As with the Marilyn Monroe calendar and me, movies early on tickle kids' imagination about the possibility of sex. In the sixties, Nancy Lathrop was still going to kids' matinees and was "spending many a Saturday afternoon wondering why it was I couldn't see that film called *Alfie* (1966), why I had to go and see some *13 Ghosts* (1960) or *Everything's Ducky* (1961), and this *Alfie* thing was getting a lot of press, and I couldn't go see it. It was rated M for 'Mature.' And *The Honey Pot* (1967) with Rex Harrison. I remember a big poster in the lobby for this. *The Honey Pot*. It was very scandalous."

Before he hit puberty, James Ford saw the 1965 film *Dear Brigitte*, about a young boy who had a crush on Brigitte Bardot. Ford "felt just like that little boy in the film. I was in love with Brigitte Bardot. Just the thought of her made me giddy. It was hard for me to look at her on the screen because of the feelings she evoked in me (which of course I didn't understand). Witness the birth of my sexual awareness. Who better than the Sex Kitten herself." Ford's crush on Bardot lasted a year or two until he saw Jane Fonda in *Cat Ballou* (1965). Fonda was "so sexy, Brigitte had to take a back seat."[2]

Paul Sbrizzi also found "Movies gave me my first exposure to sex and the strange. When I was nine, my mom took me to a Sherlock Holmes film [Billy Wilder's *The Private Life of Sherlock Holmes* (1970)] in which a famous ballerina tries to get Holmes to impregnate her. When he demurs, the ballerina asks him if she's not his cup of tea and Holmes, to get out of it, replies that Watson is his cup of tea. My curiosity was piqued but I don't think I got what they were talking about until years later." Sbrizzi also sneaked into *The Andromeda Strain* (1971), which he remembers as being rated R but was in fact rated G. He was ten and remembers "experiencing an odd feeling of giddiness when they showed the scientists stripped buck-naked."

Girls develop crushes on male stars as well. Marion Levine "learned how to fall obsessively in love by watching Dustin Hoffman chase after Katharine Ross in *The Graduate* (1967, when Levine was fifteen). In fact, I sneaked on forbidden makeup and rolled up the waistband of my skirt so just in case Dustin looked past the screen and saw me faithfully pining for him in the fourth row for the fifth time, he might think I was as cute as Katharine Ross and chase after me." "Rudie Bravo" had my "first crush on the character Billy Jack [in the 1971 film of the same name]. Billy Jack was the first person I'd ever encountered, man or woman, real or fictional, that had a *code*, a set of principles by which he lived his life. I think I still have a crush on him! I am always deeply shocked, and a little hurt, when someone criticizes any aspect of Billy Jack." On the other hand, Bravo did not respond to one of the most renowned movie love objects. She did not like the character of Scarlett in *Gone With the Wind*, nor Ashley Wilkes, and as for Clark Gable in the picture: "And Rhett rapes Scarlett and he's a 'real man.' Oh, please, don't make me sick. I was really too young to think all this cerebrally. It was more of an intense discomfort. All through grade school I had a crush on a black guy who sat next to me. The whole slavery thing, and the fact that there were *no* black people in the entire audience (there always had been, in other movies I'd seen at the Ozark), really, really bothered me." She later saw Gable in the earlier *It Happened One Night* (1934) and began to "'get' the Gable thing."

Though the idea of sex was exciting, it could also be unnerving. One of Debra de St. Jean's most memorable experiences was when she was twelve and went with her older sister to see *Saturday Night Fever* (1977). "Of course, as all the girls did, I fell in love with John Travolta. But the things that shocked me the most about the film were the language and the nudity. I had never heard such language, and never before had I seen nudity. I remember the shock I felt—it took me a couple of days to adjust." Don Ricketts was thirteen when the film came out, and his older brother took him to it behind their parents' backs. In hindsight, Ricketts thinks his brother took him "because he wanted to prove to me he had it all grooved in already with the opposite sex and it was my great fortune to learn from the master: Him. Of course he wasn't learning anything from John Travolta that he didn't already know. He was just there to guide me to pick up some pointers." But Ricketts felt the education was too early for him.

Even going to the movies with a church group could not keep a kid's mind off sex. In the early sixties, Jon Conrad's youth group leader took the group to some contemporary movies he thought would provoke interesting discussions. One film was *Dr. Strangelove*, which Conrad and the other kids "all found entertaining, partly because it was 'dirty' [Tracy Reed in the bikini early in the picture and all that discussion of precious bodily fluids]—I must have just been starting high school." After the word got around, the kids' parents "got [the youth group leader] to discontinue the plan."

Scott Oppenheimer started getting interested in sex as a kid when he would go to movies with his parents "hoping to see breasts." At the age of thirteen, he made attempts—"usually successful" he says—to see hard-core porno movies, and he later spent most of *The Exorcist* with his first love, "crawling all over her and not watching much of the movie, annoying the hell out of her, part of the time anyway." Anthony Thompson, who had the temper tantrum at *Fantasia* and threw up after *Pee Wee's Big Adventure*, had his best experience at the then-new Beverly Center Cineplex in Los Angeles. "I actually kissed a girl. The thing that was so great about it was that I even got to hold her breast inside of her brassiere. I have never felt that good since."

On the other hand, Oscar Berkovich learned early to go to the movies alone because, "If I go, for example, with my girlfriend, I can't concentrate on the picture the same way. Don't get me wrong, I love their company, but when it comes to movies, it's a different story. They're constantly asking questions or they want something to eat or drink just when the film begins to be interesting, and personally I just detest that."

Even if they are not your date, girls at the movies can still be a distraction. When he was in his teens, Richard Gonzalez and two of his friends, Lyle and Darius, went to the big old State theatre in downtown Los Angeles to see a triple bill of action pictures. In the middle of the first feature, sitting about five rows from the front, he started to get bored.

> But these girls, that had somehow managed to get into the theatre for free, sensed that the crowd was starving for "real" entertainment. To make sure that they did get the attention, the two girls raced down from the east end of the aisle of the theatre on skateboards wearing skimpy outfits. They got so close to the screen that they looked like some 3–D movie effect. I sure didn't know what to make of it, as Lyle and Darius apparently did.
>
> Those two girls were so boisterous, they seemed to resemble children the way they giggled so gaily. They sat down in the front row to the side and began to whisper to each other. They were up to something, I figured. And only then did I realize that something *was* going down when the two girls had their eyes set on where the three of us were sitting. I could eliminate any possible notion that the girls were interested in any of us. I denied the most obvious thing that was happening: the two girls walked up to our seats and asked us if we wanted to sit with them in the front row, turning my erotic fantasy into stark reality.

I was baffled. I never had a dream come true in a matter of minutes— perhaps it was the power of suggestion. Or so I thought. It turned out that the girls were only trying to get their boyfriends jealous . . . to the point of them wanting to kick our asses. But I got the best end of the deal that day. Lyle and I both scammed on those two girls that day, but the girl Lyle was with was the most troublesome. She tried to get him beat up outside the theatre. The boyfriends waited with their girls in front of the box office for us three. Lyle's date asked him for a cigarette, which he obliged. The girl took the cigarette from Lyle, and her hand brushed against his. Her boyfriend saw this and got in Lyle's face and tried to pick a fight with him. It was all a messy relationship with those girls that day. . . . Maybe *too* much cinema is bad for one's own personal life.

The girls Brad Long met at the movies in his teens were less trouble. He would get his mother to drop him off at the mall cinemas before he got his driver's license. He would meet girls at the mall and talk them into seeing the movie he was going to see. "If they wanted to see something else, I would tell them I had seen it and how bad it was. Once in the theatre, I was in my element. It was dark, the seats were close together, and hormones were on my side. I can remember making out until the credits ended and the lights were coming up. It was in a movie theatre where I kissed my first girl, felt my first breast, and had my first mutual touching below the waist, all of this years before I would have a car. A head start in life and I owed it all to the movies."

A car, of course, could take you to a drive-in theatre. Drive-ins, particularly in the fifties, got the nickname of "passion pits" because of all the sexual activity supposedly going on in the parked cars. However, more people remember the drive-in as a *family* rather than a sexual affair. Virginia Keene, who was a child in the fifties, has pleasant memories of going to the drive-in with her family.

It seems to me now that I grew up in the back seat of a station wagon at the drive-in theatre! We went often, a couple of times a week, and we saw every conceivable kind of movie, usually in double features. . . .

More than anything I remember the Westerns, perhaps because they were my father's favorites. Mother packed sandwiches and thermoses, and there were pillows and blankets. I always hung over the back seat in rapt attention, while my little sister slept in the "way back." Trips to the concession stand for popcorn were a real privilege, and sometimes there were jungle gyms and slides up front and special chairs for children to watch the movies. If it was really hot and we promised to be still, we were allowed to lie on a blanket on the hood. No matter how often we went, it was a special family event—a family picnic at the movies. I loved it more than anything.

Lisa Moncure's family had similar outings in the sixties, and "the feel of the cold metal and the sound the speakers make as they hit the glass on the window, as well as the quality of the sound they emit, take me right back to those days." Coni Constantine also went with her family, "decked out in my jammies, of course," and remembers that "there was just something about being up really late in the cool night air, watching, not one, but *two* movies on that big screen that always held a kind of fascination for me." On the other hand, Marilyn Heath, a mother in her forties who takes her three kids to the drive-in, sees the experience now from a parent's perspective: "euphoria with a little slice of hell."

The family experience at the drive-in was particularly strong in the Latino community in Los Angeles. Rick Lopez says,

> One of my earliest childhood recollections is going to the drive-in theatre with my parents to see Cantinflas movies. What had probably become a landmark for thousands of first generation Chicanos, the Floral Drive-in in East Los Angeles, was the place to go to see Mexican movies. Lines to get in were always long, and it was typical for the authorities to send people away. Although there were plenty of second- or third-rate theatres showing the same movies, people preferred to go the Floral. It wasn't so much the movies that attracted people, but the festive atmosphere during and after the screenings. It seemed as though everyone knew each other, because no matter where we parked, we would always bump into someone we knew—a friend, a neighbor, or relative . . .
>
> Ever since I was young, I always enjoyed the movies. And whether the movie was a masterpiece or a churro (a Mexican turkey) I always managed to "willfully suspend my disbelief" regardless of the commotion. One of the worst things that could happen at the Floral was fights. It wasn't until a man was stabbed to death that the city and the drive-in began to seriously prohibit alcohol.

Richard Gonzalez's parents also took their family to the Floral and it was "the only weekly ritual we never grew tired of. Looking back on it now, it seems a lot of prestige came with the fact that we were a family unit and our dad cared enough about us to take us all to the drive-in every Tuesday night. But it was kind of tacky when my mom would dress in perfect matching clothing just to go out on a drive-in date with her husband and five children. Tuesday night she cared about the way she looked."

The drive-in experience was not solely a North American phenomenon. Lizy

Moromisato grew up in Peru and remembers family outings at a drive-in there. "It was one of the few occasions that I had going out with both my parents, and also because I had the chance to have a milkshake while watching the movie. Perfect!"

David Ko had two sisters and one brother and

the four of us would just sit there on the hood of our monster Plymouth Fury station wagon watching these animated Disney features. We knew we were growing taller when the people behind us complained that we were blocking their view when we sat on the roof of the car. I remember making a big grocery bag full of popcorn and taking it to the drive-in. We would bring our blankets and pillows and set camp on the hood of that old V-8. I don't know how our parents even saw the movie with our big heads leaning against the window. The stars were shining in the sky, and the glow of the screen captivated us into a trance of wonderment. I lived in Hawaii, so it never got cold at all, and we would be cozily bundled, transfixed on the images of the screen.

Perhaps even more than indoor theatres, drive-ins call to mind eating food from the snack bar. Peggy Dilley's first moviegoing experience was at a drive-in, and her father bought her a cherry soda. "I think I OD'd on the happy adult feeling I got that my dad bought me that soda, on the sweetness of it, and on the impact of the big movie screen, because I got a sick headache—the first one I ever remember having, being too high, too much excitement and a soda that was too sweet. Even now the thought of cherry sodas bought in a movie theatre makes me feel sick."

Richard Morales moved up from going with his family to going with other kids. He remembers,

there always seemed to be a carload of kids and me at the bottom of it, hiding under a blanket. Since I was usually the smallest, they could sneak me in under a blanket instead of in the trunk, where one of my big brothers was usually put. I can remember the voice at the ticket booth, the vague lights from under the blanket, and my constantly asking, "Are we there yet?" Once inside the drive-in, there were always five or more people passing around candy, Cokes, and popcorn in and outside the car. And the same major production was happening in a hundred other cars inside the drive-in. Or so it seemed. The last few times I went to the drive-in, about two or three years ago, it seemed deserted, and going into the empty snack bar gave me a lonely and empty feeling.

Going to the drive-in with a group of friends could be fun. In the mid-seventies, Kasey Arnold-Ince took her "very susceptible" friend Robin to see *Carrie* (1976) with two boys at the drive-in. "I made some excuse to sit in the back seat, while Robin sat in the front with her brother Chris and his friend Dave. The final sequence—with its unexpected shocker—caused Robin to scream (loudly) and jump up in her seat, flinging her arms about and hitting her head on the roof. She also hit Dave in the mouth and knocked Chris's head against the car window. The cacophony of shrieks, moans, and curses was nicely punctuated by my near-hysterical laughter."

Drive-ins could be a problem for comedies. Jack Hollander and his friends, having seen the trailer for *Airplane!* (1980), somehow ended up seeing the film at a drive-in. The film was as funny as they hoped, but "the odd thing was how awkward it was to see this film in the drive-in; we *knew* people were laughing a lot, but we couldn't hear or share their laughter."

There are other pictures the drive-in setting helps. The first movie Patrician Cortazar saw was *2001: A Space Odyssey* (1968), and she saw it at a drive-in. "I have this eternal image of men floating against a white capsule that was set in deepest space that extended beyond the screen into all that night. I will never forget that moment; I have not sat through this movie once since then."

Kasey Arnold-Ince did not have such a pleasurable experience when she saw the film at the drive-in. She was then in her teens, and she was "trying to watch the film while my date attempted to exercise his options. Despite the distraction, I was so fascinated I went back later to see it again, unmolested."

Given that kids grew up watching movies at the drive-ins in their pajamas, maybe it is not surprising that when they could go without the family, sex began to enter into the process. Ervin Riggs's best moviegoing experience was the first time his father let him use the car to take his girlfriend to the drive-in. Riggs cannot even remember the film. "We had so much fun laughing, talking, and kissing, I didn't want the night to end."

Desreta Jackson has had both good and bad nights at drive-ins. One Friday she and her girlfriend did not have dates, so they cooked up some food and sneaked it in. "That hot good-tasting food, along with the giggling and laughing while we talked about men and commented on the movie, made the evening wonderful." On the other hand, her worst experience was also at a drive-in.

I was on a date. During the date, the guy kept trying to get intimate with me, but that's not what I wanted. When I refused, he kicked me out of the car. The jerk. . . . When I got out, he told me to come back, but my pride refused me to. So I walked through the lot and in front of the drive-in, where I called my mother. When she came and picked me up, she wanted to know what happened, but I was too embarrassed to tell her. I mean I wasn't a fourteen-year-old. I was eighteen going on nineteen.

Peggy Dilley was dating the man who became her husband when she was seventeen. They were both working but not making much money, and he was able to get his father's brown Corvair for the weekends.

We drove around a lot, but I wouldn't let him park, because I had this thing about not wanting to be seen in a parked vehicle with him. We wanted to be alone. I was too shy to go to social functions. He wanted me to himself anyway. I didn't like to go to his house, because his folks would sit in the living room, and all of us would stare at TV and say nothing. We couldn't go to my house because my stepfather was crazy.

So we found a compromise. We went to drive-in movies every Friday and Saturday night, almost every weekend, all year round, including winter and in the rain in Detroit, Michigan, for two years. We spent a lot of time fogging up the windows, but we watched a lot of crummy and some good movies, too.

Consensual sex happens. Derek Garubo's "most memorable movie experience was actually screwing my girlfriend in my car at a drive-in that just so happened to coincide with the love scene in the movie! I will put it this way, I could see the movie and she could not, and I laughed when the love scene came on. My girlfriend wanted to know what the hell was so funny, and I had to make up some excuse as to why I laughed. If I had told her the truth, that would have been the end of the world!"

Wil Dimpflmaier had a fairly recent experience with a drive-in, a six-pack, and a blonde:

First I met the blonde, Lisa, in Vegas and made plans to go out on an old-fashioned date, since we both lived in Los Angeles. Then my roommate bought a '69 Malibu Chevelle with his Vegas winnings. That's when I came up with the idea of the drive-in. Let me tell you, it's not easy to find a drive-in in a reputable neighborhood. After about an hour of calling around, I decided on the one in Carson.

The ride down there was great, one arm around my new girl and the other palming the wheel as we rocketed down the 405 freeway, playing the classic rock station, of course. When we arrived, it wasn't hard to find a parking spot, since the place was deserted. I wondered why more people weren't there. When the movie started, I realized why. You could barely see the screen, with all the light pollution around. We had decided to see *Men in Black* and *Nothing to Lose* (both 1997), and I was interested in seeing both movies. Well, after a few beers and Lisa's top coming off combined with the low visual quality of the screen, I kinda lost interest in the movie. . . .

The girlfriends I dated in high school knew of my interest in the movies, and they quickly understood that if *I* asked them to go see a movie at a drive-in, it was because I wanted to see the movie. The one time I had trouble in this area was with a girl that I had never dated before. "Winona" had been dating my best friend, and they had broken up. She wanted to talk to me about him, and I suggested we could drive around a bit and talk. After we made the date, I discovered that one of the local drive-ins was showing a double bill of *The Grapes of Wrath* (1940) and *Tobacco Road* (1941), neither of which I had seen. I knew from the Deems Taylor book that *The Grapes of Wrath* was supposed to be a classic film, so I suggested to Winona we see it. She agreed but must have assumed I had other things on my mind. I spent most of the Joads' trip to California removing her hands from various parts of my body. I did get to see the entire film. I did not see any of *Tobacco Road* until many years later.

I was not the only member of the moviegoing audience of the fifties that looked for serious films, and I did not have to go to nearly twenty-year-old films like *The Grapes of Wrath* to find them. What has come to be the standard view of American movies in the fifties is that it was a time of films with very little or no content or with the content put in the films in disguise (as in the science fiction films of the period, such as *Invasion of the Body Snatchers* [1956]).[3] This view comes from two sources. The first is the nostalgia industry. The fifties in particular have become a major focus for nostalgia, primarily by white males who long for the last time white males seemed to be in uncontested power. I have found no people of color and only one woman nostalgic for the fifties, and in her case, it was her own youth she was nostalgic for. By its nature, nostalgia tends to see the past as a lot purer than it really was, and the fifties were not pure.

The other source for the view that fifties films were devoid of content comes from the left-wing film historians, who assume that because of the blacklisting of left-wing writers, directors, and producers, all seriousness went out of American films in the fifties.[4] Sometimes these two points of view coincide. The 1987 documentary film *Legacy of the Blacklist*[5] points out how bland the fifties films became by showing clips from *Beach Party* movies. However, those films were made in the early sixties, but they were undoubtedly included in the documentary because the writer of three of them was Leo Townsend, who had been a friendly witness before the House UnAmerican Activities Committee. The documentary, sympathetic to those on the blacklist, could not resist a little point scoring.

Part of the problem the left has with the films about serious subjects in the early fifties is that several of these films were anti-Communist. That does not mean the filmmakers treated them in a particularly serious manner. As the blacklist developed and Hollywood came under attack from the right wing, the obvious response for Hollywood was to make films that opposed Communism. Hollywood turned out fifty anti-Communist films between 1947 and 1954.[6] Most of them were very low-budget films, most of them were awful, and very few of them made any money.

The producers did not spend money or time on the films, and the films tend to fall into clichés, with very little understanding of Communism or its appeal. Most of the films were variations on the anti-Nazi pictures of the forties, with the accents changed slightly. In *Big Jim McLain* (1952), the Communists seem interchangeable with traditional Hollywood gangsters. I saw *Big Jim McLain* when it was first released, and it seemed to me just another John Wayne action picture, with Wayne getting the bad guys once again. It was not until I saw the picture on television some thirty years later that I noticed how much of it was bad propaganda.

Besides Wayne in *Big Jim McLain*, the most notable talents who made an anti-Communist picture were director Leo McCarey and actress Helen Hayes with their 1952 flop *My Son John*. I did not see it until I was a graduate student in film at UCLA in 1968 when I was a teaching assistant in a class run by Howard Suber. He showed the film, saying it was the best of the anti-Communist films of the early fifties. The night after the screening, I wrote in my diary that it was "one of the most awful, embarrassing movies Hollywood ever made."

It became very clear to Hollywood that while there might be a conservative trend in the country, there was no audience for anti-Communist films. George Byron Sage, a longtime reader in the story department at Twentieth Century-Fox, and according to one of his bosses, "one of the dullest men in the world,"[7] was smart enough to realize as early as 1950 that recommending an anti-Communist story to the studio was not a good idea "since anti-Communist films have been rather unsuccessful financially."[8]

There were serious pictures that made money in the fifties as well as those that did not. *Sunset Boulevard* was a success for Billy Wilder, which allowed him to follow it up with *Ace in the Hole* (1951), which was not nearly as successful. One of the coldest, most sardonic films to come out of Hollywood, *Ace in the Hole* tells the story of Chuck Tatum, a down-on-his-luck newspaperman who hypes the story of an attempt to rescue a man trapped in a cave. A large crowd is drawn to the rescue site, and the trapped man dies before he can be freed. The crowd is implicated in its voyeuristic interest in the story, and the film was too harsh for audiences of the time. The last time I saw it was at a revival theatre in Los Angeles in 1993, and the audience was dazzled and stunned by the bitter wit of the film. The second feature that night was *The Bad and the Beautiful,* which seemed soft and sentimental by comparison, and it is not a soft and sentimental film.

Another serious film of the time was *From Here to Eternity,* the 1953 adaptation of the James Jones best-seller. Providing a thought-provoking look at the peacetime army, the film was the ninth highest-grossing film of the decade. In 1979, I ran the film in my History of Motion Pictures class at Los Angeles City College, and it worked better than the television miniseries made at the same time. One student, writing a comparison of the two, noted that the 1953 film was better because it did not have all the bad language and violence of the miniseries. I suggested she read Jones's novel to see how much *both* the film and the miniseries had cleaned up the material.

One of the most enduring of the serious films of the fifties is *On the Waterfront* (1954). The subject of the film is corruption within a labor union, not a common subject then or since. The subtext of the film, which was not as clear when it was released as it later became, was writer Budd Schulberg and director Elia Kazan's dealing with the impact of their friendly testimony before the House UnAmerican Activities Committee. This subtext gives the film its emotional power, because Schulberg and Kazan were making a film about something they were passionate about. Its intensity is what still makes the film compelling. Made on a budget of $880,000,[9] the film grossed $4.2 million, and it still works effectively on audiences.

As with *Sunset Boulevard* and *Singin' in the Rain,* what moves people most about *On the Waterfront* are the performances, particularly Marlon Brando's. Monica Dunlap was an acting student in New York in Uta Hagen's class when she first saw the film. She and the others in the class felt Brando was "our hero as an actor." Marion Levine was taken as a child to see the film and "fell in love with Terry Malloy [Brando's character]." Later when Levine studied acting, "I analyzed Brando's performance and made it my own paradigm of great acting. Nuance, pain, conflicting emotions, tenderness, rage, and the unexpected appearance of vulnerability—Brando made us feel his every moment." Al Gonzalez, an actor, was also impressed with Brando the first time he saw the film, but a recent viewing of the film gave him second thoughts: "With it now known of Brando's use of cue cards on the set for remembering his lines, his constant habit of looking away from the person he's speaking to in a scene is reminiscent of a cast member from *Saturday Night Live* reading the TelePrompTer in the middle of a skit, it really becomes annoying. And as for the back seat [taxi] scene, I felt that compared to some of the more realistic films of today. . . . Brando's performance seemed a little dated and a little bit false, or more to the point, stagey."

Later audiences, like audiences at the time of the film's release, do respond to the reality of the New York locations, which Richard Henrie found "interesting. I tend to be drawn more to movies that are set in New York. New York just seems so real, while Los Angeles just seems too phony." On the other hand, Albert Nazaryan, a student in his twenties, saw the movie as a teenager and thought it "a comic book." He explains, "As I was growing up, all the thugs on film and especially TV were black or Hispanic. In my neighborhood, most of the gang members were Hispanic. Juxtapose this with Marlon Brando (Marlon Brando!) . . . and Rod Steiger as 'the people from the wrong side of the neighborhood.' It seemed artificial to me, especially the goons. On top of all this, no one cursed."

Since Lilia Fuller grew up in Bulgaria in the 1970s watching Russian propaganda films, when she finally saw *On the Waterfront*, it was not "particularly my kind of picture. Maybe because I am tired of social and politico-economical films with their big messages about the injustice of the world."

Kazan and Schulberg followed *On the Waterfront* three years later with the striking film *A Face in the Crowd* (1957). Schulberg's satire of television and politics seemed almost unbelievable at the time, but most of it has come true. If anything, television has gone to greater excesses than the film shows. The film is overwrought and exhausting to sit through, and very few people did at the time. Even later, it was a difficult film for audiences, but it is rich and compelling for those willing to stick with it, and in 2000 I had a class that loved its *restraint*, especially after years of Oliver Stone and Quentin Tarantino films, particularly the media satire they "collaborated" on, *Natural Born Killers*. We can now estimate that *A Face in the Crowd* was forty-three years ahead of its time.

The first three years of the wide-screen era saw three films made in old-fashioned small-screen ratios and in old-fashioned black-and-white win the Academy Award for Best Picture of the Year. *From Here to Eternity* and *On the Waterfront* were followed in 1955 by *Marty*. The year 1955 was a good year for serious films. There was *Blackboard Jungle*, a hard-hitting, if finally sentimental, look at juvenile delinquents at a big city school. Its use of the song "Rock Around the Clock" under the main titles brought rock-and-roll to the movies for the first time and in an incendiary way. It was heard as the music of juvenile delinquents, and both the music and the film offended adults. The same year and from the same studio with the same star (Glenn Ford) was a more complex and less explosive film, *Trial*, about the trial of a Mexican-American boy accused of murder and the attempts by the Communist Party to use the case for its own ends. While the picture was one of the few anti-Communist films that was an artistic success and an even moderate commercial success, it has been virtually forgotten and undoubtedly ignored by left-wing film historians made uncomfortable by its view of the Party. Seldom revived, it almost never appears on television and has yet to be released on video.

The year 1955 was also the year James Dean became a star—first in Kazan's *East of Eden* and again, shortly after his death, in *Rebel Without a Cause*. I was thirteen and going into the traditional sulking phase of adolescence when *East of Eden* was released in the spring of the year. Having an older brother who seemed, although not entirely truthfully, to be as much of a goody-two-shoes as the brother in *Eden*, I immediately perceived myself as the unloved son, like Dean in the film. I sulked around the house for a few months, banging doors when I came and went, until one night my father said, "It would be nice if you said hello to us once in a while."

I stopped sulking overtly, but Dean's mixture of power and vulnerability was appealing, and I managed to work my way socially through high school doing either overt or covert imitations of Dean. It appealed to high school girls. Like many other boys of my generation, I had a red (well, off-red) windbreaker like Dean in *Rebel*. I was heartbroken at the news of his death, and like millions of others, I eagerly anticipated Dean's last film *Giant* (1956), which was not released until a year after he died.

Dean's image as the eternal teenager is based primarily on *Rebel*, but in fact, both *East of Eden* and *Giant* outgrossed *Rebel* in the fifties. *Giant* grossed $12 million (the tenth highest-grossing film of the decade); *Eden*, $5 million; and *Rebel*, only $4.5 million. An adaptation of the Edna Ferber novel, *Giant* is on the surface a multigeneration soap opera about a family of Texas cattle ranchers. It is about the corruption of money, particularly oil money, and the film is darkly satirical about Texas excesses. What most people now forget about the film is that a strong recurring thematic element is the relations between the white Texans and the Mexican Americans who work for them and ultimately marry into the family.

In the spring of 1986, I taught a course in the History of American Film at UCLA, and one of the films I showed was *Giant*. To a group of students in their late teens and early twenties, who had grown up with the image of the fifties as a period of cultural emptiness, it was a shock to discover that big-budget American films of the period could be *about* something.

On the other hand, the class screening was only a few months after Rock Hudson had died of AIDS, and the class had real difficulty accepting him as the macho, patriarchal head of the family. Nine years later, when I showed the film in a class at Los Angeles City College, the students there had no problem with Hudson in the part. I do not think this change was simply the difference in students at UCLA and LACC.

Time passes, attitudes change.

Opening the Sixties

In the fall of 1958, while I was visiting my brother at Princeton University, we went to see *The Defiant Ones*. It is a fifties-serious message picture about the brotherhood of man, as were most Stanley Kramer movies of the period. In *The Defiant Ones*, Tony Curtis and Sidney Poitier are two escaped convicts chained together. Poitier plays one of his patented fifties "noble Negroes," and at the end of the film, he and Curtis have literally broken the chains that bind them. Poitier jumps aboard a freight train, and Curtis is running alongside. Poitier holds out his black hand to help the white trash Curtis. From the audience of Princeton men, virtually all of them white, came a shout addressed to Poitier's character, "Let him go!" The audience cheered the comment, then booed when Poitier pulled Curtis onto the train.

Part of the audience's reaction came simply from upper-class white men looking down on white trash and another part from the audience's realization that Poitier's character showed the kind of nobility of character that the Princeton men thought they had. Yet another part of their response, however, came from the beginning of a change in reactions to films from audiences of the time. This in turn combined with a change in the nature of serious (and some not-so-serious) films at the end of the fifties. Just as American society began to drag itself out of the cultural lethargy of the fifties, so did American films, opening themselves up to subject matter and approaches that would have seemed unthinkable in the glory days of the major studios. The opening up was by audiences as well as filmmakers, each reinforcing the other.

Just as it is impossible to imagine Billy Wilder getting permission from a studio in the thirties or forties to make a film like *Some Like It Hot* (two straight heroes get into drag to avoid getting killed by gangsters, and one of the guys lets a guy fall in love with him), it is difficult to imagine audiences of earlier times responding to such a film as audiences in 1959 did when Wilder made *Some Like It Hot*. In the same year that *Ben-Hur* was the top-grossing film, *Some Like It Hot* was the fifth highest-grossing film, bringing in rentals of $7.7 million.

Wilder's film the following year, *The Apartment*, grossed even more, with rentals of $9.3 million.

Because the inspiration for *The Apartment* was an earlier film, its development suggests how films had changed. Wilder had seen the 1945 British film *Brief Encounter*, in which a married doctor meets and falls in love with a married woman. This being the forties, the couple does not consummate the relationship, but comes close one afternoon when they go to an apartment owned by a friend of the doctor. The friend arrives before the couple can do anything, and they leave in embarrassment. Wilder began to wonder about the friend. Does he lend his apartment out for this sort of thing all the time? Why? This gave Wilder a situation but no plot. After hearing about a junior agent who lent his boss his apartment for an affair with a movie star, Wilder had a plot.[1] Wilder and his co-writer, I.A.L. Diamond, set the story not in Hollywood, but in a large corporation. A senior executive uses the apartment of a junior executive, who has developed a crush on the very girl who is having the affair. When she attempts suicide in the apartment, the younger executive saves her. The story is both more cynical than *Brief Encounter* and also more sentimental. *The Apartment* won the Academy Award for Best Picture as well as outgrossing *Some Like It Hot*. Of the two films, *Hot* holds up better, at least partially because of the fascination with Marilyn Monroe. When I showed *The Apartment* at UCLA in 1986, the students felt it was the sort of portrait of a New York schnook that has been done better since by Woody Allen.

Wilder was not the only filmmaker breaking new ground. Otto Preminger had had fights with the various censorship groups in the early fifties over two of his films. *The Moon is Blue* (1953) caused concern primarily over the use of the term "professional virgin" to describe the heroine. The film seems incredibly innocuous now, not only in comparison with current films, but also with American television of the seventies, not to mention later. In 1955, Preminger made *The Man with the Golden Arm*, the first major studio film to deal explicitly with drug addiction. Both films were commercial successes. In 1959, Preminger went further with *Anatomy of a Murder*, a compelling courtroom drama that featured what was then relatively explicit dialogue about sexual activities, and used the word "panties" for the first time in American films since the early thirties, before the development of the Production Code. It was the ninth highest-grossing film of the year.

In 1959's *On the Beach*, Stanley Kramer took his usual "brotherhood of man" theme all the way to the end of the world, caused in this case by nuclear war and subsequent radiation poisoning. In spite of the implication that all its characters were soon to die, the self-promoted sense of importance about the film and its starry cast (Gregory Peck, Ava Gardner, and Fred Astaire in his first dramatic role) made it successful at the box office. That year, *On the Beach* grossed more than *Some Came Running* and *The Horse Soldiers*, but less than *North by Northwest* and *Some Like It Hot*. Seen a few years after its first, heavily promoted release, it was more striking as a star vehicle (especially for Gardner, in her best performance) than as a message picture. I saw it in a theatre in 1995, and it dated in an odd way. An early scene in the movie identifies the year it takes place as 1964, which immediately took the later audience out of the story, since we knew several things the picture does not. The world did not end in 1964. The threat of nuclear weapons continues, but not in the way the film suggests, and there has been more damage from nuclear power than from weapons. On the one hand, a 1995 viewing was a relief for the audience that knows it did not happen. On the other hand, the political events that took place between the time of the film's release and 1995 indicated the kind of stupidity the film suggests in human behavior is still very much with us, if not more so. Who knows how the film will play in another thirty-five years?[2]

Looking at *On the Beach* in 1994, Donald Chase noted, "Then, too, there's Anthony Perkins, believably 'normal' as a young husband and father, and suggesting how his career might have gone had he not played Mrs. Bates's boy a year later."[3] Perkins had begun his film career in the mid-fifties as sort of a junior varsity James Dean, playing the sensitive son in films like *Friendly Persuasion* (1956). *Psycho* changed his career, making it impossible for him to play any later role in a way that did not take into consideration that he was, now and forever, in some way, Norman Bates.

Psycho is perhaps the most obvious example of movies of the late fifties and early sixties that, for better and for worse, opened up American films. In the fifties, Alfred Hitchcock had considerable box office success with such glamorous star-laden and relatively nonviolent films as *Rear Window* (1954) and *North by Northwest*, but he found other directors being compared more favorably to himself than he might have liked. He was also tired of dealing with the demands of big-name stars, and when he found Robert Bloch's novel, he saw an opportunity too good to resist.[4] Because the studio he was under contract to, Paramount, was horrified at the grisliness of the material, Hitchcock made the film on a limited budget, using not his usual film crew, but the crew that shot his television series.

Although Hitchcock developed an elaborate publicity campaign for the film, complete with a theatre admissions policy of not letting anybody in after the movie had started, he and everybody else connected with the film, and Hollywood in general, was astonished at the success of the film. From the day the film opened in New York, there were lines around the theatres and gridlock around the drive-ins showing the film. And not only did millions come to see the film, but they reacted in ways its creators had not necessarily intended or expected.

Joseph Stefano, who had written the screenplay and seen the rough cut, took his wife and a group of friends to see the film the day it opened in Los Angeles. He told Stephen Rebello, "As the movie went on, I saw people grabbing each other, howling, screaming, reacting like six-year-olds at a Saturday matinee. I couldn't believe what was happening. I found it hard to reconcile our movie with how the audience was reacting. I *never* thought it was a movie that would make people scream."[5] Anthony Perkins told Rebello that he did not know exactly what Hitchcock's intentions were, but Perkins said, "After hearing audiences around the country *roar*, Hitchcock—perhaps reluctantly—acknowledged that it was OK to laugh at the film and that, perhaps, it was a comedy after all. He *didn't* realize how funny audiences would find the movie, generally. More importantly, I don't think he was prepared for the amount and intensity of the on-the-spot laughs that he got from first-run audiences around the world. He was confused at first, incredulous second, and despondent third." Hitchcock told Perkins that previously he "had always been able to predict the audience's reaction. Here I haven't been able to."[6] This can be seen by the fact that *Psycho* brought in rentals of $9 million, in comparison with *Rear Window*'s $5.3 million and *North by Northwest*'s $6 million.

If Judith Waxman "had known *Psycho* was about a 'sicko,' I wouldn't have seen it. Thus, I sat in an orchestra seat in a theatre on Hollywood Boulevard. Soon I was in the back of the theatre, almost leaving, something I never do. Somehow I stayed, scared out of my mind, realizing I had just seen the outer edge of madness—and a good movie." Virginia Keene, who loved horror films even in her teens, saw *Psycho* in its first run. "I saw it at the theatre right away and then three more times at the drive-in with friends. It scared me to death—in the most delightful way. I've seen it many times in every possible form—TV, cable, video—and still find it enormously entertaining. I see it as the blackest of comedies now and certainly saw nothing funny about it in 1960!" Monica Dunlap saw it "with my girlfriends when we were schoolgirls, and I remember every damned frame of it. To this day I cannot take a shower without first checking to make sure the doors and windows are locked. Every time I take a shower, I think 'why did I see that movie?'"

The murder of Marion Crane, a character we liked, played by a star we liked, forty minutes into the film—in a *shower*, of all places—is the scene that had the strongest impact. Peggy Dilley saw the film some time later and had been warned about the shower scene, but it was still so powerful she is "glad I have a glass door on my shower now rather than a curtain." Wendi Cole was "afraid to take a shower for some time. I *would not* wash my hair if I was alone in the house. Thank God for the sliding shower door!" Al Gonzalez "had trouble taking a shower after I saw it. But for a boy it's also a good excuse for getting out of having to take a bath." Javier Rodriguez found the shower scene striking in several ways: "The fact that it was a hotel [It's the Bates *Motel,* of course] thriller was a complete turn-on. And the fact that it was done in black-and-white was a plus for me. The scene in the shower is great—and very weird. And the music made the film so real and more scary. But when the blood ran [down] the drain sink. And the sound of the water with the drain made me scared to my feet."

The shower was not the only thing that scared people about the film. Richard Henrie keeps "remembering the shots of the house from the road, spooky." Rudie Bravo found that "already having developed a fear of creepy basements, this movie practically guaranteed I'd never go downstairs again." Donna Crisci saw it when she was young and could not understand why her mother thought the final "explanation" scene was "so chilling. The old corpse in the chair . . . *that* was chilling!"

For Judith Amory the whole experience was scary. She was going to a Russian-language summer school at Middlebury College in Vermont in the summer of 1960 and had to sneak off campus for dates, so her dates were not allowed to walk her back to the campus. "I had to go alone in the dark, and it was one of the scariest walks I ever took." The first two times Lilia Fuller saw the film, she did not know what movie it was. It was only later that she learned it was "THE movie made by A. Hitchcock." She finds it brings "all kinds of skeletons from all kinds of closets."

Being terrified was not the only reaction people had to *Psycho.* Desreta Jackson liked it but found it confusing. "Up to this day I've never understood if his mother was a ghost, or if he was pretending to be his mother, or was it both?" Her confusion may have come from the different prints of the film that were in circulation. Hitchcock could not decide which of two endings to use. One ends with just the close-up of Perkins, but another ends with the close-up with an almost subliminal shot of a skull double-exposed onto Perkins's face.[7]

Some people did not find *Psycho* particularly scary. Patrician Cortazar "never found it scary as a child. I was into it for the sake of it being a classic." Angela West doesn't "remember being extremely impressed with this movie. Although Anthony Perkins gave an incredible performance, I just couldn't get into the story. Somehow I remember laughing at how silly the whole thing was. The sets looked cheap and didn't really convince me."

Many people were first exposed to *Psycho* later on television. Laurel Jo Martin saw it on TV while babysitting "alone in a mountain cabin late at night. . . . When the family returned home I was shaking, I can't really explain why—because mentally I didn't feel frightened, but my nerves were shot. Today when I see it, I enjoy the psychodrama of it and am not frightened by it." Blair Woodard says his "first exposure to Hitchcock that I had was a badly cut-up TV version of *Psycho,* it was still terrifying. It is one of those films that once seen you are permanently altered."

Tandy Summers, a student in her late twenties, also saw it for the first time on TV:

> I remember as a young kid catching the end of *Psycho* on KTLA Channel 5 just before Grandma was going to watch the news. Anthony Perkins is in the holding cell talking in [his] mother's voice. I was baffled, wondering what I was watching. Was this a movie? Was it the news? Just the shot. It's like a documentary scene.
>
> I saw the whole thing, finally, after years of slasher movies when I was around sixteen. I remember getting bored with the opening plot of Janet Leigh stealing the money. Finally, the murder. And waiting long for more. And the climax. Ripping the wig off this guy. I knew it was Perkins all along. This movie was nothing compared to *Halloween II* (1981) or the first *Friday the 13th* (1980). I just thought it was this strange movie. It just seemed so dated. Too much talk, no action.
>
> Of course, *Psycho II* (1983) was just fine with me. It had young people in it, victims I could relate to. Yeah, a lot more victims. Young people ruled in movies during the eighties. There were no young people in *Psycho*. And the classic shower scene? What was the big deal? I was used to *Dawn of the Dead* (1978) and *Phantasm* (1979).
>
> I saw the film again when I was around twenty and learned to appreciate it. I got into the suspense and rich characters. Janet Leigh taking the money had become a thought I'd considered at my jobs. This was something I could relate to. It was suspense. I saw the psychological terror in the shower scene. The buildup of the guy going up the staircase and getting it from mother. The tracking shots and the weird rack shot as the guy is falling. And the overhead shot at the top of the hall where mother just barges out. I felt the eeriness of the cop in the first half. I was older and had my experiences with cops. Maybe it was the glasses and the tone of voice that made him so inhuman. I now know this was the film where all the slasher films humbly began.

Many people whose first viewing of *Psycho* came long after its initial release already knew the plot. We have, as Brian Calderon says, "that damn *Happy Days* episode to thank." Paul Sbrizzi notes, "By the time I saw *Psycho*, I already knew its plot, so unfortunately I missed out on all the good terror." Coni Constantine saw the sequels first and thinks "the difference was like night and day, and I liked the original infinitely better than the others. I only wish I could have seen it first in order to get the full feeling of suspense by not knowing what was going to happen next." D'Arcy West thinks she saw *Psycho II* first, and "the original was a big relief to my moviegoing sensibilities. . . . *Psycho* was funny, spooky, campy, and sick. I liked that the girl was killed right away. I liked and admired the use of cross-dressing homosexuals in a fifties thriller."

Skylaire Alfvegren saw the movie years after it was made, when she was thirteen or fourteen, and it had almost a nostalgic value. "Because it was black-and-white, I was happy to see such a film could be made such a long and dusty time ago. Anthony Perkins was creepy, and I didn't think he'd make too bad of a neighbor. I have a friend now whose house is just filled with taxidermied animals—rabbits, boars, even a lion and a bear. Now really, what's the difference between preserving animals and your dearly departed relatives?"

Even though Rick Mitchell did not see *Psycho* during its first release, it is so much a part of American film culture that for Mitchell, "something about it conjures up memories of late summer 1959 and '60 in Kentucky [where he was living at the time]. Just those two years, and I don't really know why except maybe that it was at the former time I first saw Hitchcock's *Strangers on a Train* (1951) and the latter was when *Psycho* was playing first run in Lexington." *Psycho* also began to affect how we looked at earlier films. After growing up in Bloomington, Indiana, I went to Yale, and a few years after *Psycho* came out, the Yale Film Society ran the 1958 Orson Welles film *Touch of Evil*. Made two years before *Psycho*, it includes a scene of Charlton Heston searching a motel room for his wife, played by Janet Leigh. The Yale audience greeted the scene with shouts of "Look in the shower. Look in the shower."[8]

The variety of responses to the original *Psycho* suggest why the shot-for-shot 1998 remake was a disaster, both critically and at the box office. Reactions to the original film changed over the years, given audiences' knowledge of the film and its place in American culture. The makers of the remake assumed that nothing had changed, both in the country and with audiences, in the intervening thirty-eight years. But nothing could have been further from the truth.

If *Some Like It Hot* and *The Apartment* led the way for American films to deal with sexual material, and if the original *Psycho* was the forerunner of what was then new explicitness in violence, then other films opened up the ways politics was shown in American films. In the fifties, there had been serious films about brainwashing during the Korean War (*The Rack* [1956], *Time Limit* [1957]), but 1962's *The Manchurian Candidate* presented the subject in surreal, darkly comic terms. The film also satirized the anti-Communism of the fifties in ways that would have been impossible in mainstream American films ten or even five years before. Because of the tone with which the film dealt with its subjects, audiences were strongly divided over *The Manchurian Candidate*.[9] The Yale audiences with whom I saw *The Manchurian Candidate* were with the film all the way. In 1988, after being out of circulation for several years, the film was rereleased, and given the dazzling directorial styles that had been developed in the meantime by directors like Spielberg, Scorsese, De Palma, and their clones, *The Manchurian Candidate*'s style seemed almost staid. What was most striking in 1988 was the wit and intelligence of Richard Condon's original idea and George Axelrod's script, simply because by then, there was not a lot of that kind of wit or intelligence in American films.

If Stanley Kramer was taking the end of the world by nuclear catastrophe seriously in 1959, by 1964 American films and their audiences had opened up so much that Stanley Kubrick could follow his instincts. Kubrick started out to do a serious version of Peter George's novel *Red Alert*, but he kept finding it funny and decided to turn it into a black comedy.[10] I first saw *Dr. Strangelove* in San Diego when it opened in the spring of 1964. I was an officer in the U.S. Navy stationed in the quintessential U.S. Navy town, and the audience was made up of people in, or very familiar with, the American military. They knew officers just as crazy as those portrayed on the screen and appreciated all of the humor. A month or so later, I saw the film again back in my hometown of Bloomington, and the audience—part university people and part townspeople—were with the film until the point when General Ripper starts talking about the perils of water fluoridation. The film lost a good portion of the audience at that point. How dare a movie make fun of the real peril of fluoridation!?

The film also lost the young Virginia Keene, whose father was in naval aviation. She first saw the film at a drive-in with her mother in 1964. She recalls, "We were not amused. We were too close to the Cuban Missile Crisis (October 1962) to see this movie clearly. We both though it was macabre, sick, and frightening. That we stayed to see the entire movie is a huge credit to Kubrick and Sellers!" Keene has "seen it many times since, and of course, time and distance have radically altered my viewpoint. I love this movie now as intensely as I hated it then."

People who saw the film at too young an age generally did not appreciate it at the time. Laurel Jo Martin saw it "on TV in a room once when I was little. I was doing something, not watching TV, but I remember the disturbing images that I saw. The general, supposedly an adult in charge, was acting very weird; the man in the wheelchair obviously is crazy. I remember being aware that the movie was mocking something, and since I didn't know what that something was, it made me feel uneasy." Jill Mitchell remembers, "My western civilization teacher in high school showed us this. I remember he loved the film and was really excited to be showing it to us. I thought it was very cool to be watching a real movie in school. Unfortunately, I don't think I followed the plot very well, because I think I sort of zoned out after a while." On the other hand, James Ford saw it as a boy, and it "awakened my sense of irony and made me realize that, even as a child, I could understand adult humor." And Marcus Franklin saw it when he was young, but recalls it as being a James Bond movie, perhaps because it was designed by Ken Adams, who designed the early Bond films, or perhaps he is just confusing it with *Dr. No* (1962).

Dr. Strangelove made fun of the macho military posturing so prevalent in America in the fifties and early sixties that it was ripe for a satire audiences could appreciate. General Ripper, in particular, was a dead-on parody of the public behavior seen in the highest-ranking officer of the Strategic Air Command, General Curtis LeMay. After the release of the film, the American military and political leaders seemed determined not to moderate their behavior but rather to live up to all the excesses that Kubrick showed. Henry Kissinger, the model for Strangelove, was at the time of the film a little-known academic, but he seemed to grow into the public image that Strangelove gave him. Lyndon Johnson seemed a lot like Slim Pickens's character Major Kong, elevated to the Presidency. The satire became the truth, so much so that the sheer audacity of the film has become almost muted over the years. Jack Hollander first saw the film all the way through in the seventies in a class he walked into at UCLA. He says of the screening,

> I don't think that I appreciated the vicious satire as much then as I do now. Perhaps none of us did. It was, after all, just after the Vietnam War ended and the "Commie" threat was still a part of our daily lives (real or imagined). I think as we distance ourselves more and more from the frightening realities of living under the shadow of "the bomb" (not that we still aren't, but we've become a bit more optimistic), that Kubrick's far-seeing satire will truly be recognized even more for the searing political commentary that is this film. I haven't seen it since the Berlin Wall fell—I wonder how I'll react to it now—curiosity, commentary, or sad truth?

When I showed *Dr. Strangelove* in my History of Motion Pictures classes in the seventies and eighties, the students just assumed that was the way American military and political leaders had always been shown, because as far as they knew, in their own lives, that was indeed how they behaved. It was not just relevant but simply the truth.

Robin Magee was familiar with the film before she ever saw it, since her father was "the hot new politics professor at a small liberal arts college in Iowa. As soon as the movie came to the town, he incorporated it into his lectures and even did a Dr. Strangelove routine (complete with black glove) when explaining Soviet policy to his students." Years later, Magee was a student activist in the early eighties and saw the film. "The ideas were still relevant, the humor still great and Peter Sellers incomparable." Bill Pulliam saw the film at an on-campus college screening in the early eighties. "As this was the time of Reagan's election and the renewal of the Cold War, it seemed exceedingly topical."

On the other hand, David Morales, who first saw the film in his teens in the late eighties, thought it was "not that relevant." David Choe, however, is now "surprised at how well this film still holds up despite the demise of the 'Red Menace.'" Paul Sbrizzi was a little worried about the audience he saw the film with in the mid-nineties.

> *Dr. Strangelove* is one of my parents' favorite movies, so I've been seeing it and enjoying it all my life. I saw it recently at the New Beverly [a Los Angeles revival house] and was particularly impressed with the acting. However, it was really disturbing to witness the audience reaction: there is a lot of really dark, grotesque humor in the movie, and the crowd was howling and belly-laughing as if they were watching an episode of *Get Smart*. To me it seemed that the film was meant to be intellectually frightening as much as funny, and the audience seemed to be making a specific effort to take the movie only at surface value. I can only ascribe this to the lightness of our times, but still you would think a revival house would attract a somewhat less brain-dead crowd.

Maybe the crowd had just taken the subtitle to heart and had started to stop worrying and love the bomb.

We certainly began to love spies, especially those who were witty and managed to live and succeed in a world not unlike *Dr. Strangelove*'s. In the spring of 1963, while still at Yale, I went to the opening-day screening of a low-budget British-made spy movie, *Dr. No*. When Sean Connery said the words, "Bond—James Bond," for the first time, the assembled Yale men made the theatre sound like a Saturday matinee of six-year-olds. Here was the ultimate in cool, and little girls, as well as bigger boys, were impressed. Actress Lisa Moncure recalls, "I loved these Bond movies as a kid. Now that I'm a grown woman, I hate to admit it because those films were beyond sexist! Completely politically incorrect, but truth be told, I was crazy for them. I wanted to be James Bond. I used to play 'secret agent' down by the creek all by myself, sometimes my brothers would tag along. . . . Even when I played with dolls, I would play 'secret agent.' I would use the front of the stereo console as the secret controls at the secret agent headquarters that the dolls would operate."

The Bond films were not the only films to bring a lighter touch to big-budget filmmaking. Audiences were not responding to the hints of seriousness in their films as the filmmakers probably wanted them to. In the summer of 1961, I saw the first Saturday-night screening in Santa Barbara, California, of *The Guns of Navarone*—the big adventure movie written and produced by the formerly blacklisted screenwriter Carl Foreman. When Gregory Peck and David Niven started their philosophical discussion of the nature of leadership, at least five different people in the audience got up and went out to get popcorn and candy. They knew they could go then without missing any of the big action to come, and they were right. Filmmakers began using a lighter touch. In 1962, *Lawrence of Arabia* used Robert Bolt's witty dialogue as a counterpoint to the spectacle, and in 1963, Steve McQueen was the epitome of American cool as Hilts, "The Cooler King," in *The Great Escape*.

Not every big-budgeted American film of the mid-sixties had that lightness of touch. Some viewers who were so dazzled by the desert in *Lawrence* may have missed the dialogue altogether while they were waiting for the intermission so that they could get something to drink. Robert Bolt returned to write *Doctor Zhivago*, one of the big hits of 1965, but one without any light touch at all. *Zhivago* was promoted almost as an art film, given that David Lean's two previous films, *The Bridge on the River Kwai* (1957) and *Lawrence*, had both won Academy Awards for Best Picture. The film did not open up to MGM's expectations in its December 1965 reserved-seat engagements, but as soon as "Lara's Theme," the film's music by Maurice Jarre, became a popular hit, audiences understood they could accept the film not as an art film, but as a grand romantic adventure, and the picture became a big hit.

High school teacher Donna Crisci saw the movie in her freshman year of high school and says it was "*the* movie" at that time.

> We went to Hollywood to see it on exclusive run. I loved it. I thought the theme (the credit theme, not Lara's theme) was so beautiful and I really liked the character of Pasha, played by Tom Courtenay. I was the first to see it in my set, but soon the whole high school was going. We all bought clothes with a Russian influence; my yearbook pictures that year were filled with Russian collars. We read the book, we thought it sad and romantic.
>
> Sometimes I show *Zhivago* to my high school kids, the same age we were. I teach all honors kids, but they don't like it. They don't understand it or see the point. We had no trouble understanding it at all. Anyway, I still retain a nostalgic affection for this film, but I no longer think it a great film as I once did. I love the production values, but Lean did not do justice to the book.

Peggy Dilley says the film is "the movie I walked around longest saying it was my favorite and still is. I loved it so much. I still do. It's such an epic story. Haunting. That music. The snow scenes. That penetrating cold. I know what it's like to be that cold. I grew up in the ice and snow. I bought a coat like Geraldine Chaplin's. I look out boxcar windows with a poet's eye, thinking about Yuri, many times too, and write music for mandolins [it was the balalaika in the film] in ice palaces." Monica Dunlap saw it in its first release and remembers "thinking how beautiful Julie Christie is . . . and how stunning the scenes were, her seduction, Zhivago and his family opening the train boxcar door in the mountains."

Jon Conrad saw it during a winter holiday vacation when he was in his sophomore year in high school. "Two school chums spent the break with my family. My father took us all to see this. I hated the music right off (still do), then fell asleep through most of the movie. The following spring, I saw it again when it finally made it out to 'regular' theatres, and though I stayed awake, I still found it boring. And HATED the music." T. Taylor, however, remembers the music and not the movie, although it is one of her mother's favorites. And Natalie Sibelman says, "*Doctor Zhivago* I didn't love: too much crying and too much snow."

Because of its grandeur and scope, *Doctor Zhivago* suffers more than many films when seen on television. Scott Hemmann saw it in its first release and "sat entranced though the entire film by the epic story, the beautiful score, the lavish sets, the majestic and rich cinematography, and David Lean's stylish direction. It is another film I refuse to watch on TV." Virginia Keene, who had been "dazzled" by it in its first run, says, "Now, on video and cable it loses that grandeur and beauty and seems slow and tedious in spots. It seems terribly stifled by the small screen."

Jack Hollander first saw *Doctor Zhivago* on TV and then later in a theatre:

One cannot say that they have seen this movie until viewed on a full, large screen (Some cable channels wisely show this and *Lawrence of Arabia* letterboxed; unfortunately, these films are so grand that although the entire screen is viewed, it is too small to be appreciated—how can you even *see* the train along that thin strip in the center of the vast whiteness as it progresses eastward?). I supposed that the greatness of this film lies in that no matter how many times I see the film, I ache for Zhivago to catch Lara as he staggers off of the streetcar at the end, and each and every time I cry when he doesn't. Every performance is so beautifully crafted (Credit, in part, must go to David Lean; even actors I don't much care for—I'm not a big Omar Sharif fan, for example, but he's so good in these two films—are so splendid in his films that I marvel at their skill), the camera work and the pacing are spectacular, and the film score is great. Another great feat of a David Lean film is that they do not seem to be that long at all while you are watching them—the time passes so smoothly. The images are also so haunting (Zhivago coming to the door with a face full of ice; Lawrence encouraging the attack with his, "Come on, then!; etc. . . .) and they stay with you forever. Even when I see these again (and again) on TV, these moments are reinforced in my memory.

Dorian Wood was first exposed to the film on television when he was young:

My father's favorite film of all time. He bought the official sound track, poster, and even the coffee mug. Of course, I had to see the film. Back then, I really didn't mind seeing the films of such large scale on the Boob Tube, and the impression that I got from watching *Doctor Zhivago* was that of great sadness and lingering, cold depression. I was probably about seven at the time, and the movie just seemed too tedious to me. I'd try to go to my room, but my dad would beg me to stay and continue watching, insisting that the next scene was going to be excellent. Even back then, I realized how important the film was to my father. I didn't know why, and I still don't. What I do know is that this film became part of his life, and from time to time he'll try to convince me to watch it with him (he owns a copy, of course), and most of the time I'll back out. The film is truly great, but it's obviously more than that to my dad. He named my younger sister Lara.

Doctor Zhivago's main competition at the Academy Awards that year was *The Sound of Music*, an adaptation of a moderately successful Rodgers and Hammerstein stage musical. By 1970, the film had passed *Gone With The Wind* as the highest-grossing film up to that time.[11] Audiences developed a love–hate relationship to *The Sound of Music* from the beginning. Donna Crisci did not like musicals and only went to see it because her best friend was working in the theatre and could get her in for free. Crisci "could not understand what all the fuss was about. Choked even then on the horrid message in 'I Am Sixteen' long before I knew I was a feminist. Was not moved during 'Edelweiss,' though I recall people sobbing around me. I still don't like this film; in Salzburg this summer, I said that aloud and was almost lynched." Virginia Keene "saw this at the theatre when the whole world was crazy about it. I hated it. I thought it was silly, sappy, sentimental drivel. It just didn't work for me on any level. I've never seen the whole thing again. I gave it a shot on cable once and disliked it as much as ever." Monica Dunlap saw it "as an adolescent and secretly believed that I was already too sophisticated for it, or it was my ambition to be too sophisticated for it. Recently it was shown on television and I appreciated it."

The first time Peter Albers saw *The Sound of Music*, he thought, "This is one of the greatest films ever made." He explains, "It was so exciting, with the intrigue, the love interest, and all the relationships working together so well; it really seemed like magic." Aubrey Solomon, a film historian who was also a producer on the late seventies television series *That's Hollywood*, first saw the film "in Amsterdam in the summer of 1967 with Dutch subtitles and was totally unimpressed. . . . I've excerpted it in shows I've done and some scenes are undoubtedly enjoyable, but I've resisted any opportunity to see it again."

When Francisco Checa first saw it, "the idea of someone who was to be a nun changing her mind for someone or something else was hard to understand, me being young and Catholic." For Patrician Cortazar, the music in the film was "the source of many productions in our backyard as children." Olufemi Samuel saw the film with his family. "The movie centered around discipline and family harmony and it was used as a yardstick in my family. I remember that my dad threatened us that if we don't stop being bad, he was going to act like the father in *Sound of Music*. This implies discipline, so we would stop immediately."

Albert Nazaryan saw the film in Armenia when he was six. "My mother took me to see *The Sound of Music*. We watched it four or five times. I remember a rectangular box filled with colors, Julie Andrews, puppet-goats, all surrounded by complete blackness. I don't remember how I felt, but it must have had a big impact on me since there are very few things I remember about Armenia. But I vividly remember those bright summer colors." Years later, Nazaryan's family had moved to Los Angeles, and he watched the film once a year on television. "I loved this movie more than anything. I always got this warm feeling as though I was one of those kids in an Austrian castle and not in a shitty house in Hollywood. Escapism at its best!"

The Sound of Music has been shown regularly on TV, and unlike other large-scale films, audiences will watch it. Scott Hemmann, who will not watch *Doctor Zhivago* on TV will watch *The Sound of Music*, at least partly because he had a crush on Julie Andrews when he first saw the film. For Robin Magee, the film was "the cause of the fastest shower I've ever taken in my life. It was first shown on TV in 1976, and my parents were going to let me see it provided I was *completely* ready for bed. I also *had* to see it because we were three weeks from production at school, and I was playing Brigita (the third youngest child)." Angela West was not quite so sympathetic to the kids. "I just wanted to shoot the children with their gold hair and happy little faces. I think the entire family should have been caught by the German police and stuck in a concentration camp for a month to give them a good dose of the real world."

For D'Arcy West, the family experience of watching the film on television was a bit unconventional.

I would watch it every year until the puppet show sequence, right when the adults started falling in love and the Nazi political thing came into play. I always thought the best musical numbers were in the beginning. Then I'd turn it off and stand in front of the mirror and scream all the song words I could remember and make up the rest. I would get my sisters in on this, too. My mom would catch us watching *The Sound of Music* and tell us to turn off that terrible movie. I finally asked her why she hated it, and she said because Julie Andrews is so 'dykey.' I've watched the movie all the way to the end in my adult years, and it's not bad. In fact, the last half is probably what lends the movie any depth at all.

Like D'Arcy West, Blair Woodard has changed his views. "As I have grown up with it, my ideas about the backdrop of Nazi-occupied Austria have changed. The ideas of personal freedom and having to sacrifice for it have become more important, while the beauty of the music has stayed the same." Nancy Lathrop's changed reactions have been more extreme. As a kid, she saw it in the theatre and liked the first part with the kids, then as a teenager began to appreciate the romance, and then discovered the political story. "It was like a whole different movie. I hadn't seen this one. I'd seen some other version of it when I was a kid." And for some people, the movie just remains beloved. Jack Hollander has seen the film several times, and in college he wrote for the band newsletter of the UCLA marching band. Once he asked his fellow members of the band what their favorite films were. "The consensus among this musical bunch gave the nod to *The Sound of Music*."

Because of the enormous commercial success of *The Sound of Music*, Hollywood decided that the way to get the audiences to turn out was to make large-scale musicals. *The Sound of Music* was followed shortly by *Doctor Dolittle* (1967), *Star!* (1968), *Hello Dolly* (1969), *Paint Your Wagon* (1969), and others. With a few exceptions (*Funny Girl* in 1968), they were disasters at the box office. The average weekly attendance at the movies dropped from 44 million in 1965 to 17.5 million in 1969.[12] About 1968 or 1969, I was at a party with a choir my wife sang in. One of the women in the choir was complaining that they did not make any good movies like *The Sound of Music* anymore. I asked her if she had seen any of the musicals that had come along after *The Sound of Music*. She had not.

"Why not?"

"Well, they weren't the same."

Alfred Hitchcock was later quoted as saying that *The Sound of Music* was one of the biggest disasters that ever hit Hollywood because of all the money the imitations lost. He was right, and it paved the way for a change in the way Hollywood made movies. And a change in the audiences who went to see them.

Television and Movies

Let us take a brief pause, as they say in television, to discuss just that—television, or at least moviegoing on television. From the fifties on, many moviegoers saw their first movies on television. Olufemi Samuel began that way.

> I started watching movies at an early age. An age too early to recall what I first saw. I was one of those kids that watch TV from morning till night. I had such a bad habit of watching TV that my father once said, "They could steal the whole house while Femi is watching TV, and he wouldn't even know it's been stolen." That was how terrible I was. I also remembered my first word was "Ssshh" instead of "Mama," beckoning people to be quiet. And what do I watch TV for? Simply movies! Movies! Movies! Movies! I love movies for no reason whatsoever, I just love them; maybe because it gives me the opportunity to put myself in a "trance." It takes me to this other world for two hours, in which I experience love, romance, action, comedy and tragedy. I just love it!

Not surprisingly, to this day Samuel watches most of the movies he sees on TV and video, as do many others.

Regular moviegoers make the transition—sometimes earlier, sometimes later—to watching movies in a theatre. Wil Dimpflmaier was four when his father took him to his first movie theatre. As Dimpflmaier's father later told him, after about twenty minutes, "I stood up on my chair and told him I wanted to change the channel. I didn't quite get the theatre concept. My father had to explain to me that everybody paid to watch just this one show and there were no other channels. For some reason, I thought there were big dials on the side of the screen where I, and only I, would change what was on. I've gotten past that." Joaquin Berndt grew up in South America watching movies on television and saw his first movie in a theatre at the age of seven. He was addicted to TV as a younger child, but then his brother took him to see a movie when they were visiting a big city. The place they went looked more like a house than a theatre, and the chairs were very "rustic." Berndt sat down and saw the large screen and "wondered until the movie started why we were all gathered in this place looking at the same empty wall, then it started. The film was black-and-white, and I watched it and fell in love with it."

Sometimes the transition from television to film can be a shock. Edna Gabbard spent her childhood in the Philippines in a country town. Her first experiences watching a movie were on TV, and she could not figure out how they could get the little people into the box.

I cried when it was a sad movie and screamed to death when it was a scary movie. My mother didn't allow us to watch a movie, so my sister and I escaped the house all the time just to see a movie on the TV. My mother believed that watching a movie will teach us only immorality, and she was always telling me that. That was impacted into my mind, and I grew up having no interest in going to a movie theatre. . . .

I was at the age of sixteen when my mother allowed me to go to a theatre and see a movie with a group of my cousins. My mother allowed me only that time because I was the only one in all of those children who had never been in a theatre. I was so naïve inside the theatre and scared that I might get lost in the dark, I grabbed my three cousins inside.

My nervousness got too intense when I saw those running horses on the screen and the huge train appeared to be coming through the audience. I screamed, and everyone was all laughing at me. I felt very embarrassed! I told the story to my mother that I was behind the children of my age because I never go to a movie theatre. It was hard to convince my mother until I lost interest in seeing a movie in a theatre. I remember that my mother only allowed me to see a movie if it was a karate movie because I played karate at the time. At least I could save my school allowance to see a movie and watch all of Bruce Lee's movies.

Watching television in America, particularly in Los Angeles, can affect how you view the movies. Sam Frank used to watch a late-night movie program in Los Angeles, hosted by a comic named Paul Gilbert. Frank saw the movie *Sylvia* (1965), in which Gilbert played a female impersonator in a nightclub. "*That* shocked me at age thirteen, and I was never able to watch that guy again without thinking of the pervert he played in that movie." For some people, such as Michael Behling, just the fact that movies were competing with the other shows on television was enough to turn him off movies on TV. "I think this was because I had a very short attention span, and the two hours of airtime that a movie took seemed like a very long time during which I could watch several other shows. So most of the feature-length films I would see would be with my parents in a theatre." Don Ricketts has adjusted his viewing to fit television. "I watch about two to three films to completion each week. A lot of times I will watch, if on TV, just pieces of movies. I surf the channels a lot. Mixing movies with news, commercials, sports, sitcoms, nature documentaries, and MTV. Sounds confusing. Only if I change the stations too fast."

Rocio Vargas's family had a black-and-white television set, and when her parents took her to see the movie *Mary Poppins* (1964) in a theatre, "It was a truly wonderful experience. I remember crying when leaving the theatre, because I wanted my mother to buy that big television set with the crispy colors. From that point on, our black-and-white TV set, that until then was the best thing at home, took second best to the magic of the big screen." Rudie Bravo has movies that she watched on her mother's black-and-white television set that she still has not seen in color. She was "literally *awed* the first time I saw John Boorman's *Excalibur* (1981) in color on TV, and again when I saw it on the big screen."

Joaquin Berndt explains why he and others will go out to see a movie rather than watch it on TV. "Movies are the real thing. Why would you go to see a concert when you could watch it on MTV? Because it is the real thing! When you are smashed by the gigantic screen, when the stars look at you and you feel the thrill of being showered by the lights of the story that happens right there . . . ." Octavio Jimenez agrees: "The reality of the matter is that the best place to see a movie is in the theatres, because you get audience participation, the effects of sound in an enclosed room, and the benefit of seeing the picture on a giant-sized screen. . . . Television . . . will always be second best." Terrence Atkins adds, "I think that I was robbed by being raised in the video/TV generation."

Watching films on television has all kinds of drawbacks. Bill Pulliam recently saw *Dr. Strangelove* on TV and was disappointed that the various sight gags in the backgrounds, such as the bombs labeled "Nuclear Warhead—Handle With Care," were not legible on the small screen. Photographer Alix Parson thinks movies are "always better in theatres. The television robs so much from films—their impact and power, the sound, the theatre experience (in technical and aesthetic terms). What I dislike most about movies on television is all the distractions that come with watching a movie at home—the phone, what's going on outside, etc." Jean Ferguson agrees. "I think this is a matter of focus—folding the laundry while watching a film or answering a telemarketer's call breaks the concentration."

Albert Nazaryan adds, "For better or worse, you are forced to give the film your complete attention in a theatre. Everything is black except for the screen. It is truly an *experience*. Television is not an experience. It is a distraction." Richard Henrie concurs. In the year before he replied to the questionnaire, he saw about fifteen films in theatres, but over a hundred on TV, and "It's strange, because I can't remember the films I saw on TV."

Rocio Vargas finds the relationship between seeing a film in theatres and on television more complex.

> I have noticed that for me action–adventure movies lose their magical impact on the small screen. However, if I go back and watch them again on the big screen, the emotional impact comes back again almost with the same intensity as it did when watching them for the first time. On the other hand, movies dealing with complex plots, social issues . . . such as *J.F.K.*(1991), *Malcolm X* (1992), *The Godfather, Dead Again* (1991), *The Conversation* (1974), *The Ten Commandments* and others never lose their magic, whether I am watching them on the television set or at the movie theatre. . . .
>
> *The Sound of Music* had much more emotional impact on me when I saw it in black-and-white instead of in color. I think it was because black-and-white added to the dramatics of it all, while the color softens it, making the movie more of a fairy tale kind of thing, taking away a lot of the realism that for me made it such an interesting movie to watch. To my disappointment, I have never seen this movie on the big screen either.

Kasey Arnold-Ince, the mother of a six-year-old, says in response to the question about watching movies on television,

> Movies on TV? They have that? Why didn't I know? (Probably because I've been going to bed at 9:00.) I don't get premium channels, I don't get *TV Guide*, and the TV is not turned on Monday through Friday (with occasional exceptions), so that Max and I can read, play games, build stuff, sculpt, etc. Consequently, I have no idea what's on the tube in the way of movies. (I know, I sound too virtuous to be true, but it's a self-defense measure in a world that is intent on turning my child into an aggressive, ignorant boor.)

Watching movies on TV can also bring the family closer together. Peter Albers remembers that movies were a big part of his family's Christmas holidays.

> When I was a little older, my middle sister would come home from college at vacation, and we would stay up until all hours of the night watching the fundraising Christmas movie festival on WNET-PBS. There would always be great old movies, particularly Fred and Ginger, who were our favorites. It was a magical time every year, and what made it particularly

wondrous is that, not only did it build wonderfully right up to Christmas, but it would keep Christmas going on past New Year's. Heck, we could watch *Top Hat* (1935) ten times. It just got better and better.

Among the joys moviewatchers like Albers discovered with television were old movies. Ira Katz started getting hooked on old movies on television as a kid, when "it was possible to sit there and watch movies all afternoon every Saturday and Sunday. So that's exactly what I did. I loved all the old movies with Cagney, Bogart, Tracy, and Stewart. At an early age (like many other people) I identified with James Dean, Montgomery Clift, and Marlon Brando. I didn't have a clue as to who they were, but I always enjoyed watching them."

The old movie that most people were probably introduced to on television was *The Wizard of Oz*, if only because its regular network showings were (and still are) family events. Bryan Cawthon's family had a small thirteen-inch TV set, and the channel showing the film did not come in well, so his first memory of the film is of his mother yelling out the window "better" or "worse" as his father adjusted the antenna on the roof. The first time Rigo Fernandez saw the film he was six years old and attending a birthday party at his grandparents. "The kids were running around making noise and walking in front of the TV screen, so I did not really get the storyline, but I did get pulled in by all of its colorful magic. . . . I remember the surreal characters (the scarecrow, the tin man, and the dwarfs) being very much animated and almost three-dimensional." The movie made Valerie Hornig "want to become part of it, to live the magic." It gave her "the impression that whoever made this movie sure knew what I was dreaming about."

Rick Lopez dreamed about *The Wizard of Oz* afterwards. He also saw the film for the first time on TV when he was six but was scared by the witch and the flying monkeys. "There's something about bizarre skin colors and hair that have always scared me. I've had several nightmares with blue or green human-meat-eating monkeys. I think *The Wizard of Oz* has contributed to those nightmares. In terms of the story, I've always hated it. I wish Dorothy would have stayed in Oz. The credo 'There's No Place Like Home' no longer has any relevance; especially if you don't have one."

Lisa Evans saw the film with her family when she was six and thought it was scary and that the Munchkins were "eerie and demented." When her parents praised Judy Garland's singing, "I burst out crying. Shocked, my parents asked me what was wrong, and I exclaimed that I could sing too. In actuality, I was jealous that my parents were fawning over another little girl." It was then that Evans decided to become an actress. She has never come to love *The Wizard of Oz*. "To me, it's like a bizarre drug trip, and I think that song 'Over the Rainbow' is the most annoying song in the world. OK, 'Tomorrow' from *Annie* is the most annoying song, but 'Rainbow' is close. Wouldn't you know that I've choreographed both of those shows for children's theatre too? Yuck!"

Steven Krul watched *The Wizard of Oz* "religiously" every year and hopes someday to see it in a theatre. "The movie always was an emotional roller coaster to watch as a kid. Along with thinking Judy Garland was kind of a babe, those scary Flying Monkeys, the Wicked Witch of the West, it was all an exciting trip. The movie going from black-and-white to color is something that really stood out to me. I loved the music as well and found a record album of the sound track at a library, which I would listen to in between yearly viewings."

Al Gonzalez always saw the movie on TV and "enjoyed it each time it came on. . . . However, after five or six viewings over my young life, and by the time I was about thirteen, I'd pretty much had it. I do think, though, that as I get older I may come to enjoy it again." Blair Woodard watched it every year as a kid and "saw it recently at a friend's house while their kids were watching it, and it was great to *see* their reactions to some of the scenes that I had enjoyed and to realize that the film still worked."

For many people who grew up with black-and-white television sets, finding out the film was in color came as a surprise. When Rudie Bravo finally saw the film "in color on a big screen, I was shocked at how different it made the movie. For one thing, Dorothy looked old. But I also felt like I'd been watching only half a movie." Jack Hollander knew it was in color, and since his family "may have been one of the last 'middle-American' families to join the color revolution," he made the point one year to visit a friend with a color television set the night it was shown.

Virginia Keene saw *Oz* for the first time in color when "I was confined to a hospital bed in New York City in 1974! Imagine my astonishment when I watch Oz explode in color for the first time, as though I'd never seen the film before." Rick Mitchell saw it first on TV in black-and-white around 1958, and "my memory is that my fascination at the time was more with the special effects, an area in which I had a developing interest, and I only really liked the adventure sequence involving the Wicked Witch's castle." He did not see the film in color until he came to Los Angeles, by which time he had developed an appreciation for musicals, which he had not had before.

Peggy Dilley had been reading the book by Frank L. Baum when *The Wizard of Oz* was shown on television for the first time.

The Wizard of Oz is another movie that I've lived, in my head, on and off in my life. . . . I was maybe ten, just the right age to become Dorothy. It was on until past my bedtime, and I remember falling asleep and missing the very end. The next day, all my neighbor friends came over and we chose parts and started acting them out in my grandparents' backyard, on the swings, in the dollhouse, on the picnic table, etc. I got to be Dorothy. We acted out the story for months, and I finally finished reading the book, because I had to see how it ended.

This movie continued to affect and motivate me. It made me move to California from Madison, Wisconsin, in 1979. I came with just two suitcases and my dog Benji. He looked like the movie Benji, but he was like Toto to me. I wore a yellow and white checked shirt, because it reminded me of Dorothy's checked dress. I had my picture taken wearing braids in front of the Hollywood sign. When I walked in the Hollywood Hills, I was following the yellow brick road. Hollywoodland was Munchkinland. The Hollywood Reservoir was The Emerald City and The Observatory was the wicked witch's castle.

Gone With the Wind is another film many people made their first acquaintance with on TV. Wendi Cole first saw it on TV and thought, "It was the most glorious thing I had ever seen. I thought Scarlett O'Hara was so beautiful. I don't really remember much, because I was so young. I just remember thinking that the dresses Scarlett wore were gorgeous, and I wondered what it would be like to live in that time." Marcus Franklin saw it when he was young and hated it, "and I hate it more now than when I saw it when I was young, since I really understand what was taking place in that movie."

Tandy Summers remembers being rather unimpressed upon her first viewing of *Gone With the Wind* and says she was

around seventeen or eighteen when Ted Turner's TBS started regularly playing *Gone With the Wind*. Back then I'd watch maybe a few minutes of it, then get bored. Back then I saw it as just an old period movie with not a lot of action. I never stuck around long enough to watch the action. My grandma loved it. She saw it back when it first came out. I thought it was for girls, like a soap opera. But around twenty-one or twenty-two, I sat and watched the full movie. It's a great movie.... The epic shots of all the soldiers wounded, hundreds and hundreds of them. "Who cares," I was thinking around seventeen or eighteen.

Eva Mahgrefthe watches *Gone With the Wind* "religiously each year when they play it on television. Watching it for the first time I became so absorbed in the story and so involved with the characters, even the ever-intruding commercials did not disturb me. 'Fiddle-dee-dee' with a Southern accent and a saucy attitude became my phrase of choice for the next several weeks. I fell in love with the film and, since the age of ten, began collecting books and memorabilia related to it. Never has a viewing of it not left me in tears, and I have seen it at least fifteen times."

The film had been Scott Hemmann's mother's favorite film, so when it came to a revival house, the whole family went. Even though they misread the show times in the paper and got there in time for the intermission, Hemmann still liked the film and has seen it many times in revival theatres. However, he refuses to watch it on television. "It just wouldn't be the same."

Other films made different kinds of impact when seen on television for the first time. Nancy Lathrop saw *Citizen Kane* on a television set with bad sound, so she "did not understand what he said when he dropped the globe in the beginning, so the entire film I was searching along with them for his final words, and when the sled burned, I didn't make the connection." By the time Tandy Summers saw *Kane* at age sixteen on cable TV she had

> heard about it as a great masterpiece in interviews with Spielberg, Lucas, and Kubrick. I watched it and was glued from start to finish. The moody music and scenes in the beginning. Was this a horror movie? The amazing visuals are what stuck out the most. It didn't matter it was black-and-white. In fact, it was better being that. I don't remember if I got it all the first viewing, but I knew it was about this guy who had everything and lost it all. I thought back then it was such a profound movie. Only later did I begin to appreciate the humor in it. But Kane was such a likable guy. Back then it was sad to see this guy's life turn out so tragic. I think the scandal with the other woman flew over my head. Yeah, I was a pretty dumb guy. I just kind of wondered why this guy didn't get elected.

Another classic film that was shown a lot on television was *Casablanca* (1942). As much as Scott Hemmann loved the film when he saw it on television, he "didn't fully appreciate it until I saw it last year in rerelease at the Mann's Chinese Theatre with a full house." Robin Magee first saw *Casablanca* "in bits and chunks on late-night TV in high school, as my dad absolutely refused to give up the TV when it was on. Finally, in college (at the film society) I saw it in its entirety. *Wow!* I was stunned! An intelligent movie, with snappy dialogue and all sorts of double-crossing." Adam Ozturk "tried to watch it and could not. . . . I turned it off because of the terrible acting of the French colonel [it's not clear if he means Conrad Veidt as the German colonel or Claude Rains as the French police chief] and others also. The fakeness of the scenery and the set, I didn't believe it at all."

Peggy Dilley caught up with *Sunset Boulevard* on television. "I may have seen it, or parts of it, many times before in my life, but this was the time I most remember, because it was the first time I started to see myself in the lead female character's shoes. And it seemed very sad and tragic—sad when each of us comes to realize that those magic days of youth, when you think the world will always be your oyster for the taking, are really going to end someday if they haven't already."

Lisa Moncure enjoyed *The Birds* (1963) on TV more than she might have in a theatre. "My mother had already seen the film and warned me that it was scary. We were eating cabbage with dinner that night. Our TV trays were in place, right in front of the TV. I had told my mother to warn me ahead of time about the scary parts so I could cover my eyes. The thing I didn't tell her was that I hated cabbage. So when the scary parts came on, I excused myself and secretly took the cabbage with me and threw it out. So Alfred Hitchcock kept me from having a balanced diet as a child."

Kalani Mondoy saw *Jaws* first in a theatre, then on television, where "it just didn't seem that scary. I think it's because of two reasons: (1) I already knew what was going to happen and (2) there wasn't any audience around to scare me by screaming their heads off."

Watching movies on network television has its own aggravations. Oscar Berkovich, Susanna Serrano, and Daniel Barr object to the editing of features for network showing, with Barr noting that "the editing tends to be so Presbyterian." Scott Renshaw also objects to network cutting, admitting, "I'm a film snob, not so much in terms of genre or subject matter, but in terms of the quality of the holistic film experience and the opportunity to see a piece of art (and I do consider film an art) the way the artists involved intended it to be seen, to the extent that that is possible."

Eva Mahgrefthe admitted above that *Gone With the Wind* was so compelling that the commercial breaks did not bother her, but for other viewers on other films it can be a problem. Edwin Castro finds it difficult to "keep the same tone of emotion or excitement" about a scene if it's interrupted by commercials. "It's a good way to lose interest in a movie."

For some viewers cable is the answer, although as Oscar Berkovich says, "They're always playing the same films over again and it does get mighty expensive." Peter Albers does not mind seeing the same films over again on cable, even bad ones. "When watched like that, even a movie that's awful to begin with takes on a comfy, familiar feel—like a piece of furniture, or a painting you've had on your wall forever." Skylaire Alfvegren does not have cable, because "my already meager free time would be gobbled up getting bleary-eyed taping the screen gems of the centuries." However, she does try to catch up with cable when she visits her grandmother, who has "the 'super-fabulouso' cable package." For "Glinn Leevitt," "The only people I know with cable are my parents. In order for me to watch a movie on cable, I also have to endure my parents. So naturally, I do not watch many movies on cable."

Sangbum Lee alternates between cable and non-cable TV movie watching.

If the movies I really want to see are on the cable, then I will use the cable, but if the movies I really want to see are on the non-cable television, I will watch those—even though I cannot stand the commercials—since it saves me money on renting cassettes.

Sometimes, the non-cable television will suddenly put on a movie I really want to see but was not even thinking about, and I like the surprise effect of this, so I watch it, despite having to put up with all the commercials. But sometimes putting up with all the commercials gets to be too much, so I will stay away from non-cable television for a while.

Kurt Knecht did not go to movies until he was in high school. "My father never took me, and I never went by myself. We did have HBO though, and I incessantly watched films from there." D'Arcy West found her family's cable connections perhaps more entertaining than her parents imagined. "We had 'Z' channel [a legendary Los Angeles cable movie channel in the seventies] when I was growing up, and we lived in sort of a remote canyon area of L.A., so when we got bored, like we so often did, my sisters and I would watch soft-core Emmanuelle movies or the Pink Panther movies [1963–1983] over and over."

On the other hand, it was not necessary to get cable to find yourself sexually aroused by movies on television. Sam Frank, who grew up to write the book *Sex in the Movies*,[1] remembers that one of the local Los Angeles independent broadcast stations used to run the same movie all week. Frank "watched *Damn Yankees* [1958] all nine times because Gwen Verdon as the seductress Lola got me incredibly horny. I spent the whole week watching the movie on my mother's bedroom television masturbating to 'Whatever Lola Wants.'"

Closing the Sixties

Even before *Bonnie and Clyde* was released in the late summer of 1967, it had begun to strike a nerve in viewers—or rather, *a lot* of nerves. Curtis Lee Hanson, the editor of *Cinema*, saw the film before it was completed and wrote in the summer issue of his magazine that "even in rough cut, *Bonnie and Clyde* is the most significant American movie in years . . . [the filmmakers] have produced, while working within the Hollywood studio system, an extremely personal, meaningful film; the best to come along in quite a while. . . . *Bonnie and Clyde* will be a commercial hit. Young people will throng to it."[1]

Bosley Crowther, the august film critic for the *New York Times*, did not share Hanson's opinion.

> It is a cheap piece of baldfaced slapstick comedy that treats the hideous depredations of that sleazy moronic pair as though they were as full of fun and frolic as the jazz-age cut-ups in *Thoroughly Modern Millie*. . . .
>
> Such ridiculous, camp-tinctured travesties of the kind of people these desperados were . . . might be passed off as a candidly commercial movie, nothing more, if the film weren't reddened with blotches of violence of the most grisly sort. . . .
>
> This blending of farce with brutal killings is as pointless as it is lacking in taste, since it makes no valid commentary upon the already travestied truth.[2]

Bonnie and Clyde, with domestic rentals of $20.25 million, outgrossed such expensive 1967 musical attempts to duplicate the commercial success of *The Sound of Music* as *Thoroughly Modern Millie* (rentals of $14.7 million), *Camelot* ($11.9 million), and *Doctor Dolittle* ($6.2 million).[3] Michael Medved thinks it was the "youth pictures" of the late sixties that drove down the average weekly movie attendance to approximately twenty million, where it has stayed ever since.[4] I suspect it was the flop *Sound of Music* wanna-bes, as well as the continuing impact of television, that reduced the family audience for movies. Hollywood did not desert its traditional audiences, as Medved claims, as much as the audiences deserted Hollywood. Filmmakers began to respond to the audience that remained passionate about the films—the youth audience. And within a year of his *Bonnie and Clyde* review, Bosley Crowther had retired.[5]

One of the few reviewers of the time who paid attention to audience reactions to movies, at least at this stage in her career, was Pauline Kael. While the writers of *Bonnie and Clyde*, David Newman and Robert Benton, had been influenced by the changes in European films of the early sixties,[6] Kael noted that "when an American movie is contemporary in feeling, like this one, it makes a different kind of contact with an American audience from the kind that is made by European films, however contemporary."[7] Kael describes the audience at the screening she attended:

> *Bonnie and Clyde* keeps the audience in a kind of eager, nervous imbalance—holds our attention by throwing disbelief back in our faces. To be put on is to be put on the spot, put on the stage, made the stooge in a comedy act. People in the audience at *Bonnie and Clyde* are laughing, demonstrating that they're not stooges—that they appreciate the joke—when they catch the first bullet right in the face. The movie keeps them off balance to the end. During the first part of the picture, a woman in my row was gleefully assuring her companion, "It's a comedy. It's a comedy." After a while, she didn't say anything. Instead of the movie spoof, which tells the audience it doesn't need to feel or care, that it's all in fun, that "we were only kidding," *Bonnie and Clyde* disrupts us with "And you thought we were only kidding."[8]

Monica Dunlap may well have been in the audience Kael saw the film with. Dunlap saw it in New York when it was released. "It definitely made an impression—a new kind of Hollywood film is the way I think I thought of it. Hip in some new Hollywood way, but the brutality in this movie was also new, and I didn't particularly like it. I didn't think of it as a good film but more as a slick one." Peggy Dilley was also divided about the film at the time and remains so to this day. "Being politically who I'd become by the time it came out and who I still am and wanting to have an affair with Warren Beatty real bad, I'd like to like it, but it still bothers me. It's not *quite* tragic, but I don't think I like Oedipus putting out his eyes either. I want the good guys to win. . . . Let's have a revolution that succeeds."

Al Gonzalez saw it in a theatre as a kid and was not pleased with the experience. "The loud guns scared me. As an adult, I've seen this movie twice, once on video and another time on TV. I still don't like it much, and the loud guns no longer scare me." Virginia Keene saw it "only once, when it first came out. I was so horrified by the endless slow motion death scene that I left the theatre and was in the lobby until the film was over. It troubled me for a long time. I remember little else about the movie except that I thought the title characters were jerks. I think it's time to check this out again," especially since she recently liked such films as *Reservoir Dogs* and *Unforgiven* (both 1992).

Some people responded more to the suggestion of sex in *Bonnie and Clyde* than to the violence. Marion Levine was fifteen when she saw it in its first release and "learned the fine art of seduction by watching Faye Dunaway smolder. . . . In fact, all my friends and I were just like Bonnie. We dressed like her, walked like her, smoldered just like her. The only discernible difference was that we, unlike Faye Dunaway, were trapped in the bodies of middle-class teenagers whose only viable criminality lay in shoplifting lipsticks from Rexall instead of sticking up banks."

Albert Nazaryan responded to both the sex and the violence when he saw the film at the age of sixteen and thought it was "awesome. . . . Entertaining, violent, and Faye Dunaway in the seminude." He had heard that in the original script, there was a ménage a trois between Beatty, Dunaway, and the character eventually played by Michael J. Pollard (the scenes were cut after Pollard was cast.[9]) "I was appalled. Was nothing sacred? I knew my pubescent thoughts of Faye Dunaway's golden nude flesh would be forever marred." James Ford also remembers Dunaway. He went to the film "with my girlfriend in high school who happened to look quite a bit like Faye Dunaway. . . . Made me appreciate my girlfriend even more . . . for a while." Arnold Quinlan remembers only the beginning—"Faye is in the window half-naked. One of the sexiest shots I had ever seen"—and "then the slaughter at the end. No other shooting sequence has come close. . . . It is interesting how movies are remembered through youthful eyes." But when twenty-three-year-old Javier Rodriguez first saw it on TV, "The shootout at the end was so fake that I turned the TV off."

Richard Bogren saw the film with a group of friends while in college, and "We all thought Michael J. Pollard really made the film." Adam Ozturk also liked Pollard—"what a character, what a laugh, what a funny bunch of noises came out of him"—and was sad when Bonnie and Clyde were killed. "It's funny how I couldn't care about the cops or civilians they killed, but I wanted them to keep going; the anarchist in me."

The elements that made *Bonnie and Clyde* seem fresh and daring in 1967 very quickly became a standard part of American film. The violence of the shootouts was deepened by *The Wild Bunch* (1969), and the sexuality was intensified by *Last Tango in Paris* (1973). The combination of comedy and violence became a staple in action films. And for the next decade there would be many low-budget variations of *Bonnie and Clyde* set in the thirties with old cars (e.g. *Bloody Mama* [1970]). Daniel Barr, in his twenties, saw the film on TV in later years and thinks it "doesn't hold up . . . today it looks like a bad Movie-of-the-Week. On recent viewing, I noticed it looked very 'seventies' [sic]."

Ted Cantu grew up with a love of gangsters, so he enjoyed watching *Bonnie and Clyde*.

> We used to imitate Cagney and run around the neighborhood with sticks (pretending they were machine guns). The fascination continues with *Bonnie and Clyde* and *The Godfather* films. After 1967 we could approach the real gangsters and not rely on fictional fantasy. *Bonnie and Clyde* was great because it dealt with violence at a realistic level. . . . The ending really scares me when the farmers peer into the windows looking down at the bodies. That's the first time the point of perspective changes and it just ends. It stops as if the camera ran out of film. It bothers me just as much as it did when I first saw it; it's very haunting.

Pauline Kael noted at the time of its release that "*Bonnie and Clyde* brings into the almost frighteningly public world of movies things that people have been feeling and saying and writing about, and once something is said or done on the screens of the world, once it has entered mass art, it can never again belong to a minority, never again be in the private possession of an educated, or 'knowing,' group. But even for that group, there is an excitement in hearing its own private thoughts expressed out loud and in seeing something of its own sensibility become part of our common culture."[10] Perhaps this is why the film still works for some viewers.

For all its impact on the culture, *Bonnie and Clyde* was topped at the box office in 1967 by Stanley Kramer's star-laden but stodgy message picture, *Guess Who's Coming to Dinner?* ($25.5 million), and by the highest-grossing picture of the year, *The Graduate*. The latter pulled in rentals of $43.1 million, almost as much as *Bonnie and Clyde* and *Guess Who's Coming to Dinner?* together.

The first reaction I heard from a viewer of *The Graduate* came from the husband of one of my wife's friends. We ran into Len in the middle of Westwood Village, the area next to the UCLA campus. By late 1967, it was on its way from being a campus suburban movie theatre area to becoming one of the predominant first-run exhibition areas in Los Angeles (a result of the recent completion of the Santa Monica and San Diego Freeways. Westwood was nicely situated at the intersection of the two freeways. The Santa Monica Freeway brought people from the east and west, and the San Diego Freeway brought people from the San Fernando Valley in the north.). As I recall, the large theatres on opposite corners were playing *Guess Who's Coming to Dinner?* and *Doctor Dolittle*.

Len, however, was raving about a little movie he had seen and was encouraging us to see. It had just opened; he loved its satirical take on contemporary society, and he was sure it would not be playing for too long. It was too intelligent, he thought, to make too much money.

Finding *The Graduate* was not easy. It was not playing in Westwood. It was not playing on Hollywood Boulevard, the other first-run area in Los Angeles. It was not playing in Beverly Hills, the first-run area that was being overtaken by Westwood. The only theatre the film's distributor, the small Avco-Embassy company, could put its film in was the Four Star, which was on Wilshire Boulevard well east of Beverly Hills. When my wife and I went to see *The Graduate* the following Saturday night, the theatre was packed.

The audience loved the film, laughing all the way and cheering Benjamin's attempts to get to Elaine in time. They hardly seemed to notice that Ben and Elaine did not really have anything to say to each other in the final shot. So much of the film was drowned out by laughter that I went back to see it again at a weekday matinee, figuring it would not be as crowded. The theatre was not *quite* as full, but the nature of the audience was different. The Saturday night crowd had been younger people and couples. The matinee crowd was mostly women in their thirties and older. The daytime audience was more involved in the relationship between Benjamin and Mrs. Robinson, did not laugh as much at the film, and was not cheering Benjamin on in the final scenes, but simply seemed resigned to the story ending this way.

As the film grossed more and more over the next few months, I noticed that attitudes about it began to change, especially at UCLA. I was now in the graduate program in the Theatre and Film Department, and the students there in those days tended to look down on American film. While originally my fellow students were nearly as enthusiastic as Len had been, a few months into the run they were saying the film was all right, but "flawed." By midsummer of 1968, they thought the film's director, Mike Nichols, had become a "sellout" for making such an obviously commercial film. Not a frame of the film had changed in those six months.

Some people saw the slickness immediately. A woman who saw it at the time felt the film was "a little like *Bonnie and Clyde* to me in its lack of soul and slick, similar style. The use of popular music in the film made an impression, but this film to me was another woman-disparaging film in a sort of subtle way. I couldn't say that even in my own mind at the time, but I remember feeling it. I think that I thought I liked it on a surface level at the time." Peggy Dilley picked up on similar vibrations, but in a different way. She was "about eighteen when I saw this. I wanted to lynch Mrs. Robinson. It was probably pretty exciting sleeping with her, though. It's too bad she had such a pretty daughter. I wanted to come live in a big house in California, and laze in swimming pool sun, and party in sunset bright multilights, and drive up a winding coast in a red convertible sports car, and live in Haight Ashbury and go to school at Berkeley. I wanted it so bad I eventually had to do it because I believed in Simon and Garfunkel."

Jon Conrad was "exactly the right age, supposedly, to be affected by this, a junior in college. I saw it in a big theatre next to our campus, with a full and appreciative audience. They mostly gave it a standing ovation at the end, but I didn't get it. Some of it was fun, some seemed dumb and pointless, and I certainly didn't see what made it so special to everybody else." His reaction changed when he saw it years later. "I was better able to appreciate the style and timing of its comic acting, especially in the early scenes. But it still seemed to me to have no resonance with real life whatever, and I still can't understand the devotion some people have to it."

Virginia Keene was twenty-two when *The Graduate* came out, and she "identified with the main characters and their dilemmas, and of course I was crazy about it! It seemed custom-made for my friends and me. The music by Simon and Garfunkel already belonged to us." She's seen the film since, and "it seems as fresh and poignant and funny as ever." Ira Katz was in his early teens when the picture opened. "It was easy to relate what Ben was going through at the time because we all (myself and the people I was associated with) just seemed to be floating, unsure of what direction to take for our future. The music did and still does play a large part in the meaning of the movie. It seems to communicate the inner thoughts of the character. I have seen it on television since then and much of the emotional impact is still there for me." James Ford saw it in high school and "started to become aware of my own future after high school. Plastics. I didn't think so either."

Some viewers could not relate to the film culturally. Richard Bogren had grown up on a "farm and relatively poor," and the lifestyle was simply too different at the time for him to appreciate. Rick Mitchell's "background is essentially midwestern middle-American middle class with little racial orientation. While attending Transylvania College in Kentucky in the sixties—one of the few black students there—I hung out primarily with kids from Connecticut and New Jersey and heard enough about prep schools to have no problems with *The Dead Poets Society* (1989), for example. However, while I enjoyed *The Graduate*, in December 1967, I hadn't had enough exposure to the unique L.A. Westside culture it depicted to be as affected by it as many others apparently were."

Jack Hollander was too young to see the film when it was first released but did see it later. He thinks the age you are when you see it affects how you respond to it. "I believe that my age has directly influenced my appreciation for this film—I liked it most when I was Hoffman's character's age (just post-college). Perhaps this is the *Catcher in the Rye* of movies—don't we appreciate

Holden Caulfield more as adolescents than we do as adults? In any case, any film that has Katharine Ross in it can't be all bad. Again, so much of this film has become 'icons'—just say the word 'plastics' in conversation and there is a mutual acknowledgment that the word refers to this film."

Lizy Moromisato was in college when she first saw it. The movie club near her college was running a Dustin Hoffman week, and she and her best friend went. "We felt very identified with the character . . . we were still young and disoriented about what we really wanted to do in life. But more than the movie itself, we just fell in love with Dustin Hoffman, and we missed school that whole week." Lisa Evans, who was born in 1968, saw *The Graduate* in college and "found that I could relate to much of the film. I thought it was an amusing film, but the mood it established made me kind of sad. I don't know if it was because of the music or the fact that it was so obviously dated in the sixties. The 1960s always seemed like such a sad yet magical decade to me. This movie really captured that time to me and . . . every time I see the film, I feel as if I am in a time warp."

Kurt Knecht came to *The Graduate* in 1989 when he was in his twenties. "The film was so powerful for me since I was able to identify with Dustin Hoffman's character. I remember driving to USC [where some of the "Berkeley" exteriors were filmed] and imagining myself as Benjamin Bradock looking for Elaine. I went to the same fountain that Dustin Hoffman had sat by during the film."

Shaun Hill-Kret "loved it. I loved it the next time and the next. This movie struck a cord with me." Wajeeh Khursheed was in his teens in the eighties when he first saw the film.

> It was the talk of the town, a movie was out on tape that had sex and among people we would never imagine. Sokoto, Nigeria, was a small town and a conservative town, and we as children could not just get our hands on just any film; our parents made sure that we didn't. But curiosity was at its peak, and somehow we did get to watch it. It was one of the most exciting periods of my teenage years. Watching this movie on TV recently wasn't as exciting as it was the first time, although I was looking for the same scene that excited me when I watched it the first time.

Tandy Summers first saw *The Graduate* on TV as a kid and did not understand it, although she remembered the seduction scene between Hoffman and Bancroft. The movie seemed to her "like a sitcom. A lot of it had to do with the music playing in the background during that seduction scene." When she was twenty-six, she caught it one night on TV. "I don't think I'd been wrapped into a film so deeply or rooted for the character like this in a long time. . . . I related so much to Hoffman's character now. All the ambitions my relatives had for me."

Like Summers, Glinn Leevitt didn't get as much out of the film as a child as he did when he saw it as an adult. He says that his older sister

is a big Paul Simon fan, don't ask me why. Anyhow, as a result, she was always watching *The Graduate*. The first time I saw it, I was way too young to appreciate it. I think my initial thoughts as a kid were that I was watching a bunch of lazy upper-class rich people who live by their pool. Since growing up, I have seen it again and do like it a lot. It seems to me I was half right about what I remember in seeing it the first time. It is very much about the leisure of the rich, but also about the youth growing up in this complicated society.

Bill Pulliam was too young to see *The Graduate* when it first came out, but when he saw it years later, he thought it was "excellent" and realized that all those years he had not had a clue what the song "Mrs. Robinson" was about. Daniel Barr did see it as a very young boy and "found it exciting erotically. Perhaps it was the similarity between the older woman in the film and my mother and grandmother. It struck a deep oedipal chord within me as a child. I would like to see it again, as it has faded from memory." Rick Lopez thought Hoffman should have run off with Mrs. Robinson, because "the daughter seemed so boring!" When Kenneth Hughes saw the film, he "wanted Mrs. Robinson and her daughter. I related to all the alienation, even though I was never rich and universitied. The alienation was mine, and screwing peoples' moms would handle it all perfectly."

Jill Mitchell, whose mother started taking her to Woody Allen movies when she was three or four, took her to see *The Graduate* at about that age. Mitchell remembers very little from the first screening, but when she saw the film again fifteen to twenty years later, "I got these intense feelings of flashback, especially during the pool scene. I think that seeing huge visuals as a small child influences one enormously. When I saw this the second time, it didn't feel like I suddenly saw something I'd seen a long time ago; it was more like I had unearthed a visual from my subconscious. This may sound a bit dramatic, but the feelings I had for this film were much more familiar to me than a distant memory."

Several younger people came to the film long after its first release. Angela West is in her twenties and calls *The Graduate* "one of the grooviest movies I've ever seen. . . . I think this movie was so good because it really spoke for a generation. I was enlightened by the entire movie and understood my parents' values a little more." D'Arcy West's "good friend's dad is [the actor who played] Benny the make-out king of *The Graduate*. Whenever we're near a window, we pound on it and scream 'Elaine!' My friend's dad still looks like he did in the movie—all slick and blond and creepy." Appropriately enough, she thinks, "the best part of the film was the very end, sitting on the bus, and they don't say anything. I love that they don't say anything to each other. That kills me."

Dorian Wood saw the film in the eighties when he was in his early teens and "really could not get it. The guy looked a lot like Dustin Hoffman, but back then I knew that he was an old guy and this guy was young . . . the movie just seemed too 'seventies' to me." Brian Calderon, now twenty-five, saw the film when he was twenty-two, and while he liked it more than he thought he would, "Parts of the film reminded me of a music video."

Even films not specifically intended, in subject matter or style, for the youth audience were often more appreciated by that audience in the late sixties. The most obvious example is Stanley Kubrick's *2001: A Space Odyssey*, which he began working on in 1965, long before Hollywood began thinking in terms of the new youth audience. When the film was released in 1968, it split the audiences as *Bonnie and Clyde* had done the year before. Many viewers wrote letters to Kubrick, and some of these were printed in *The Making of Kubrick's 2001*,[11] which was published two years after the film was released.

Before asking the noted moviemaker if he could borrow one of the space suits for his home-movie sequel, fourteen-year-old Randy Clower wrote in his letter to Kubrick he "loved every minute of *2001*. Anybody who says it was dull is an idiot. How can a movie so different, like *2001*, be dull? Oh, well, some people are dumb." Joel Robin Burcat, a thirteen-year-old from Philadelphia, wrote, "It was, in short, the best movie I have ever seen. Even though I am considered bright, I could not understand the last part of the movie." Jody Adams, a senior at Radcliffe, wrote "*2001* was WOW FUN, NEAT, KEEN!" Therese Kustra, nineteen years old, from College Point, New York, was not as impressed. "I must tell you it is the worst picture I have ever seen. . . . My girlfriend and I watched the audience's reaction as the people were leaving the theatre. Some people stared at each other and said nothing, while others laughed."

The grown-ups were often angry at Kubrick. Mrs. Elsie M. Gutwald of Lutherville, Maryland, wrote, "I was relieved during the intermission to overhear numerous couples express their disgust at the picture and to hear it made no sense to others, either. Many people left during the intermission. I have always had a high regard for MGM and stayed to the bitter end. My faith in MGM has been totally destroyed."[12]

Ansel H. Smith of Monroe, Louisiana, had just seen the film before writing to Kubrick. "My wife and I drove fifty miles to see it. During the return trip, we tried to discuss calmly what we had seen, but we invariably ended up screaming at each other. Had we lived another fifty miles from the theatre, we might possibly have worked something out—some sort of conclusion that we would have lived with." He had enjoyed the first part of the film, but "It was only when you started waving that damn black two-by-four all over the screen that I got a little uptight, as they say. Being a conservative, I found HAL 9000 [the computer "character" in the film] a little uppity." Virginia M. Dominick of Cambridge, Massachusetts, also mentioned the computers. "I enjoyed seeing a scientifically accurate description of space life and computers of the future. However, one thing did escape me (as it did all of my friends, many of whom have doctor of philosophy degrees)—the plot. Was there one?"

Not all adults hated the movie. Milton B. Schlenoff, a friend of Kubrick's father, wrote to him about the younger Kubrick's film. "My conclusion is that the entire picture is marvelous. For those adults who cannot enjoy this picture, I must agree with the sage who said, 'You cannot place pearls before swine.'" And in San Francisco, the home of counterculture, Anna Belle Neal wrote, "You say in effect that a true artist can't be a transcendentalist. I find you to be both. You are a genius and I also expect to (I hope) brush with you in the starry heavens when we are all reposing on our way to becoming (hopefully, again) the energy and spirit that is, do you think, Nietzsche's superman?"

As the letters would indicate, *2001* provoked both great and awful moviegoing experiences. Bryan Cawthon saw it with his father.

> My father, for as long as I have known him, has subscribed to *Popular Science* and *Popular Mechanics*. For this reason, I believe he was compelled to see the movie *2001: A Space Odyssey*. It was just me and my dad and my first time seeing a film in a theatre. I was five, and I remember being very much overwhelmed and scared. The tension was intense and the sound was all around me. . . . My mom wasn't there [as she would have been if they were at a drive-in] in a relatively quiet car, with a speaker box that could be controlled. The experience was traumatizing and I'm sure I have been scarred emotionally.

Although Al Gonzalez later came to enjoy the film, his first viewing of *2001* turned out to be one of his worst moviegoing experiences. Watching the film with his girlfriend, he soon realized

> the length and subject matter of the film was not conducive to my girlfriend's interest. From early on in the picture, in so many words, she tried to let me know that she could not understand my wanting to see the film. I have to admit that at some point in the movie I was getting a bit fidgety myself, but I had picked the film, and I was determined to ride it out. Unfortunately, my girlfriend didn't have this same gung-ho attitude.

In fact, halfway through the movie (or for that matter, at about the time that HAL started getting nasty), she looked over at me, nudged my arm, and in a last ditch effort, near tears, begged me, "Baby. Please let's go."— Sniffle, sniffle.

Well, it's bad enough when I pick a movie that I find hard to sit through (because I'll make myself watch it all). But when the person next to you (who came mainly to be with you) is driven to pitifulness and tears— well, a barbarian I'm not.

The second time Donna Crisci saw *2001* was the most memorable. She had loved it the first time and went back to a midnight screening in July 1969. "The same day, man would walk on the moon for the first time, and this was how we were ushering the day in. I remember people cheering during the film, everyone high [as opposed to the kinds of highs that many viewers of the film chemically acquired during its first-run engagements]. And afterwards, we all went out on Hollywood Boulevard and pointed up to the moon and said, 'Tonight! Oh, tonight!' Magical."

If *Bonnie and Clyde, The Graduate*, and *2001* started the youth revolution in American movies in the late sixties, the film that confirmed it all was 1969's *Easy Rider*. For a variety of reasons, I did not see the film until well into its run, and it never grabbed me the way it did others of my generation and those slightly younger. Peggy Dilley was there for an early screening.

My husband and I were living in married student housing at Michigan State. We went to the theatre just across the street from the campus. It was packed with long-haired, hippie-looking, radical students. They cheered and booed in all the right places and had a rousing good time, but we all walked out in a depressed hush at the end. Another hero taken away. Par for the American course.

Oh, I want a revolution. I want to smuggle pot and smoke it around a campfire in the open on a big screen, as if it were legal or something, and get a heady sensation like we were getting away with it. Let's start something new! I want to go live in a commune in the desert. I want to sleep in a cemetery in New Orleans. I did take pictures in a couple of them. I got that much. And I want to beat up all the ruddy rednecks who want to do me in, even if my family is from the boonies. [For those who smoked too much dope while watching the movie and missed them, she is referring to scenes from the film.]

Ira Katz saw *Easy Rider* in a theatre when it was released. "It was a statement of 'Our Generation.' The music was of 'our' time. To me and many other people it had all the desires we felt inside. The idea of getting on motorcycles and just riding around the country with long hair flowing in the wind was what I and so many others of us wanted to do. It also reflected our fear of the 'establishment' out to get us."

By the time of the film's release, Virginia Keene was

living in a commune called "The Matilda Street Madhouse." We went to see this movie en masse, and it became our anthem. Seeing this film was akin to a religious experience for us. It inspired daydreams of dosing the water supply with acid and building geodesic domes in the wilderness! I've seen it only once since then (on video), and it seems painfully long and dated. The endless improv in the New Orleans cemetery seemed so intense and relevant then—like the poetry we wrote on acid! Both seem inane now. The sound tracks are still great, the bikes are classics, Nicholson is as funny as ever, and the ending packs a punch, but as a whole the film is a relic from the Haight.

Marion Levine saw *Easy Rider* at a drive-in with her first boyfriend, who had already seen it. "He had his two-year-old niece in the back seat, and she was crying and wetting her diapers and it didn't matter. The movie totally transported me. I didn't care that these guys were drug dealers—they still represented all that we thought we were or aspired to be: scruffy rebel outcasts. When I saw the movie again in my twenties, I couldn't believe how flaccid the pacing was and how stupid the story."

Monica Dunlap first saw *Easy Rider* during its initial release and was impressed by it. "It mirrored my anti-establishment feelings, and I was very moved by Jack Nicholson's character and performance. To me his short role was the heart of the film, and I felt a real appreciation and gratitude to the actor. That performance remains for me his most honest and moving performance, but I have never seen the film again." James Ford was "disappointed. Wanted to love the film like all my friends did. I didn't. Liked Jack Nicholson. Thought the movie banal and unimpressive. Did not mind characters taking drugs, hated the thought of romanticizing drug dealers."

For Donna Crisci, who was "a basically conservative, sweet little thing at the time (I've changed), I hated this film! Too anti-establishment! Almost evil. Couldn't stand anyone in it. And would you believe, one of the times I went and saw *Cleopatra*, this was the second feature? Real programming genius there. I've never watched this again; I like the evil niche it fills in memory, the film all the bad, anti-Vietnam people liked, the weird hippies—not decent Americans like me."

Aubrey Solomon saw it in the sixties and thinks, "It was good in its time, insufferable in later years." Jack Hollander was not quite old enough to see the film when it first came out, but caught up with it in the early eighties, "but by then, Dennis Hopper was already remolding his public image as a rebel, Nicholson was too well known and Fonda's potential as an actor was never realized. This film *had* to be seen in its cultural setting to be truly appreciated." At the time, Marilyn Heath thought it was "a good yarn, broadened my horizons." She thinks now, "I would like to own this one for nostalgia, having been a young hippie in the sixties and seventies."

Al Gonzalez saw the film later and thought the "sight of the bike getting mangled was a great ending with a lot of impact and meaning." He saw it again years later and remembers, "enjoying the movie as much as the first time. This is probably due to the long time span between viewing such that there are certain details I hadn't remembered." Kevin Kennedy saw *Easy Rider* in the eighties, just after high school graduation, "with a few friends. One of them and I decided we would ride motorcycles across the country together. It took a few years, but we watched the movie again in the summer of 1986, the night before we left Connecticut for the ride. Fortunately, we never came across two old guys in a pickup, carrying a shotgun." Nancy Lathrop has "never been able to get through it. I don't have the proper drugs. I have yet to find the LSD dealer who can get me through that film." She has tried, but only gets up through the death of Nicholson's character and then "back in the box, back to the store."

Wil Dimpflmaier, now in his twenties, saw it when

in fact I had stepped up to an apartment shared with a girlfriend in a relationship so serious we had a cat. We enjoyed one of the liberties of not living at home, which was being able to smoke pot openly in any room of the house whenever we wanted to. Thus, with the reputation *Easy Rider* had, it seemed like the right movie to rent. The part that I remember best is when they got Jack Nicholson high, and he stared spouting off about aliens living among us. I don't know if it was just because I was in the same frame of mind as him, but he was making a lot of sense.

Bill Pulliam was too young for *Easy Rider* when it came out and "didn't appreciate the culture at the time. I found Doonesbury's parody much funnier. I haven't seen it as an adult."

Released in June 1969, *Easy Rider* had brought in $7.2 million in rentals by January 1970. It was outgrossed in 1969 by Disney's *The Love Bug* ($17 million; family audiences had not *completely* given up on going to the movies), *Butch Cassidy and the Sundance Kid* ($15 million), and *Goodbye Columbus* ($10.5

million),[13] but its success, particularly in view of its small budget (under a million dollars), persuaded Hollywood that low-budget films by young filmmakers for young audiences was the way to go. It did not entirely turn out that way. Most of the "youth pictures" that followed in *Easy Rider*'s wake were virtually unwatchable. Have *you* ever seen *Cover Me Babe* (1970)?

Dark and Golden

Of course I'd heard the rumors. The studio had picked up a book before publication for a cheap price but never really intended to make the movie. They'd made a movie like it a few years before and it was a flop.

Then the book became a bestseller and they had to make it. Then all the best directors in town turned it down. They eventually talked a young hotshot director into making it, and more than once they nearly fired him. The studio hated the rushes. The release of the film was delayed from December to the following March—always a bad sign. Even before it opened in New York, it was announced that it would be released nationwide in more theatres more quickly than normal. This was before the days of wide first releases, and it was usually a sign the studio knew it had a turkey and wanted to make as much money as quickly as they could, before word-of-mouth killed the picture.[1] But then when it opened in New York, the reviews were ecstatic. Could the reviews possibly be right?

The day the film opened in Los Angeles in 1972, I took a bus up to Westwood—by then *the* first-run area in Los Angeles—and managed to find a seat down front on the left in the crowded theatre. As I was wondering if the film could live up its reviews, the lights went down. The curtains opened, the title of the film came on, accompanied by a few notes on a trumpet, and then out of the darkness came the first line of dialogue. "I believe in America. . . ." One hundred seventy-five minutes later, *The Godfather* ended.

I was not entirely convinced it had lived up to its critical hype. It seemed a little longer than it needed to be, and Brando gave one of the most god-awful technical performances in the history of movies, but the performance seemed to work within the picture. I have since seen the picture several times, of course, shown it in my film history classes a few times, and grown to like it better than I did the first time, although I still think Brando's performance is abysmal.[2]

I had not read the novel when the film came out, so I came to the film with no expectations. (I subsequently read it and thought it was a lot better than many people give it credit for.) Donna Crisci had read the book and "was so pleased with what they had done with it. I was moved and angered and awed .... [Francis Ford] Coppola had all these little touches (peas in the spaghetti!) which brought back memories of my own Italian grandmother." Nancy Lathrop was only in junior high school when she read the book, but it was, "in junior high, one of those books that around page twenty-four, everybody's copy of it opened right up, because that's that scene with Sonny and the bridesmaid [having sex]. Nobody really read the whole book. So going to the film, I couldn't wait for page twenty-four to come up on the screen. Better in the book, as most things are."

Carlos Aguilar was slightly older than Lathrop at the time, and he and his friend had one copy of the book, which they traded off with each other, and told each other the story as they went along. *He* remembers the Sonny and the bridesmaid scene as being on page twenty-seven. "From the opening frame I knew that Coppola had captured the emotions of the book. It was like watching old friends. I knew everyone so well. I felt like I was watching old Super-8 movies of past family outings."

Marion Levine was an acting student in New York when the film came out, and it was her first look at Al Pacino, whom she had heard about in class. She enjoyed certain aspects of *The Godfather* but "didn't understand the complexities of filmmaking. Although I was caught up in the grand emotional sweep and physical spectacle of the film, I didn't truly understand the incredible vision and ambition that went into its making. For me, it was a movie about wonderful scenes and set pieces. Perhaps it's asking a lot for a twenty-two-year-old girl to identify with a pack of money-hungry, cold-blooded killers. With the exception of Brando's performance in the last sequences of the film, I was left pretty much unmoved."

For all the hype about the film, some went without any particular anticipation. Scott Hemmann "only went because a friend wanted to see it, and I had nothing better to do that weekend. I didn't really know much about it except that it was a gangster picture (which I had no interest in) and it starred Marlon Brando (whom I didn't like). I hadn't seen Marlon Brando in anything since I'd watched *A Streetcar Named Desire* on TV, and because his appearance had changed so much, it wasn't until the final credits rolled that I knew which part Brando had played. I was very impressed with the movie."

For many viewers, *The Godfather* was so overwhelming an experience, it changed their thinking and behavior. Francisco Checa, now a forty-year-old electronic engineer, remembers "thinking about organized crime in a whole different way from before. I saw these gangsters in particular as good guys, when before all gangsters were bad guys to me." Tandy Summers was eighteen when she finally saw it on video and it "made me feel like becoming a cold-blooded gangster. Their whole honor code and respect I wanted to emulate." So far she has not become a gangster. Olufemi Samuel saw the film, and he and his friends went to school "to start our own Mafia organization in junior high. I was the don, and we would beat other kids just to get respect. One of my boys turned against me, and I tried to tell him that he's not supposed to touch the don, but he still beat the daylights out of me." Steven Krul, a student in his twenties, "grew up in Rhode Island, and I can't tell you how many people I knew were influenced by this movie. From wanna-be mobsters to the real thing, they all had that coolness and cockiness that you know they got from the movie. This movie is to mobsters as the Grateful Dead is to Deadheads. Except the mobsters bathe more."

Debra de St. Jean and Lam Yun Wah first saw some of *The Godfather* on television as kids but in different circumstances. De St. Jean saw it in America.

> I remember when *The Godfather* was aired on television. I was sent to bed early so that my parents could watch the movie. Of course, I didn't stay in bed; curiosity had gotten the best of me . . . I had to sneak a peak. So I snuck into the living room to catch a glimpse. I walked in on the part of the film that the one Mafia member [it's actually the head of a movie studio] finds the head of his prized horse in his bed—needless to say I was scared to death. I had not seen anything so horrific before. I had nightmares for weeks and kept a close eye on my dog. As an adult, I finally did see *The Godfather*, which was good, but once was enough—violence is not my genre of films.

Lam Yun Wah was eleven years old, living in Hong Kong and going through his movie phase when one of the local TV stations ran both of the first two *Godfather* films one Sunday night. "Although it was dubbed in Chinese, I simply fell in love with the images. Because I had to go to school on Monday morning, I'd only watched about three-fourths of the first episode. I didn't know then it was such a great film. The next time I saw them was a few years later when Francis Coppola released a TV version called *The Godfather Saga*. I went crazy."

Like me, other viewers found the film worked better for them as the years went by. An extreme example is Lawrence Dotson, who liked gangster movies in general, but the first time he tried to watch *The Godfather*, "I couldn't. It was too long and dark and boring. I guess after growing up in a violent city like L.A., I became jaded by the violence, so it became easier for me to sit down and appreciate *The Godfather* for what it was: a cold-blooded gangster flick. It is now one of my all-time favorite movies."

Another fan of the film, who saw it when it was first released, is Virginia Keene.

I heard the hype, and I read the book and was braced for disappointment, but this time the movie far surpassed the novel for me. It was one of those unforgettable cinema surprises! The whole package worked in every way for me—there were new stars for our generation—Pacino, Keaton, Duvall, Coppola! It was really very exciting. This numbered among my favorite films of all time the first time I saw it . . . and it still does, in all of the same ways, except that I can no longer separate it from the whole saga. I knew this was a great movie the first time I saw it, and I feel the same way now, though my respect has deepened with the addition of two films and the passage of over twenty years.

Keene of course went to see the sequel, *The Godfather Part II* (1974) and was pleasantly surprised.

I saw this one the instant it opened, of course. I had my fingers crossed, but sequels are sequels. I never dreamed it was possible: this film was even better than the first! It filled in the gaps and added depth and new dimensions. The history was wonderful; De Niro was wonderful. This was movie heaven. . . . I've seen if often since then, and I can't separate I and II in my mind. They blend and flow together as a single piece and take on a certain grandeur and dignity that I don't associate with many films of my generation. If anything, they've gained stature with the passage of time, not merely "held up well."

Keene is right that the first two *Godfather* films have "gained stature" with viewers over time, whereas we have seen that *Bonnie and Clyde* and *Easy Rider* have not. Part of that increase in stature is the depth and artistry of the films, but another part of it is the way they have become part of our culture. When I showed *The Godfather* to my film history class in 1996, it struck me how much of what we think we know about the Mafia comes from this film. The film has to explain what a consigliere is, but we all know, and the reason we know is because of the film. And is there any one of us who has not used the phrase "Make him an offer he can't refuse"?

Another person who was looking forward to the sequel was Marion Levine, who had been taking acting classes with Lee Strasberg, the legendary acting teacher of the Actor's Studio. For Levine, "The most exciting thing about this film for me was seeing Strasberg acting. . . . He discussed working on the film, relating it to our work in class, so it was a thrill to see. The filmmaking is brilliant and perhaps unequalled in modern American cinema, but I never got truly swept up in it on an emotional level—there was no one to identify with." Jon Conrad also saw *The Godfather Part II* when it first came out and found it "not the visceral experience the first one was, but highly affecting and memorable."

Javier Rodriguez saw the first film and liked the story and the music, but did not like the second film because of "its story. And the way it went from past to future. And the way there was not one main character, but two. But the music was so beautiful and full of life. Also, I liked how the story went more in depth than the first movie."

Aubrey Solomon had seen the first *Godfather* at a prerelease screening at USC, but *The Godfather Part II* is "one of the few major pictures I saw on video first. Big mistake. I can't remember much about it except the scene in the boat [where Fredo is killed]." Eva Mahgrefthe originally saw both of the first two films on television, and "the magic, created by the story and enhanced by Coppola, pulled me right in. When an injustice was done to the Corleones, I cried for revenge."

In 1977, Coppola cut the two films together, added several sequences cut from the theatrical films, cut some of the violence and nudity, and the result was shown on successive nights on NBC under the title, *The Godfather Saga*. Al Gonzalez was still a kid at the time and "caught glimpses of it, having known (even as a kid) that this was a 'big' film." Jack Hollander was in high school when the original *Godfather* came out and is grateful he did not see it at the time. "I would *never* have appreciated it." By the time he did see them, they had been shown as the *Saga* on television, but at the insistence of his older sister, he watched the films

as they were released [as two films]. I'm sure that I saw them on the big screen for the first time (again, at the revival houses) and possibly together as a double bill. Perhaps it was because it was too much to handle, but it took several viewings for me to rate these films (especially the first one) as one of the greatest films of all time. I think that it is the compelling nature of the movies. I can remember watching the first film on cable one night when I was working in Pasadena. I knew that I had to turn the TV off and go to bed (to go to work the next day), but I couldn't reach for the "off" button. It was almost as if someone would know that I turned off *The Godfather* and that I would be visited by strangers in the night who would make me pay for my indiscretion. It's so *compelling*! I am breathless each time I see the movie. The second movie has the greatest performance of all the films—Robert De Niro as a young Marlon Brando. We *know* what the young Brando was like at that age, and De Niro isn't it, and yet we are absolutely convinced that that man on screen will grow up to be the Don Corleone that we are, by now, so familiar with.

Needless to say, like many fans of the first two *Godfather* films, Hollander went to see *The Godfather Part III* when it was released in 1990, sixteen years after *Part II*.

Perhaps it is my absolute devotion to the first two films and the compelling urgency conveyed in each that leads to my reaction to the third installment. . . . We just don't care. Most importantly, we don't care about [director Francis Ford Coppola's daughter] Sofia Coppola as Michael's daughter, so that when she dies, we're not agonizingly crushed (which we *must* be in order to make this film work). . . . I kept waiting for the only music I know from *Cavelleria Rusticana*, the "Intermezzo." I was initially disappointed (and surprised, frankly) when the opera was over and this music hadn't been heard. I was pleasantly surprised when this music was utilized (and quite appropriately I felt) for the final scene—it is *so* gorgeous a piece of music that I couldn't imagine it not being utilized.

Al Gonzalez saw *Part III* "at the theatre the day it came out. I was disappointed. The cinematography and the settings were the only things that I liked about this film, and that's not why I went to see it. The cast just seemed lighter, the plot was lame, and casting Sofia Coppola finished off what was already proving to be another ordinary film. It was nothing to compare to the previous two." Jon Conrad avoided the Sofia problem by not seeing *Part III* at all. He had noticed Sofia Coppola in an earlier Francis Coppola film, *Peggy Sue Got Married* (1986), did not think she was that good, and deliberately did not see *Part III*. Angela West also did not like Sofia Coppola but did "think Andy Garcia gave a good performance, and I must say I was extremely interested in his acting when he took his clothes off. Oops! Who said that?"

The industry audiences for the film were even harsher than the public. Aubrey Solomon saw it "at an Academy screening at Paramount, and many people in the audience (viewing it for nomination consideration) started laughing when Sofia got shot at the end."

Some viewers not only liked the movie but liked Sofia Coppola as well. Laurel Jo Martin "thought Sofia Coppola was wonderful; maybe she can't act, but she was a welcome change from the plastic kids you see in a lot of movies. When she was shot, I thought it was tragic."

I was disappointed in the movie, having had the first two films—especially the first one—grow on me. However, I felt the problem with Sofia Coppola was not so much that she was a bad actress but that she was badly directed. Her father often shoots her in loving close-ups but does not give her any direction as to what to do. He was directing her more as a father than as a director, but he has often not been good with actresses. Two years later she was charming and delightful under Jeffrey Levy's direction in the low-budget film *Inside Monkey Zetterland* (1992), and her own directorial debut, *The Virgin Suicides* (1999), shows she has some of her father's directorial genes. And she is even better than he is with actresses.

D'Arcy West thought the film was so bad, "I apologized to my boyfriend after the movie for making him come see it with me," but when Virginia Keene "first saw this in the theatre, I was quite ambivalent. I felt disappointed that it was confusing and that Coppola's sweeping story seemed to lose its way in Rome. I also ached for poor Sofia, and so she was an enormous distraction. Still, the story did captivate me—especially the Vatican intrigue—and it was a joy to see old friends again. I've seen it twice on video since then, and I've warmed to it more each time. Now it does seem a continuation of the *Godfather* world, and I don't think it could have stood alone."

Wendi Cole loves all the *Godfather* movies, even *Part III*, and "If they made a *Godfather IV* (God forbid!) I'd go see it." Most of us who have now spent over twenty-five years with the Corleones probably would, whether we would admit it or not. They keep pulling us back in. . . .

One reason audiences continue to be drawn toward these films is their seriousness, typical of the early seventies. If the films of the late sixties, such as *Bonnie and Clyde* and *Easy Rider*, struck nerves in the audiences—especially the younger audiences—the films of the early seventies went deeper and became more complex *and* found an audience. As we have seen, it was a smaller audience than in preceding decades, but it was also a more *intense* audience. Marion Levine says that her "addiction" to movies "first took hold in my twenties, when movies were of an age (in the 1970s) that I can only describe as golden. Informed by intelligence and subtlety—where having a message was the point—those movies of my early adulthood still burn in my brain when I rub up against life's more uncomfortable challenges. I think to myself, what would the Jack Nicholson of *Five Easy Pieces* (1970) do in a situation like this? If he could tell that diner waitress where to put the chicken salad, couldn't I tell off all the assholes making problems in my life?"

Levine is not the only person to suggest that that this period in American films was something of a golden age. I implied this in my 1988 history of screenwriting, *FrameWork*,[3] and in 1993, the magazine *Movieline* had a special issue on the seventies. The article began with David Thomson's article "The Decade When Movies Mattered" and included an article on the twenty movies of the seventies "to kill for." The magazine also noted that it was not all perfect in an article called "The Squalor of the 70s."[4] The squalor and the richness of the period were sometimes combined.

Richard Morales was about twelve when this period in American films started.

The Fox Theatre (in Orange County, California) used to show movies for ninety-nine and sometimes forty-nine cents. The best movies I'd seen there were *Woodstock* (1970) and *M*A*S*H* (1970)—good music, good laughs, and pubic hair. We'd seen plenty of G- and GP- [the early version of what became the PG rating] rated movies, but it was the double thrill of finding an adult stranger to accompany us into an R-rated movie that was most memorable. At night we would walk into the drive-in by our house to watch movies, very often without a speaker and in the cold. It was this way that I saw the first scene of *Clockwork Orange* when it was still rated X. Besides the nudity, I was intrigued by the whole movie, and for the longest time, for whatever reason, I called it my favorite movie. What little I heard of the sound track had sparked an interest in classical music, and shortly after I was checking out the Time-Life records of Beethoven.

Other movies of the time had serious messages. Patrick O'Leary saw "*Midnight Cowboy* (1969) and *Taxi Driver* (1976) when I was younger [in California]. But after living as an adult in New York for a number of years and seeing them again, I understood different things in them and recognized subtle details that had truth about living in New York." Even a piece of sincere schlock like *Billy Jack*, struck a social chord in the then-teenage Lisa Moncure.

Billy Jack was probably the first film that had my mind thinking about social injustice. I really identified with the people in it. Probably because there were lots of young white women in it with long hair like mine. I'm convinced that all people are narcissistic and really like looking at themselves in movies. Regardless, this movie stirred me up, and the song that came with it ["One Tin Soldier"] kept reminding me of its message. "Go ahead and hate your neighbor, go ahead and cheat a friend. Do it in the name of heaven, you can justify it in the end. . . . " Since I lived in the middle of the Southern Baptist belt, this really hit home.

The seventies combination of schlock and seriousness often showed up in its scarier movies. Hollywood had always made movies that scared people; they generally had no more serious pretense to them than scaring the audience. *The Exorcist* seemed to connect with the audiences' feelings about religion, children from hell, and green pea soup. Even the *trailer* for the film was so scary that when he saw it at age twelve, Peter Albers "didn't sleep for years because of it. In fact, when I finally saw it —on the same night as I first saw *The Shining* [1980], for god's sake—I was twenty-three, and I slept with my light on for days."

The early screenings of *The Exorcist* became legendary for their effects on audiences. Scott Hemmann remembers one.

The film that had the most profound emotional effect on me was *The Exorcist,* simply because it scared the hell out of me. I remember seeing it as clearly as I can remember any film I've ever seen. I saw it with a girl-friend at the Cinerama Dome [in Hollywood] shortly after it opened. I had read the book a year or two before and enjoyed the story, but reading it in no way prepared me for the sensory onslaught that bombarded me. The film was like a roller-coaster ride through hell for me, and I was to-tally drained by the time the final credits rolled. I recall the sound being turned up so high that it kept me in a constant state of anxiety. I was literally on the edge of my seat from the beginning of the film to the end. I was twenty when I saw the movie, and I lived alone at the time. I slept with the light on and the radio playing for months afterward to help me sleep. I didn't sleep very well for a long time, and if "Tubular Bells," the theme from *The Exorcist,* were to start playing on the radio, I'd wake up immediately and have to turn it off. This film made me realize the power there could be to a movie. I've never been a fan of horror or monster movies, but there was something in that one that struck a chord deep inside my dark subconscious. I've never seen the picture since that first time. It's not because I'm afraid it would have the same effect on me; I know it wouldn't anymore. I don't want to see it now, because I'm afraid I'd be disappointed in it, and I want to remember it as the affecting film it was for me twenty years ago.

Virginia Keene saw it early in its run as well as many years later.

I remember every detail of the first time I saw it—at the Coral Theatre in Miami. We stood in line in the hot sun for a long time, and we were shocked at the admission price. It was the first time we'd every paid five dollars for a ticket! The movie scared the daylights out of me. I couldn't sleep alone for several days and needed a night-light for a long time, but it was a roller-coaster scare, not the nightmare psychic wounding of *Catch–22* (1970). This was the best horror since *Rosemary's Baby* (1968) and before that, *Psycho*! Now, on video it seems even better than it did then. The novelty of the sensational special effects has worn off, and the sexuality and language aren't quite so shocking any more. With the cheap thrills skimmed off the top, the raw power of a truly fine movie shines through. I love the preface now, and its stylistic difference works well for me. Twenty years ago it just seemed weird. The screenplay is far better than the novel, the acting superb. I really care about these characters. This is a finely crafted movie, and I think it's another one that looks even better with the passage of time.

Marilyn Heath had not planned to see *The Exorcist*.

I was dragged to it by my boyfriend and his religious fanatic chess partner. All my friends said it was great. That afternoon the UCLA Bruins
were on their eighty-second game of their eighty-one-game streak [in
basketball] that I was following avidly, even though I am not a sports
person and do not even know the rules. This streak had me completely
swept. [But] I saw *The Exorcist* instead of the game. From the beginning,
it was so sick I watched the audience instead. A young black woman next
to me was so frightened she asked me to hold her finger. My religious
friend was frantically shaking his fists at the screen with a gruesome almost strychnine-like grin. I looked behind me—a child of about five years
was looking traumatized at whatever was going on. I heard a noise I could
not identify and looked at the screen—it was her neck snapping while
her head spun. Yuck. There was too much subliminal stuff in this flick,
oughta be against the law. The Bruins lost, and I will always blame *The
Exorcist*. I had to go get apple pie à la mode at the Bright Spot restaurant
to shake it off.

Donna Crisci also saw *The Exorcist* in its first run in Westwood. She had been
"riveted" by the book. "The lines in Westwood for the film were enormous; it was
raining and the then-new McDonald's near the theatre did a booming service in
the line. The media at the time was reporting people sick in showings and running out in hysteria: I saw the film many times at the theatre and never saw any
such thing. People did react and scream with horror at the events on screen. But
they left admiring it." There were people who did throw up, although perhaps
not as many as legend and the media of the time had it. William Peter Blatty, the
author of the novel and the screenplay,as well as the film's producer, attended the
press preview in New York. "At a certain point, a young woman came up the aisle
and, walking by me, was a little unsteady, and I heard her saying, 'Jesus, Jeeeeesus,'
and I thought, 'Oh, boy, we're dead. She hates the picture.' But I marked the point
at which she left. And that's the point at which *everybody* got ill and at which I
always have to lower my head: it's when they're giving Regan [the possessed girl]
the arteriogram and the needle goes into her neck and the blood comes out.
That's the moment it's always been."[5]

Because the film dealt with Catholic theology, however shallowly, it had a
particular impact on Catholics. Rocio Vargas grew up Catholic in Costa Rica,
hearing stories about exorcisms. She saw the film in a theatre there.

The Exorcist not only scared me, but also caused me to become much
more interested in understanding the whole mark of the beast. However,

looking back, I remember that when I was watching the movie, my intellectual mind shifted back and forth from that of a well-collected superachiever to that of a very scared little girl. I remember nodding my head in approval when the priest and principal actor were quoting a passage from the Bible, which to my surprise was somehow connected to the idea that the anti-Christ will be born into a family involved in politics. I was just ready to indulge on the idea, when my analytical mind was jolted by the horrifying sensation of eternal entrapment and helpless persecution of a priest running desperately back and forth inside his room trying to escape from an unseen force that he could not control. I can still close my eyes and see him trying helplessly to protect himself from this evil with Bibles and crucifixes.

This movie for me also had some offensive moments, such as the time in which a crucifix was used by the possessed girl in very sexual ways, or the times in which profane and very blasphemous language was used against God. However, I did understand that these scenes were necessary to make the point of the movie. Anyway, what else can you expect from someone who is possessed by the devil? What is very interesting to me is that a movie designed to scare the audience half to death would have such an intellectual impact on a young person such as myself at the time.

Anthony Thompson was just "glad I was going to a Catholic School at the time, so the priest could protect me." For Skylaire Alfvegren, the movie was "frightening beyond belief—particularly because I had a fervently religious mother who had given me detailed accounts of possessed people she had come in contact with in her work for the ministry."

Given that the film was so scary and was rated R, it is surprising the number of kids who not only went to the film, but whose parents or family members took them. Al Gonzalez was in the fifth grade when he saw it.

Me, my older brother, and a cousin begged my father to take us to see it. Having already seen the movie, my father advised us against it. Despite this the begging continued, and my father eventually took us, with the warning, "You're sleeping in your own room tonight."

"Okay, okay, let's go."

What I remember of that experience is that I watched half of the movie through my fingers. I also remember green vomit, shaking beds, a cracking neck that twisted in the night, slamming doors and drawers, and the girl's messed-up face. Father knew best. I had trouble sleeping for the next two weeks.

Gonzalez saw the film later on video and enjoyed it as a horror film, but "it had nowhere near the effect on me it did as a kid. In fact, I remember laughing at some if it."

When Bridget Sweet was ten, her best friend Shelly went to see the film and told her friends about it at school the next morning.

> I could not believe the things she was telling us. I'll never forget that day on the school bus. There were about thirty kids around her just listening to seedy details. Shelly was the only kid in school who had seen that film, and that made her the most popular girl in class. I wanted to be popular, too. I also wanted a large crowd of people surrounding me, so I asked my mom if she would take me to see *The Exorcist*. She said, hell no!
>
> I was so jealous that my friend got all that attention from viewing a grown-up film like that. I got so tired of kids saying things like "Shelly, tell us about the devil girl" or "Did her head really turn around backwards, Shelly?"
>
> From that time on, I have always wanted to see movies that were not for viewers under eighteen. I felt I was missing out on something. And to this day, I tend to view films that are naughty and violent.

Nancy Lathrop was in junior high when the film came out and says,

> Who can forget being in junior high and having the ultimate experience of going to see *The Exorcist*, which you had to talk your parents into, or lie about? It was not so much about the movie. It was about going and waiting in line. . . . It was on the news about the lines. Going to it and going with your little junior high school friends and trying not to be grossed out and feeling like you'd really gotten away with something by getting into that film. I will just never forget the notoriety of it. I remember having seen an ad for it—probably for the book—and did not know what an exorcist was, looked the word up, went out and got the book, read the book. If I had gone to that film the first week it opened, I would have had to have lied to my parents to get to it, and then suddenly the thing exploded. That was something you had to do. You had to do it. But it was a lot of fun, and I wasn't grossed out.

Wajeeh Khursheed was twelve years old when he saw the movie. He and his parents were visiting Pakistan to attend his grandfather's funeral.

> *The Exorcist* was just released and my thirteen-year-old cousin wanted

me to go along with him to watch it. The theatre was only a block away from my grandfather's house, so we both walked to the show, which was at about 9:00 P.M. On the way back home after the show, my cousin, who did not watch many films, had a very tough time walking home without looking over his shoulders. He was really scared, and surprisingly I wasn't. I found it very funny the way he was behaving; he couldn't even go the bathroom at night alone and had to wake up his mom to go along with him. That was the time that I really got him by sneaking over to the window and making all sorts of scary noises. The entertainment of that movie did not end after the show for me, but went on for days as I scared my cousin every night. I still laugh about it whenever it comes across my mind.

Michael Thomas's Catholic mother refused to let him watch it as a child. "After seeing it, I finally understood her reasoning." He finally saw it in college and felt then it was "just good scary fun." James Ford had read the book and finally saw the film "in a theatre filled with sailors, while I was stationed in Australia. Pretty scary, but I was in a fairly macho state of mind. Still, Mike Oldfield's "Tubular Bells" make[s] me look over my shoulder."

Aubrey Solomon kept "waiting for the scares, but they were more of a freak-show variety than anything terribly shocking. I couldn't help but think how *Mad* magazine would lampoon this." Jon Conrad felt it was not "much more than a scary movie that sometimes tripped over into the ludicrous. I recall that at times I was the only one in the theatre giggling."

Scott Hemmann was right about the sound being cranked up very loud in the first-run engagements. Both the sound effects and the volume the film was played at had a huge role in *The Exorcist's* success during its first six months in theatres. When it eventually moved out of first-run theatres and into subsequent-run theatres, where the volume was not kept as high, the box office take declined somewhat.[6] In the late seventies, I ran the film in my film history course and deliberately kept the sound at a "normal" level to test my theory. The class did not find it as scary as original audiences had.

Nat Segaloff, the biographer of William Friedkin, the director of *The Exorcist*, noted that the film "has also, understandably, not played widely on television and loses most of its impact on video."[7] Given the kind of collective audience experience the film became known for, he might think so, but even on TV the film retains its impact for some viewers. John Slipstone saw it on TV and "literally pissed my pants. Once again, my Catholic upbringing played into my fear." As for Peggy Dilley, "I was too chicken to see [*The Exorcist*] until years later, tamed by the small screen. All that talk of people barfing and passing out, and there probably are real demons, and if you see that movie they'll get inside you, and not even an exorcist will be able to get them out. Hysteria. My mom came to visit me, saw I had read the book, thought I was demon-possessed . . . (no ma, just schizophrenic—it's a fad we're going through) and took the book home and burned it."

David Bromley was twelve and had just successfully seen *Poltergeist* (1982) when his brothers (the ones who used to get him to swap his dime for a nickel) "dared me to watch *The Exorcist* with them on TV. I said 'Sure, I love scary films!' thinking I was being cool. It scared the shit out of me! That night while I was lying in bed, wrapped like a mummy, sure that Regan was under my bed, I decided mom was right and therefore was done with scary films. Needless to say, I slept with my mother for about three months after that. Oh yeah, my brothers, the evil twins, [were] grounded for a month." When Bromley saw it again, he was twenty, "It still scared the hell out of me! I can't imagine seeing it in a theatre; man, that would be intense. Of course, I would have to go and see it in theatres even if it would be intense."

Angela West was too young to see *The Exorcist* in the theatre. "I probably wouldn't be alive today if I had gone to see it in a theatre." A few years later, the movie was shown on commercial television, considerably censored. "I was still too young, so my parents sent me to bed early. I remember sneaking out of my bedroom and peeking quietly into the living room. Unfortunately, I peeked right when Linda Blair did her incredible head-turning sequence. It was the scariest thing I'd ever seen in my life. My mother had to sleep with me every night for the next week, because every time I closed my eyes, all I saw was a greyish-green head staring back at me."

Once, when Wendi Cole was a child, "*The Exorcist* came on TV. I would *not* turn the TV on the channel that movie was on. I would turn the knob *backwards* just to avoid *any* glimpse of that movie. I saw it later on videocassette, and I just laughed all the way through it. . . . The things that the demon (was it Satan?) did were hilarious." For Lilia Fuller, *The Exorcist* was the kind of movie she liked in her mid-teens, "especially the vomiting scene and the one with the turning head. Wonderful, full of mystery and secrets, occultism and surreal beings." Terrence Atkins couldn't sleep for weeks after seeing it, and then "I met Linda Blair years later and kept waiting for her to vomit on me."

Dorian Wood first saw the film on video, with his entire family, "in broad daylight. . . . My mother had unsuccessfully objected to renting this film for my sister and me, but my dad, being the deranged lunatic he is (well, at least when he wants to be), brought it home. I had nightmares for weeks, and my mother's efforts in trying to laugh through the movie to make it seem a lot tamer than it was, proved to be unsuccessful as well. Ironically, years later, my mother told me that her favorite book back in high school was, in fact, *The Exorcist*, and that I should read it as well. Go figure."

Black and Dark

If part of the reason audiences turned out for *The Exorcist* was to deal with the real-life horror of Nixon, then it is not surprising that one group who went to see the film was African Americans. African American audiences liked horror films, especially those that transformed other, more realistic horrors into exaggerated cinematic ones. Given the influence of religion in the African American community, several of the seventies horror films that appealed to black audiences dealt with pseudo-religious subjects. In addition to *The Exorcist,* another favorite in the black community was *The Omen* (1976), about the return of the anti-Christ. I cannot tell you the number of student-made horror films from African American students I saw in the late seventies and early eighties that used on their sound tracks the music of Orff's "Carmina Burana," which was used in *The Omen.*

By the seventies, moviegoing was beginning to become integrated, but that had not always been the case, particularly in the south.[1] African American film historian Rick Mitchell grew up in Lexington, Kentucky, and remembers the theatres there as well as what he later learned about them.

My earliest moviegoing experiences took place at the Lyric, a "black-only" theatre in Lexington, Kentucky. . . . Although the hardtop theatres in Lexington were not integrated until 1961 (blacks could then sit in the balconies of two of them), the area drive-ins were *always* integrated, without separate restroom facilities even. In the mid-fifties, two new drive-ins opened as first-run venues, and films with a strong appeal to black audiences like *St. Louis Blues* (1958), *The Defiant Ones, Anna Lucasta* (1958), and *Porgy and Bess* (1959) would be booked there rather than in the downtown houses.

In 1948, two modern (for the time) neighborhood theatres were built in Lexington—one for whites, the other for blacks. For years, I remember the Lyric as having only five hundred seats; later I found out it was closer to nine hundred. Because there were a lot of black traveling variety shows in those days, the stage was built with a proscenium, which made in possible for them to put in a CinemaScope screen in 1954. (The white theatre, the Ashland, was smaller and built to accommodate [a screen with a ratio of 1 (height) to] 1.37 [width. It was as narrow as the Roxy in Bloomington, Indiana, had been]. After integration I discovered [the Ashland] ran *everything* [regardless of how it had been filmed] at [1 (height) to] 2.1 [width]!) [Mitchell is also a projectionist, as you may have guessed, and *very* concerned about proper presentation].

For as long as I could remember until February 1963, the Lyric had three weekly program changes, almost always double bills. Sundays were major A features in second run, usually one to six months after they'd played first run in Lexington [at the white theatres] (and two to three months after they'd opened in L.A. and New York). The Wednesday change was second-run or older films with more of an adult appeal. . . . The Friday-Saturday change was kid-oriented, mostly science fiction and horror films, which had supplanted Westerns in popularity with kids in the late fifties, often on triple bills. In the late fifties, there was usually a serial chapter on the program, from Columbia Studios, whose serials are considered the worst. And on some Saturdays, there were special programs of twenty cartoons and two features. In the early sixties, there were successful Friday-Saturday triple bills of science fiction/horror films, juvenile delinquent films, and Tarzan films. In February 1963, the Wednesday program change was eliminated.

Why certain pictures played the Lyric when they did and others not at all I now know has to do with the vagaries of rental charges. I don't know if the Lyric played any films on percentage, but I know the Friday-Saturday films in particular were on flat rates—usually the lowest, considering we often got films I can't prove ever existed. And the delay in getting some films for the Sunday change was due to their second-run rates initially being too high for the Lyric, especially the major studio ones. The films were not booked by the manager but by a booking service in Cincinnati.

We never got a lot of MGM films, non-rock-and-roll musicals, or the higher-profile Disney films. We did get practically everything Universal released, most of Columbia's lesser films, and everything from American-International and Allied Artists. . . .In September 1962, I started working at the Lyric as a relief projectionist, primarily doing Saturday and Sunday afternoon shows until the theatre closed in March 1963, after running *West Side Story* for a week to virtually no business. Integration of the downtown houses was a factor as was the increased tendency of the older audience to stay home and watch TV. The building was not torn down, however, and in 1984 was reopened as a homeless shelter.

Before the seventies, segregated theatres played films—usually made on very low budgets—aimed specifically at African American audiences.[2] What changed in the seventies is that films that were aimed at such audiences found their way into integrated mainstream theatres. Valerie Hornig remembers the impact of one of those films.

Although I must have been fifteen at the time of its release, the first movie that I remember going to was *Cooley High* (1975). This movie made such an impression of me. Beyond the fact that I was attracted to the moody, bluesy flavor of this film, the aspect that really moved me was that it was a "black film." At this point in my life, I was so used to seeing white faces on television, from Shirley Temple in *Heidi* (1937) and Elizabeth Taylor in *Cleopatra,* that merely to see real black actors in a movie just "blew my mind." And this is not to take away from the talents of the aforementioned actors, but when I saw Glynn Turman and Lawrence Hilton-Jacobs on the big screen, it really brought a new type of realism to the forefront—to me Black Cinematic Realism. I suppose that everyone wants to be represented, and finally I was. I remember the following week at my junior high school, that movie was the talk of just about every student who had been fortunate enough to see it over the weekend. Everyone was asking, "Did you see *Cooley High*?" The question, as far as I can remember, was one of both curiosity and pride.

Many other black films of the time were not as genteel as the charming *Cooley High*. A whole genre of the period's films came to be known as Black Exploitation, or Blaxploitation. Some African Americans look back on those films with mixed feelings. Richard Henrie, now a thirty-seven-year-old truck driver,

can't believe I was so hung up on those films. They were shallow, but still that's what I grew up watching. Now if you ask me what I thought about *Shaft* (1971), *Superfly* (1972), *Shaft's Big Score* (1972), *Foxy Brown* (1974), *The Mack* (1973), etc. I could go on and on. . . . Later in life when I saw a lot of these Black Exploitation movies on cable or TV, I was amazed at how awful these films are. The scripts were horrible, and the acting was terrible. I idolized guys like Richard Roundtree and Max Julien; now I look at these films and can't believe how bad they were in these roles.

Bridget Sweet, now in her twenties, will never forget the first movie she saw.

"I was about five years old, and the film was called *Superfly*. . . . That film had such an amazing effect on the African American community. Before the film *Superfly*, most black males wore Afros or their hair shaped low. *Superfly* started a new hair craze. When we arrived at the show, mostly all the men in our community had their hair permed just like the Superfly character. At that time, I didn't realize how much of an influence cinema can be."

Another film Sweet saw at the time was *The Mack*.

> I totally idolized the main character called "Goldie," and at that time I did not know the film was about pimps and street hookers, prostitution. I didn't even understand what these people were all about.
>
> At that age, all I could see were good-looking men in nice clothes and big fancy cars with a lot of girlfriends. The women in the film had money and dressed like movie stars. Back then I thought, "I want a boyfriend like that when I grow up." I thought it would be interesting to view *The Mack* as an adult, so I recently rented the film. When I viewed the film as an adult, I hated the movie. I was outraged. The film degrades women and glamorizes pimps and drug pushers, and the film exploits the community. . . . I felt ashamed of myself to think this film, *The Mack*, was such a great movie, but I was a little girl, impressionable, and I just didn't know any better.

Some black audience members still buy into the aesthetics of the Black Exploitation period. Anthony Thompson, now twenty-two, says, "I like black films. If it is not a black film, I want to see some action, some people dying, and some tits and ass wiggling."

White audiences of the seventies did see the Black Exploitation films and had a variety of responses to them. I saw Melvin Van Peebles's *Sweet Sweetback's Baad Asssss Song* (1971), one of the most violent and antiwhite of the films of the period, with a predominantly white, middle-class audience in a Los Angeles-area beach town. They had not a clue what the movie was about. I also saw white audiences cheer the black heroes of *Shaft* and *Cotton Comes to Harlem* (1970) when they outwitted the dumb white cops, crooks, etc. Those films worked in the traditional American way of making the audience root for the underdog. I am sure the audience reaction at the time was helped by the civil rights movement, which was seen to have helped bring increased fairness and equality to American life. Those attitudes began to change in American audiences—both black and white—with the increased political conservatism of the eighties.

While audiences of all races could enjoy the outrageousness of the Black Exploitation films of the seventies, the more realistic and more realistically violent movies of the eighties and nineties produced different reactions. Because many films, not only those aimed at black audiences, deal with violent themes, such films often attract an audience already prone to violence. For example, Bridget Sweet, who had liked *The Mack* when she was young, saw the 1988 film *Colors*, which deals with both black and Latino gangs in Los Angeles. "It was intermission time, and this film just went off. All of a sudden a group of people tried to start a fight with us because we were wearing red (our school colors). Now this is in Indianapolis, Indiana, where there are no gangs, but because these troublemakers just saw the film, they were motivated. Their school colors were blue and gold."

When Javier Rodriguez saw the exploitation picture *Crack House* (1990),

> there were so many gang members there. There was so much noise and chaos that it was unreal. The way they were writing on the walls and on the seats. They even had a shootout in the theatre that day. And a young black girl was hit by a bullet. The reason, I found out later, was because she had a red shirt on. And the guys she was talking to were gang members. There was also smoking drugs inside the theatre and drinking beer. What made matters worse was the fact that someone was throwing ice. The noise level in the theatre was higher than the sound system. And all you could hear was bad language, back and forth.

A film does not even have to be about gang activity to attract a gang audience. Shawn Taylor saw *Nightmare on Elm Street Part 3: Dream Warriors* (1987) with some friends at a theatre in downtown Los Angeles.

> We were doubtful in going because of the atmosphere in downtown. As soon as we walked in, there was an aroma of marijuana. As soon as that wore off, there was a stale musty odor in the air. Now how could one watch under those conditions? [Well, in the sixties, with *Easy Rider* . . .] But as youngsters, since we paid we were going to manage. Then a fight broke out between two rival gangs, forcing the police to come in and break it up. Two of the guys were fighting right in front of the screen. . . . That's when we said enough is enough and went back to demand a refund. We got it and vowed never to watch a film in downtown again.

Rick Mitchell also tired of downtown Los Angeles, "where, aside from the condition of the theatres, crying babies, and screaming kids, the real danger was fights among members of the audience, particularly when the combatants were of different races and other members of the audience were expected to take sides along racial lines."

Mitchell noticed the problem even earlier in the theatres along Hollywood Boulevard, particularly with the legendary second- (or third- or fourth-) run house, the World. Writer Pleasant Gehman remembered the heyday of the World.

In the late seventies, the World showed four movies for a dollar, gradually increasing to two bucks, and eventually three dollars as inflation took its toll. Not only was the admission cheap, making the World the perfect place for bums to snooze or broke punk rockers to spend an afternoon, the films they showed were amazing, uniform in their low-grade, cheap horror sleaze: they were badly dubbed, horribly shot, and inevitably, the World's prints were scratched, with warped sound tracks and edits that seemed to have been made by a moron. Films like *The Tingler* [1959], *The Corpse Grinders* [1972], *The Last House on the Left* [1972], *Honeymoon Killers* [1970], and *Two Thousand Maniacs* [1964] were shown with alarming regularity—and this was before so-called "splatter films" had even achieved cult status. They were just gross movies that few people wanted to see, which was fine for the discerning audience at the World, where the bathroom was notorious for being a good place to score drugs (if you couldn't cop there, you couldn't cop anywhere), and where live sex acts were frequently committed in the back row, up against the wall of the projection booth.

The World may have been the only movie theatre that routinely employed armed security guards. Everyone who was coherent enough to speak would talk back to the screen, and fights broke out on a regular basis. Patrons often switched their attention from the screen to the row from which the dispute came, often jumping atop their seats to get a better view as the fights became physical and rolled down the aisle; once, a guy even took bets and collected cash, the brawl went on so long.[3]

Hollywood Boulevard was, and still is, one of the first-run areas in Los Angeles. That was where Virginia Keene had one of her worst experiences as a moviegoer, when she went to see the critically acclaimed 1993 film about violence in South Central Los Angeles, *Menace II Society*.

It was the only time I have ever felt threatened by an audience. I was aware that this film had the potential to kindle volatile feelings, but it never occurred to me that I wouldn't be safe at the Hollywood Pacific at a Sunday matinee! I arrived early and sat toward the front, so I was unaware of the nature of the audience until it was too late for me to leave gracefully. It seemed that the entire unsavory element of South Central had migrated for this performance. The theatre was crowded, and all seats surrounding me were occupied. The audience was talking in conversational tones even at the beginning of the film, but talking became yelling and hurling of epithets at the screen. As the volume increased, they began jumping up and down and cheering the murder of the Korean grocer each time it was shown [on the store surveillance tape the killer had taken and continues to replay during the film]. I usually ask people to be quiet or change my seat if people talk, but this time I didn't dare do either. I just curled down into myself and wished the movie to be over. I felt very conspicuous, very white, very alone and very vulnerable. I'd felt the barest hint of animosity at some of Spike Lee's films and *Boyz N the Hood* (1991), but that was slight discomfort. This was fear. Fortunately, no one antagonized anyone else, and the movie ended without incident, but I was shaken.

The one time I felt threatened by an audience was also in a Hollywood Boulevard theatre in 1976, but the audience was almost exclusively young white males. The picture showing dealt with a violent urban world, and the audience got into the intensity of the film, which continually threatened to get violent but did not until the end. By the end, the audience members seemed ready to tear somebody apart, anybody. The climax of the movie, however, was a bloodbath in which the main character shot and killed a large number of people. This seemed to relieve the tension a little for the audience, but I got out of the theatre as quickly as I could. The film was *Taxi Driver*.

Violence also eventually worked its way out to Westwood. The increase in films aimed at younger audiences in the late seventies and early eighties brought larger numbers of teenagers to Westwood (as opposed to the college and Westside yuppie crowd that came in the early seventies), and in January 1988, a young woman became the victim of a random shooting on the street. This was followed in 1991 by a riot on the opening night of *New Jack City*. Anthony Thompson was there and remembers that "the movie was very good, but violent. Afterwards, the Westwood riots broke out. People were looting stores, breaking windows, and fighting each other. The worst part was when a gunshot went off, and a crowd of at least two hundred people ran my way. I ran for dear life, trying not to get trampled." What was not emphasized in many of the news reports of the incident was that the crowd was upset because the theatre had oversold the late showing and could not admit everybody who had bought tickets into the theatre.

Westwood has been trying to recover ever since, with only moderate success; although since it is no longer as crowded, it is a much nicer place to see movies. In November 1996, *Set It Off*, a film about four black women who get back at society by robbing banks, opened nationally. On the opening Wednesday night in Lakewood, a Los Angeles suburb, gunfire erupted between gangs inside the theatre. Three people were injured, although none by gunfire.[4] The following Saturday, there was a shooting outside a Torrance (also a Los Angeles suburb) theatre showing the film, although this involved not people who had seen the movie, but gang members waiting to see the film.[5]

Two days after the Torrance incident, I caught an early matinee of *Set It Off* in Westwood. The audience was not large—maybe thirty people—and most of them were black women. We enjoyed the film enormously as an example of the rather small *Thelma & Louise* (1991) genre of women's action revenge picture. While I was one of the few people in the audience who did not at some point or other shout out "Go, girl" during the film, I never felt threatened by anybody in the audience.

As I left the theatre, I ran into a television crew from the local NBC station, and I could see the reporter's eyes light up when he saw me. He had obviously been sent around to various theatres to get responses to the film in view of the shootings, and here he had a middle-aged white guy coming out of the film. I agreed to an on-camera interview and watched the reporter verbally dance around while he waited for me to deliver a sound bite. I eventually admitted I was a film historian. After he processed that information (and probably realized it would make him look good to his bosses for actually having *tracked down* an authority figure to comment), we redid the interview. In the final story on the news that night, he paraphrased my comments on how violence is the audience's fault, not the film's, and the only sound bite he used was the most outrageous example of an act of violence after a film that I could remember off the top of my head—a man who killed people after seeing *The Ten Commandments*. Don't believe everything you hear on television.[6]

If *The Exorcist* scared a lot of people, two years later *Jaws* scared even more. As Al Gonzalez says,

> When *Jaws* came out, I remember the words of one critic, "*Jaws* has people running out of the water like *The Exorcist* had people running into churches." That's right. And I was one of them. I was twelve and a half when I saw this movie, and I had trouble swimming in a pool, much less in the mud holes we had for lakes in Texas. So of course I could understand people on the coasts who refused to jump into the oceans.
>
> But what a great adventure movie it was. The seventies were a great time for the movies. Along with all the antihero vehicles, there were also movies like *Jaws* and *The Exorcist* that really did for their genres what hadn't been done for some time. . . .
>
> It was great on first viewing. I saw it again later that summer, but it never had the same initial impact.

Wendi Cole saw *Jaws* when she was five, but it did not make the impact on her then that it did later. Seeing it later, "I have not been able to convince myself that this is just a movie the same way that I did with *The Exorcist*. I am terrified of sharks." D'Arcy West found that *Jaws* did not scare her as much as *The Exorcist* had. "There was nothing dark about *Jaws*; it was clean, sunny, summery fun. However, I still to this day have nightmares about *Jaws II* (1978) that I am in the raft being circled by a shark and someone keeps pounding on the underwater cable. The shark biting into and being electrocuted by the cable is an incredibly strong image in my mind."

Brian Calderon saw *Jaws* when he was eight, and it became his worst moviegoing experience. "My father's hand was on my thigh. . . . As the shark bit down, my father's hand clamped down on my thigh. I told him he was hurting me. He didn't realize he was doing it. My mother tells me I had nightmares after I saw *Jaws*, but I don't think it was about the shark." Jill Mitchell saw the film at about the same age while visiting her father in Los Angeles. "I was scared fishless, and I had to run up the aisle a couple of times to avoid implosion. My sadistic daddy insisted on taking me out on his dinghy in the harbor the next morning. That was one of the most frightening experiences of my life. I was *sure* that morning would spell the end of me and my foolish father."

For Michael Thomas, seeing it with his father was a slightly different experience.

> I was eleven years old. I remember waiting in the long lines with my father. Typical of a New Jersey summer, it was hot and unbearably humid. The film was selling out everywhere, and I just hoped we would get in. I had never seen so many people line up to see a film. I told my father once we go in, I would run to save us seats. The second my ticket was torn, I bolted into the theatre and grabbed two prime seats. It was a madhouse. I knelt on the armrests looking for my father. A few minutes later, he arrived with popcorn and candy. *Jaws* seemed especially real to me because I grew up on the Jersey shore and often went fishing with my father and sometimes caught small sharks just beyond the breakers. I think I had more fun watching *Jaws* than any other film in my life. I was at just the right age.

Kevin Kennedy was eleven or twelve when the film came out and originally planned to see it with some friends, but those plans did not work out. A week later, his parents were going and invited him to come along. Being at that age, "I decided to be cool and sit a few rows in front of them. When the shark first appeared while Roy Scheider was scooping 'chum' into the water, I swear I must have flown back to my parents' row out of fear. We all got a good laugh about that afterwards, but it took me quite a while before I would go swimming at night!" Anthony Thompson saw the film with his mother and does not "know who screamed more like a woman, my mother or me."

Javier Rodriguez had read the book by Peter Benchley before seeing the film in a theatre, so "I felt cheated of a movie" and that "the plot . . . needed work."[7] But he was still impressed "with the way the shark was evil." Jack Hollander had not read the book, but when he saw the film in its first run, "Unfortunately, I went to see it with several people who had already seen it. In their defense, they tried to contain themselves at the 'shocking' scenes, but their efforts to try NOT to give away the secrets ended up spoiling a scene or two anyway (but not much)."

Donna Crisci remembers that everyone in the theatre was still

eating popcorn when the shark claimed its first victim—poor Chrissy, out there swimming alone. This scene totally devastated me; my own popcorn sat uneaten forever on my lap, and I remember being aston- ished that people were still stuffing theirs down while shrieking for the girl. I don't know why this memory has stayed with me . . . it had real impact, almost aside from the rest of the film. I just kept thinking about her for days, that poor girl, with that unseen menace worrying at her out of our sight. I used to have to push the image out of my thoughts.

Just as *Psycho* had turned people off showers, *Jaws* turned people off water in many of its forms. Brian Hall was a child when he saw the movie, and "like every other kid, I was terrified to even take a bath after I saw *Jaws*. Whenever the water turned dark in the tub, fear would grip my heart, and I would be asking my mother if I could get out of the tub." Steven Krul also saw the film at a young age, thinking it was going to be "a shark documentary. It ended up scaring the shit out of me. I was afraid to even walk near puddles in the street after seeing it."

For most viewers, *Jaws* caused fears of the ocean. Terrence Atkins grew up in Florida. "Before *Jaws,* I spent half my childhood in the ocean. When I walked out of that theatre, my 'pearl diving career' was over. I can remember going into the bathroom and being worried that the shark was going to come out of the toilet and get me. And believe me, I was no stranger to sharks. I had seen them firsthand in Florida. . . . But *Jaws* created something in my mind that could never be taken away." David Ko was growing up in Hawaii when the film came out and says it "had a profound impact on me. I used to swim in the ocean every day and never feared the deep end until *Jaws*. I was never the same after seeing it. Till this day I get a creepy feeling when there isn't anybody around me when I swim. . . . In a way I wish I never saw that movie, because I'll never view the ocean [the same way] again."

The opening scene also affected Rocio Vargas and "had a lot to do with my decision to quit my swimming lessons and never swim in the ocean again. Until now every time I get into a pool I can't help thinking of sharks coming from underneath me ready to rip my legs off." Actor Ira Katz had the same reaction to the first scene, and although the fear "later diffused and then disappeared ... to this day if I go into the ocean, I am still fearful of anything around my feet." Angela West saw *Jaws* in a theatre and "was extremely disappointed that I paid $2.75 to see this movie. Maybe it was that I simply wasn't into sharks that ate people or bikini bathing beauties that were too stupid to stay out of the water. Whatever the case, I felt the movie lasted way too long and I wanted so desperately for Jaws to attack Steven Spielberg."

The film gave Wil Dimpflmaier "a phobia of the water that I couldn't shake, and it still acts up once in a while. My father hates that movie with a passion; as a boater and a diver, he feels it wrecked a lot of people's love for the water. Seeing that movie as a kid and then having to water-ski at the next family weekend outing just sucked." He got back into surfing at seventeen and still occasionally watches *Jaws* when it is on television. After he has watched it and is out surfing, however, "that damn sound track pops into my head. Then instead of comfortably sitting on my board with my legs dangling in the water below me, I lay on it, getting the maximum amount of my body out of the water, and paddle towards the closest surfer just to increase the odds. Yeah, great movie."

When she was growing up in Kentucky, Alix Parson "put off seeing *Jaws* until I was eighteen. Even with the movie being that dated and the hype long gone, I still can't go into the ocean." Blair Woodard also did not see it when it first came out. "I remember the ads for the film on TV and was freaked out by them. I didn't see the actual film until I rented it some years ago." Arnold Quinlan found the poster with the shark coming up underneath the swimmer just as scary as the movie, and David Bromley was so scared by the trailer that he initially did not see the movie. His brothers hummed the theme and convinced him, at age six, that sharks did indeed live in the lakes in Michigan where they went swimming. Bromley eventually saw the film on television at age thirteen and was "like, that's it?"

Peggy Dilley was smart enough that "*Jaws* couldn't sucker me in enough to go see it. I didn't want to worry about sharks. I'd spent two years swimming, from age five to seven, year round, off the coast of Miami Beach, and I didn't want to believe I came close to being eaten. I love the ocean: don't make it a taboo, scary place. But it did. I couldn't help it. I'm so suggestible. I saw *Jaws* all cut up on TV years later, and sometime in the process, I gave up surf swimming. Or maybe it's fear of skin cancer."

Film student Tandy Summers saw the ads in the newspapers and at age six wanted to see it, but when her dad took her to the drive-in, she fell asleep during the cartoons and missed it. Four years later when it was rereleased, she saved her lunch money and "snuck out of school one day and saw it. I ended up seeing it about ten times in the three weeks it played. I just couldn't get enough . . . . I knew the first time I saw it I wanted to do something in movies." For Carolyn Backer, *Jaws* also interested her in the art of cinematography. "I don't remember how old I was at the time, but I remember some shots as if I saw it only yesterday."

Virginia Keene saw the film when it opened and loved it. "I still love it on video today. It doesn't work for me at all on commercial TV. I watched part of it once, but the commercials weren't just exasperating, they ruined the suspense for me. I gave up on it because it wasn't fun. The key to *Jaws* IS fun, I think. It has a kind of cartoon feel and lots of comic relief." For David Morales, the film did work on TV. "The music struck instant fear. Feared for my feet and lower extremities even on the couch."

Jaws "did the job on" Jon Conrad "beautifully, it worked completely. I saw it early on. I remember being surprised that it seemed to be in every theatre in the country the week it was released, not realizing it would be a pioneer in the wide-release strategy that's now so prevalent." *Jaws* was only one of the films that persuaded Hollywood that first-run films should be released in a large number of theatres simultaneously. Paramount's wide release of *The Godfather* started the trend, and *Jaws* cemented it. When I mentioned earlier that *Jaws* scared more people than *The Exorcist*, it was in reference to this distribution pattern, since as noted, *The Exorcist* played limited engagements for several months before being widely distributed. By putting *Jaws* into a large number of theatres, Universal was able to make the hype and the interest pay off. By January 1976, less than a year after its release, *Jaws* had pulled in domestic rentals of $102.65 million, while *The Exorcist* had only $71.715 million.[8]

In spite of D'Arcy West's comment that *Jaws* was "clean, sunny, summery fun," it and *The Exorcist* were hardly lighthearted movies, as the reactions to them show. The films of the early seventies tended toward the darker side. As previously noted, some of this began in the films of the late sixties, such as *Bonnie and Clyde* and *Easy Rider*. *The Godfather* films dealt with political and social corruption as well as violence. It is not surprising then that the early seventies saw a revival of film noir—dark and violent films about corruption and violence in American society.

If you look at any current film history textbook or read any of the thousands of essays about film noir, you will be under the impression that it was one of the most important and popular film genres of the late forties and early fifties.[9] However, it was not well-received by audiences in its time. Of the 211 films of the forties that brought in rentals of $3 million or more, only nine were film noir, and those tended to be major studio productions with big stars such as

Double Indemnity (1944). Of the 287 films of the fifties that grossed that much, not one was a film noir.[10]

When Arthur Knight wrote his film history *The Liveliest Art* in 1957, he did not use the term film noir, which was originally used by the French in the late forties, to describe American films of crime and violence. Knight's discussion of this type of movie comes in a section on the increased realism in postwar films and the increased use of violence in films that evolved out of the films, newsreels, and documentaries of the war.[11] In the 1971 first edition of Gerald Mast's *A Short History of the Movies* there is no listing for the term in the index, but by the time of the sixth edition in 1996, there are twenty-two listings in the index.[12] There are reasons film noir made a comeback in the seventies and has remained a popular style.

While the dark cynicism of film noir appealed to *some people* in the late forties, it appealed to a larger audience in the social upheavals of the late sixties and seventies. The combination of an unpopular, unsuccessful war and Watergate put American audiences in a mood to accept the view of American society as corrupt—a major element of film noir. Noir returned in such seventies films as *The French Connection* (1971), *Klute* (1971), *The Godfather, Serpico* (1973), *Chinatown* (1974), *The Godfather Part II*, *The Conversation*, *Farewell My Lovely* (1975), and *Taxi Driver*, all films that were commercially successful and nominated for one or more Academy Awards in major categories.

Film noir also returned for two other reasons. Film noir has always seemed to me to be, along with science fiction, one of the most male adolescent of all film genres. Many of the younger, baby boom generation who were hitting their teens and twenties in the late sixties and early seventies were the people being made cynical by the social problems of the time (and the fact that the youth movements did not provide them instant gratification: the American soldiers did not get out of Vietnam until 1973, and it took over two years after the Watergate burglary to get Nixon to resign). Film noir has a male adolescent's paranoia about the adult world, and in many cases it includes a male adolescent's fear of adult women's sexuality. A ruling principle of film noir seems to be that if a guy hangs out with a dumb, innocent blonde virgin, he'll be OK, but if he has actual sex with an adult brunette, he'll die. As someone who has been married to a brunette (although we are now both graying a bit) for over thirty years with no serious side effects, I have always found that aspect of the film noir a little preposterous.

The second reason for the return of film noir was nostalgia. If the films noir of the forties and fifties were at least nominally realistic, many of the films noir of the seventies looked back on the past with nostalgia. Of the early seventies films noir mentioned above, *The Godfather* films, *Chinatown*, and *Farewell My*

Lovely are all set in the past. Both the *Godfather* films and *Farewell My Lovely* are set in the forties and fifties, and Robert Towne, the writer of *Chinatown*, moved its story from the teens, when the events that inspired it actually took place, into the thirties of the Hollywood gangster movies. Watching vintage forties and fifties films noir in class and in revival theatres, it has struck me that audiences of the seventies, eighties, and nineties enjoyed the films because the stylistic excesses—both verbal and visual—made them camp.

Because of the social upheavals of the sixties, nostalgia became a dominant force in popular art in the seventies, especially the movies, as people tried to smooth out the turbulence of the previous decade. Nostalgia in films had previously run in twenty- to thirty-year cycles. The fifties looked back at the twenties and thirties. *Bonnie and Clyde* in 1967 looked back to the thirties. What happened in the early seventies was that middle-aged audiences looked back to the period of time before the upheavals of the sixties; they looked back to the fifties. This happened to coincide with the childhood and teens of many of the baby boomers, so the fifties became a source of nostalgia for them as well.

The film that made the transition was the 1973 picture *American Graffiti*. Officially set in 1962, it *feels* more like the fifties: small-town adolescents drive around at night, two of whom decide over the night whether they are going college the next day or not. I lived through those activities in the late fifties in Bloomington, a town not unlike the California town in the film, and many others in the audience had lived through similar experiences in their towns (and cities too, although the film struck its strongest chord in those of us from small-town America. And probably in those of us from small-town America who had moved to big cities).

Aubrey Solomon saw the film at a prerelease screening at the film school at USC, and he has "never seen an audience go wild for a movie like at this screening. They were hooting, hollering, and cheering all the way through. I later viewed the movie at a theatre in Montreal where the response was enthusiastic but nothing like the USC screening." While part of the enthusiasm at USC may have been that it was made by one of the first USC Cinema alumni to make it big, George Lucas, most of the feeling was very much a generational reaction. While the film brought about a heavy load of fifties nostalgia to the movies and television (*Happy Days* and its spin-offs grew out of the success of *American Graffiti*), it was one of those films like *Easy Rider* that never quite had the same impact later or on a different generation of people. It has had almost no reissue value and has never been particularly successful at revival theatres.

I found it ironic, and still do, that the opening song on the sound track of *American Graffiti* was "Rock Around the Clock." In *Blackboard Jungle,* it was a song demonstrating the ferocity of alienated urban teenagers. By 1973, it was being used as nostalgia for the "good old days" of "good" teens of the fifties, who were only slightly alienated. Perhaps it was an attempt by Lucas to suggest a depth that the film did not have.

Even in the seventies films that were dark and serious, elements of previous films and film styles showed up. To take the five films nominated for Best Picture for 1976, *All the President's Men* was a film noir/docudrama that recalled Frank Capra's 1939 *Mr. Smith Goes to Washington*; *Bound for Glory* came out as bravely against the excesses of the Depression as the 1940 film *The Grapes of Wrath*; *Network* owed a lot more than it admitted to the 1957 film *A Face in the Crowd*; *Rocky* was a smart mixture of *On the Waterfront* and *Marty*; and *Taxi Driver* recalls any number of films noir.[13] The question, particularly after *American Graffiti*, was whether the nostalgia would overpower the seriousness.

The question would be answered shortly. Something else was out there, on its way in, about to overshadow everything.

Star Wars

The first reaction to *Star Wars* I heard came in 1976. One of my students at Los Angeles City College was taking a course taught by the science fiction writer Alan Dean Foster. The student, who shall remain nameless because of his on-going successful film career, mentioned that Foster had shown the class some production sketches from George Lucas's new film. The student's reaction was that it looked like the most stupid stuff he'd ever seen.

In November 1976, Jack Hollander joined some other filmgoers who

> were invited to the Avco Theatre in Westwood to see the new film *Nickel-odeon* for the special price of—a nickel! I vaguely remember the film.... It had something to do with the early days of filmmaking in Hollywood. What was memorable about this five-cent experience was that before the film, they showed a trailer. The trailer opened with a black screen and words (in blue) across the screen reading "A long time ago, in a galaxy far, far away..." Even after *Nickelodeon* finished screening, people were leaving the theatre talking about the *Star Wars* trailer ("I wonder if that's all the effects," "looked neat," "can they really DO that?" etc.... The anticipation from just that two-minute snippet was enough to help build the anticipation for the film that would not open for six months, and is still the only trailer I can recall where and when I first saw it.

Kasey Arnold-Ince saw the same trailer. "It just came on, out of nowhere, a flurry of images unlike anything I'd ever seen, a live-action comic book with that big, blustery sound track. I don't remember any dialogue, just images and music. And then it was over, with a little note: 'Coming This Summer.' I turned to my date and said, 'What the hell was that?' and we both agreed that it looked like a real 'dog.' Sometimes it's good to be wrong."

I don't remember the first time I saw the trailer for *Star Wars*, but when I did, I was struck by how little of the film it showed. There were no special effects, which is what led to the comments Jack Hollander heard. There was no substantial dialogue, and the music, which was not the John Williams score we associate with the picture, was rather generic. The trailer *did* promise some swashbuckling (Luke and the Princess swinging across a chasm of some sort) and some humor (R2–D2 falling over, going "Uh-oh."). I learned later from another former student of mine, Mary M. Lind, who worked on the film and the trailer, that they did not use the special effects because (a) Lucas did not want to, and (b) many of them weren't finished yet.

The first screenings of the not-quite-completed *Star Wars* are now legendary.[1] Lucas showed it to the head of the studio, Alan Ladd Jr., who was relieved it was not the disaster he had feared, but he wondered if kids would like it. The same audience included the advertising and marketing staff, who loved it, but the next screening was for a group of Lucas's filmmaker friends. Lucas recalled to his biographer, "They all thought it was a disaster," and those who did not say so expressed sympathy to him that it did not work.

Meanwhile, the trailer was still in the theatres, doing its job. On March 12, 1977, the Los Angeles International Film Exposition ran a program of trailers called "Son of Coming Soon!" It featured trailers from such classics as *Tammy and the Bachelor* (1957), *Queen of Outer Space* (1958), *Exodus* (1960), and *The Boys in the Band* (1970). Nearly all the trailers got enthusiastic reactions, laughter if not cheers, but the biggest reaction was for the *Star Wars* trailer.

Aubrey Solomon was working at Twentieth Century-Fox that spring, and he saw the film at the studio "on the weekend before it opened and bought Fox stock Monday. It was fun, but after reading the hyped-up story in *Time* magazine, I must have been expecting more."

Since *Star Wars* was to be the first film I knew of that had an on-screen credit for one of my former students, I decided to see it on opening day—May 25, 1977. My daughter Audrey was twelve and wanted to come along, so I figured we could catch the 5:20 P.M. show at the Avco in Westwood. When we got there, most of the line was inside, and I was more than a bit put off that the admission price, which had been $3.50 for nearly a decade, was now $4.00. And I should have been suspicious that the $4.00 sign was hand-lettered. The theatre had obviously raised the price when they saw the kind of crowds they were getting. I never entirely forgave George Lucas for being even indirectly responsible for the rise in admission prices.

The theatre was full and eagerly anticipating the film. Part of their enthusiasm may have been chemically induced. I wrote in my diary that night, "let's put it this way, when the lights went down, the lights went up," as some people started smoking funny-looking cigarettes. The audience cheered the Twentieth Century-Fox logo, and cheered even louder when Lucas used the old Alfred Newman CinemaScope fanfare under his Lucasfilm title. The audience dutifully read the crawl explaining, as my friend Tovah Hollander put it, "what happened in the first twelve chapters." There was an appropriate "awwing" when the camera panned down to the planet and the first rocket ship zipped across the screen. Then the nose of the cruiser began to appear and got larger. And larger. And LARGER. The audience went wild and was, I wrote in my diary, "noisy and enthusiastic all the way through." They remained noisy throughout the long final credit roll.

Audrey and I loved the picture. She later got an autographed photo of Carrie Fisher as Princess Leia, which she still has somewhere. I, however, wrote in my diary, "had second thoughts almost as soon as I left the theatre: it really is a film for twelve-year-old film freaks. It has a certain sophistication about how we respond to old movie types (it uses a lot of them), but an enormous naïveté about people. It seems the ultimate film students' film: technology and old movies are the answer to everything."

My then-current students, not surprisingly, loved the film—many had seen it several times opening day—and it was all they talked about the next day, although one student had the same kind of second thoughts I did.

On vacation in Washington, D.C., at the time, Jon Conrad also saw it on opening day. "Looking around for things to do in the *Washington Post*, I saw a rave review of the picture that was opening that night. . . . It looked like fun, and I got there for the 5:00 P.M. show. I sat through the whole thing twice (it always helps to see big movies at the Uptown in D.C.—big screen, great sound and projection). One of my typically dopey predictions on the way out: 'Gee, I enjoyed that a whole lot, but I wonder how many other people will.' Duh."

As Jack Hollander notes, the *Star Wars* trailer produced "awesome" anticipation. "This couldn't possibly be as good as the trailer. Of course it was, and then some. . . . I remember being carried away with the rest of the audience with the great spectacle that was this film. . . . This is the first and only movie that I paid to see four times in its original run in the theatres—I couldn't get enough of the stuff. I could quote lines, discuss camera angles, etc."

Rick Mitchell's anticipation, along with other science fiction fans, came from having read the novelization. He "felt that if Lucas got 50 percent of what was in the novel on the screen, he'd have a hit, as this would be the film that those of us who were turned on to science fiction, both in film and fiction, in the fifties had long wanted to see. I first saw it in 70mm at the cast-and-crew screening at the Academy and felt he had more than succeeded."

However, the trailer for *Star Wars* had not worked for Donna Crisci.

I really didn't want to see this. I had heard no hype. I love science fiction but not fantasy, and I had seen a trailer that said the film was about a robot and a boy and a wizard . . . the wizard thing lost my interest in the film. But then it opened, and everyone was talking, and my sister and I went out to Westwood one day to see it. I remember there were business-men in line who had already seen it and were back again, and that sur-prised me. I looked at the stills from the film, and one of them—a shot of Han assisting Luke in the garbage bin—struck me for some reason: I think it was the idea of a friend helping a friend, and I remember thinking I might like the film after all, if it avoided too much magic.

Well, I was captivated by shot one! I don't think kids today can realize how those opening scenes looked, that endless ship, the words floating off into the stars, the incredible grabbing blast of the music! I was hooked at once, but I didn't fall in love with it forever until the scene of Luke gazing off at the double suns as the beautiful Jedi theme, filled with yearn-ing and nobility, swelled behind the scene. I remember consciously think-ing to myself at that moment, "I love this movie. . . ." When I came out of the theatre, I can recall looking at this world, at telephone poles and streets and cars and thinking, "No, this doesn't look right!" I don't think any film ever transferred me to another world like this one.

Scott Hemmann also intended to avoid the film. When he saw the first ads on television, "I thought it was going to be a cheesy rehash of those 1950s drive-in B movies. I remember thinking the character of Chewbacca looked like he was wearing a costume made of recycled mop heads. After the movie became such a hit, I grudgingly allowed myself to be dragged to it and was surprised at how much I enjoyed it." Steven Krul "almost didn't go to see it because of *Jaws*. My father showed me a full-page newspaper ad for *Star Wars* with a picture of all the characters. Once I picked Chewbacca out of the crowd, I said no way am I going to see this thing rip people apart through the whole movie." When they got to the theatre, he "started thinking that maybe this won't be so bad if all these kids are here waiting to go in, and the ones coming out from the previous screening were smiling and jumping around still psyched from the movie. When I finally got in, I was pleasantly surprised to find out Chewy was with the good guys, and the movie was about everything I used to dream about as a kid: trav-eling through space, seeing creatures from other worlds, and being the hero."

A friend of Laurel Martin's was "shocked that I hadn't seen it yet." They went to the Chinese Theatre in Hollywood, and by the end of the film, Martin "was a crazed fan of that film. I went with anybody who'd go see that movie."

Peter Albers remembers "being very upset when I first sat down in the the-atre for my first viewing of *Star Wars*, thinking we were way too far back. Later that evening . . . as I pulled some of the weeds I had blown into by the film out of my hair, I thought we might just as well have been six inches from the screen, it was just so effective and involving." A woman who now works in the industry admits, "There may be something missing in me, but the main feeling I had watching it was that the sound was too loud and it bugged me," although she did enjoy the cantina scene. Paul Sbrizzi read the reviews and went with high expectations but was "horrified to realize I'd gone to see a big-budget Saturday morning kiddies program." He would have been seventeen at the time.

Because the film was such an immediate and continuing success, there were lines waiting to get in. Long lines. Rocio Vargas saw the film in San Jose and remembers that "people waited for up to three hours before the movie started just to get a ticket." Nancy Lathrop did not "enjoy the experience of going. I understood waiting in line for *The Exorcist*, but at *Star Wars* there were those goofy people out front, dressed as those characters, and they were playing with their little swords, and we were in line forever in Westwood. We got in, and we were in a corner over here in the packed theatre, and the film lost me about fifteen minutes into it." Lydell Jackson and his friends obviously waited long enough to see the film, because when they went, "There was no one there and so the manager let us go in free. He gave us free popcorn and cokes!"

Terrence Atkins was spending that summer with his father in Loveland, Colorado, and saw the film twenty times. "Thank God it was showing at the local theatre. Movies like this give people in towns like Loveland, Colorado, a reason to get out of bed in the morning."

Al Gonzalez saw the movie months after it had opened and had high expectations because of the hype. "It's a shame, because I know I would have really enjoyed it if I could have seen it without any advance notice . . . when I finally saw it I remember thinking 'No big deal.'" Virginia Keene was out of the country when it was released, but "there was a lot of excitement about it even in the Caribbean. I returned six months later, and it was still playing in the theatres. I was duly impressed by the special effects but was frankly surprised and disappointed by a sophomoric story and dreadful acting. I've seen it only once since, and for me it has suffered with age."

Aubrey Solomon went back to see the film several weeks after it opened to "see it in a theatre . . . just to see it with a paying audience. The movie did play very well right from the in-your-face title card. I enjoyed the sound track (music and sound effects) probably as much as the picture." I went back to see the film the first week of August and sat through two matinee showings simply to examine the visual effects and the sound effects, which did much to create the worlds of the film. I also noticed at those August screenings how much the film had become part of the culture. When Sir Alec Guinness first said, "May the Force be with you" in the opening day screening, there had been no particular reaction to the line. At both of the August screenings, the line was met with cheers and applause.

Rudie Bravo's second viewing of the film came almost fifteen years after her first. She went in Pasadena and was "with the biggest group of science fiction geeks ever, and the sparsely filled theatre contained even more geek-boys (all with plastic pen protectors in their button-up shirt pockets and Swiss army knives in their survivalist tool belts). There was another girl in the group I was with, and just before Harrison Ford makes his first appearance, she leaned over and said, 'Now we'll find out how many other women are here.' Sure enough, as soon as Han Solo appeared, female catcalls were heard from different corners of the theatre."

Richard Bogren waited only ten years before he went back to see it again. The first time was in a small, mall theatre, but the second time was in a theatre with a "BIG" screen. Most people went back to see it a little sooner. At age six, Ricardo Lopez had seen the film several times "at third-rate theatres," but a friend's father took Lopez and the friend to see it at Mann's Chinese, and "it was like seeing it for the first time again . . . it was like seeing a different movie. I remember the huge screen . . . bright, curved, and in one piece. The image was bright and colorful. The sound loud, clear, and coming from every direction. And most importantly, the audience was actually there to experience the film—they were courteous and quiet. At the time, it was the most awesome experience of my life." Maryanne Raphael saw it first at the Chinese, and then later "in a small theatre on the big island of Hawaii. It seemed like another movie." The first time Kulani Jackson saw it, he was "totally into the merchandise," but on later viewings, he thought the film has "pretty bunk effects."

For many kids in the seventies, like Marcus Franklin and "Moe Gardener," *Star Wars* was the first movie they saw all the way through. When Franklin saw it at the drive-in, "My father was waiting for me to go to sleep all night, but . . . I was very excited by the movie and even yelled and cheered during the final battle." For Gardener, it was the first "complete experience" of seeing a film. His father piled them into the family car during a cold spell, then turned up the heater so all the kids were sweating, and "I still remember my sister reading me the words at the beginning of the film. The next day on the school bus, I remember telling everyone on the bus about this cool movie I had seen, and the kids telling me how many times they had seen it. I could not understand why anyone would want to see a film twenty or thirty times. I have never seen *Star Wars* again."

Gary Demirdjian's brother took him to see *Star Wars* when he was seven, and "I believe from that point on, I was changed forever. Here was a silly science fiction film that took itself seriously, and I believed in it. It was raining that day, and during the movie when my brother had to use the bathroom, I went as well. And while I was waiting for him, I was marching around the bathroom like a storm trooper, the umbrella in hand for a laser gun. That movie drove me crazy; I was actually addicted to a film!" Javier Rodriguez responded to another element. He was "a little kid with a big imagination. I remember being so amazed at the spacecraft and space. And the way I felt it was so true and there really existed an alliance."

Mia Gyzander was about ten when she saw *Star Wars*, but "for some reason, my only memory from this movie is the little robot." Teddi Lawrence was about seven then: "My favorite uncle, Uncle Jim, took my two brothers and me to see *Star Wars*. There were three big thrills in this: the first was my uncle taking us to the movie, the second was that he said we could get whatever candy we wanted (I think I ate two boxes of Snow Caps, plus popcorn), and the third was that when we left the theatre, we all wanted to see it again, so right then we bought more tickets." Tandy Summers saw it at age eight and a year later saw it again, making her grandmother sit through it twice.

In June 1977, Scott Renshaw and his brother wanted more than anything to see *Star Wars*.

For a month [after it opened] we had been pleading with our parents to let us see it, but they responded only with the ever popular, "We'll see." One Sunday afternoon after church, we drove to the little shopping center where the supermarket my mom usually used was located. It seemed like a fairly ordinary shopping trip. However, *Star Wars* was showing at the theatre in the same shopping center. After we picked up a few things at the supermarket, my parents put the groceries in the car. My brother and I were ready to get into the car when my parents turned around and started walking very casually towards the theatre. After a few feet, my mom turned around and said, "Well, are you coming or not?" To this day, that may be the most transcendentally cool thing my parents have ever done.

Renshaw saw the film three more times that summer.

Lawrence Dotson's mother "took us to see *Star Wars*, the first time she had been to the movies in years. She still talks about it to this day. I guess she was as impressed as I was!" By the time the movie came out, Peggy Dilley had children of her own and took her son to see it. "My son liked it. I liked the music. It was stirring. We bought him *Star Wars* dolls for Christmas. But enough was enough .... I didn't really want to see the next two installments, but my son talked me into it. Good and bad. But then I saw Joseph Campbell [the philosopher who inspired George Lucas—and in later years more would-be screenwriters and Hollywood executives than he should have] and saw a picture of that little guy with the powers over a door in the used book section of The Bodhi Tree [a Los Angeles bookstore specialized in metaphysics and New Age books], and I had to give in. Yes, I believe in the force too, Luke."

Lilia Fuller, who was so entranced by the film as a child in Bulgaria that she decided to study English, started collecting the toys when she was young. For Blair Woodard and his friends, they did not even need toys. He remembers that that summer the games on the playground went from "wars to Star Wars." For David Martinez, watching the film even today is "like an old friend from your childhood that will always be there." Coni Constantine loved it as a child, but seeing it later on video found it was "sort of a letdown. However, Luke, Han, Chewie and the rest of the gang were as great as I had remembered them."

Lisa Evans saw the film at age nine with her brother, who was seven, and it "pretty much ruled our young life. My brother went away on a camping trip, and while he was gone, my mom wallpapered his room in Star Wars, hung up Star Wars curtains and put down Star Wars bed sheets and pillowcases. It was the coolest thing my mom ever did, and my brother was the hot kid on the block because of that room." They had all the toys in their house, but "although I wasn't a tomboy, I didn't think it was fair that almost all the Star Wars merchandise was geared towards young boys. It was sexist; girls like Star Wars too, but admittedly, boys liked it even more. . . . " The family had a tree in the front yard they played Star Wars on, and one day her brother fell out of the tree and "got a fat lip. The force wasn't with him that day I guess."

> Many years later, upon coming home from college, I was talking to two young girls in my mother's front yard. We were talking about trees, and I told them, "We used to have the best tree before it was cut down; we always played Star Wars in it," and one of the girls looked at me dumbfounded and said, "Star Wars?" I realized at that moment that there is a generation gap of young kids and teenagers that have never seen Star Wars and couldn't care less. By dissing Star Wars, these kids were dissing my childhood, and I suddenly felt very old. It's strange when a movie represents a big portion of your childhood, and it's sad when you realize it's time to kiss that movie and your youth goodbye.

By the end of 1977, Star Wars had pulled in domestic rentals of $127 million, making it the highest-grossing film of all time up until then. Jaws was in second place with $121.36 million; The Godfather was third with $86.11 million; The Exorcist was fourth with $82.2 million; and The Sound of Music now fifth with $78.66 million; followed by The Sting (1973) and the longtime top grosser, Gone With the Wind, which with its various reissues now had rentals of $76.7 million.[2] But Star Wars kept on pulling in the money. In the following year, 1978, it added over $38 million, and in 1979 it added another $11 million plus.[3] By the end of its 1997 reissue, it had grossed more in its five reissues than it had in its original run.[4]

Needless to say, the anticipation for the next chapter in the story was building. The trailer showed up in theatres in late 1979 and immediately promised more. Unlike the original trailer for *Star Wars*, the trailer for *The Empire Strikes Back* emphasized special effects, specifically the chase through the asteroid belt, which told audiences immediately that the special effects would go beyond what the first film had done. But Lucas was also up to his old tricks. In the original *Empire* trailer, there is no sign of Yoda.

I had not planned to see *The Empire Strikes Back* on its first day, May 20, 1980, but my daughter the fifteen-year-old fan wanted to see it. The line at 2:30 for the 5:30 show at the Avco was not too bad, and Audrey actually found a place in line with a friend of hers from school. I waited in line with him while she did some shopping, and he beat the pants off me at the simple pocket computer game he had. I think I had, at the most, only a dimmest suspicion that the game was the wave of the future.

The crowd inside was, I wrote in my diary, "just as wild as the first-day audience for *Star Wars* had been, if not more so. This audience began applauding at the sound beep before the movie began." (There is a sound beep on the leader of the film before the film itself starts; projectionists usually try to avoid letting it be heard—they can see it on the film and know to turn on the sound then—but I have the suspicion this projectionist was playing with the audience.) There was not the marijuana smoking there had been the first day at *Star Wars*, but there did not need to be. The audience was primed. On the other hand, the audience Marilyn Heath saw it with was smoking the weed.

My reactions to the film were somewhat similar to the first one, as I recorded in my diary: "I have to admit I enjoyed a lot of it and laughed at some of it and with some of it, but it left me uneasy. Part of it is the reservations I had about the original: I distrust a movie that goes to such lengths to work me [over] emotionally over sub-adolescent fantasies. A bigger problem with this one is that it now seems to take itself seriously. At least *Star Wars* didn't pretend to be a tract on moral philosophy. This one does, but the philosophy's on the nursery school level. . . . At least I get to see [Fellini's] *8 1/2* (1963) tomorrow [in the film history class I teach]."

I had a hard time getting up the next morning "between the overcast weather, a headache, and depression over *The Empire Strikes Back*." The class did not like *8 1/2*, and in the class discussion the next week, "We got off the film itself and into the differences between 'commercial (narrative)' and 'arty (time jumpers)' flicks and audiences' attitudes towards each. I got in my licks on *The Empire Strikes Back,* and they got in their licks at Antonioni and Fellini."

When he was twelve years old, Brian Hall saw *Empire* the first time with an appreciative audience.

The theatre was packed with Star Wars fanatics. Whenever the main characters were seen for the first time, everybody went wild. That is the only sci-fi movie that ever had me totally wrapped up in its world. I loved that cocky Han Solo and that fur-ball Chewbacca. I almost cried during the scene where they tortured Han. The theatre was so quiet you could hear a pin drop. I hated the fact that I had to wait another three years before I could see what was going to happen to him. But because of this, I became a Star Wars fanatic. I used to go around the house and pretend I was a storm trooper or a rebel soldier so much that it made my mother sick, and she wondered if I knew the difference between reality and fiction. In school, I always daydreamed that my desk was an X-wing fighter. And one time during an earthquake, I ran around the house pretending I was in the belly of the space worm the Millenium Falcon was in the movie. I've seen *Empire* ten times in the theatre and about ten times on video.

Gary Demirdjian, who spent part of *Star Wars* marching around the bathroom using an umbrella as a laser, was in the lines at the Avco to see *The Empire Strikes Back*. "Needless to say, *Empire* blew my mind. Here was a sequel that could actually compete with the original!" Aubrey Solomon thought *Empire* "was better . . . than the first one, even though the story was darker and inconclusive. It was striking in concept and effects and a marvel of technical prowess. The opening 'Snow Walker' scenes were probably the best in all three movies." Rick Mitchell saw the film at Fox and thought "it was a richer improvement on the first—until the cliffhanger ending, which at the time annoyed me." He enjoyed the film more over the years, and it became "another all-time personal favorite." When Dorian Wood finally got around to seeing the film on tape, he found the ending so frustrating that every time he watched, he pushed the stop button on the VCR when Han Solo was frozen.

The Empire Strikes Back is high school history teacher Donna Crisci's favorite film of the three,

because it is the least cartoonish, the most epic and serious. I also think it is a physically beautiful film; the scenes with Yoda raising the cruiser in the swamp, the framing of the duel scenes with Vader and Luke, all blues and oranges, absolutely wonderful. I can look at this film and love it. I liked the good guys hopelessly down, and the wonderful mythic element between father and son that was introduced.

When it ended, I groaned, "Three more years!" which seemed endless before *Jedi [Return of the Jedi (1983)]*. We argued endlessly those three years: was Darth really Luke's father? Who was Yoda's "other"? These films were before VCRs were in: you couldn't buy films like this. I had a student who bootlegged copies, and the week before *Jedi* opened, I showed both during lunches, waiting for *Jedi*. Kids came in and jammed the classrooms, sitting up on cabinets and every inch of floor space. The anticipation was incredible.

As could be predicted, Crisci was there for one of the first showings of *Return of the Jedi*.

We went the night before, everyone ditching work. People had to sleep out on Wilshire Boulevard [outside the Avco theatre], and I can still see long lines of folks camping out on grass lawns, puzzled drivers going past all night. Once in the theatre, the atmosphere was nothing short of electric; never have I been in a place where people were so high, excited, happy (well, maybe Beatles concerts. . . .). At *Jedi* we sat and cheered everything, even the custodians in the theatre. We shrieked to the Twentieth Century-Fox fanfare and logo and brought the house down at the first presentation of the ad for the THX sound [quality control] system, the organ rattling the theatre as we were told, "The audience is listening" for the first time. Were we ever! I think about this every time I see the THX deal to this day and smile every time. We damned near died waiting for Luke to stop pounding on his father and for Darth to save his son, everyone yelling at the screen, "Luke, stop!" or "Darth, help him!" It was unreal. I myself was so excited when Darth moved to assist Luke that I did not see what happened to the emperor. Later, driving home on the freeway, I had to ask what the heck happened. The funny thing is that I didn't like *Jedi* much! I was faintly disappointed in it. But the experience of seeing it that morning with a roomful of fanatics was probably the most exciting movie experience of my life.

Brian Hall, who had loved *Empire* so much that his mother did not know if he could tell reality from fantasy, was also anticipating *Jedi*.

It was a long three years' wait for *Return of the Jedi*, but I made it. I remember sitting in church one Sunday before it came out. My pastor was preaching about how one day Jesus is going to come back and rapture the church away. And I was sitting there thinking, "I hope he doesn't come back before I can see *Return of the Jedi*." I remember that I could hardly sleep that night of the opening weekend. I got up extra early, got on the bus, and stood in line for an hour or two. I was so excited. The moment I had been waiting for three years was finally here, and it was well worth it. (But personally, I think *The Empire Strikes Back* was the best of them all.) Everyone cheered, and I got goose pimples as Luke Skywalker rescued everyone from Jabba the Hutt.

My daughter had moved out and started college by the time the film was released, and I was out of town, so I did not get around to seeing it until four or five days after it opened. I did not feel a lot different about this one than I had about the earlier ones. Rick Mitchell saw it in its first run in Hollywood and was "disappointed by this film, which helped elevate my opinion of *Empire*." Aubrey Solomon also found it "a real disappointment . . . after Jabba blows up, so does the movie." Alix Parson was "pretty disappointed in *Return of the Jedi* . . . . I thought that things were wrapped up a little too neatly. And the last scene with everyone arm-in-arm hugging and singing was total cornball. Like with most things, I think it was more exciting anticipating the third *Star Wars* movie than actually seeing it." After seeing the film, Karpis Termendzyan felt "there can never be another one like this. Everything made sense to me; all three movies were perfect."

Michael Thomas was working as a projectionist at a theatre in the Los Angeles suburb of Marina Del Rey when *Jedi* opened. The theatre had just been outfitted with projectors capable of handling 70mm prints, and *Jedi* was the first film to be shown there in 70mm. "When we finally screened the film, I felt such a letdown. *Jedi* did not grow and mature with the audience that made *Star Wars* a smash hit six years earlier. The fuzzy Ewoks had marketing strategy written all over them. At any moment, I expected to see a price tag show up behind a furry ear. *Jedi* had all the technical razzle-dazzle but played it safe and lost a fan. Maybe I had just grown up."

Peter Albers enjoyed *Jedi*, but "that ending made me really, really angry, and the more I think about it, the angrier I get. The 'Blub-blub' song? How dare he end one of the two or three greatest Hollywood movie series of all time with a bunch of teddy bears (and I *love* teddy bears) running around, purring cutely and singing 'The Blub-blub song.' I still get hives thinking about it." Michael Behling is even more brutal. He loved the first two films, but "the fucking Ewoks! I came expecting to see a monumental battle along with spiritual insights culled from the world's religions, and what do I get! A moronic, very 'Hollywoody' script, and a bunch of dancing teddy bears."

One thing Jack Hollander liked about the film was that "Leia is allowed to do some serious mayhem (no passive woman in this film!)." But by this point, Bill Pulliam "was becoming really annoyed with the softening and 'feminization' of Princess Leia (in the first, she was taller than Skywalker; by this one she was shorter)." Derek Garubo liked the philosophy, which "attracts me I guess because of my beliefs in Taoism. These beliefs are that we all have the energy of the universe flowing in our bodies and that we break out of the pettiness of humanity by becoming one with it. It is a quite beautiful philosophy and the movie reflects it almost identically." Jon Conrad, who had seen *Star Wars* on the first day, "was rather late getting to this. . . . This was a bit of a letdown after the first two (the very end seemed weak for the signoff to a trilogy), but still fun."

For all the disappointments that viewers may have felt for the second two films of the trilogy, they still turned out to see them, some of them many times. In its first year of release, *The Empire Strikes Back* brought in rentals of $120 million, which made it the third highest-grossing picture up to that time, behind only *Star Wars* and *Jaws*.[5] In its first year of release, *Return of the Jedi* brought in rentals of $165.5 million, moving it ahead of *Empire*, which had added another $21 million to its grosses in the intervening years. *E.T. The Extra-Terrestrial* (1982) had overtaken all the *Star Wars* films by that time with a gross of $209.6 million, but *Star Wars* was now second with $193.5 million, with *Jedi* third and *Empire* fourth.[6]

The *Star Wars* trilogy became part of people's lives, but in varying ways and in varying degrees. For Michael Behling, the films—the original *Star Wars* in particular—were "always amazing to me for creating a complete WORLD that was to me completely believable and intricate as well as interesting and beautiful." Douglas Choe just felt that Lucas had seen "too many Kurosawa films and Joseph Campbell books for his own good." Wendi Cole had never seen the films and stayed up one night to watch them all on cassette. She liked them, even though "I had never gotten into the *Star Wars* thing. When people were going nuts about Darth Vader being Luke Skywalker's dad, I was clueless. I'm glad I watched them. Now I know what the big deal is. Although, I still think it was stupid the way Luke told Princess Leia that they were brother and sister and she says that she knows. Yeah, right!"

I had always thought that Princess Leia was one of the weakest characters in the films, and as a feminist I was irritated she did not get to *do* anything until the middle of *Empire,* when she was fixing some of the ship's plumbing. In the mid-eighties, there was a woman student in her mid-twenties in my class, who thought that Leia was really a feminist heroine because she held her own against the guys. Marion Levine dismisses the *Star Wars* films, although she saw them and loved them, as "'guy' movies and just not for me." Susanna Serrano loved the films, but the "only character I fell in love with was the robots of the movie. R2–D2 was my favorite."

David Bromley did not see the first film right away, but when he did see it he was not impressed. He liked *Empire* "a lot more than the first. I only saw it once but I did like it. Of course, all my friends thought I was from Mars or something [for not liking it more]." He loved *Jedi* and guesses "I just had to grow into the whole Star Wars frenzy, or maybe I was just older and was into films more or Princess Leia! I love the little Ewoks."

Edward Pina was a kid at the time of the *Star Wars* films and thought they were "the most memorable movies of my generation. After seeing each movie, I was just like every kid. I went through the *Star Wars* phase. Playing roles at school during lunch with my friends. Buying the *Star Wars* lunch box and collectors items." *Star Wars* "programmed" Alex Kuyumjian "to go crazy on the merchandise. To this day I have mint-condition characters of all three movies intact in storage. This past (1997) release [their value] skyrocketed. I expect they will go even higher when the new saga is released."

James Ford had his own children by the time the trilogy was originally released, and while Ford could "take them or leave them," his children "loved the movies though, so I have seen them many times. I helped make Lucas rich by purchasing many action figures." Angela West was too young to see the films in the theatres but saw them later on video, where they still affected her. "It [*Star Wars*] created a desire in me to have a Princess Leia lunch box, which I must brag happened to be one of a kind in my second grade class. . . . Of course, I carried a crush around for Luke Skywalker for most of the second grade. I told everyone he was my boyfriend."

Wil Dimpflmaier thinks the trilogy "was just the best thing going when I was a kid." He collected all the toys after the first film came out, when he was four, then when his older brother took him to *Empire*, he fell asleep during the cloud city sequence. "When *Return of the Jedi* came out, I was old enough to go with my friends, and I can remember the day like my dad remembers the day JFK was shot." He later saw the whole trilogy in one day in Germany. "It was cool to do once, and only once. The most entertaining thing was the crowd. Europeans are a little wacky as it is, but this was the cream of the wacky crop. A lot of people looked like they could fit right in at a Trekkie convention, and some were in full costume. There was a storm trooper sitting behind me and an obscure crimson guard sitting in front of me. I realized I'm still a fan of the movies, but I lost the infatuation when I stopped playing with the toys."

Dennis Wilkes was impressed with *Star Wars* and liked *Empire*, but when it came to *Jedi*, "By this time, I'm eighteen and a little bored." Virginia Keene felt the films declined, although she was still standing in line to see *Jedi*, mainly because the friend she had seen *Star Wars* with had become her husband. She says, "These films have not worn well for me. They were really one-shot movies." By the time he answered the questionnaire for this book, David Morales had to admit that "the *Star Wars* trilogy is mushed together in my head."

Jack Hollander was a fan of the trilogy and found that seeing the earlier installments changed his perception of them in view of the later ones, notably when seeing *Empire* again after seeing *Jedi*.

> The near idiotic "I love you" . . . "I know" becomes far more palatable after its resurrection in the third film (one of the saving graces of the

third film is that Lucas and other filmmakers were obviously paying attention to all of the speculation frenzy and decided to listen to the public to guide them in making the film). We see the "question mark" scenes differently after we have the answers in *Return*. I, for example, fully expected that Darth Vader WAS Luke's father and that Luke would "turn him to the good side." However, I thought the "other" referred to that character (Luke's father, Anakin)—I didn't anticipate Leia's relationship to Luke —although that did solve the other "ménage" problem.

Eva Mahgrefthe saw all three films in theatres and says, "seeing the films later on cable took away the grandeur of some of the battle scenes, but gave more focus to the psychological aspects of the films—the true meaning of good and evil and the forces for both which exist in every man."

For Marilyn Heath, the trilogy has become very much a family affair.

My eldest daughter was born the year *Star Wars* came out. I saw it by myself with Gracie in my arms the last week it was playing at the Chinese Theatre. It had played for a whole year, so the print was a little rough, but I love science fiction. The movie created a whole world to escape into. . . .

[*Empire*] became my favorite *Star Wars* movie for a while because Darth Vader stole the show. I loved the theme so much I bought it on record, but I cannot play it unless I really need to because then my five-year-old son has to hear it over and over. Kids love Vader more than the heroes; he's a father figure. . . .

I saw *Return of the Jedi* with a film buff friend, who preferred only serious adult movies. I placated her by pointing out that the Empire could represent the imperialists and the rebels, the people. Years later it was the first *Star Wars* picture seen by my son, when he was three years old. We got it on tape late at night and woke him up to watch it. His expression was beautiful; he was in heaven.

Writing in 1994, Gary Demirdjian admitted he had only been to the movies twice in the previous eight months. "To me, the movies that come out now are . . . usually pale imitations of movies that were already made in the past with some slight twists. . . . I think subject matter also influences me a great deal as far as 'My God, I have to see this film' type of excitement. I guess I haven't felt like that in a while. But when the next *Star Wars* or Indiana Jones rolls around, I will be in a theatre."

When Aly Kourouma came to this country in the early nineties, a friend of his was astonished that he had never seen the *Star Wars* films. Kourouma says, "I don't know what, but something in the movie definitely and irredeemably kept me out of it. What? I don't know . . . but I think that this is a good illustration about how this film is really a part of the American heritage—so American that everybody else will be unable to get into it." Perhaps, but in the initial years of their foreign releases, *Star Wars* brought in $215.7 million, *The Empire Strikes Back* brought in $192.1 million, and *Return of the Jedi* $124.2 million.[7]

Many people, especially film critics, assumed that the trilogy was a one-time phenomenon and after the first few years would have no reissue value. In an effort to prove to Lucas they could handle the distribution of the next trilogy, Twentieth Century-Fox arranged to rerelease the first trilogy in early 1997. With the company's 1996 release of *Independence Day*, they attached a trailer for the reissue. It began with scenes from the films in a small section of the screen with tiny sound, with a narrator saying this had been the only way to see the *Star Wars* trilogy for years, but now it was coming back to the big screen, whereupon the image increased in size, as did the sound. But what followed was very much like the original trailer: Luke and Leia swinging across the chasm, R2–D2 falling over with an "Uh-oh," plus several special effects shots. The trailer was appealing to *Star Wars* fanatics and to their nostalgia for films that had, twenty years previously, worked at least in part because of their use of nostalgia for old films and old film genres.

It all worked again, better than anyone connected with the film expected. Tandy Summers, who had made her grandmother sit through the first rerelease of *Star Wars*, saw the new edition four times. As a kid, her favorite character was Luke Skywalker, but now in her twenties it would be Han Solo, "the cool pirate." Steven Krul had seen it originally and the 1997 release was only his second viewing. "It brought back memories. I still got the same feelings I did when I first saw it, which I don't know if it's a good or bad sign. Even though I knew how it was going to end, I still followed the story through like I've never seen it before."

In March 1999, my wife and I had dinner with an old high school friend of hers. While the two women caught up on old times, the friend's ten-year-old son and I talked *Star Wars*. I asked him which *Star Wars* toys he owned. Thirty minutes of inventorying later, I understood how Lucas had managed by then to sell 4.5 billion dollars worth of toys in the previous twenty-two years.[8] Then I asked the boy how he had first heard about the movies. He had learned of the characters, particularly Boba Fett (a particular favorite of kids), from a Nintendo *Star Wars* game. One day in 1997, when the first trilogy was back in the theatres, his older brother noticed him playing the game and said, "You know, there are some movies with those characters in them." They went off to see the films. The next generation was hooked.

After the questionnaires for this book were completed, *Star Wars: Episode I The Phantom Menace* opened in May 1999. If you read the newspaper stories and checked the online chat rooms, you would have been forgiven for thinking that the film was universally despised, especially the character that represents the ultimate result of Lucas's Joseph Campbell-inspired, whiney, adolescent white-boy narcissism, Jar Jar Binks. Within two months, the picture had become the third highest-grossing film of all time.[9] Like Coppola and the Corleones, they keep pulling us back in.

On the summer day in 1997 that I finished the rough draft of this chapter, I went out later for a walk. Finding myself at the nearby Westside Pavilion mall, I wandered into the Suncoast Video store and saw they had a life-sized cardboard cutout of Princess Leia in her *Return* harem outfit, promoting the upcoming video rerelease of the trilogy. I also could not help but notice that Carrie Fisher was browsing in the store.

By the time I left the store, the cutout was gone. I have no idea if Fisher bought it, or if they gave it to her. Or if she just asked them not to display it. Or if its disappearance had nothing to do with her. But would *you* want a cutout of yourself, only partially dressed, twenty years younger than you were today, on public display?

Time passes, people change.

Film Education

I have watched movies and, as you can tell, movie audiences since I was a child, but in the late sixties I began to watch both from new perspectives. We are now going to take a pause from the historical continuity to look at those perspectives. I started graduate school at UCLA in 1967, where I became professionally interested in film history. I began to become aware of how the movies of the past played to present audiences and how the films of the present played in relation to the films of the past.

At UCLA I took a number of film history courses. I've already mentioned seeing *My Son John* there. In the same course, *The Grapes of Wrath* was shown, and unencumbered by anyone sitting too close to me, I noticed a strange reaction to the film. When the Joad family, trying to escape the Dust Bowl, talked about going to California as if it were the promised land, there was a sort of half-snicker from the audience of sixties California college students. It was only a half-snicker, I suspect, because many of the students in the class were from out of state and had come to California as a potential promised land for would-be filmmakers.

That UCLA course eventually led me into a project run by Professor Howard Suber called the Oral History of the Motion Pictures, in which he corralled a group of graduate students to conduct oral history interviews with successful longtime filmmakers. While other people interviewed directors and animators, I ended up talking with the great screenwriter, Nunnally Johnson, who had written both *Jesse James* and *The Grapes of Wrath*, among others. When Johnson and I discussed *Jesse James*, I told him how I had gotten hooked on movies because of it, and he told me that when he was a boy in Columbus, Georgia, he had gotten hooked on Jesse James by watching a stock company melodrama about Jesse. I later heard from an old friend of his, Daisy Tucker, that what really hooked Johnson was watching the audience reaction to the show when he was older and was working as an usher in the theatre. I did not mention my first experience with *The Grapes of Wrath*.

Nunnally and I did not watch his films together, but one night we stopped the interview early because he wanted to watch John Ford's *Cheyenne Autumn* (1964) on television. He had not seen it before, and since he was working on a screenplay for a "big two-[shows]-a-day" Western,[1] he thought he might be able to learn something from Ford's film. The film was not good, and after an hour and a half, he turned off the television, saying later, "Nothing you could learn from a thing like that."[2]

The oral history project led me to a one-year research associateship at the American Film Institute's (AFI's) Center for Advanced Studies. I did a series of interviews with people who had worked with Nunnally Johnson at Twentieth Century-Fox,[3] and this involved occasionally screening films at the AFI before the interviews. Although the Center was supposed to be for advanced studies, I noticed more people turned out for the rousing pirate film *The Black Swan* (1942) than for Darryl Zanuck's serious message picture *Wilson* (1944). On the other hand, there was at the AFI that year a prerelease screening of Don Siegel's odd Civil War gothic film *The Beguiled* (1971). This was an audience that knew Siegel's work on first-rate B pictures like *Riot in Cell Block 11* (1954), so they understood what an expansion of his repertoire this was for Siegel. I doubt if the film, which was not a commercial success, ever had a better audience than it did that day.

One of the advantages—and disadvantages—of watching movies in Los Angeles is that you run into people connected with movies *at* the movies. It was great to listen to Siegel talk about his film at the AFI, but it was depressing to watch the 1975 flop *Lucky Lady*, directed by Stanley Donen, sitting across the aisle from Fred Astaire. Astaire had worked with Donen on *Funny Face* (1957) and did not look happy as he watched the mess Donen had made of *Lucky Lady*. I generally find industry screening audiences the least interesting audiences, if only because everybody in the room has an agenda, and those agendas often have little to do with the film.[4] Nancy Lathrop used to go to screenings for cast and crews of films shortly before the films opened and thought those audiences were the most respectful of films of any audiences she had seen. I can see her point. I saw Woody Allen's *Zelig* (1983) the day it opened in Westwood, and the audience of devoted film buffs appreciated the special effects work more than an audience I saw the film with later.

Living in Los Angeles, you run into people connected with your favorite movie. Sam Frank is a devoted fan of the 1960 George Pal production *The Time Machine*. In 1995, he saw the film's star, Rod Taylor, at a Thrifty drugstore in Studio City in the San Fernando Valley.

I did a double take, asked him if he was Rod Taylor, and said, "You made the movie that made me fall in love with movies, and I have been dying for thirty-five years to tell you this."

He replied, "I'll bet the movie is *The Time Machine,* and please tell me more." I told him how I saw George as my intellectual stand-in, and what his defeat of the Morlocks represented to me, and that no matter what else he ever did as an actor, this was the role for which he would be remembered. His face lit up as I spoke, and when I finished, he shook my hand, turned around, and walked down the street to wherever he was going with a self-confident bounce. No matter that he had probably been told this countless times and that he had made dozens of movies since then; he was hearing confirmed yet again that he had made none better or that would have a greater or longer-lasting impact than that one.

While at UCLA, my summer job in 1968 was as a tour guide and tour bus driver on the rather slapdash MGM studio tour, which consisted of a couple of rattletrap buses and some college student tour guides. The studio had an extensive set of back lots that impressed the tourists, but that summer there was very little filmmaking activity at the studio. The one feature being shot was *Marlowe* (1969), and one morning as I was driving a group through the sound stages, I noticed one of the film's stars going toward the dance rehearsal stage. Rita Moreno looked a little baffled as the bus speaker system not only identified her for the tourists but also gave a nearly complete list of her credits.

Two years later, MGM was auctioning off its properties and costumes prior to selling off its back lots to developers (since everybody assumed that studios were dinosaurs that were going to be replaced by *Easy Rider*-type productions). I went back to the studio, which was open for the public to browse among the items being auctioned. As I got to the costumes, I happened to fall in behind Adolph Comden and Betty Green, who had written *Singin' in the Rain* and other classic MGM musicals. They could remember that Cyd Charisse had worn that *particular* dress, but in what movie?

In addition to the films and film programs at UCLA and the AFI, Los Angeles also had then, in the days before videocassettes, a number of revival theatres. Older films even played regular theatres. In May and June of 1971, the Los Feliz theatre in East Hollywood ran a complete series of Buster Keaton silent comedies, which had only recently been rescued from the vaults. They still worked beautifully for audiences. I saw them, even though it was a long drive. I almost skipped *Seven Chances* (1925), since I knew nothing about it and could not find much information on it. It turned out I already knew at least one thing: it was the Keaton film that had him sitting alone in the church, the still of which had been printed in the James Agee article over twenty years before. And as a bonus, the film was one of the funniest of the lot. It is the one with Keaton dodging the rocks that Arnold Quinlan remembered in the first chapter of this book.

Driving up Vermont Avenue to the Los Feliz, I passed the main entrance to Los Angeles City College, where I had unsuccessfully interviewed for a job the year before. This spring they were hiring again—this time for someone to teach a course in film history. I started as a part-time instructor in the fall of 1971 and became full-time in 1972. I have taught the History of Motion Pictures course since then, working with instructors who teach other sections of the course. We select films that will not only educate the students about film history but that we think will make some connections with them.

Over the years, as I have watched and listened to the students respond, or not respond, to what we show in class, I have seen how older films work, or do not work, for modern audiences. The earliest films we show are very short comedies, made before or just after 1900. They are simple slapstick gags, and the gags still get a laugh. *The Great Train Robbery* (1903), the first story film and the first Western (sort of), still amuses, but it does not excite the audience the way it did at its first showings.

 The obvious choice of a D.W. Griffith film is *The Birth of a Nation* (1915). The first time I taught the course, I ran this film with a bit of fear and trepidation because of its justly deserved reputation for being a racist film. In the early seventies, however, the audience, including the black students, could laugh at the film, at least partially because the civil rights movement of the sixties had made it seem as though things had changed since the Reconstruction. During the Blaxploitation era, I even had audiences (black and white) cheering the black characters in the films in their fight with the Klan. By the end of the seventies, the country was turning conservative and the laughter for *Birth* was dying out. Discussions of the film in the eighties and into the nineties were often only about the racism of the film.

After serious silent films, we turn to the study of silent comedy. From the first, I have shown several Buster Keaton films, including *College* (1927), which was partially filmed at what is now LACC.[5] *Seven Chances* generally plays as well to the class as it did at the Los Feliz. An exception was when we showed a Douglas Fairbanks swashbuckler before the Keaton film, and *Seven Chances* became too much of a good thing.

Chaplin's films do not play as well to a contemporary audience, even though there are those that love him much more than Keaton. Women often dislike Keaton's portrayal of women and like Chaplin's idealization of women, although I have had women students who prefer Keaton's realism about women: he does not idealize them, knows they can be crazy, and loves them anyway. When I have students write papers comparing and contrasting one of the films seen in class with a recent film seen outside of class, the papers often compare Keaton or Chaplin to modern comedies, nearly always to the detriment of the more recent films.

The two Chaplin films that I have found play the best are *The Gold Rush* (1925)—at least to some extent because the woman in the film is the vivacious, non-waifish Georgia Hale—and *The Great Dictator* (1940), although I gave the latter a bit of help with the context in which I showed it. In my History of Documentary Film course the day before *The Great Dictator*, many of the same students saw Leni Riefenstahl's documentary about the 1934 Nuremberg Nazi rally, *Triumph of the Will* (1935), which Chaplin specifically parodies. I doubt if *The Great Dictator* ever had a more appreciative audience than one that had sat through all 110 minutes of Riefenstahl's film the day before.

Many of the early sound films date badly for contemporary audiences, such as King Vidor's all-black 1929 musical *Hallelujah* and Lewis Milestone's 1930 *All Quiet on the Western Front*. But several of MGM's all-star vehicles still amuse, such as *Grand Hotel* (1932) and *Dinner at Eight* (1933). Greta Garbo still enchants in the former, but audiences who have the image of Joan Crawford as *Mommie Dearest* (1981) are astonished at her youthful vitality in the same film. The Capra films of the thirties continue to play well; however, an audience I had in the seventies for *Lost Horizon* (1937) gave an audible gasp at the brief glimpse of what is supposed to be Jane Wyatt's bare back. The audience had grown up with Wyatt as everybody's favorite mom on *Father Knows Best*, so seeing this scene was like catching your parents in bed. The Capra comedies have enough substance for stimulating class discussions, as in the one I had with a class on *Mr. Smith Goes to Washington* (1939) shortly before Nixon resigned. We were discussing whether Nixon identified more with the corrupt Claude Rains character or with the Jimmy Stewart character. The class's immediate choice was, of course, the Rains character, but as the discussion went on, they changed their minds. After all, Smith is alone, outnumbered, convinced he is right, and the object of attacks in the media. Nixon would have felt right at home.

The Preston Sturges comedies play well, particularly *Sullivan's Travels*, not surprising with an audience of would-be filmmakers. *His Girl Friday* (1940) dazzles, and I do not think I have ever had a compare-and-contrast paper that rated any modern comedy better than *Friday*. Given the number of Latino students we have, and the occasional Native American student, John Ford's *Stagecoach* (1939), with its stereotypes of both, plays badly, but his and Johnson's *Grapes of Wrath* usually works, especially with Latino students who have done farm work with their families. In the seventies, most students who had seen the film before on television had seen it with the first twenty-five minutes cut out to make room for commercials, which meant all the exposition about the Dust Bowl conditions was missing. They were fascinated to learn *why* the Joad family was going to California. After videocassettes, this was less true. Every few years, I will have a class that finds Ma Joad's first scene in *Grapes*, in which she asks Tom if he's been made "mean mad" in prison, funny. I know if the audience starts laughing at that point, the movie will be lost for them. Johnson's *Jesse James* also generally plays well, even though it is not violent enough for some contemporary action fans, and Nancy Kelly's performance as Zee has dated badly, to put it politely.

And then, as it must to all film students, comes *Citizen Kane*. Since several people who responded to the questionnaire for this book were either current or former students, and since I put *Kane* on the list of films as one of the older films to talk about, some people wrote about their response to seeing the film in class. I have often thought that we should not have to show *Kane* in class, since surely anybody who reached college age and had an interest in film must have already seen it. A surprising number of students have not seen it before class, but nearly everyone has heard of it. Francisco Checa "only saw it recently in class, but by then I had heard so much about it that it was very difficult for me to form an unbiased opinion regarding the film." Laurel Jo Martin had heard of the film "long before I ever saw it. I read about it in a book about old films my mother bought me. In fact, I read *The Citizen Kane Book* at least two years before I saw it.[6] The movie never wowed me, because I'd read so much about it before I ever saw it. My love of it has grown; the more I see it, the more I enjoy it."

Some students had seen *Citizen Kane* before. Douglas Choe was "a card-carrying member of the 'Orson Welles is overrated club' until watching this film in class. Now, I have a greater appreciation for the incredible precociousness of its filmmaker and the depth of his achievement." Patrician Cortazar was "too young before to grasp it—the time we saw it in class was absolutely inspiring." Virginia Keene went through a similar transition:

> My mother made me do it [see the film]. She meant well, but it was like taking medicine. I knew it was good for me, but it tasted bad. I was sixteen and couldn't relate to it in any way whatsoever. Who cared about a musty old black-and-white movie about a dead man and a whiny opera singer? I longed for romantic daydreams, not death and decadence. *Breakfast at Tiffany's* (1961) and *West Side Story* moved the earth for me that year. Poor mother. Bad timing. The next time I saw it was in this class, and it was reinvented for me. My feelings made a 180–degree turn. I've seen it twice since the class. New doors open for me each time.

For Shaun Hill-Kret, even being twenty-five was no help. "I was bored stiff and have no intention of every watching it again."

Younger students often knew Welles only from his later appearances. D'Arcy

West remembers "being confused, because up until then I had only seen Orson Welles on wine commercials and The Magic Castle TV specials. I thought he was a very fat magician. I felt sad and embarrassed that that was how I knew him, and that was probably how a lot of people knew him, because *Citizen Kane* was so truly amazing." For Wendi Cole, "It was interesting for me to see Orson Welles not fat. Although you could see that he was going to be. I guess the thing I'll remember most about this movie is the fact that I thought Orson Welles was kind of handsome (if not a slight bit odd)."

One of the advantages of seeing older films in a classroom, at least at LACC, is to be able to see them not on video, but on film on a big screen. This is particularly true for *Citizen Kane*. Derek Garubo is a professional photographer and found *Kane* "mesmerizing" on the big screen. For Javier Rodriguez it was the special effects created "with no modern equipment" that impressed him. Seeing it on the big screen in class made Dorian Wood realize it would not be the same film on the small screen, although he wished he'd seen it with "an uneducated audience, to see and feel a truly spontaneous and natural reaction, instead of an overeducated group of brooding intellectuals." (That is the first and only time I know of that LACC students have been called "an overeducated group of brooding intellectuals.") Albert Nazaryan had a slightly different reaction, "marveling . . . at the fact that here was an old movie that wasn't boring the ____[sic] out of me. I didn't notice even one thing we discussed . . . as film students. Instead, it was a terrific movie with a great story."

What Marion Levine liked most about *Citizen Kane* was "the photography, the lighting (and shadows), and the camera angles. Watching the film yet again in class, I was struck by how hollow the acting is and how the story functions in an archetypal way instead of a personal one, but every time I see it, I find something new to admire." Eva Mahgrefthe saw it for the first time in class and "found it to be shallow character development enriched with trick shots."

Rick Mitchell, the projectionist and film historian, saw *Kane* in a class not at LACC, but at USC. He had not seen it before and

did not see it until after I came to L.A., naturally in a film appreciation class at USC. I was disappointed. I'd been hearing for years about this "great" film, but everything I thought it was going to be was in the newsreel at the beginning, while the rest turned into a soap opera about how a rich and powerful man nearly lost it all because of a blonde airhead. As for the technique, I was not particularly awed, as I'd seen it all before, though not as explicitly overdone. Every technical innovation claimed for *Kane* can be found in Warner Brothers pictures of the early thirties, especially those directed by Michael Curtiz, on which I'd had a steady diet the tube in Lexington in the late fifties and early sixties.

Jill Mitchell (no relation to Rick) had first seen *Citizen Kane* while dating the grandson of its co-writer, Herman J. Mankiewicz. "I rented it and after seeing it, felt like I had missed something. After seeing it in class, I know I hadn't missed anything; I just don't like the film."

Another film we often show is *Casablanca*, which most students have seen at least part of on television. For Octavio Jimenez, seeing it in class was the first time he had seen the entire film. When he saw it on television, "a lot of the detail was lost, I could not understand all the dialogue, and the shadows that made the movie eerie were not on television. When I saw *Casablanca* on the big screen, all the little details such as sound, dialogue, shadows were suddenly on the film, and it made the difference because since then I've enjoyed the film."

Virginia Keene also saw bits and pieces of it and thought of it as one of "those 'passing through' movies. That is, we catch pieces of it while passing through the living room on our way to somewhere else. Television has ruined a lot of movies for me that way. I always thought this movie was beautiful to look at, but it never involved me. The first time I saw it on the big screen, in class, I was completely absorbed and I actually cried at the end."

Rigo Fernandez had avoided *Casablanca* before class because even though "everybody has seen it but me," he did not have "the gumption enough to rent it because it just does not appeal to me. Sobby [sic] melodramas don't appeal to me that much." Shaun Hill-Kret still thinks she's too young for the film: "An okay movie that my parents like a lot more than I ever have. . . . It never moved me emotionally." But twenty-two-year-old Desreta Jackson enjoyed the film because of "the relationship Bogie and Sam had. Because during that time, blacks and whites didn't interact very well, and I really like to see things like that."

One of the most interesting reactions to *Casablanca* I ever heard came from a student during the class discussion. She said she liked *Casablanca* because it was "deep." *Casablanca* is many things, but deep is not one of them. What I think she meant was that, in comparison with contemporary films, *Casablanca* is a very rich film: full of plot, full of characters, full of atmosphere. Many contemporary films seem thin in one or all of those areas. And the film is about something—fighting the Nazis—in a way that most later action movies are not.

We also occasionally run some of the social comment pictures of the late forties and early fifties, and one that holds up surprisingly well is *Pinky* (1949). It was an enormously popular film in its time, but it was also criticized for having its leading role of a young black woman who passes for white played by Jeanne Crain, a white actress. Since most of today's students have no idea whether Jeanne Crain is black or white, the issue is a relatively minor one in the class discussion, and the strength and nobility of all three major women characters—played by Crain, Ethel Barrymore, and Ethel Waters—has great appeal, since nobility is not a character trait found in many contemporary films.

Arnold Quinlan first saw *Sunset Boulevard* in class and then "made a point to show this film to my then short-term roommate. Hoping that she would make some kind of connection with Norma [Desmond—lead character in the film, played by Gloria Swanson]. Unfortunately, she lacked as much understanding as she lacked range. Both as an actress and a person. This, of course, made me seem ever closer to Joe Gillis [lead character in the film, played by William Holden]. In circumstance as well as mindset. Fortunately, I got rid of the roommate before I got shot." Wilder's follow-up film, *Ace in the Hole*, often plays better with contemporary audiences, and that includes my classes.

Along with *Citizen Kane*, it is almost impossible to instruct a course covering the history of American film without showing *On the Waterfront*. You can teach almost everything there is to learn about American films of the fifties from the film—the House UnAmerican Activities Committee, the influence of Italian Neorealism, the rise of independent production, the influence of the Actor's Studio, etc. About the only thing you can't teach from it is the development of wide-screen processes.

For some people the film does not hold up. Douglas Choe had seen *On the Waterfront* years before the class and "thought it was mediocre at best. After seeing it in class, I have even a lesser opinion. I found the performances, other than Brando's, unbelievable and the script preachy and simple. I also did not agree with the message of the film, as abuses of management were not addressed at all in the film. The incredible advances and sacrifices made by those in the Labor movement far outnumbered the corruption inherent in it. The cartoonish way in which the labor organizers [they are union administrators rather than organizers] were portrayed contributed to the unbelievability of this film."

The first time Blair Woodard saw *On the Waterfront* was in class; he had not known beforehand that Karl Malden played the priest. "I always associated him with [the seventies television series] *The Streets of San Francisco*, and I could see how the series producers had wanted to cast him from his role in this film." Woodard is the not only student I have had to react to Malden off of his TV work, and as seen previously with Jane Wyatt, he is not the only actor familiar to students from television appearances. Soap opera fans recognize Ruth Warrick in *Citizen Kane* from *All My Children*, and primetime viewers know *Kane's* Agnes Moorehead from *Bewitched*. Also in the film, older students recognize Ray Collins from the original run of *Perry Mason*. The reaction to these familiar faces is mostly enjoyment, rather like seeing an actor you know playing different parts in a stage repertory company.

D'Arcy West enjoyed *Waterfront* in class because "I had never seen a young Marlon Brando in a movie until I saw it.... And he was really cool. Cooler than James Dean. And now I know why people are still in awe of him, and pay him millions of dollars to be in *Superman* (1978) for five minutes [his scenes run a *little* longer than five minutes]." Derek Garubo "loved the simplicity of Marlon Brando's character and how he portrayed him," while Paul Sbrizzi, seeing the film in class for the first time after hearing about it for years, thought it had "about as much subtlety and nuance as your average *Models Inc.* [1994–1995 TV primetime soap opera] episode."

Dorian Wood was more impressed, thinking the film was "so full of action, drama, suspense and controversy" that like *Citizen Kane*, he wished he had seen it "with a big bag of popcorn and with people that don't really care about lighting, camera angles, and production flaws." Virginia Keene had seen *Waterfront* on television as a young teenager and was not impressed, but seeing it in class, "I love the performances, the photography and the writing, but from a distance (perhaps partly due to the [Leonard Bernstein] score, which I found to be very irritating and distracting). I wasn't deeply moved by the film and found this a bitter pill to swallow. I liked its tough grittiness, and it was fun to see so many of my favorite actors in one movie."

In all the years I have taught the film history course, we have only shown Hitchcock's *Psycho* once. The students in the class are also taking their first filmmaking course. The one time we did show *Psycho*, over half the final projects in the filmmaking course dealt with people killed in showers, bathtubs, and in the wittiest version, a lawn sprinkler. For the sake of the budding creativity of our students, we have never run the film again.

Many of the revolutionary films of the late sixties do not play well to the class. By the time I showed *Bonnie and Clyde* in class in the mid-seventies, there had been so many imitations that it seemed old hat. We tried *Easy Rider* once, but with the exception of Nicholson's twenty-four minutes, there was nothing but derisive laughter. We have tried *Five Easy Pieces* only once, in the mid-eighties, and it seemed to leave the class cold. Since a number of our students work as waiters, the class was—not surprisingly—much more sympathetic to the waitress in the famous diner scene than they were to Nicholson's Bobby.

Two films from the time do continue to work. *Alice's Restaurant*, from 1969, because it shows how the ideal hippie community can fall apart, is both more convincing and more touching than other films of the period. It also helps that the characterization is sharper, as well as some of the satire. The other film is *The Graduate*. Since our students are middle to lower class, they love the satire of the Beverly Hills types, and the two romances in the film still work. When I taught the equivalent course at UCLA in 1986, the students felt it still mirrored their lives. The only thing they questioned was why Benjamin's father was cleaning his own swimming pool. Didn't they have pool cleaning services way back in the sixties?

Many of the now-classic films of the early seventies continue to work for the audiences in my class. Jane Fonda's performance in *Klute* still stuns an audience, especially those who only know her later from her exercise videos. *The Candidate* (1972) is now just as smart about the political process as it was then, and so realistic that when I showed it at UCLA along with the 1960 documentary *Primary*, students in the discussion groups had trouble remembering what was in which film. *The Godfather* is. It just *is*. And probably always will be. Coppola's *The Conversation* seems better and deeper as the years go by, but some students feel Coppola and editor and sound designer Walter Murch's playing around with time and sound is too "student film." I tell them I would be delighted if they would make one like that.

A nonclassic seventies film that works better in the class than it did in the theatres is the 1975 exploitation flick *Crazy Mama*. In theatres it seemed like the last of a long line of imitation *Bonnie and Clydes*, with a touch of *American Graffiti* thrown in. It starts out in Arkansas in the Depression, as a family is thrown off its land, then jumps ahead to Long Beach, California, in the fifties, when the family decides to return home to reclaim the land. Seen in class as a sleazy farcical response to *The Grapes of Wrath* (and not an unknowing one: one of the characters in the film is seen reading another book by John Steinbeck), it gains from its class context, as did Chaplin's *The Great Dictator*.

Context, of course, is crucial to a film history course, which explains why it is difficult to select films of the eighties and nineties for the end of the course: too many of them suffer in comparison with what has been seen before. I thought *Tootsie* (1982) would be sure-fire: it was critically acclaimed, had popular stars, and was an enormous box office hit. It bombed in class. When you see it after having seen Keaton, Chaplin, *His Girl Friday*, and *Some Like It Hot*, it does not seem quite as sharp. The same thing happened, only more so, with Spike Lee's *Do the Right Thing* (1988). As with *Crazy Mama*, I knew the minute I saw it in the theatre that I would eventually have to run it in class. That semester we started with *The Birth of a Nation*, stopped midway with *Pinky* and ended with *Do the Right Thing*. The general reaction among the students, some of them black, was that *Pinky* was better and that Lee was still using the same old stereotypes of lazy, shiftless, oversexed black people D.W. Griffith had used, albeit with more of a sense of humor than Griffith had.

Learning about—and seeing—the films of the past, whether they are on television and videocassette, or especially in a film history course, changes how you perceive films. In a film history course, you tend to see the best of the past, and the large mass of contemporary films suffer in comparison. This creates a kind of nostalgia for the past that many students know only through the films seen in class or on video. That, and the studying of film as an art and means of social communication, changes how you look at all films, both past and present. As one of my former students, Oscar Berkovich, put it, "You never look at films the same way once you start studying film." Peter Albers was a student at the University of Wisconsin at Madison before he was a student of mine. "Madison had the single largest on-campus film screening program in the country at the time—over four hundred movies a year were shown. Over the course of nine months, I saw an awful lot of movies that I had not heard of before or since. This was when I first started developing a more critical eye towards film."

Albert Nazaryan is not so sure such knowledge is a good thing. "In a way, I hate understanding how movies work. As a kid, they were either good or bad. Now when someone asks me if I liked the film, I might talk about how the director couldn't compensate for the crummy script. Or the acting sucked, but the cinematography was great. I've bitten the apple, and I miss the innocence. But once in a while, when the movie's really good, everything becomes black around the screen again, and all I see is the light on the screen."

Angela West said in the fall of 1993 that being a film student has changed her view. "Before I was a film student, I could merely sit and watch and become ultimately swept away. I still catch myself doing that sometimes. I do, however, think the quality of American films has gone down the tubes in the last half decade. Are we embarking on cinema experiences that will be remembered through history? I would be embarrassed to know our culture is going to be viewed by people fifty years from now by them watching *Jurassic Park* or *The Last Action Hero* (both 1993)."

I have taught film for so long that by now, some of my former students are teaching films. One of them, Nancy Lathrop, taught English and a cinema elective in middle schools in Los Angeles for several years, and we talk once a year or so about how the kids reacted to various films. As an English teacher, she "hoped to God" there was a film based on the book being read in class, since one of the top five questions students ask her is, "Are we going to see a movie?" Not only does she use films of books read in class, but she also will bring in films connected to themes being discussed. When the discussion one day turned to the issue of mutiny, Lathrop took a break from the lesson plan and showed the 1954 film *The Caine Mutiny*, which she found had a strong enough plot and structure to capture the students' interest. "We all did Captain Queeg for a week and went around saying 'Strawberries, strawberries.' This was the class that for my birthday gave me two little silver balls, so I could just walk around and do this [roll the balls in her hands as Queeg does when he is agitated]."

She has also shown *Some Like It Hot*, and while the first half hour is tough for the kids, "Once Marilyn's in it, and they're all in drag and on the train, it's a piece of cake. It goes very well. They think it's funny. They howl at the closing line. It still works very well." On the whole, the middle schoolers do not like musicals, although they liked the storyline of *Hair* (1979) but thought the musical numbers got in the way. Both versions of *Little Shop of Horrors* (1960 and 1986) worked with her students, and while her kids "don't have a real good sense of camp and kitsch, they managed to get through [the musical version]." Lathrop tries to select films that revolve around issues that the kids deal with or that have kids in them with whom they can identify. *The Hunchback of Notre Dame* (the 1939 version, one of Lathrop's favorite films) only worked once, much to her surprise, since she thinks "Quasimodo *is* every seventh grader." Part of the problem is that younger kids are resistant to films in black-and-white. *Gone With the Wind* sometimes works for her, but it takes five days of one-hour periods to get through, and they get squirmy in the last hour (as did Bill Pulliam, when he saw the film in the fifth grade in Atlanta. "The subtleties of the Rhett-Scarlett relationship were beyond me." Needless to say, in Atlanta, "We saw it as local history lesson as much as an art lesson").

Within a year after I started at UCLA, film critic Pauline Kael spoke to a screenwriting class I was taking, and after her talk I noted that she had said that audiences tended to go to movies to watch stories and characters and not artistic style. I asked her if she didn't think the increase in the number of film courses in colleges would change that. She gave me her "you silly boy" look and said that I underestimated the ability of academics to squeeze the life out of a subject. Over the last thirty years, I have tried to do my part to stem the tide she warned against, since as Jimmy Stewart says in *Mr. Smith Goes to Washington*, the only causes worth fighting for are the lost causes.

Directors 11

Have you noticed how infrequently the people responding to the questionnaire for this book have mentioned directors when they talk about films? This lack of discussion of directors so far is not just my cutting and editing of replies to the questionnaire. For all the hype and critical discussion over the years about directors, when asked to talk about movies, it's movies audiences talk about, not their directors.

This is even true of film students. As Kasey Arnold-Ince puts it, "Despite attending two film schools, I was never a 'responsible' moviegoer. . . . In general, I don't go see a movie because of a star, or a director, or a producer. I go to see the story. *Story is it.*" Needless to say, there are moviegoers, especially film students, who *do* develop a taste for directors. Alejandro Munoz started out going to movies to see the stars, but "soon realized . . . it was not necessarily the actor I was following but the director. As a result, this brings me to my current state of affairs, in which I view movies principally based on the director involved. Indeed, I tend to follow directors who illustrate a sort of consistency for choosing particularly interesting screenplays and merging them with unique directing styles."

Susanna Serrano is more interested in the subject matter of the film and doesn't "really care who the star or director is. That for me comes at the end. When I see the movie, then I want to know who directed it." Oscar Berkovich notes that "even if the movie has gotten bad reviews but has a good director, I go anyway to support them and really be the judge myself."

Michael Cohen began his real moviegoing experiences at the age of twelve, when his father took him to the movies every night for a year and a half. Cohen developed an interest in directors at the time by reading Andrew Sarris's *The American Cinema*[1] the classic examination of the *auteur* theory (the idea that the artistic value in a film all comes from the work of the director) as it applied to American films. "We used the book as a guide, and through it I gained knowledge of the *auteur* theory, which was to serve me well later on."

For most movie audiences, directors are a relatively small concern. This has always been true of American films.[2] At any given point in the history of American film, there have been only a few directors whose names meant anything to the moviegoing public. In the teens, it was Griffith. In the thirties, it was De Mille and Capra. In the fifties and early sixties, it was Hitchcock, in part because Hitchcock promoted himself (especially with his television show) and in part because Hitchcock, like Capra and De Mille, became known for making a particular kind of picture. He made himself a brand name.

Certainly those of us who were Hitchcock fans at the time anticipated *North by Northwest*. Virginia Keene has no specific recollection of seeing the film in a theatre when it was first released, "although I'm sure it must have been in the theatre, because every new Hitchcock picture was eagerly anticipated and a guaranteed delight. Hitchcock was an important part of my childhood, as Disney was for some people. My family watched both of his TV series [the half-hour and the hour series] religiously and never missed his films." Monica Dunlap "saw this film when it was released and many times since (whenever it's on television), and [I] never get tired of it. I love its wit; it's like *Casablanca* in that way." Marion Levine also saw *North by Northwest* on its first release, and "all I remember of the film when I saw it as a teenager was the airplane sequence and Mount Rushmore. When I saw it again a few years ago, I was bowled over by Hitchcock's storytelling ability. He wastes no time plunging us into Cary Grant's problem, and the tension never ever lets up."

Alejandro Munoz, now in his twenties, "viewed the film after having established myself as a fan of both Alfred Hitchcock and Cary Grant. And I remember considering it an entertaining movie. However, having grown up in a time when moviemaking was already more sophisticated in terms of cinematography and special effects, it was at times unbelievable." Jack Hollander finally caught up with it in the eighties, and "I must say that although I had seen the crop-dusting scene before, seeing it in context really made me appreciate it more. . . . Hitchcock attempts in this film to put some 'Joe Average' in a life-threatening situation in which he must struggle to overcome all odds to save himself. . . . My problem is that none of the lead characters reminds me of anything 'average.'" Hollander tends to prefer Hitchcock's *Rear Window*, as does Marcus Franklin, who thinks it is "the best of Albert's [sic] films."

North by Northwest struck Paul Sbrizzi "for its almost caricaturized view of America by Hitchcock—having a chase end up on Mount Rushmore had to be some kind of joke—and also for its over-the-top sexual metaphor in its final shot. Like other Hitchcock films, I enjoyed it a lot without it making a big impression on me." On the other hand, Wil Dimpflmaier recalls seeing it "as a kid, with my father in front of the television. He had to convince me to watch it . . . but once I started watching *North by Northwest,* I was riveted to the TV set.

Even as a kid, I was affected by Hitchcock's psychological barrage of events on that roller coaster of a movie. A couple of years ago, I rented it and was even more impressed again."

Jill Mitchell caught the film in Paris in the eighties. One of the theatres had a Hitchcock festival that lasted nearly a year. While remembering the crop-dusting scene, she does not recall the rest of the film so much as the whole festival "being so neat. We were American teenagers in the eighties, and we were looking forward to the next Hitchcock release as much as anyone did thirty years earlier." A little later, Teddi Lawrence saw a collection of earlier Hitchcock films at UCLA. "I watched Hitchcock progress through the decades from silent film to color. Hitchcock to me is a master of meaningful shadows. I liked the fact that it was all of his films so that they could be watched comparatively rather than in isolation."

James Ford "respects Hitchcock, don't like his movies that much." He owns some of the storyboards (sketches drawn for individual shots before filming) for *North by Northwest*, which he likes "more than the movie." Hitchcock is so much a presence in film history that although Lawrence Dotson hasn't seen *any* Hitchcock films, "I've seen all the famous scenes, including the shower scene from *Psycho* and the airplane scene in *North by Northwest*."

As previously mentioned, Hitchcock himself was baffled at the reaction to *Psycho*, because for the first time in his career, he had been unable to guess what the audience reaction would be. Perhaps because of his misjudgment, and perhaps because he was getting older, Hitchcock began to shift his attention from the general audiences to the audience of critics (particularly the French critics who already adored him), whom he could manipulate more easily. Robert E. Kapsis in his brilliant book, *Hitchcock: The Making of a Reputation*,[3] shows how Hitchcock hustled the critics and historians to promote himself in the sixties as an important artist. Hitchcock managed to influence what could be called the "critical book" on himself. Just as the "book" on a racehorse gives the general opinion of his strengths and weaknesses, the critical book on a filmmaker is the general way critics and historians talk about him.

With the exception of *The Birds* in 1963, the pictures Hitchcock made after *Psycho* simply did not connect with regular audiences. I remember watching both *Marnie* (1964) and *Torn Curtain* (1966) and listening to audiences grumble about the cheap special effects in the former and express shock at the obvious studio set of the little hill in the park in the latter. When Virginia Keene saw *Torn Curtain*, "I was sad . . . because I felt it signaled the beginning of his decline." You would not have been able to tell this from the reviews of Hitchcock's later films, which promoted them as works of genius. Hitchcock's last film *Family Plot* (1976) brought in $6.8 million in rentals but was outgrossed that year by *All the President's Men, The Omen, Hustle,* and *Marathon Man*.[4]

If there was any other director in the fifties, aside from De Mille, who competed with Hitchcock in the public's mind, it was Elia Kazan. Kazan's reputation was first made as a stage director of *Death of a Salesman* and *A Streetcar Named Desire* in the forties. He won his first Academy Award as the director of the 1947 message picture *Gentleman's Agreement* and did the film of *A Streetcar Named Desire* in 1951. Whereas De Mille was known for his spectacle films and Hitchcock for his suspense films, Kazan was known as a director of actors. Three of his actors in *Streetcar* won Academy Awards, and Kazan was given credit for making a star of Marlon Brando. In 1955, Kazan directed *East of Eden*, which made James Dean a star and grossed more than Kazan's *On the Waterfront*, a multiple Oscar winner the year before.[5] By the mid-fifties, Kazan seemed more attuned to the public's interests than any other director except perhaps De Mille and Hitchcock. He never had another major hit.

Kazan had entered the film business as a director for the major studios in the last days of the studio system. Like most directors, he chafed at the control over his work that the studios exercised.[6] As the business changed in the early fifties, he looked for independent production as a way to more fully express his personal vision. What this led to were films where he did not have the counterbalancing force of a strong producer, such as Darryl Zanuck on his Twentieth Century-Fox films, or Sam Spiegel on *On the Waterfront*. Kazan's *America, America* (1963) and *The Arrangement* (1969) are personal films—the first about his relatives coming to America, the second about his relationship with his father—but neither one connected with audiences.

Kazan's career has become the unfortunate model for a large number of directors in the post-major studio period of the independent production: a director works well with collaborators, makes pictures that are successes, becomes convinced that he knows it all, and makes films that "express his personal vision" that do not connect with audiences. Sometimes the director can recover, and sometimes, even if the director never has another popular success, he can still do interesting work but often not at the level of public acceptance of the earlier work.

John Frankenheimer had a large commercial success in 1962 with *The Manchurian Candidate*, followed by other commercial successes such as *Seven Days in May* (1964) and *Grand Prix* (1966), but later films, such as *The Extraordinary Seaman* (1968), *The Gypsy Moths* (1969), *Prophecy* (1979), and *Year of the Gun* (1991), were not hits.

Like Frankenheimer, Arthur Penn had considerable success in the sixties, notably with *Bonnie and Clyde* and to a lesser extent with *Alice's Restaurant*. *Little Big Man* (1970) grossed $15 million in comparison with *Bonnie and Clyde's* $22 million,[7] but Penn never had such a high grosser afterwards, although he made such interesting films as *Night Moves* (1975) and *Four Friends* (1981).

Douglas Choe considers Penn and Mike Nichols "two of the major talents going" in the sixties but thinks "someone put a pod next to Mike Nichols's bed in the eighties . . . how else to explain *Working Girl* (1988) and *Postcards From the Edge* (1990)." However, contrary to Choe's opinion, *Working Girl* was in fact something of a commercial comeback for Nichols. He had hits in the sixties with *Who's Afraid of Virginia Woolf?* (1966) and especially *The Graduate*, but in the seventies Nichols slipped into self-indulgence with *Catch-22* (1970) and especially *Day of the Dolphin* (1973) and *The Fortune* (1976). He had some medium success in the eighties with *Silkwood* (1983) and *Working Girl*, but did not have a major commercial hit until *The Birdcage* (1996). It was a remake eighteen years after the original of *La Cage aux Folles*, a French-Italian coproduction that was one of the highest-grossing foreign films in the United States in the seventies. Perhaps it took eighteen years of cultural change for mainstream American audiences to accept what art house audiences had accepted in 1978.

It is generally assumed that *The Wild Bunch* was Sam Peckinpah's biggest hit, but it brought in rentals of only $4.2 million and was only the twenty-third highest-grossing film of its year (1969), being outgrossed by *Butch Cassidy and the Sundance Kid* as well as two John Wayne Westerns—*True Grit,* and the more conventional *The Undefeated.*[8] The film did help establish Peckinpah's reputation as a director of violent movies—so much so that his softer, delightful *The Ballad of Cable Hogue* the following year failed to bring in even the minimum $1 million in rentals necessary to make *Variety*'s year-end charts. His violent *Straw Dogs* (1971) brought in $4 million,[9] and *The Getaway* the following year brought in $17.5 million.[10] After that, Peckinpah's films get less coherent and more baffling for audiences,[11] with a decline in the grosses. His last film, *The Osterman Weekend* (1983), brought in only $2.5 million in rentals, being outgrossed that year by *Strange Brew, Metalstorm: Destruction of Jared-Syn,* and even *Smokey and the Bandit III.*[12]

Carlos Aguilar is a fan of Francis Ford Coppola. "It can be said that Coppola has never made a bad film. Every one of his films is uniquely what he wanted it to be. Studios may bicker, critics may disagree, and the public may stay away in droves, but they are his vision. Not good or bad, but artistically what he intended them to be. It doesn't matter to him that they are loved or despised. As long as in between the studio jobs there is some money left over for his next personal work."

Certainly Coppola's personal films can connect with the audience, as *Apocalypse Now* (1979) did. Moe Gardener saw the film in two entirely different circumstances.

I was living on the campus of Texas A&M in 1979. The school showed old films under the stars where popcorn was free and people sat on bales of hay. The new films were shown in a formal auditorium. This school has the largest ROTC cadet corps outside of the service academies. This brought with it a lot of bizarre traditions. Well, when Francis Ford Coppola's *Apocalypse Now* was screened, you would expect an event to be made out of it, but this was beyond compare. The cadets marched into the film in full dress uniforms, including cavalry boots. They let out a few battle calls and all sat down in unison. The hissing and cheers were not what the director would have expected. This was drastically different than when I saw the film this summer [in the mid-nineties] at the Castro in San Francisco. Although there were lots of men in uniforms for both screenings, the audience made the film completely different.

Douglas Choe, continuing with his observations on Penn and Nichols, says that "while someone may have put a pod next to Nichols's bed, a little too much wine, food, drugs, money for Coppola." Albert Nazaryan also sees a decline in Coppola but in more poetic terms.

I can't fathom how the same person can make *The Conversation* and *The Godfather I* and *II*—films on the same level as any of Mozart's composi-tions or Van Gogh's paintings—and then follow with complete wastes of energy like *Godfather III* and [*Bram Stoker's*] *Dracula* (1992). The thing about Mozart is that what he wrote, in today's terms, would be critically acclaimed mega-hits; everyday people hum the music because it's "pretty," while the intelligentsia hail his work as one of the pinnacles of western culture. What *Godfather II* has in common with Symphony 40 in G Mi-nor is that everyone, from thug to professor, is enchanted by the work. I'm still educated now enough to at least glean Walt Whitman, but I still enjoy and marvel at *Godfather II*. My football-player friends liked *Godfa-ther III*, but the other ones (those who can and do read) hated it.

Nazaryan may be unpleasantly surprised to learn that *Bram Stoker's Dracula* was one of Coppola's most financially successful films, bringing in rentals of $47 million in its first two months of release.[13]

While Carlos Aguilar may be right about Coppola's films being personal, part of the director's commercial problem from the eighties on is that, like many successful film directors, he had lost contact, if not from reality, at least from the reality of the audience.[14] Peter Cowie, Coppola's biographer, men-tions that Coppola has never seen *The Godfather* with a paying audience.[15] Like most directors, he isolates himself, often creating what seems at the time like an enchanted working environment. Michael Cohen, who had grown up reading

Sarris, had the experience of being there in the early eighties when Coppola was trying to re-create the old studio system.

> At that time, Francis Coppola's Zoetrope Studios were across the street from my junior high school. As part of a school district-sponsored program, Zoetrope "adopted" our school and set up an apprentice program. About forty students were chosen to work with cast and crew of *One From the Heart* (1982). I didn't make the selection, and August, Francis's brother, gave a consolation talk to us, encouraging us to continue with our love for film. Afterwards, I went up to August and talked film for a few minutes. Next day I was pulled out of class and taken to the studio, where I found out that I was to be Francis's apprentice.
>
> This was a magical time. I would go to school, go to the studio, and then to see films. An odd synchronicity developed. One day I was talking to Francis about Jean-Luc Godard; on the very next [day] I met him. I took my father one day; it was the happiest I had ever seen him. Another day I was roaming around, as was my habit when the camera wasn't rolling, when I saw an elderly man sitting on the steps of a bungalow. I introduced myself. He told me his name was Michael Powell and that he was a filmmaker . . . best known for *Peeping Tom* (1960). The next night, that film was playing and I was stunned. I had met another genius.
>
> Francis became like a father to me in ways I did not understand at the time. The studio was always a safe place for me. My fondest memories are probably of Gene Kelly, who would always greet me with, "Hi, Champ." Seeing him again recently in the "I Got Rhythm" number in *An American in Paris* reminded me of Gene's special way with children.
>
> *One From the Heart* was a financial disaster, and with the studio in bankruptcy, the apprenticeship program ended. I watched the movie recently, however, and it was clearly ahead of its time, too kind and gentle for the Rambo eighties.

It was not so much that the film was too "kind and gentle" for audiences of the time, but rather that Coppola had gotten so far into the technology of filmmaking that he had lost the heart of what the film was about. Coppola directed the film from what was called the "Silver Fish," a trailer equipped with the newest film and videotape technology. He would work with the actors on the set and then retreat into the trailer and run the shooting like a director in the control booth in a television studio, speaking to the actors over a loudspeaker system. Another future student of mine, Tamra Davis, worked on the film and thought Coppola's method seemed very impersonal, since it made it virtually impossible to work intimately with the actors. Davis learned her lesson well:

she went on to become a feature director herself, most notably with *Guncrazy* (1992).

Martin Scorsese was one of the most critically acclaimed American directors of the last quarter of the twentieth century, especially by his hometown New York critics, but he has batted a little less well with the American public in general. Scorsese's 1976 film *Taxi Driver* was commercially successful, but it was outgrossed that year by, among others, *One Flew Over the Cuckoo's Nest, All the President's Men, The Omen*, and *The Bad News Bears*.[16] *Raging Bull* was one of Scorsese's most acclaimed films and later considered by critics to be the best film of the eighties (which tells you more about the critics and the eighties than it does about the film). It was released in late 1980 and grossed a little over $10 million, being outgrossed in 1981—the year it made the *Variety* box office charts—by *The Cannonball Run; Cheech and Chong's Nice Dreams; Fort Apache, the Bronx;* and even Bo Derek's *Tarzan, the Ape Man*.[17] Scorsese's highest-grossing film was one of the least critically praised—his 1991 remake of the 1962 film *Cape Fear*. It brought in rentals of over $39 million, more than the $20 million his *Goodfellas* brought in the year before or the $14.5 million *The Age of Innocence* earned in 1993.[18]

With respect to his audience, one problem with Scorsese's films is that he gets so inside both his own vision and his own directorial techniques that he forgets how the audience is actually going to take the film, as opposed to how he thinks they should. *Casino* (1995) is an example. Carlos Nino had one of his worst experiences as a moviegoer seeing the film. Not only was the theatre "very full, very hot . . . the movie was not at all what I like to watch. It was a paranoid mess of extravagance and violence," which could be said of a number of Scorsese's films. I also think that Scorsese was so into the tragic, melodramatic view of gangsters that he did not understand that for everybody living west of the Hudson River, the story was basically a comedy: "Goodfellas Go to Vegas and Get Their Clocks Cleaned by a Bunch of Cowboys." *Casino* was outgrossed in its year by *Waterworld, Pocahontas*, and *Se7en*.[19]

After making a number of smaller films, director Robert Altman made his first box office splash in 1970 with *M*A*S*H*. With film rentals of $22 million, it was second only to *Airport* in 1970 grosses, beating out *Patton, Woodstock*, and Mike Nichols's *Catch-22*. Altman's subsequent films grossed considerably less, and in the early seventies, at the height of his critical acclaim, he seemed to go out of this way to annoy audiences. I watched audiences boo and throw things at the screen at *Thieves Like Us* (1973), where Altman, like Scorsese on *Casino*, failed to understand what audiences liked about what is in effect the Bonnie and Clyde story and which he managed to drain all the excitement out of. I heard people demand their money back because they could not understand the dialogue in *McCabe and Mrs. Miller* (1971).[20] I saw people skulk out of the theatre in irritated silence after *Images* (1972). As with Coppola and *Dracula* and Scorsese and *Cape Fear*, one of Altman's highest-grossing films, *Popeye* (1980), was also one of his most heavily criticized.[21]

Peter Bogdanovich, a former film critic and historian, also made a great impact with audiences in the early seventies with such hits as *The Last Picture Show* (1971), which calls to mind the John Ford and Henry King small-town films of the thirties and forties; *What's Up Doc?* (1972), which is reminiscent of the great screwball comedies of the thirties, particularly *Bringing Up Baby* (1938); and *Paper Moon* (1973), which evokes thoughts of some of the Shirley Temple films of the thirties. The problem was that he alienated most of the people he worked with and became convinced he could do anything, which led to such flops as *At Long Last Love* (1975), a disastrous attempt at a thirties musical, and *Nickelodeon*.[22] Bogdanovich was the perfect example of Hollywood being haunted by its own past. He later had a modest popular success with *Mask* (1985), a film based on real life, not on older films.

Two enormous hits of the early seventies—*The French Connection* and *The Exorcist*—were directed by William Friedkin. After the success of both films, Friedkin became convinced he knew what audiences wanted. He was astonished when his next film, *Sorcerer* (1977), a remake of the fifties French art house hit *The Wages of Fear* (1952), flopped.[23] Pulling an Altman, Friedkin set the opening scenes of the film in a variety of foreign countries, with all the dialogue in languages other than English. Theatres showing *Sorcerer* had to post signs outside to tell the audiences that although the first sixteen minutes were subtitled, the rest of the film was indeed in English. The picture cost $22 million and brought in domestic rentals of only $5.9 million,[24] with the worldwide gross of $9 million not helping much.[25] Friedkin has yet to experience another substantial commercial success.

Michael Cimino had a moderate hit with his first film, *Thunderbolt and Lightfoot* (1974), and then a major success with *The Deer Hunter* (1978), which won the Academy Award for Best Picture. Like Friedkin after *The French Connection* and *The Exorcist*, he was given complete freedom and came up with an even bigger flop than *Sorcerer*—the legendary 1980 disaster *Heaven's Gate*.[26] Cimino continued to get work after *Heaven's Gate*, and his directorial style was just as grandiose, even when the material did not call for it. His 1990 film *Desperate Hours* was a remake of a modestly scaled 1955 hit about a trio of escaped cons who hold a typical middle-class family hostage in their own home. In Cimino's version, the story, originally set in Indianapolis, takes place in the West, with several outdoor sequences that kill the claustrophobic atmosphere of the original. The very functional family of the original has become completely dysfunctional, and Cimino somehow managed to get a stupifyingly awful performance out of Anthony Hopkins as the father. The film pulled in only a little over $1 million in rentals—less that year than *Lambada*, *Delta Force 2*, and *Leatherface: Texas Chainsaw Massacre III*.[27]

After some early low-budget satirical comedies, director Brian De Palma began to gain critical attention in the early seventies with obvious rip-offs of Hitchcock films. *Sisters* (1971) rehashed *Rear Window*, and *Obsession* (1976) did the same with *Vertigo* (1958). With *Carrie*, De Palma's most successful film until then, it looked as though he might be going beyond Hitchcock by dealing with the less conventionally Hitchcockian story material of Stephen King's tale of teenaged angst. Richard Henrie was a teenager when the film came out, and it became one of his most memorable moviegoing experiences. "I really don't remember what was impressive as far as cinematically; all I know is that this movie scared the hell out of me." He adds, however, "As I look at it today, it just seems adolescent." In the 1980 film *Dressed to Kill*, De Palma seemed at the beginning to go beyond *Carrie*'s focus on adolescence, in that he was using Hitchcock's style to get at adult sexuality in a way the older director never had. I saw *Dressed to Kill* on its opening day in Westwood and heard the audience's disappointment rather than shock when Angie Dickinson was killed in the elevator. We all thought we were into something new with De Palma, but as the similarities to *Psycho* continued to pile up, the life seemed to go out of the audience.

In 1984, De Palma did yet another rehash of both *Rear Window* and *Psycho* called *Body Double*. It cost $19 million and only brought in $3.7 million in rentals.[28] Susan Dworkin's account of the making of the film, *Double De Palma*,[29] which was completed before the film was released, makes clear, perhaps unintentionally, why the film did not work. De Palma is seen to be much more obsessive about the visual details and the style of the film than about the story or characters.

One can see the same mistakes being made in the more famous study of De Palma at work, *The Devil's Candy*, by Julie Salamon,[30] about the production of *Bonfire of the Vanities* (1990). Pauline Kael, a longtime defender of De Palma, is quoted in a blurb on the back of the hardcover edition of the book as saying, "It's probably the best book yet on how a big studio can shape the content of a movie. This wasn't a case (like *Heaven's Gate*) of the executives losing control; this was a case of executives who were so controlling—so 'responsible'—that they gradually drained the satiric fun out of the material." This was a lead that a number of the reviewers of the book took, but while the studio (Warners) does not come off well in the book, the failure of the film is mostly De Palma's. Salamon followed the production all the way through to the completed film, but then in a spectacular failure of nerve, declined to criticize the film itself. Early in the preparation of the film, she tells of De Palma discussing the project with the studio executives: "They were pleasantly surprised by the intellectual analysis that came naturally to him. He explained that he wanted to present the story as a broad satire, a dark farce on the order of Stanley Kubrick's *Dr. Strangelove*, a comedy about nuclear warfare. He told them he thought the way to convey the spirit of Tom Wolfe's [the author of the novel on which the film was based] exaggerated, energetic prose would be through exaggerated, energetic imagery."[31] One look at the film can show you that De Palma was much more concerned about getting the "exaggerated, energetic imagery" (e.g. the long Steadicam shot near the beginning) than he was with obtaining the kind of precise, pinpoint accurate performances that Kubrick got and were necessary to tell the story correctly.

De Palma's other "serious" film, *Casualties of War* (1989), failed for the same reasons: the performers were simply not believable, since apparently De Palma does not have a clue how real American soldiers actually behave. Not surprisingly, De Palma's overheated directorial style has worked best with audiences on more lightweight material, such as his two rehashes of old television series, *The Untouchables* (1987) and *Mission: Impossible* (1996), where characters and plot are of less concern.

The eighties also saw the first impact of Spike Lee's directorial work, most notably with *Do the Right Thing*, but then Lee fell into the trap that Altman, Friedkin, and others had. For a sequence in *Crooklyn* (1994), an otherwise charming coming-of-age story, Lee shot one sequence with an anamorphic lens (see chapter 2 for a discussion of anamorphic lenses), which he then had projected without a similar lens, distorting the sequence by squeezing the image. Theatres perhaps had learned their lesson with *Sorcerer* and had signs already printed to put outside the auditoriums telling the audience the effect was intended. Audiences were still baffled and upset by the distortion. Lee shot *Get on the Bus* (1997) in a variety of film stocks that became equally annoying to watch.

Quentin Tarantino made his first impression in the nineties and condensed the process we have seen with other directors by delighting and irritating members of the audience in one film—his most successful, *Pulp Fiction*. Mario Franco felt it was "a definite good [example of] the movie experience in the movie theatre ... Quentin Tarantino's attempt to interconnect several stories about all aspects of L.A. style was effective, entertaining and humorous." Steven Krul had not seen a movie in a theatre for two or three years when he saw *Pulp Fiction*. "It had been a while since a movie gave me the wild ride that *Pulp* did. It was the first movie I had seen with overlapping story lines. I ended up seeing that one a few more times. . . . I had never heard of Quentin Tarantino before and checked out his other films, which I don't think were as good, with the exception of *Reservoir Dogs*. It got me excited into going to movies again."

Moe Gardener liked the film so much he "rented it to see it again and was surprised to find I liked the film better. It seemed to hold together better than the first time I saw the film." The first time Alex Kuyumjian saw *Pulp Fiction*, he "didn't really care for it at all. I was thinking what the hell was that? But the second time, I really liked it. I even saw it a third time in the theatres. It just seemed I didn't get it the first time, but later I understood it fully."

Carlos Nino had mixed feelings about *Pulp Fiction*. "I liked this movie a little more than *Forrest Gump* [which came out the same year]. I liked Samuel Jackson's character. I don't care much though for flashy dialogue and violence . . . . I liked Harvey Kietel, but nothing more than the delivery; he wasn't the movie. I really don't like John Travolta." Marcus Franklin thought the picture was "garbage," while for Jill Hakansson, it and *Natural Born Killers* (the 1994 film Tarantino cowrote but did not direct) are "simply too much for me. It's too extreme, and I don't like the new 'cool guys' on the screen. There is too much violence, and I don't like the cinematography. I remember a lot of strange low angles that didn't make sense to me." T. Taylor lists *Pulp Fiction* as her "least favorite film. Although the look of it is trendy, slick, and appealing, and there are some unique artistic twists and concepts, I detested the violence. I hope this filmmaker, who has such mass appeal, will be more socially responsible in his future endeavors. . . . It pissed me off!"

Michael Behling "must admit I love the film. However, the praise it got was ridiculous. It is a great film and perfect crystallization of the zeitgeist from when it came out. A clever postmodern film . . . but why must everyone be so postmodern? I prefer individuals who tweak the zeitgeist rather than simply feed the flames." James Ford "did enjoy the movie, thought the music played a big part. Don't think it's one of the all-time greats. Pithy dialogue. A little too hip. Maybe I'm rebelling against the Tarantino bandwagon."

Spielberg

The most commercially successful director, and certainly the best known by the public, since the seventies is Steven Spielberg. Spielberg first came to the public's attention with *Jaws*. Bryan Cawthon's friend had heard something about the movie, and the two of them went to see it. Cawthon remembers, "There were not any special banners promoting the film or crowds waiting to get into the theatre. We just went to see another movie. I remember jumping out of my seat each time Spielberg decided I should. . . . A short time after we saw the film, it became huge. The promotion became more apparent, and the lines were long." But not everybody was impressed. James Ford was "disappointed" with *Jaws* and "am usually disappointed with Spielberg's films. Want to like them. I do a little, but not enough. Recognize his talent. Master of suspense, among other things."

The mention of Spielberg as a master of suspense suggests that he was about to take over Alfred Hitchcock's place as a brand name, but he was smarter than Brian De Palma. Spielberg's next film had suspense, but it also had wonder. Sangbum Lee's parents took him to see it when he was about five.

> The first film that had any real impact on me was Steven Spielberg's *Close Encounters of the Third Kind* (1977). I was totally overwhelmed by the intense visuals of both the earthlings and the alien spaceships and the dramatic interactions between the characters. When the main alien spaceship landed at the end, I was totally mesmerized, feeling that I myself was part of a momentous event. However, I must admit that I did not understand the movie the first time I saw it . . . when I was much older, I rented the cassette and watched the movie again, and this time I could really grasp what was happening in the movie . . . I fully comprehended the meaning of a first contact between aliens and the human race. I have enjoyed all the Steven Spielberg movies since that time, but *Close Encounters* still is the one that is most memorable and significant for me.

Dorian Wood was three years old when his parents took him to see the film. "They decided to see a film that I considered to be incredibly boring. I remember that the theatre was packed and that all eyes were completely glued to the screen—in a rather eerie way, I thought. I slept through most of the picture, but I was abruptly woken up by some strange music near the end. I recall having seen a bunch of lights, which seemed to fascinate the entire audience. I really could not see what the hoopla was all about. Anyway, it was years later that I had the chance to see that film again, this time on video, and I really regretted not having enjoyed it in the theatre."

Rigo Fernandez was five when he saw *Close Encounters* with his mother. "I remember coming out of the theatre after watching it and having a somewhat philosophical conversation with my mother all the way home about the universe and extraterrestrials. I guess for the first time, I realized how minute and insignificant I really was . . . compared to the rest of the world. It was not a gloomy or negative feeling; it was more of a revelation, a reinforcement of all my childhood fantasies realized. I now believed that almost everything that I heard and saw through 'the tube' was or could really happen." Don Ricketts was a little older and "wanted so much to meet an alien and did while watching Spielberg's classic. . . . The cosmos is great and full of unbelievable friendly things. I was so grateful that life wasn't only confined to earth. WHY I believed and trusted the aliens I have no clue."

Michael Thomas remembers "at the time I was really into UFOs and Bigfoot. I would read all kinds of stuff on the subject, so the film was a natural for me. I remember liking *Close Encounters* more than *Star Wars* at the time. *Star Wars* was exciting and fun, but *Close Encounters* seemed more human and real to me . . . it seemed possible." Later, in 1980, he saw the *Special Edition* of *Close Encounters* and was "disappointed. I missed the footage they took out to accommodate the new scenes. The thing I liked most about the original was that the ending was left to the imagination. . . . I felt Spielberg should have respected the audience and given them credit for drawing their own conclusions."

I was probably too old for *Close Encounters* when it first came out. There was enough of the twelve-year-old boy in me to like *Star Wars*, but when I first saw Spielberg's film, I had seen enough "creatures from outer space come to earth" movies to think that *Close Encounters* was basically two hours of foreplay. The *real* story is what happens *after* they land. At first, I attributed my negative attitude toward the film to having seen it in a theatre that did not have Dolby Stereo, so I made a point of seeing it again in a theatre that did. It did not help. I also tried the *Special Edition* in 1980 but had the same problems Michael Thomas did. I even gave the version that Spielberg prepared for television a watch, and it still did not work. I doubt if I will try any more Special Editions he may release.[1]

For *Close Encounters,* Spielberg had used his success with *Jaws* to turn what had started out as a $2.7 million budget into a $19 million production.[2] Fortunately, the picture was another blockbuster at the box office, although not quite of *Star Wars* proportions. By January 1980, *Star Wars* had brought in domestic rentals of over $175 million, while *Close Encounters* grossed $77 million.[3] For his next film, *1941* (1979), Spielberg followed Friedkin's path and spent even more: $27 million.[4] While the grosses were better than those of *Sorcerer,*[5] and the foreign grosses were enough to give the film a slight profit,[6] *1941* was seen as unsuccessful compared to his two previous films. Spielberg seemed to be following all those other directors, but unlike them, he was smart enough to go to work for a producer who could rein in his spendthrift ways. He went into what industry analyst Art Murphy calls professional "rehab," proving he could work on a limited budget.[7] The producer was George Lucas, and the picture was *Raiders of the Lost Ark* (1981).

Raiders was intended as a tribute to the Saturday afternoon serials moviegoers like Judith Amory and I had enjoyed as children and to those like Richard Bogren who had seen them on television. Nancy Lathrop saw the connection as well. She went to the movie assuming she would not like it but came out thinking, "Boy, are they going to go back and make movies like this? This'll be cool." Both Spielberg and Lucas were picking up on the nostalgia for past films and making it work in contemporary terms.

Michael Behling was "about fifteen when I saw it, and I'm male, so how could I not love it? Great inventive action in front of a fantastic (in both senses of the word) backdrop." Maryanne Raphael saw it at a drive-in "with my son and two teenage nephews. We all had a grand time, but I don't think I would have cared nearly as much for the movie had I seen it in a regular movie house without my young companions." Peggy Dilley was in her early thirties when she saw it with her son and thinks, "It's a children's movie. Too short, too much action, and not enough substance. I think I outgrew Saturday matinees. I can't even appreciate them. But if it had been made when I was a preteen, I'd probably think it was wonderful, too." Virginia Keene was in her mid-thirties, and we "stood in another line for this one [after having done the same for the *Star Wars* movies] and couldn't even find seats together, but this time even I was hooked. . . . This was fine, tight filmmaking. *Raiders* was the good old bigger-than-life, Technicolor American superhero adventure film. Yup. We do have this on video, and it still makes me laugh if my spirits are low and boosts my morale if I'm feeling troubled."

Gary Demirdjian was about eleven when he saw it. He and his brother and sister were ready to see another film, "and my uncle told us to see this one movie that was full of action and adventure. He said screw the movie you're about to go see, go see this other one instead. Well, we said screw you and went ahead with our original plans (the movie sucked; I forgot the title). But the next week, we remembered what he said, so we saw this action movie. It turned out to be *Raiders of the Lost Ark*, and, well, we flipped over it."

Blair Woodard remembers "going to see it several times in a row when it first came out. I still don't think there is a film that has been able to romanticize an occupation as tedious and meticulous as archeology the way *Raiders* did. After it came out, all of my friends and I wanted to become archeologists. It is incredible to me that Harrison Ford has been able to continue to act after playing so many recognizable characters, yet he is still able to change parts over and over. To me it says a lot about his ability as an actor." As a teenage girl, Robin Magee also appreciated Ford but for a different reason: "Harrison Ford—what else can I say? Harrison Ford being adventurous, daring, sweaty, and beating the bad guys. I saw this *many* times!" Jon Conrad saw it once, "enjoyed it well enough, but once was enough. The use of religious symbols for thrill effects seemed insensitive to me, even though I'm as big an atheist as there is." Michael Thomas saw a year after it was released, and it was "probably the last Spielberg film I really enjoyed without reservations."

Jack Hollander saw *Raiders of the Lost Ark* on the weekend of its release and enjoyed it, but he began to have some doubts.

I have probably seen this film more often than any other movie ever made (except, perhaps, *Casablanca*). I saw it the first weekend it opened at the National Theatre in Westwood and again a few days later with my sister. I discovered that there were all sorts of things that I didn't "get" the first time. In fact, each and every time I saw this film the first few times, I saw something that I had missed earlier. I looked at characters differently . . . . I caught lots of errors . . . , but mostly, I continued to have a good time with the film even after multiple viewings. Let's face it, the first time we see the opening ten-minute "roller coaster," it is absolutely thrilling. Even knowing what is going to happen doesn't alter (too much) the excitement inherent in the film.

"Steven Spielberg and the Incredible Vanishing Plot"—Let's face it—Spielberg is the P.T. Barnum of filmmaking. Let me explain. Indiana Jones swims out to a *submarine*. We then see the mystical red line tracing the sub's path over many, many nautical miles. Then there's Indiana Jones in the naval shipyard. Now, I know (from reading the book [the novelization]) that he lashed himself to the back of the periscope with his whip and hoped that the sub stayed at periscope depth (which it does). In fact, in the film, Indy does not have his whip in the scene after this ship ride. I also know (from reading various magazines) that Spielberg filmed a scene where Indy lashes himself to the periscope. I also know that the scene didn't work very well. Spielberg's solution—leave it out and pretend no one will notice the serious plot gap (right!). Of course, he's right—even those who noticed didn't care. . . .

Don't get me wrong—generally speaking, I love Spielberg's films and the films he has produced [which Hollander notes have the same Vanishing Plot point problems]; but this nagging problem of assuming that the audience is too slow to notice plot gaps and script inconsistencies is really annoying.

The plot and continuity problems Hollander found did not bother Javier Rodriguez. He saw *Raiders* first on television and thought he "should have seen it on the big screen. I liked the way the story was so real. The character Indiana Jones was also amazing. I mean he was kind of like a believable hero. . . . And the music was so wonderful and loud." Tandy Summers thought the stunts in *Raiders* were "real and believable," especially when compared to the sequel, *Indiana Jones and the Temple of Doom* (1984), where the stunts in the opening sequences were "just too much. I don't know. Maybe I'd enjoy it if I was twelve. I was just fifteen when I saw *Indiana,* and I didn't buy the whole movie." Marci Kozin *was* twelve when she saw *Indiana,* and it was one of her best moviegoing experiences. "My brother waited outside the ticket box at our local theatre for hours before the tickets went on sale. . . . My brother didn't have his driver's license yet, so he rode his bike to the theatre (skipping school, by the way). The theatre was jam-packed, people were sitting on the floor, the audience was incredible, the action was so exciting, I was loving it. Ahhh, the big screen."

Plot gaps and continuity problems and all, *Raiders of the Lost Ark* was a massive hit. Lucas kept Spielberg to a budget of $20 million,[8] and by 1985 the film had domestic rentals of nearly $116 million, with *Indiana Jones and the Temple of Doom* right behind with $109 million.[9] A second sequel, *Indiana Jones and the Last Crusade* (1989), outgrossed the first and almost matched *Raiders* with $115 million.[10] Unlike other directors, Spielberg had learned his lesson: you do not have to spend an unlimited amount of money to make movies that people want to see. For his next film after *Raiders,* he spent only $10 million.[11] And the film brought in rentals of over $209 million.[12]

E.T. was Conrad Hilton's

most memorable movie. To me this was what every young boy at my age at the time would want. A creature from outer space that you could bribe with a bag of Reese's Pieces. It was like a dream come true to see E.T. come alive on screen. Everything about the movie felt so warm and seemed so real that the best way to describe it would be "the willful suspension of disbelief."

I was almost in tears as I sat in the theatre watching E.T. seem to die, and when all hope seemed to be lost, the flower came alive and filled my heart with joy as I saw the red light glowing again in E.T.'s chest.

I believe everyone, young and old, would have liked to fly up in the sky on a bicycle with their friends, which was another amazing scene in the movie. In my opinion, there hasn't been an alien-meets-human relationship to have the impact that *E.T.* had on me.

Skylaire Alfvegren was about five when the film came out. "I just adored the creature. I remember being totally enthralled with the alien and immediately began collecting every piece of *E.T.* merchandise around. A plush *E.T.* doll, soap, plastic figurines, drinking glasses, a TV tray. . . . I still have these things, and I wonder if my interest in UFOs has been fostered by that movie." Alfvegren saw it at a drive-in, as did Glinn Leevitt, but the only thing Leevitt remembers about his experience with the movie was being cold.

Michael Behling remembers seeing *E.T.* in his early teens "with my parents and coming out of the theatre crying along with everybody else. I think I cried because everyone else seemed to be crying; it was kind of a group thing. Because really I don't recall it being that sad, but then again I can't remember anything about the movie at this point. I only remember it at all because it seems so idiotic to me that I cried from it, and I always remember my most embarrassing moments." Shawn Taylor enjoyed the movie at age six with his family and

smiled, laughed, and cried during this film. I wasn't getting up from my seat; I didn't want to miss anything in the movie. I would have wet my pants if that's what it took. But as the ending of the movie neared, I began to cry. I asked my mother why did E.T. have to go back home. She said, "Because he must go home and see his family." I wasn't too worried by the answer. I was surprised to have looked over and seen my ever-so-bullish brother wiping his eyes of tears. My mother then replied to me, "Don't worry son, everything is going to be all right. E.T. will be safe at home with his family." Then she wiped her eyes with a tissue.

Lizy Moromisato also saw the film with her brother. "My brother must have been about eight at the time we saw it. I loved the movie, but I guess my brother got more involved with it, because days later I found a paper with the title *E.T.*; he had written the whole story so he would not forget it! I sometimes tease him about that." Brian Hall was about fourteen when he saw the film and "got caught up in *E.T.* fever like everyone else. . . . This was a particularly special film to me, because I was going through a rough time in my life, and things like this helped me out in little ways."

E.T. was the very first movie Edward Pina ever saw. "I remember I sat next to my dad. I was a little scared because of all the loud noise, but I got used to it after a while. Just looking up at the giant TV and watching a boy find a friend from outer space and crying when he flew into the sky. My dad was holding me and telling me that he would come back." *E.T.* reminded Lawrence Dotson of *Snoopy, Come Home* (1972) "because it had to do with losing a good, non-human friend." D'Arcy West's mother made her take her sister, and "I hated it. I felt manipulated and angry when everyone started crying, and I thought E.T. was ugly, and I thought Drew Barrymore was a hideous child."

For Michael Sampson, *E.T.* "conjured up nostalgic feelings of my childhood when I used to listen to fairytales." Jon Conrad was in his early thirties when he saw the film "on the Sunday of its first weekend. It was fast and entertaining and I was enjoying it, when I suddenly realized that tears were coursing down my cheeks and wouldn't stop. It started up during the flying-in-front-of-the-moon sequence and kicked in for the whole last scene. I have never been so glad for a long final credits sequence so that I could collect myself. It has affected me the same way again any time I see it in a theatre." David Bromley "wished I could find an E.T., and for months I kept looking out my bedroom window up at the stars trying to see if a ship would land."

Virginia Keene does not remember when and where she first saw *E.T.*, but she "loved it. I'm sure I did, because later I bought the video for our collection. When I watched the video, I was surprised that it seemed overly sentimental. Perhaps I've outgrown it. It never again moved me as deeply as the first time. The *deus ex machina* of the flying bicycles for the getaway always bothered me as being preposterous, especially in a film as well made as this. If I were Spielberg, I would be embarrassed by my cop-out. It amuses me that he made it his logo [for his Amblin' Entertainment company]."

Richard Cross was a father when the film came out and took his five-year-old daughter. "Although I consider myself a tough guy, her tears were contagious. A touching, uplifting movie." Monica Dunlap saw it with her brother and her niece "at a suburban multi-cinema complex in Rocky River, Ohio, when it first came out. The audience was full of little kids squirming and all excited. They all greeted my brother in whispers, because he and my little niece had seen the film before. 'How many times have you seen it, Annie?' 'This is my fourth time.' All the other kids whispered the number of times they'd seen it. It was a great film experience for me, because I love this kind of audience involvement and loved [the character of] E.T." During a screening, Marilyn Heath, then in her thirties, and her mother "laughed when E.T. was dying hooked up to all those machines. Appalled six-year-olds turned and gave us offended stares. That made it worthwhile."

For Noel Obiora, who was visiting America from Nigeria, *E.T.* was the first film he ever saw in this country. "It was the first time I ever saw a complete audience stand up at the end of the movie and applaud enthusiastically as if a live performance had just concluded and the performers were taking a bow. The entire experience, not just the quality of the picture, did things to me." He eventually moved to America.

Michael Thomas was just starting his career as a projectionist the summer *E.T.* came out, and "I liked the film, but after seeing it several times while I worked, I became rather sick of it." Nancy Lathrop saw the film late in the run, so because she knew the story and the impact it was having, she "felt like I'd seen it before I even walked in. I pretty much had. Not a complex plot." Still, she "was manipulated like everybody else, but walked out feeling very ashamed of myself for being manipulated, but my overwhelming impression of it was, 'This is making how much money?'"

Marion Levine admits, "I know I'm too cynical, because I didn't care for *E.T.* It changed styles in midstream and went for the obvious emotional buttons. I'm sure I cried—I cry watching AT&T commercials—but I wasn't moved on a deeper level." Jack Hollander saw it the week it opened, then a second time two weeks later. "The second viewing was (at least) one too many. I shouldn't be critical—I liked the music, I liked the character (E.T., not anyone else), and there were a few clever script devices (the alien only speaks English phrases he has heard). I suppose that my biggest complaint is that the scientists are not portrayed as menacingly as they should be. In fact, I found myself rooting for them half of the time."

Bill Pulliam saw *E.T.* after it had run a while and "after hearing about it excessively. I still enjoyed it but always get annoyed at extraterrestrials that look like slightly modified people (don't those FX [special effects] folks have any imagination?)." Douglas Choe's reaction to E.T. was "Jesus said he would be back; he just didn't say what he would look like."

Throughout the eighties, Spielberg continued to make the obvious crowd-pleasers, like the two *Indiana Jones* sequels, but he also tried to deepen his work, with only varying degrees of success. *The Color Purple* (1985), *Empire of the Sun* (1987), *Always* (1989), and *Hook* (1991) reached audiences of various sizes, but none were as large as the audiences for *E.T.* Or for his 1993 film *Jurassic Park*.

Like Nancy Lathrop at *E.T.*, when I saw *Jurassic Park* at the end of its first week's run, my reaction was, "How much money was this making?" The final domestic rentals were $208 million.[13] The reason the success surprised me was that I thought it was one of Spielberg's worst pieces of direction. The continuity is constantly off (the shots of the opening sequence do not cut together smoothly, and there's the mystery of what Jack Hollander might call the In-credible Vanishing Blouse: what happens to Laura Dern's blouse, which sud-denly disappears near the end of the picture?) and the acting is uneven (Spielberg never explained to Sam Neill that he was going to have to do *something* to hold the screen against kids and two different types of dinosaurs, the computerized ones and Richard Attenborough). Still, the dinosaurs were impressive, and the success of the film suggests that Spielberg's instincts about the story in relation to the audience were on target: get the dinosaurs right and we won't care much about anything else. Scott Hemmann had a reaction similar to mine. He thought *Jurassic Park* "is just *Jaws* on land and not nearly as good. The computer-gener-ated special effects were awesome, but I think Spielberg should have remem-bered the human cast. Laura Dern, usually a wonderful actress, is awful and the others aren't much better."

Valerie Hornig found that "reading the book beforehand almost ruined the movie for me until I resigned myself to the spectacular special effects and real-ized that this was what this film was all about—fantasy. And with this under-standing, I could enjoy the tour." Although Coni Constantine "can't claim that it was this movie that made me decide to become a paleontologist, it was re-leased at about the same time that I made the decision, so of course I was very excited to see it. The dinosaurs were very real looking even if they weren't all taxonomically correct. It made the concept of dinosaurs more real to me and has been in inspiration." Virginia Keene was looking forward to seeing *Jurassic Park* at the theatre

as soon as the crowds ebbed, because the whole concept screamed for a big screen. I was enthralled by the fabulous special effects, but felt sad that this movie could have been so much more than just good-looking. Spielberg found a new toy. He got the dinos right but not the people. It really didn't bother me so much at the time, because I was concentrating on the smoke and mirrors. While I was watching the film, I was reminded of seeing Cinerama, or 3–D, or IMAX for the first time. [*Jurassic Park*] was more a technological event than a cinematic event for me. I really didn't concentrate much on the story and didn't care about the charac-ters (except for Jeff Goldblum). They seemed to me to be cardboard cut-outs, and the story was shallow ... and didn't have to be! Too bad Spielberg didn't use his source material more. The book was so much better. . . . There were all the ingredients for a great film here. This seems like a missed opportunity.

Lizy Moromisato worked "for a model kit manufacturer, and we released four kits of the dinosaurs featured in the movie. Doing the preproduction research for the kits gave us a lot of access to the special effects aspect of the movie, so by the time I saw it, I already knew how the dinosaurs had been made and how they moved the way they did. The first impression I could have gotten from seeing the movie is that it had been spoiled, but I was still amazed at how natural it all looked in the movie." Marguerite K.A. Petersen thought "the dinosaurs stole the show. I almost wanted them to win."

Shaun Hill-Kret rates it "right behind *Star Wars* as the best roller-coaster visual fantasy I've seen. If I saw it as a kid it would probably be my all-time favorite, but as an adult the story had serious flaws, and Laura Dern's character was a token part." Dinosaur-lover Donna Crisci first saw *Jurassic Park* as an adult and says she is

> someone who would hawk her soul to see a real *Tyrannosaurus rex*, who used to stare at dinosaur pictures for hours, who watched *Lost Continent* [pick your version: 1951 or 1968] thousands of times to watch the dinos, who never forgave the makers of *King Kong* (1933 or 1976) for thinking a gorilla could kill a *T. rex*. This film was great fun, but what I really loved about it was the dinos themselves. When Sam Neill reacts to seeing the first great beast, he had my expression on his face [Neill's one great acting bit in the film]; when he fell to his knees when told a *T. rex* existed, it was exactly how I felt at the moment. I could watch this film forever for those moments. I wish I could have seen it as a child! Oh, to be terrorized by the greatest beastie of them all. I had resented the novel for making the raptors the real menace and was thus surprised and delighted when Spielberg restored the real king of the dinos to his rightful place in that wonderfully triumphant attack on the raptors—the *Tyrannosaurus* tossing his head and roaring his power. ZAP! I was a cheering kid again!

Darrin Burrell "didn't get a chance to see *Jurassic Park* at the theatre, but I did rent it and watched it over and over . . . again with my six year old son, James, who is a dinosaur fanatic. I enjoyed the brilliant magic created by the special effects department. The dinosaurs were truly believable, especially the herd scene where they are chasing the people. I still get an enjoyable experience when I watch this film."

Many people saw the film on opening day or soon thereafter. Kalani Mondoy was there for opening day. "I had the pleasure of seeing it with a bunch of young children. I was laughing more at the children's reactions and probably had my mind more fixated on them than on the story itself." Dorian Wood and his mother and sister also went on opening day. We "went to the premiere in a second-rate multiplex in Florida, which was full of pimple-faced Valley Kid-wanna-bes (who am I to talk?) who just would not shut up throughout the entire film. We managed to enjoy it, despite the racket. . . . It was the premiere of something historic, and I was there. And I've got the ticket stub to prove it."

It took Aubrey Solomon three tries to completely appreciate the film. The first time was "one of the worst moviegoing experiences in my life. I went to a theatre and walked out three times to get an usher to keep the Spanish-speaking family behind us from doing a simultaneous translation. The usher was Spanish-speaking and did little to help. It totally ruined whatever enjoyment there was in the movie. I saw it again at a WGA [Writers Guild of America] screening and thoroughly enjoyed it. It was like I hadn't seen it before. Then, I watched it again at Universal in four-track DTS [Digital Theatre Sound] and marveled at the technical skill that went into it. The acting wasn't great, the story wasn't the most adept, but as sheer entertainment it worked roaringly well." Luis Garcia saw the film at the Chinese Theatre and was also impressed with the sound. "The theatre trembled as the sound echoed all around the room. The sound made the movie more enjoyable and excited."

Glinn Leevitt liked *Jurassic Park,* "because for me it was the first movie that has truly been frightening to watch in a long time. I thought the story was really good, but that has more to do with Michael Crichton [the author of the original novel] than anyone else. However, the more I watch it, the more I dislike it. The second time around, the dinosaurs looked really fake. I think sometimes it is best to watch a movie only once and hang on to those notions and ideas you get from seeing it the first time." It took Rocio Vargas three times to see the film "completely. The first time I went to see this movie, I spent more time crunched in my seat screaming, counting the wrinkles on the palm of my hands, than watching the action on the screen. I missed the whole thing. It was a horrible but magical experience." When she finally "saw" the movie, she thought the scenes of the dinosaurs were "breathtaking."

Wendi Cole saw it "the night it opened at the theatre. I loved the fact the dinosaurs look so real. I was on edge during the entire movie. The thing that I liked though was that my anxiety was left in the theatre. I didn't have nightmares or anything." She did not like the "peaceful" ending where the "fact that they were almost *eaten* by dinosaurs is completely forgotten. What kind of chump do I look like? I can't believe Spielberg went for such a sorry ending." The film did give Daniel Barr nightmares. It left him "quivering and cold. . . . It struck a chord of primal fear, the fear of being eaten by a dinosaur, a monster, or a boogey man. The story sucked; it was an impressive CD adventure game created as a tool for the marketing empire to sell its wares. I don't respect Spielberg on sociopolitical or economic grounds; he is a pandering little brat. Unfortunately, with a lot of power and financial support."

Because of the hype for *Jurassic Park*, which caused many people to rush out to see it in its opening days, there was something of a backlash against Spielberg and the film. Rick Mitchell says, "By the time it opened, I was so bored by the hype I really didn't care if I saw it or not. I finally did see it for free at Universal and was really not impressed. . . . I also felt that . . . Spielberg's heart really wasn't in it and he was just going through the motions."

Kevin Kennedy was rather disappointed in the film and only went because a woman he knew

> dragged me out to see it with her. We went to the Hollywood Galaxy Cinemas on Hollywood Boulevard. That was a mistake. After buying the tickets, they told us we had to wait in line on the sidewalk. The line was so long that I suggested we get our money back and go another time. While we were walking back to the box office, we found ourselves behind the first group of people being seated in the theatre. The next thing we know, an usher told us to stay in line and just keep going. I was about to explain to him that I only wanted to return our tickets, but my friend quickly shut [me] up, and we continued with the group into the theatre. After seeing that "trash," I wish I had spoken up. I will never see that film again, at least not voluntarily.

Angela West was "so excited when I heard they were going to make a movie about dinosaurs. I was so disappointed when I actually saw the movie. I give two thumbs up to the genius of the creature creators, but that wasn't quite enough to save the entire picture for me. I felt I would have gotten more of my money's worth if I had gone to the La Brea Tar Pits [a site in Los Angeles where dinosaur fossils have been found, marked by large model dinosaurs]." Peggy Dilley "couldn't believe how bad it was when I finally saw it under very bad conditions at the Vine Street Theatre [a second-run house] on Hollywood Boulevard. There was nothing to it. . . . Maybe if I'd seen it at the Chinese, I'd have a better attitude."

Blair Woodard will "always remember *Jurassic Park*, as it was the last film I saw before heading to Guatemala for the Peace Corps. I thought it was appropriate to watch a film that takes place in Central America before I left to go there. It was one of those films that, in my opinion, did not live up to the hype. It was also interesting to be able to see it released in a foreign culture several months later. I actually watched a bad print of it in Guatemala and was still not that impressed." Or, as Peggy Dilley says of *Jurassic Park*, "It wasn't *Schindler's List*."

Domestic rentals of *Schindler's List*, Spielberg's other 1993 release, had only reached a little over $38 million by May 1994,[14] but while not as widely attended as *Jurassic Park*, critics and audiences liked it better. As he had between *Jaws* and *Close Encounters*, Spielberg once again shifted his style. He simplified his style in respect for the material and the audience, foregoing several of the dazzling camera moves he was noted for. While Spielberg had always worked well with actors and was able to elicit entertaining performances from them, one of his weaknesses was a lack of interest in character. But *Schindler's List* possesses more in terms of characterization than any other Spielberg film, and the result was enormously moving. Jack Hollander, who had problems with Spielberg's previous films, recalls a typical screening in Orange County.

> I will never forget the experience of seeing [*Schindler's List*] with a crowd of people. One lady sitting behind me started audibly sobbing about thirty minutes before the end of the film and never stopped. One could see and hear people's reactions to the emotion of the film throughout. What was wonderful about this film (and the great success of the film, in my opinion) was that the strongest reactions were not left for the horrible scenes (the random shootings, the children hiding in the out-house, the Auschwitz scene) but for the beautiful ones (the end sequence, the great drama of the list writing scenes—"The list is life!" I started "losing it" when the survivors were donating the gold in their teeth for a token for Schindler).

Not every audience or audience member was so moved. In fact, *Schindler's List* provoked some of the strangest reactions in the history of movies. In January 1994, a group of Oakland high school students was taken on a Martin Luther King Jr. holiday field trip to see the film, but the students were not prepared for what they were going to see. As previously discussed, the context in which a film is seen can be crucial. Without being familiar with the historical context, the students laughed and talked during the scenes of the horrors of the Holocaust and eventually had to be removed from the theatre.[15] A striking explanation of their reaction came from Kevin Weston, an assistant editor of a journal on San Francisco Bay Area teen life. "They were laughing not at the Holocaust, but at the movie. The truth is, few African Americans go the movies—even 'serious' movies like *Schindler's List*—expecting a seven-dollar epiphany. We're used to distancing ourselves from what we see on the screen, not identifying with it. We're used to laughing. How else can we deal with the absurdly degrading portraits of ourselves we see on the screen—or with our total invisibility?"[16]

In response to the story about the Oakland incident in the *Los Angeles Times*, a man who had worked at a theatre in Los Angeles wrote in with details of a similar incident. An elderly woman came to the theatre on her birthday for a showing of the film, but not all her relatives showed up, so she gave several of the paid-for tickets to people in the shopping mall. Some of them were teenagers who did not stop talking and jeering during the film.[17]

The most bizarre reaction came in San Diego, where a man shot and critically wounded a woman in front of him during the scenes in which Nazis were shooting Jews. When the police arrested the man, he told them that he had recently changed his religion from Catholicism to Orthodox Judaism and wanted to test God and protect Jews in general from harm.[18]

In 1997, Spielberg returned to dinosaurs with the sequel *The Lost World: Jurassic Park*, a better film than the first one (the acting was more consistent, as was the continuity) that racked up $229 million at the box office but was still second that year to *Men in Black*.[19] Perhaps people had been turned off by the hype for both the original and the sequel as well as the problems people had with the first *Jurassic Park*. Or it may just have been that *Men in Black* seemed fresher and more imaginative. Still, *The Lost World* outgrossed all other films that year, including from the year's top ten *Liar, Liar; My Best Friend's Wedding;* and *Face/Off*, which suggests the better quality of the sequel overcame audiences' problems with the original.

Perhaps mindful of the strange reactions to *Schindler's List*, Spielberg made a particular effort in promoting his 1998 film *Saving Private Ryan* to set the context for the film, so audiences would know what to expect, specifically in the gory D-Day sequence that opens the film. There were not the kind of strange reactions *Schindler's List* had elicited, and the timing of *Saving Private Ryan* provoked a widespread outpouring of discussion about World War II. Veterans who had not talked about their experiences found the film a way to open up to their friends and relatives, and the film equally provided a stimulus for younger people to talk to their elders who had served in the war.[20]

Like *Schindler's List*, *Ryan* showed Spielberg as a director at his less flamboyant (with the exception of the desaturated [color was removed from the image in the printing process, giving the film a faded look] color[21] and the occasional playing with the film speed) than in his "lighter" films. Perhaps he had taken to heart the words of the great director John Ford: "Anybody can direct a picture once they know the fundamentals. Directing a picture is not a mystery, it's not an art. The main thing about directing is: photograph the people's eyes."[22]

In 1986, the Directors Guild of America commissioned Chuck Workman to make a film commemorating the fiftieth anniversary of the founding of the Guild. The film was *Precious Images*, a seven-minute compilation of shots from hundreds of movies, including four of Spielberg's. I saw it many times in theatres and have run it several times in class. It never fails to amuse and, more noticeably, move an audience. The interesting thing is that almost none of its impact comes from any flashy directorial touches, such as elaborate camera movements. The impact comes instead from the faces of the actors and the memories we have of the parts they were playing in the movies. The dynamics of *Precious Images* is in the editing of those images, which had not been shot by their directors to be cut together in this way. The film is a tribute as much to the actors and to Workman's editing as it is to directors.

Of course, in most of the shots of the actors, the directors *have* photographed the eyes. . . .

Studios and VCRs

And now a pause in the more general discussions to return briefly to the historical pattern. The emphasis on directors in the late sixties and early seventies—both in Hollywood and in the critical and historical press—brought about a backlash in Hollywood in the eighties. Most of the directors had behaved liked raging egomaniacs, and very often the targets of their excessive behavior were the junior executives at the studios.[1] By the early eighties, those junior executives were now in charge, just at the time that Hollywood's focus shifted from the more personal projects of the seventies to the potential blockbusters that *Jaws* and the *Star Wars* films had introduced. This change in emphasis meant a return to the system of strong producers that had dominated the studio system before 1948, which would have been wonderful for filmmaking if the producers had been the caliber of Irving Thalberg, Darryl F. Zanuck, and Hal Wallis. But who we got instead were, just to name a few of the many, Julia Phillips, Jon Peters, and the worst of the lot, Don Simpson.[2]

Like many people, Simpson had gotten hooked on movies early, claiming he caused a stir at the age of five when he saw De Mille's 1952 circus film *The Greatest Show on Earth*, saying he would not leave the theatre until a happier ending was provided.[3] He became an executive at Paramount in the mid-seventies but was fired because of his drug and alcohol use. He was given a production deal at the studio, probably with the assumption on the studio's part that nothing would come of it. However, even with his shortcomings, Simpson did look at movies from the audience's point of view. Screenwriter Robert Towne, who worked with Simpson, said of him, "Don had specific ideas on what an audience wanted to feel, when they wanted to feel it, and what would be transporting for them. He prided himself on being a member of the audience. He always said, 'I buy my popcorn and watch a movie and want to feel something.'"[4]

In the mid-eighties, Simpson and his partner Jerry Bruckheimer produced a number of large-scale commercial hits. One of them, *Top Gun*, was the highest-grossing film of 1986,[5] but Simpson was so sloppy about the accuracy of the Naval Aviators Top Gun training program that the retired admiral assigned as the technical advisor said to one of the real instructors, "I'm just trying to keep them from turning *Top Gun* into a musical." Given the amount of rock music on the sound track, he may have failed at that as well, although he did admit, "Most of the decisions they made, made the movie better than reality. They just knew how to make it work."[6]

Octavio Jimenez, who was in his teens at the time, seems to have been the audience Simpson and the retired admiral were both aiming at.

> *Top Gun* really brings patriotism to its highest form in the sense that this movie was really done to promote the U.S. through the eyes of a hotshot pilot who happens to be the best in the world at what he does, and shows it by defeating the communist threat to peace. I have to say that this movie did its job on me, and because I am so drawn by planes, this movie really knew where to hit me when it came out in theatres. I was amazed when the fighting scenes came out in *Top Gun* and was saddened when tragedy hit and Goose died in a plane accident. But what really made the movie great was the music associated with the movie, which in combination made the movie a classic in my mind.

I could see what Jimenez meant about the hotshot pilot. When I was in the navy in the mid-sixties at the U.S. Naval Air Station in San Diego, I used to ride to work in a small boat with Naval aviators. The film bought into their self-serving romanticism in a completely uncritical manner, unlike the way the 1939 film about airmail pilots, *Only Angels Have Wings,* undercuts the bravado. I was teaching the film history course at UCLA the spring *Top Gun* was released, and if it had not been too late in the quarter, I would have added *Dr. Strangelove* to the course to show the class where *Top Gun* thinking would lead.

Virginia Keene "found the situations and relationships (especially the romance) to be contrived and unbelievable—probably because my father was a naval aviator. The only things that worked for me were the spectacular flying scenes and a good song. This didn't work on any other level. I've seen parts of it since on cable. I had forgotten that it launched the careers of Val Kilmer, Meg Ryan, and Tim Robbins, so I guess it had some value." Keene thought it was initially so successful because of Tom Cruise. "This was a star vehicle if there ever was one." Daniel Barr definitely responded to Cruise and the time period, calling the film "pure eighties. Cruise was the young icon that inspired me as a young man and actor, as it did the rest of the world. It will always be his best performance for me—heroic, fresh, vulnerable. It is a corny film and looks dated now, but it had an innocence and energy that transcended its political limitations. Perhaps because it was made before his ego and Scientology got hold of his soul."

Seeing *Top Gun* at the time of its initial release, Jack Hollander was "very disappointed in this film—I found the acting blasé (probably due to the weaknesses of the script), the plots totally unbelievable, and the action sequences a bit hard to follow (although generally exciting). I suppose my initial reaction on viewing this had something to do with the unbelievability of the contrived combat between the good guys (red-blooded Americans) and the bad guys (those pesky red Commies). Haven't we beaten this horse to death yet?" Al Gonzalez "saw this at a theatre when it first came out. I thought it was stupid. I saw it again on video. I liked it a little better. I don't know why. But I still laughed at some of the heroic, formula aspects that made the movie what it was." Dorian Wood "never really liked *Top Gun*. Maybe it had to do with the fact that I saw it in a cheap hotel room while on a cross-country trip to New York. I was pretty cranky and completely exhausted. Nevertheless, years later I saw it again, and I still hated it."

A lot of people in the military responded to *Top Gun*. When Michael Sampson "first saw *Top Gun*, it was a very enjoyable experience. At the time, I was in the United States Navy assigned to an aircraft carrier. When I first saw the movie, I literally felt that I was a part of that movie. It was a piece of art I could relate to. Strangely enough, I recently watched *Top Gun* for the second time, and the experience was totally different than what it was like when I was in the military. I did not feel like a participant but more like a spectator." Ervin Riggs was a jet mechanic in the air force when he first saw the film and "it seemed like I was right out there on the launch pad as the mechanics taxied out the aircraft. I could just feel what they were going through as they launched and recovered the jet fighter aircraft."

For Blair Woodard, *Top Gun* "holds a lot of high school memories. It came out my junior year, and I saw it at least six times over the summer. Having seen parts of it recently on video, I was not as impressed as I remember being at the time. I think that to really appreciate the flying sequences one needs to see it on a big screen, but I was also not into the characters as much anymore. I chalked it up to maturity on my part." Paula Lampshire was in her late teens when she saw it and "really liked it, because I always wanted to join the navy and fly a fighter plane for the experience and the personal challenge. But I never did join. So I experience the idea of it every time I see *Top Gun*."

Lampshire was not the only woman who liked the film. As Mia Gyzander says, it was "Well, kind of nice for teenage girls." And not just teenage girls. I ended up seeing it with a former student of mine in her twenties, who had dropped by my house to pick up her shoes (don't ask—it's not nearly as interesting as it sounds) and was *dying* to see the movie. She loved flying and spent more time bouncing in her seat over the flying sequences than over Tom Cruise. And stewardess Shaun Hill-Kret thought it was "the best adrenaline movie I've

seen. . . . Wouldn't want to see this movie if I was thinking of joining the marines, 'cause they'd get me for sure."

That is more or less what happened to Peter Albers. "I'm embarrassed to say
I called the marines the next day after seeing the film. Not that I didn't have
problems with the film—the whole last act of going to fight the commies dis-
gusted me right at the time. Flying just looked like so much fun, and women
dig you! When I think of how close I came to going to Platoon Leaders Camp
because of that damn film, I get physically ill." Edward Pina was also caught up
in the "great adrenaline rush of a movie. All those jets flying at top speeds,
flying all over the sky, blowing up other jets. After watching *Top Gun,* you wanted
to become an air force pilot and fly with Maverick, Keman, and Viper."

Kenneth Hughes saw the same association that Peter Albers did. "What can
I say? I like chicks and planes, etc. . . . Play me for the boy I am." Bryan Cawthon
also got the connection. "It had technology, it had big egos, and it had the sex
scene with the beautiful woman." Having heard rumors about the actors involved, Dennis Wilkes had a little trouble with the sex scenes. "A closeted actor
and a closeted actress playing lovers. But they clicked, unlike Richard Gere and
Jody Foster [with *Sommersby* (1993), there were the same kinds of rumors about
those actors as well]." For Arnold Quinlan, who either had not heard the rumors or did not care, "Kelly McGillis was yummy. Basically your adolescent
nocturnal emission type of movie. Big bad plane, big bad motorcycle, and big
bad Kelly McGillis." (This perhaps shows the advantages of market research on
a film like *Top Gun.* At early screenings of the film, test audiences demanded
steamier love scenes between Cruise and McGillis, and they were shot and edited into the film.[7])

The people who saw the links between sex and planes were not alone. And
unlike Shaun Hill-Kret, Peter Albers, and Edward Pina, many male viewers knew
it was not the marines and air force the film was about, but naval aviation.
Applicants for the program increased, and many of the navy flyers who partici-
pated in the Tailhook scandal in 1991, where women were molested in a Las
Vegas hotel, had been inspired by the movie. The official report noted that "the
movie fueled misconceptions on the part of junior officers as to what was expected of them and also served to . . . glorify naval pilots in the eyes of many
young women."[8]

As is apparent from earlier discussions and some of the comments about
Top Gun, beginning in the eighties, more and more people were seeing movies
on videocassettes. The possibilities of videocassettes had been around since the
sixties and seventies, but they exploded in the eighties, although not in the way
most film industry people thought they would. Most of the self-serving as-
sumptions within the industry in the seventies were that people would want to
own cassettes of films. Virtually nothing I have found written in the seventies

indicates anybody had any idea of the potential of the video rental market. By 1998, a year in which the domestic U.S. box office for American films was $6.88 billion,[9] spending on video rentals was $8.1 billion, while my best estimate of the spending on video purchases was approximately a mere $6.85 billion.[10]

The success of the video rental market comes from two indisputable facts. The first is that people do not necessarily want to own every movie. The second is that, with the exception of Alcoholics Anonymous meetings, the video rental store is the greatest pickup place since public laundromats.[11] Since I normally go to my local Blockbuster in the mornings, I had not noticed this until I dropped by one Friday afternoon at five. I was slapped in the face by the combination of aftershave and perfume as soon as I walked in the door. I simply looked at the behavior of the customers; it was easy to figure out what was going on. You can see why. If you are a guy, you can approach a woman in the drama section and tell her your ex-girlfriend had suggested you see that love story that gets mentioned in *Sleepless in Seattle* and does she remember the name of it. If you are a woman, you can approach a man and tell him that your ex-boyfriend suggested you see that war picture that gets mentioned in *Sleepless in Seattle* and does he remember the name of it.

David Ko takes even further advantage of the fact that films are available on video.

I used to rent at least one or two movies a night a couple of years ago. I associate videos with raw sex. My favorite way to get together with a girl is to ask her to come over and watch a video. It's usually after we've already seen one movie at a theatre or talked on the phone for a long time. I would set up my TV in the bedroom, and I had a roommate who slept on the couch in the living room. I'd bring the girl over and say, "We can't watch TV in the living room, because my roommate is sleeping." So we'd go into the bedroom and watch videos there. There wasn't any couch there, so we'd lie on the bed and "watch" movies. Of course, when two youngsters lie in a dark room on a bed, it's not much after the titles start to roll that nature takes control. My favorite line was, "Let's turn the lights down; I like to watch videos like that." Also, videos were the cheapest date. I used to go to a video store that was $1.07 per video. I guess, looking back on it, I wasn't manipulating anyone. They were in my bed not because of the video, but because they wanted to [be there]. But it sure did seem to make things easier.

Teddi Lawrence, on the other hand, rents because "I often avoid social situations and other people, thus the best place to be is at home cuddled on the couch. Also, a large number of the films that I come to want to see are rentals only." Richard Morales has a complicated, changing relationship with videos:

Because I can't get at the good movies in the theatre, I depend on videos for watching old or obscure movies. The two years preceding this one I was living with other people who had VCRs, and so I got in a lot of movie watching. And living with someone else tended to drive me out of the house and escape to the movies more than it does now, living alone. I was watching about two to three movies a month in theatres, but on video at this time I was watching about three videos or more a week. With the selection of movies that video had, I don't think I was watching any TV movies then. I could see movies at the time I wanted, without commercials, and feel assured that they were uncut. I was purposefully trying to get in all the movies that I had always wanted to see, because once I lived by myself I knew that the videos would be cut to nothing. Although I have nothing against videos, I don't like having a TV in my own house. And even though they both demand my attention, it is television I don't want to give my attention to. Television, unlike videos, has no limit on your time.

The advantages of seeing movies on video are many and varied. John Slipstone does not have the cash to see a lot of first-run movies, thinks cable and regular TV are "moronic," and finds that "my saving grace is the video stores. I do love film and adventure, and I seem to quench this thirst with a rental cassette." The video store he frequents has "a wonderful array of the most obscure films in one room." After Rudie Bravo stopped working in movie theatres, including several revival houses, she "compensated by watching two, and sometimes three, videos a night during summer when school was out. This was about six years ago, and since then I have favored videotapes to theatre because it is much more convenient. . . . Even Landmark [which has several theatres running revival programs] in its heyday would only run *An Affair to Remember*, or *Nosferatu* (1922 or 1979), or *Repo Man* (1984) once a year."

Alex Kuyumjian finds watching cassettes more comfortable. "I really don't care to pay to sit in a stiff chair for two hours and watch a movie unless it is for a presentation that I really want to see. I get a little restless in a chair for long periods of time. I think I'm just trying to say that I prefer home viewings over theatre ones." On the other hand, Laurel Jo Martin "vows I'm going to see a movie in a theatre, then I wimp out and wait for the video. I'm not real thrilled with this because I love the big screen and dark theatre. TV is just sitting at home. But I'd say I saw three movies in a theatre last year and probably rented a hundred or more on video. I say rented rather than watched, because sometimes the action movies that I rent for my husband I don't view."

Susanna Serrano often sees a movie in a theatre when it first comes out and then sees it again when it comes out on cassette, because "I must see it again, or I didn't want to pay the $7.50 to see it at a movie theatre because it didn't seem worth my time and money." I have a similar kind of hierarchy: films that I feel I have to see when they first come out in theatres; films I have to wait until my wife can go because she will kill me if I see them without her; films I am willing to pay twice to see in theatres (only one or two of those a year); films I wait for until they come out on cassette; films I wait for until they show up on free network television (I had cable for three months in 1983 and gave it up because the service was so bad I could never get through an entire film without the cable going out), and films I'll tape off the 3 A.M. showings on the local independent stations. As I get older and am prone to prostate problems, I also agree with the much younger Lizy Moromisato, who finds that one of the great conveniences of films on video "is that I can stop the machine if I feel like going to the restroom." The other side of the coin for her is that "renting movies is so much more affordable that now I am very picky about which movies I will go see in a theatre." Glinn Leevitt has similar feelings:

> I tend to see movies at home rather than the theatres. It is not a matter of preference, just convenience. I do not like watching a movie in a theatre with lots of people, nor do I like having to sit through two hours straight. Most of all I do not like paying $7.50 to see a movie that I may not like. This is why I am partial to watching them at home. I can watch a movie in silence. With a videotape, I can stop it to go to the bathroom or get something to drink. I can rewind it to a part I like or fast-forward it through the boring parts. The only time when I insist on seeing a movie in a theatre is when they are rereleased, such as revival theatres do. I have seen *2001*, *Queen Christina* (1933), *Akira Kurosawa's Dreams* (1990), *Casablanca*, and many greats on the big screen. I believe that seeing pictures like this in a theatre are the only ones worth paying an outrageous amount for.

An acquaintance of mine almost never sees movies in theatres. He and his wife rent videos so that they can constantly rewind to play a great bit of dialogue over and over. They drove their adult daughter screaming from the room by constantly repeating Judi Dench's great line in *Goldeneye* (1995), "If I want sarcasm, I can go home and get it from my children."

Lillian Khan buys videos "that I would not mind seeing again. It has to be especially interesting for me to buy a film. I do not intend to view the film immediately, but to create a library of the best, which I can look at from time to time as I feel like seeing again." Virginia Keene sees the same benefit in video rentals as well. She says that her and her husband's first VCR "and the movie rental orgy that followed all amount to a 'best' experience. Suddenly there was the opportunity to see movies again and again at whim. When I was growing up, if you didn't catch it at the local theatre, you didn't catch it all—ever. Now we can explore areas that were totally unavailable to us: foreign films, silents, documentaries. I'll never take videos for granted. They've made new realms of movies available to me. It's like having a smorgasbord at my beck and call!"

Michael Thomas also uses video "more as a tool for film analysis than entertainment. The distinction between the big screen and television is profound for me. I can enjoy a movie on video, free TV, or cable, but it is nowhere near the same as watching it in a theatre. . . . Why rent *The Godfather* films when I can see them playing around town at least once a year?" Armando Sanchez is also aware of that difference. He sees about five movies a week at his house, "if possible in the wide-screen format. I hate the pan-and-scanned version. Most of these formatted videos seem to be missing the magic you get at the theatre. Of course, nothing compares to the environment you get at the movies. . . . But you do get the full viewing space of the image as you remember seeing at the theatre." Albert Nazaryan likes the laserdisc player he bought with his first credit card for the same reason: to rent films in the wide-screen format.

Dennis Wilkes prefers video for foreign films, "then if I miss a subtitle, or a visual clue to reading the subtitles, I can go back and watch the segment again." It also helps that many videocassettes are subtitled in yellow, which makes them easier to read than the white subtitles on most films. And some cassettes even use the letterbox format to put the subtitles on the black band under the picture rather than on it. Other film instructors and I have found video a great way to study films, not only with the rewind and fast-forward functions, but with the single-frame pause.

Videocassette recorders also support family viewing of movies. Richard Bogren, now in his forties, quit cable eight years ago and "bought a VCR. We rent a lot of movies, but most are chosen by my sons. For many years, my wife and I avoided renting movies we felt might be unsuitable for the kids, and to some extent we still do (perhaps to avoid embarrassment rather than be censors). The kids' tastes in movies are eclectic; they often bring home 'oldies' that I enjoyed 'way back when.'" D'Arcy West's remembrance of *The Wizard of Oz*

is primarily my memory of my younger sister's obsession with that movie.

We had it on tape, and my little sister would watch it over and over, silently mouthing the dialogue all the way through. And even though we owned the movie, she would sob every time it was over until my mother would rewind it and start it up again. My sister would continue this until she exhausted herself. I would sometimes watch it with her, but I would watch her break into song and dance and then settle into her silent recitations of dialogue. When I see it today on TV, it feels very comforting to watch, and I surprise myself by knowing most of the words, too. (The only other movie my sister was so fascinated with was *Mommie Dearest.*)

Kurt Knecht grew up getting hooked on movies on cable, since his family did not take him to movies. Then his father "disconnected the cable, because he said we watched too much television. Somehow I got him to purchase a VHS machine." Knecht would scrape up the money to rent films and quickly got hooked on horror films on tape. However, not everybody was getting tapes legally. Skylaire Alfvegren remembers "seeing a bootleg copy of *The Rocky Horror Picture Show* (1975) at the age of seven, courtesy of my best friend's father's business trip to Japan. We giggled at the adult scenes, and I look back at our early repeated viewings of this and blame it for my lifelong fascination with drag queens."

Of course, there are disadvantages to watching—or trying to watch—films on video. Debra de St. Jean enjoys "renting videos more than going to a theatre to see a movie. . . . What I usually find happens is that I will go to the video store to rent 'a' movie and end up renting two or three movies, thinking I'll watch them over the course of the weekend—and I end up watching none of them." Kevin Kennedy's VCR was broken for a year, but at least "I always have free TV." Patrician Cortazar, a writer, appreciated video, "because I can view anything over in slow motion hundreds of times at my discretion and eat, which I love to do during a good film," but her moviegoing habits decreased in the nineties.

I have become "overinformationalized." With two telephone lines, an answering machine, a TV, VCR, Macintosh [computer], a fax, modem, cable. . . . I felt that I was becoming overindulged with unnecessary, frivolous information. I tried for a while just unplugging the TV and cables, so the automatic reflex action of going for the remote when one walks in the door was affected. But not enough. So I did the obvious right thing—I gave my TV and VCR to my homeless friend down the street so she could sell it to some poor unsuspecting soul. I did keep my tapes, though—PBS specials, science, documentaries on Bali, animals, Joseph Campbell, *Alice in Wonderland* (1951), *Dumbo* (1941), and *Apocalypse Now* were treasures that I did not want to part with.

Sang Sang Taing does not like to see movies on cassette because of the bad visual quality created in the duplication process. Anthony Thompson refuses to rent movies at current prices. "Whatever happened to new releases for ninety-nine cents? . . . The only time I watch movies on cassette is when somebody else pays." And sometimes the concern is not the money but the clerks. When Arnold Quinlan only recently got around to renting *Gone With the Wind*, "I found myself having to explain the reason I was renting this particular movie to the rental clerk. It just seemed embarrassing to be renting this movie to watch alone. As if I had picked it out myself. You know, instead of having a wife (or girlfriend) pick the film up to watch."

I have had similar experiences. Explaining you are a film teacher can cover a lot of strange rentals, and especially strange mixtures of rentals, like the time I rented in one haul a tape made up of Eadweard Muybridge's nineteenth-century photographs of movement, Michael Caine's seminar *Acting on Film*, two Russian silent films from the twenties, and Russ Meyer's *Vixen* (1968). Even one of the normally unflappable clerks at Vidiots, the best video store in Los Angeles, could not avoid wondering about the connections among those. (Oh, all right. The Muybridge and Russian films were of significance to me as a film historian, the Caine was educational in learning about film acting, and if I was going to watch all that heavy-duty stuff, I really needed a palate-cleanser to watch in the middle of them. Think of *Vixen* as a cup of sherbet. A big cup.)

Many people use the VCR to learn about film history, such as Scott Renshaw, who uses "video to fill in the gaps before I was a regular moviegoer, to see the acknowledged classics of the years before I was even born." Video also works to create nostalgia for films never seen before, as in Renshaw's case. When Dorian Wood first saw *Casablanca*, "it was a true crime—in color. On my living room couch, munching on greasy potato chips, I could not help but ponder through the entire film on how wonderful it must be to see this film in black-and-white. The pale pastel colors used would often distract me from what was going on. The film, nonetheless, was exceptional."

Seeing a classic film again on videotape may create the same feeling the film originally did. For Lilia Fuller, viewing on tape "is almost like the first time, simply because I would never rent a video if I didn't expect to be mesmerized by the movie." Richard Morales has rented *Casablanca* several times, always trying to "see if I can put together better what is happening between Rick and Ilsa, but I always get caught up in the interesting characters and great performances. I like the bartender, the German waiter, and probably most of all, Claude Rains. As a kid, I had always seen a fatter Peter Lorre in monster movies, but I only came to appreciate him in the skinny movies he was in—*The Maltese Falcon* (1941) and *Casablanca*."

Video can even motivate people to see a film again in a theatre, such as Donna Crisci, who loves "the experience of being in a theatre and will go see a film on screen that I have a video copy of at home." Alejandro Munoz saw *Citizen Kane* for the first time on video and "must admit that this experience in no way compared to the second viewing of it on a big screen." D'Arcy West saw the first two *Godfather* movies "back-to-back on tape. These are my favorite movies ever. I've since gone to see them in the theatre, like special engagement showings, and loved them so much. . . . I re-rent them every time I meet someone who hasn't seen them, and I make them watch it with me."

Antonio Olivas "first saw *Casablanca* on TV and later at a movie house, and the difference was astounding: almost magical. Conversely, seeing *Top Gun* at the theatres was 'way cool,' but seeing it on TV was only 'OK.'" Other films can seem different when seen later on tape. For Edwin Castro, *Star Wars* on the small screen "lost its magic. Things were not so lifelike on TV." But sometimes the change can be for the better. Susanna Serrano says, "Most of the movies that I have seen on tape more than once, I always seem to get a better picture of the movie in my home watching it over and over. My views of the movie *Raiders of the Lost Ark* changed when I saw it on video, because I got more of the field of the meaning of the story line than when I saw it on the big screen." Brian Calderon has *Citizen Kane* on tape at home and "every time I watch it, I get something different out of it."

Shawn Taylor says, "A film that worked for me on both big screen and videotape was *Speed* [1994]. It must be because the film didn't necessarily thrive on special effects. This is, of course, excluding the bombings. . . . The nonstop action was 'fun-filling' and a sense of suspense dawned over me, like I was wondering what's going to happen next. . . . One film that also worked both on film and videotape was *Schindler's List*. I was deeply touched by the graphic scenes in the film." Taylor saw *Batman* (1989) in the theatre and hated it, although he sort of liked Jack Nicholson's performance. "I really appreciated his performance even more on videotape. Because I had the luxury of reviewing his parts over and over and forwarding through the rest of the hideous film."

David Bromley "actually liked *Pulp Fiction* better on video. I really don't know why, maybe because of the scenes that Quentin Tarantino showed at the end of the film that had been edited out from the final film." Marcus Franklin was "glad" he saw *Independence Day* (1996) at home on video, especially since he had not paid to rent it. It was a "bad movie, but decent since I saw it at home." Five years after Kurt Knecht saw and enjoyed "the little gags" in *The Gumball Rally* (1976), a film about a cross-country car race, Knecht "got my local video store to purchase a copy in order for me to rent it. The film was ultra-bad. I couldn't believe that I had reveled in this film five years before. I felt embarrassed for having recommended the film to my video store."

In the late eighties, Sam Frank was a professional film critic. He had seen *The Tall Guy*, a 1989 British comedy, in the critics' screening and loved it.

When I saw *The Tall Guy* again on television, and by myself, it moved slowly. What I had found hilarious the first time didn't even make me chuckle the second. I can tell you why. Comedy needs an audience. I had seen it with two-dozen other critics the first time, and we were sparking each other with laughter. Without that audience, it died on a small screen. Conversely, *Shadowlands* (1993) is a literate biographical drama in an academic setting I wanted to be part of myself. Seeing this movie on a screen with six hundred other adults, it captivated me and made me cry.

A week ago, I saw it again on my TV via tape, and by the second hour, it was agonizingly slow. Reduction to a nineteen-inch screen and lack of a theatre audience to react with had the movie putting me to sleep. Home video is far more convenient than all the time and expense of seeing the same movie in a theatre, but there are many times when we pay the cost of being bored by a story that would otherwise have us in its grip.

I, on the other hand, not only laughed at *The Tall Guy* in theatres, but laugh at it every year when I look at it on video.

David Morales says, "With most movies, my take on them stays the same whether I see it in the theatre or on video. The big exceptions are action-type movies or movies with lots of grand scenery. Those are just so much better on the larger-scale medium of the movie theatre screen. All other movies I think look better on the big screen, too, but not to the same degree and not so radically." There is no question that the big, noisy action films of the eighties and nineties can work supremely well in the theatre. Oscar Berkovich remembers

a couple of years ago, back when I was a kid, that I had to beg my big brother to take me out to see *Rambo Two* [technically it was *Rambo: First Blood Part II* (1985)] the first day. I told him that it couldn't be just in any ordinary theatre—it had to be at the Mann's Chinese, and so it was. I can clearly recall it as if it were yesterday. Waiting in line for about four hours to go in. All the audience sitting quietly and patiently for the film to start, and all of a sudden when the curtains went up, the roaring and screaming of the audience was unbelievable. It was amazing. Every adventure that he undertook and every breath he would take, I would take it with him. I remember constantly getting up from my seat and sharing my emotions with the audience when Rambo was saving the POW. The combination of those action sequences and the music beautifully blending in really

turned me on. For me it was an unforgettable experience. I was screaming and slapping my hands so loud that for a second there I thought that
Rambo was really hearing me and responding to my physical and emotional reactions. Not all movies hit me like the way this film did.

Because the industry was hoping for that kind of reaction, it was making
movies that piled on the action, the music, and the noise. While they made
money, the films were losing some of the qualities that had made American
films so memorable that audiences were nostalgic for them. Chuck Ross proved
the point in 1982.[12]

Ross was the literary trickster who a few years before had typed up a manuscript version of Jerzy Kozinski's National Book Award-winning novel *Steps*
and submitted it under a pseudonym to fifteen different publishers, including its original publisher. All of them turned it down. In the early eighties, he
tried the same thing with Hollywood agents (since studios generally do not
read material unless it comes in from an agency). He typed up the screenplay
for *Casablanca*, changing the name to the title of the play it was based on,
Everybody Comes to Rick's, attached his usual pseudonym, and sent it to 217
agencies. Ninety of the agencies did not read it, because they do not read
unsolicited material. Eighty-five of them read the script. Thirty-three recognized it as *Casablanca* and wrote back to Ross, saying things like "Have some
excellent ideas on casting this wonderful script, but most of the actors are
dead." Three agencies that did not recognize the script wanted to represent
Ross. Eight agencies noticed it was similar to, but not the same as, *Casablanca*
and made criticisms and suggestions. Forty-one rejected it. Among the comments were "too much dialogue, not enough exposition, the story line was
weak," "dialogue could have been sharper," "too much dialogue for amount
of action." One agency noted that action-adventure movies were selling better now, and said, "A new writer today, unless you can come up with an action-adventure type of thing, I mean T&A, I'm talking Tits and Ass type of
show...." Another pointed out that "the biggest success today is *Raiders of the
Lost Ark*. It's purely escape.... It's not gory, it's not morose, it keeps you on
the edge of your seat. You completely forget the outside world, you completely forget your troubles. You're wrapped up in identifying with the people
up there on the screen."

In a sidebar to Ross's article, Richard Corliss expanded on the differences
between *Raiders* and *Casablanca*, noting that "*Raiders of the Lost Ark* was all
show; *Casablanca* is mostly tell." He thought, and probably rightly so, that
Casablanca could not get made in 1982, and he explained why. "The script lacks
or evades hot B.O. [box office] elements for 1982. The sex is all innuendo. The
special effects are limited to a few animated maps. There is only one teenager in

the story, and she is Bulgarian. The one chase scene lasts but a few seconds; the climactic fight lasts one punch. . . . People talk instead of acting. Or, rather, talk leads to action. This is a romantic melodrama that operated in the cloudland of ideas and ideals." American culture had changed, and with it American audiences for new theatrical films, regardless of any nostalgic feeling they may still have held for *Casablanca*.

14 *Promoting Habits*

The screenplay of *Casablanca* did not fit what Hollywood was making in 1982 at least partly because of the change in the pattern of distribution of films since *Casablanca* was made. In the heyday of the major studios, films were shown first in the largest cities (New York, Chicago, Los Angeles), then several weeks later in smaller cities, and later still in small towns. Thus, over a period of weeks or months, a film could build up a reputation, facilitated by critical comments, newspaper advertising, and most importantly word-of-mouth discussion. Some films were given a wide release, but they were generally the bad ones from which studios wanted to bring in as much money as quickly as they could, before the bad word of mouth spread too far.

In the seventies, the distribution pattern began to change, and wide release of films became the norm. Early in the decade, there were wider releases for such films as *Billy Jack* and *Magnum Force* (1973). In 1975, *Jaws* opened in 409 theatres at the same time and was an enormous success, which led to even wider releases. In 1978, *Grease* opened in 902 theatres.[1] By the late nineties, simultaneous openings in over 2,000 theatres were not uncommon; in the 1998 Christmas season, ten movies opened in over 2,000 theatres each.[2] However, to support such saturation openings, it is necessary to promote the films with heavy advertising to create instantaneous widespread awareness. National television advertising is needed to support a nationwide opening of a film. So as the costs of making a picture increased, the cost of marketing films increased. In 1974, the cost of making an average studio film was $2.5 million, and the cost of marketing it was $1 million. By 1995, the average cost of a studio film was $34 million, and the average marketing cost was $16 million, and most of the increased marketing cost was from television advertising.[3] This is not surprising in view of the fact that a 1994 Gallup poll conducted for *Variety* showed that most people learned more about individual films from television than from any other source.[4]

All of this affected which movies got made and how they were made. As producer and former head of Twentieth Century-Fox Lawrence Gordon said in 1991 about his selection of material, "I want to be able to see how we can make a trailer from that script. And if you can make a picture that will fit that trailer, then I know how we can sell the picture."[5] Justin Wyatt, in his excellent book *High Concept: Movies and Marketing in Hollywood*,[6] shows how filmmaking itself in the eighties was focused on finding the various marketing hooks to help sell the film. These included the use of strong images and quick cutting in the trailers, strong visual images that can be transferred to print ads, and increasingly, the use of music—not only in the film and trailers but also on records and CDs—as promotion for the film. By the nineties, Hollywood was the undisputed Land of Hype and Glorification. I was mildly amused when on a trip to England in the summer of 1994 I heard people complain about a few too many posters advertising *The Flintstones*. I restrained myself from telling them what it was like in Los Angeles that summer: *The Flintstones* were *everywhere*— in television ads, in movie trailers, in toys at fast-food outlets—not just on a measly couple of posters.

The principal way movie audiences get their hype is through trailers of upcoming films, whether they see them on television or in theatres. Not surprisingly, trailers have changed over time. MGM marketing chief in 1991, Greg Morrison, said, "They've gotten much more sophisticated. At first [in the thirties], trailers were like book reports, spiced up with flaming words and a stentorian narration. They were simply a synopsis of what was coming. But in the late sixties and early seventies, they were transformed from an informational tool to an advertising tool. The studios realized you could shape the trailer to produce a very attractive product—and systematically weed out segments of the film you didn't want to show."[7] To that end, the makers of trailers use the same kind of market research to test trailers that producers use to test films. Testing showed that audiences were not getting the joke until a third of the way through the original trailer for *The Naked Gun* (1988), so the trailer was recut to emphasize the humor.[8]

Producer Rob Cohen particularly stresses the value of the theatrical trailer: "What makes a trailer so important is that it's the first time a paying audience is exposed to your film in the venue where it's going to play—it's on the screen and in the dark, bigger than life. So you're trying to present your film the way you'd present yourself at the front door on a blind date. You want to put your best foot forward."[9] Sometimes you succeed.

Movie audiences have grown to expect, know, and sometimes love trailers. Robin Magee says, "Generally you can judge how good a movie is, whether you should just rent it, or whether you've just seen the entire movie (the good-parts version). The best trailers are the ones that *don't* tell you the whole movie and even make fun of themselves a bit. The one for *In the Line of Fire* (1993) was great, didn't give too much away. The *Wayne's World* (1992) preview that pretended to be *The Addams Family* (1991) was also good." Rigo Fernandez has come to "believe they have grown weak in disguising the film's shabbiness if the film is truly shabby. At the same time, they do tend to help in choosing your film before you go . . . the ones I loved to see were the ones for horror films; just watching them gave me the chills." Which helps explain the continuing production of horror films by the studios: they are incredibly easy to cut trailers for.

Michael Thomas, a one-time projectionist, remembers several trailers. "The one for *Jaws* comes immediately to mind. The John Williams score would fill the speakers as the voice-over soundtrack would say something like 'when God created evil, he created Jaws.' The visual was a murky underwater POV [point of view] of the shark. It was actually a simple trailer by design but very effective. I remember the trailer of *Apocalypse Now* from television. Wagner's 'Ride of the Valkyries' echoed as a series of stills from the film were rapidly cut together in a patchwork effect on the screen."

Like Thomas and the *Apocalypse Now* trailer, Valerie Hornig remembers the trailers that are "fast-paced, intense like the ones for *Jaws, The Exorcist, Jurassic Park, Speed, Fatal Attraction* (1987), *The Hand That Rocks the Cradle* (1992), *Terminator 2,* (1991), and *Aliens* (1986)." Darcie Cushwell remembers the trailers for all the *Jaws* movies, primarily because "I always wanted to see more and they hardly showed the shark." Actually, the original *Jaws* trailer is not quite as quickly cut together as Hornig and others remember it. Looking at it today, what is striking about the trailer for *Jaws* is that Spielberg's name is never mentioned and appears only in a general list of the credits at the end of the trailer. The reason is simple. Before *Jaws*, Spielberg was an unknown. Afterwards, of course . . .

When I taught the film history course at UCLA, I ran a group of trailers from the UCLA Film Archive, including one that had been a personal favorite of mine, the trailer Bud Smith cut for *Sorcerer*.[10] It is an extraordinary piece of film editing, and it was the only one of the bunch that made students ask me about the film, since by then the 1977 film had been forgotten. A few of the students saw the film on tape on their own and agreed the trailer was much better than the film.

Another trailer that caught the public's eye was the one for *Star Wars*. Michael Behling remembers seeing the original trailer for the film when he was about seven. "Leaving the theatre, I told my parents that I really wanted to see *Star Wars* and that I was very impressed by it. My dad (and my mom I think agreed) was surprised and thought the movie looked absolutely terrible. Perhaps I remember this incident for some sort of Freudian reason, because it felt very satisfying to be right against my dad."

The trailer for *Return of the Jedi* followed the same pattern as was used in the trailers for the first two *Star Wars* films: a lot of detail but leaving out some-thing crucial, in this case Jabba the Hutt. In the fall of 1998, the first trailer for the fourth *Star Wars* film made its debut in theatres, and the anticipation was so strong that people stood in line just to see the trailer, leaving before whatever film was playing started. I did not catch the *Star Wars: Episode I: The Phantom Menace* trailer until a couple of weeks into its run, and by then there was a curious reaction: none. There was a *big* reaction to the trailer that was shown after it—a brilliant parody of the *Star Wars* trailers that turned into a trailer for the next Austin Powers movie, *Austin Powers: The Spy Who Shagged Me* (1999). As it turned out, the anticipation for the next episode of *Star Wars* grew so much over the next few months that in the immediate run-up to the film's May 1999 release, Fox figured they did not have to advertise as much as it might for a less-anticipated movie. And they were right. In the weeks preceding the re-lease, Fox spent only $10 million in advertising, as opposed to the expected $15 to $20 million.[11] And the picture still opened to record grosses.

The trailers for *The Shining* (1980) and *Poltergeist II* (1986) stand out in Paul Sbrizzi's mind because of their "tag lines": "Heeeere's Johnny" and "They're ba-ack." However, Sbrizzi thought the trailer for *Marathon Man* (1976) was "a work of art in and of itself, the way it took the clips from the movie and ar-ranged them into a sort of paranoid poem." Similarly, Patrick O'Leary remem-bers two trailers "very strongly (and in one case, turned out to be better than the actual film). They were for *Looking for Mr. Goodbar* and *The Exorcist II: The Heretic*, both from 1977. These probably seem like odd choices, but I think the reason these trailers worked for me was because there was no dialogue or voice-over in them, only music and images. I remember the editing and music made them both interesting and different from other trailers."

In some cases, the stunning image in the trailer started with the trailer and only later got into the film. For the 1991 film *Robin Hood: Prince of Thieves*, Seiniger Advertising, the company that made the trailer, created a shot of an arrow's point of view as it flies through the air to its target. The image was so striking that the bit of film was cut into the picture.[12] Which didn't impress Ira Katz, since because of the bad critical reaction to the movie he never saw it, but he loved the trailer and "the way the arrow was filmed. It said so much with so little." Katz was not the only one who loved the image. It showed up two years later in parody form in the trailer for Mel Brooks's *Robin Hood: Men in Tights* and also in the film *Hot Shots: Part Deux*. As Brian Fox, whose agency created the ads for *Hot Shots: Part Deux*, said, "Movies are basically the same stories being reexecuted over and over with different twists. If the story lines don't change that much, why should the ads?"[13]

Another element of the original *Robin Hood: Prince of Thieves* trailer struck Scott Renshaw: "It used the score from *Willow* (1988) and made a really bad film look interesting." Using previously composed music is a common practice for trailers, for the same reason it was used in this trailer. Joel Wayne, then senior vice president of worldwide advertising at Warners, said, "When we did the initial trailer, no one had composed any music for the feature, so we had to improvise. Tony Seiniger, who was doing the trailer, came up with the idea for [using the music from] *Willow*, which created the perfect adventure atmosphere and really sold the images we had from the film."[14]

If one knows the original source of the music, this borrowing can be irritating. I love Thomas Newman's score for *Little Women* (1994), but it seemed irritatingly sentimental when used on the trailer for *Something to Talk About* (1995). On the other hand, the use of Edvard Grieg's music from *Peer Gynt* in the original trailer for the film version of Stephen King's *Needful Things* (1993) brought out a satirical edge that the film's score, added to the later trailers, did not capture. After seeing the first trailer, I had thought I might see the film, but I decided against it after seeing the second one. If they were dumb enough to screw up their picture with a bad score when they could have used Grieg, I was not about to give them any money.

The potential blockbuster films of the eighties and nineties came to depend on their trailers. Scott Renshaw remembers one trailer that stands "head and shoulders above the others. That would be the trailer for *Batman*, which began appearing in theatres about six months before its release in June of 1989. Everyone in the theatre went absolutely nuts. It was one of the most skillfully crafted trailers I had ever seen and did exactly what it was supposed to do . . . create anticipation for the film itself." The trailer—and the promotion for the film—hyped the film into becoming a box office success.

One of the most vivid trailers of the nineties was the one for *Independence Day*. After the film opened, Darrin Burrell wrote, "I am still fascinated by the blowing up of the White House. I guess since this trailer has been shown for so long in the theatres, it had a lasting impression on me, making me want to go see this movie as soon as it was released in the theatres." David Bromley also remembers "how they hyped it for months and everyone else seemed to be copying it!" Not everyone was copying it; it just seemed that way. The best rip-off was so good it fooled Michael Behling. "It was an *Independence Day* trailer at first. It said something like 'they're coming . . .' There was all this buildup in Dolby Stereo, and then just as it climaxes and as the audience waits expectantly for something amazing, such as a spacecraft—maybe even a spacecraft destroying the White House—a huge Technicolor smiling face appears, and the speakers blast out the Brady Bunch theme song and advertise that movie. So apparently the projectionist spliced those two trailers together. It was hilarious." It was not the projectionist. It was just a brilliant parody of the *Independence Day* trailer by the creators of the trailer for *A Very Brady Sequel* (1996).

With the nonpotential blockbuster—the film with a limited audience—the job of selling the film is even more challenging. The flashy techniques do not necessarily fit the film, and subtler ways have to be found. The Miramax Company, headed by Harvey and Bob Weinstein, specialized in the nineties in promoting offbeat films to surprisingly large box office results. They took a moderate hit in England, *The Crying Game* (1992), and turned it into a phenomenal success in America. However, Miramax's technique of making the film's secret plot twist a publicity point did not work when they tried it again two years later with *The Advocate.* Audiences who thought Jaye Davidson was cute as a button did not really care that the advocate's client was . . . a pig. Mark Gill, who was the head of Columbia's publicity department before he went to Miramax, put it this way: "Working at a [big] studio, you learn how to put up the biggest tent. Only at Miramax, they're trying to do the same thing on much less money."[15]

Gill later recalled one person's reaction after a critics' screening of Miramax's 1996 film *The English Patient.* "You have to make it commercially successful? Good luck!"[16] Gill and Miramax spent between $27 and $30 million on promoting the film, which is not exactly a small tent, but they spent wisely. According to Miramax marketing executive Marcy Granata, Miramax's goal with *The English Patient* was to "make this an event film not like *Independence Day* or *Twister* (1994), but an emotional event." They wanted to avoid selling the film "as a small, precious film" but as an epic "with big emotions, sweeping environments and story of intrigue, romance, and betrayal."[17] In other words, not another *Casablanca*, but a nineties equivalent of *Casablanca*. The initial marketing campaign focused on the romantic story elements and the visual sweep. Research showed that while women were interested in seeing the film after the first ads, men were not yet. The promotion shifted focus to the wartime action a few weeks before the film opened, and the film became a major box office success with both men and women.

Trailers for art films can be just as striking as trailers for big audience films. Angela West thought the trailer for Sally Potter's 1993 *Orlando* was "spectacular," since it was "done to entice the audience to see this movie. The reason being that after seeing the trailer you had no idea what the movie was about." Daniel Barr thinks the best trailer he ever saw was for *Howard's End* (1992). "I knew nothing about the film or many of the actors except that I had heard some of their names. When I saw it, it made all the hair on my body stand on end. I have never experienced anything like it before or afterward. It was a sublime experience." I was more irritated by that trailer than dazzled. It was a collection of stills with no dialogue, although it was obvious that the film was going to have literate dialogue. The probable reason the trailer did not include dialogue is that there were sound problems with the film, which were not entirely solved in the first stereo mixes of the film.

In the nineties, selling films about African Americans—to either predominantly African American audiences or predominantly white audiences, or to both—was complicated. In 1991, Columbia managed to sell *Boyz N The Hood* to multiracial audiences. The first ads were focused on the African American audience and focused on the hard edge of the story.[18] Shawn Taylor saw one of the earliest ads for the film. "It was first broadcast on Superbowl Sunday. It had an inner-city flavor to it and seemed very interesting. All the action scenes were shown on the trailers. It was presented to be a violent inner-city-based film. But to my surprise, it wasn't only that." When the studio wanted to broaden the audience, the ads began to focus on the critics' praise of the film.[19] Two years later, New Line started its ad campaign for *Menace II Society* with the emphasis on the violence in the story, then shifted the focus to the personal stories of the characters, including the love story.[20] The earlier trailer attracted Ervin Riggs. "I was so eager to see the movie, because the previews reminded me of the lifestyle I used to live when I was growing up. It's kind of sad, because selling dope, gang-banging, and shooting at people was just a way of life where I grew up. It's like a tunnel vision if that's all you see and that's all you are exposed to, then that's all you think exist. I just thank God I was able to escape that lifestyle of living."

Not everybody loves trailers. Virginia Keene is very emphatic about her feelings:

I loathe and despise trailers and try my damnedest not to see them. I avert my eyes and try to mute the sound in my head because they've spoiled so many movies for me. They either distort the movie or reveal it by showing the best bits. *Groundhog Day* (1993) is a good example of distortion. The trailer made it appear to be slapstick—a shallow *Saturday Night Live*-vintage Bill Murray skit. I almost stayed away because of the trailer. Perhaps I'm mistaken, but it seems to me that trailers didn't used to be this manipulative and invasive. I do know that they didn't always enrage me! Still, I remember few of them well. I do fondly recall the trailers for *Psycho* and *The Birds*, William Castle trailers as a group [Castle was a fifties cut-rate Hitchcock who used gimmicks such as electric shocks administered to some theatre seats to hype his films], and fifties Westerns as a group. It seems to me they used to entice us and tease us with glimpses and bold sweeping titles and hyperbole. They don't tease me now; they assault me, pummel me. Now only Woody Allen seems to respect that tradition of sweet secrecy. I love his trailers. They merely tell me there's a "Woody" on the way!

The one trailer I will always best remember is the one for Coppola's *Bram Stoker's Dracula* and that's because I DIDN'T watch it. It wasn't easy, but I was forewarned and determined to be surprised by the film. I vowed never to look at the trailer. I looked away from the TV, closed my eyes at the movie theatre . . . for MONTHS! I couldn't close my ears, and so the words were committed to memory long before the film opened, but I never saw the insidious little thing. I even videotaped it with only the sound cues for reference, because by that time I was curious to see if it was worth all of the self-restraint involved. Until then, I had no idea how omnipresent and how tantalizing the nasty things are! Well, I held out. Although the film was a general disappointment, it *was* a visual banquet, and I *was* pleased that I'd never seen any of it before. As I thought, the trailer did indeed cheat the audience by revealing some of the best bits.

Scott Hemmann is not quite so fanatical: "A movie trailer can have the power to make me want to see the film or totally turn me off of a film."

People in the industry are aware of the delicacy of the problem. Joe Roth started his career cutting trailers for television and went on to head film production at Twentieth Century-Fox and, later, Disney. He said in 1991, "A bad trailer can hurt much more than a good trailer can help. When I see a bad trailer, you'll never get me back, no matter how many TV ad buys you make. As a moviegoer, I've already made up my mind. You just can't recover from that."[21] That same year TriStar put the first trailer for *Hudson Hawk* into theatres, and audiences were baffled by the combination of action and comedy, so the company did a second, all-action trailer. It did not help, and the picture bombed.[22]

As one might expect, trailers are often tested in Los Angeles theatres before they are widely shown. Nancy Lathrop recalls one example—the first trailer for the 1980 version of *The Blue Lagoon*, starring Brooke Shields.

The audience was in hysterics. It was the funniest trailer, unintentionally. We were just howling, because it had all those little Brooke Shields lines. It would be Christopher whatever-his-name-is standing with a loincloth or doing something. Cut to Brooke looking at him with her big eyebrows and then back to him saying, "What are you looking at?" and she'd say, "Your muscles." And this was in the trailer, like this would make you go and see it. And I can remember we just thought it was hilarious. And then as we walked out of the theatre, we got hit up by a marketing firm asking us our opinion. I mean, obviously the studio wasn't real sure, either. And we told him. The guy said, "You're real polite," and he showed us what everyone else had said. And I remember that the trailer was pulled. I feel very lucky to have gotten to see it.

Lathrop later worked for Kaleidoscope, a company that made trailers, which gave her a "heightened awareness" of trailers. She gets suspicious if the trailer is too good and doesn't go to the movie, because she thinks she's seen all the best parts. If the trailer is not good, then "it may mean the movie is good because it's got plot and some complications, something they can't squeeze into three minutes."

The rationale for putting the best of the film in the trailer is explained by Bob Israel, the cofounder of Aspect Ratio, the largest independent company working on trailers. "One thing we hear is 'How can you give away the best jokes?' The fact is the studio has an average investment of $50 million to $60 million. If you don't pull out all the stops, then you don't get people in the seats for the first weekend. And then it's very hard for the movie to build to a successful level."[23] Unfortunately, the films often do not live up to the parts shown in the trailer. Carlos Gabriel Nino says, "*Cape Fear, Malcolm X, Twister, RoboCop* (1987), *Higher Learning* (1995), *Boyz N the Hood*, and *Terminator 2* are all movies I wanted to see from the trailers. They either had good music, intriguing images or controversial contents. I liked a few of them, but I really liked the trailers!"

Julio Carmona grew up in Los Angeles and remembers

we usually got all the trailers and all the propaganda, so the extra excitement was always there. . . .

My worst movie experience was when I saw the first *Batman* movie. I remember all the commercials and trailers. The buildup was just too much. I was looking forward to seeing this movie for a while. Finally, on opening night a bunch of friends got together and went to see the movie. There was definitely a lot of excitement inside as the audience sat down to get ready for the feature. When the movie was over, I was really disappointed. The picture itself was terrible. Everybody left the theatre silent. The movie experience definitely taught me that you could not always believe advertisements. You have to learn how to choose a picture you are going to like.

Peter Albers had a slightly different reaction to the hype surrounding *Batman Returns* (1992). "Often the glorification of violence in the trailers in some movies—despite the fact that that may have nothing to do with what the true sentiment of the film is—can keep me from enjoying the film. I thought *Batman II* [*Batman Returns* is the official title] was a very entertaining film, but the fact that I was sitting in the audience with a lot of seven- to twelve-year-olds, to whom this film had been marketed, really gave me the heebie-jeebies."

Patrician Cortazar does not "like it when trailers give a false impression of the movie just to sell it. *The Hunt for Red October* (1990) is one that I recall. For once, I wanted to see an action film, and they utilized all three explosion scenes in the trailer, making it look like an intense film—not so." The focus on action in the trailer came from Paramount's market research, which showed that their target audience was put off by the political elements of the story, which were eliminated from the ads.[24] For Debra de St. Jean, "It was not the movie *My Life* (1993) that had an impact on me but the trailer is what I remember." The trailer Eric Joyner remembers best was "the biggest flop of the decade (*Waterworld* [1995]). I remember all of the hype surrounding this film, how it was the most expensive film ever mad [I think he means "made," but with *Waterworld,* I would not bet on it] and it ended up being horrible."

Moe Gardener thinks "the best trailer I have ever seen was for *Mission: Impossible* (1996). The trailer was fast-paced, exciting, and sexy—everything you look for in a throwaway film like this—except the film was slow, confusing and stale." Sangbum Lee saw the same trailer, "but I never went to see the movie, because I perceived that the movie was going to be nothing but a collection of such action scenes, and I don't like a movie that just tries to overwhelm me with action."

What should be apparent from the reactions of these moviegoers is that sometimes the hype for a film works and sometimes it does not. Bill Pulliam and his wife saw the trailer for *Rush* (1991) on the video of *Thelma & Louise,* never having seen Jason Patric before. They hunted down *Rush* and all his other films, and he has become their favorite actor. On the other hand, Terrence Atkins says, "I'm pretty typical in respect to catching most of the big blockbusters. If it's got a lot of hype on television or in the trades, I'll go." But he also admits, "*Strange Days* (1995) had a *great* trailer. Ralph Fiennes speaking directly to the audience like a drug pusher. Although it didn't draw me into buying a ticket."

Very often, when the hype does not work, it flames out in spectacular fashion. In 1978, Paramount tried to promote *Sgt. Pepper's Lonely Hearts Club Band* the same way it had with the hit *Grease* the same year. As Justin Wyatt points out, "Although the research proved that the film had an unusually high level of preawareness, word of mouth was uniformly negative. [Producer Robert] Stigwood's film possessed excellent marketability, but very poor playability."[25] Columbia Studios spent between ten and thirteen million dollars in 1982 to promote the film *Annie* (including such film tie-ins as Annie dolls in the Sears, Roebuck and Company back-to-school catalogs, Swensen's "Annie" Flavor-of-the-Month ice cream, and tie-ins with F.A.O. Schwartz department store in New York City), but it did not help.[26] The film was outgrossed that year not only by *E.T.* but also by *Rocky III, On Golden Pond,* and *Porky's.*[27] A year later, Warners tried four separate ad campaigns for the critically acclaimed *The Right Stuff,* but none of them worked.[28] *The Right Stuff* was outgrossed by *Trading Places, Staying Alive,* and *Porky's II: The Next Day.*[29]

The year 1990 was particularly bad for highly hyped movies. Beginning in the summer, with the disastrous attempt by producer Don Simpson to do "*Top*

Gun in racing cars" with *Days of Thunder*, the year saw such box office disasters as *RoboCop II*, *Rocky V*, *Another 48 HRS.*, *Air America*, and *Havana*. Ironically, this last film was yet another attempt to duplicate *Casablanca* but brought nothing fresh to the material, unlike *The English Patient*. The failure of such hyped pictures proves William Goldman's famous dictum about the movie business: "Nobody knows anything." By that he means that "not one person in the entire motion picture field *knows* for a certainty what's going to work."[30]

The converse of the overhyped flops are the "sleepers"—the pictures that do much better than expected. They have always been part of the movie industry, but in the age of hype, their successes are all the more surprising. Nikki Finke, writing in the *Los Angeles Times*, thought *Mystic Pizza* (1988) "may have been a movie that succeeded in spite of its ads, not because of them, thanks to a lot of word of mouth. Several experts believe the early campaign didn't tell viewers strongly enough why the movie was special or why it would appeal to adults."[31] Seven years later, the thriller *Se7en* (1995) knocked such highly promoted films as *Jade*, *Strange Days*, and the Demi Moore version of *The Scarlet Letter* down the box office charts. Surprised by its success, the marketing people responsible for *Se7en* generally thought it was the film's originality that made it a hit.[32]

A survey by the National Research Group in 1994 suggested that word of mouth was not nearly as important as television advertising, but their question was about *awareness* of a film. Their survey showed that 55–60 percent of the awareness of films came from television advertising, but only 15–20 percent was from word of mouth.[33] Word of mouth probably has more of an influence in peoples' decisions to see a film, but not in the simple way we usually think. Traditionally, word of mouth is thought of as basically one person recommending a film to another. But it is more complicated than that. What happens as a film builds to its release, as well as *after* its release, is that everything about the film—trailers, radio ads, critical comments, publicity, stars on talk shows, news stories, discussions on the Internet, as well as traditional word of mouth—builds up an image of the film. Or rather several images. One is the general image for the public as a whole, but individual filmgoers develop their own impressions, which may be different from the general image. Those images, rather than just the promotional efforts of the distributor, determine whether individuals and groups will see the film. As Lew Wasserman, a longtime studio head, was reported to have said, "If they don't want to see your film, you can't make them."[34]

Charles Champlin, the film critic and, later, arts editor for the *Los Angeles Times*, once threw a line into one of his columns stating that movies exist by the "consent of the entertained," which struck me as one of the most truthful things ever said about film audiences. The relationships between films and their audiences are often thought of as straightforward: films persuade us to do whatever the filmmaker wants us to do. But even some of the earliest research into movie audiences shows us that has never really been the case. In 1928, the Reverend William Short, executive director of the pro-censorship National Committee for Study of Social Values in Motion Pictures, wrote a four-hundred-page document regarding all the evil things said about the influence of movies. He realized that he did not have the evidence to back up any of his charges, so he got a $200,000 grant from the Payne Fund to have social scientists study the impact of the movies. This produced the multivolume Payne Studies in 1933, which, unfortunately for Reverend Short, showed that more often than not, movies did not affect attitudes. The good Reverend was not happy,[35] and if you look closely at the research that has been done since, rather than at the politicians and antimedia peoples' claims about the research, you will find that social scientists usually come to more or less the same conclusions the researchers in the Payne Studies did.[36] The above sections on trailers and their persuasiveness and *lack of persuasiveness* demonstrate most clearly how that happens in real life.

Again, the relationships between the movies and the audiences are incredibly complex. To begin to get a deeper sense of the range and complexity of how we deal with film, we will now look at the wide variety of habits, experiences, and emotions of moviegoers before returning with a final look at a star/filmmaker and his audiences, followed by a concluding thought or two.

Let us start with the moviegoing habits of audiences. Like questionnaire respondent Lilia Fuller, I could describe my own moviegoing habits as "vigorous." In 1998, to take a typical year, I paid to see 134 movies in theatres, saw another 14 for free at various screenings, rented and saw 60 more on video, and watched another 63 on free television or on videos that I already owned. I see big movies, little movies, new ones, and old ones. And because I am a film historian, I can deduct the costs on my income tax return.

Kalani Mondoy sees a large number of movies and describes his habit:

During the summer and winter holiday season, I try to see as many movies as possible. . . . I often read or listen to different reviews of some movies, and sometimes they change my mind as to whether or not to see a particular film. . . . And I like to see something different in the context of the story.

The summer season is so saturated with new films I can usually see a new one every weekend. Especially after payday. Sometimes I'll see two movies on the weekend, but that usually happens when there are a lot of movies that I want to see immediately before they go into limited theatres, which are usually smaller. I also try to keep track of what movies I want to see, find out exactly when they come out in order to plan which movies I should see first. If there is a lot of commotion about a certain film, I may go see it first rather than one with lesser promotion.

Scott Hemmann tends "to lose interest in movies after they've been out for a while, and if I haven't seen one within the first couple of weeks of release, I generally decide not to see it at all, even if it's a film I've really wanted to see. I love the moviegoing experience. It is important to me to arrive early enough to get a good seat on the aisle—not too close to the screen and not too far back. The coming attractions are important to me. After the movie is over, I like to stay through the final credits."

When Richard Morales is "at the theatre, I feel more committed and so rarely walk out on a movie. . . . I can splurge on a movie or two a week, but I don't always splurge on the two or three hours it takes to watch a movie . . . I depend a lot on the recommendations of friends and even the critics before I go see a movie." Conrad Hilton works as a barber and gets "many opinions on the different films and usually know what they are about before I go see them."

While growing up in San Francisco, Kulani Jackson would check out the reviews of such critics as Gerald Nachman (Jackson liked him for providing "the most vicious reviews") and Judith Stone, then "I would call the appropriate friend for the type of movie I was to see. If it was an arty film, I would wear a scarf and dress conservatively. If it was a slick Hollywood production, I would go casual. The friend I brought usually matched both the movie and the dress code. So I would literally wear 'drag' to the theatre!" When he moved to Los Angeles, he was "aghast at the way people dressed here," but he soon got into the casual L.A. style as well.

Skylaire Alfvegren, who went on to become a freelance writer and occasional film critic after filling out the questionnaire, tends "to get dressed up to see a new film. I mean, at seven dollars one should make it an experience. I am a connoisseur of bad film and weird exotic stuff, so I tend to avoid the big Hollywood blockbusters." Virginia Keene is also selective and careful in her preparation to see a film.

Planning the event has become far more methodical and fun in itself, like a strategy game. I skim the reviews and read first and last sentences only (no cheating! I read them only *after* seeing a film) and make decisions about what I want to see. I get the local papers on Thursday and sit down with a cup of coffee early Friday morning to coordinate my Movie Attack. I plan possible strategies on three by five cards. Running times and bus schedules have become very important. How many movies can I squeeze in without wasting time? Can I catch the last film in time to grab a bus and be home before dark?

Yes, some people in Los Angeles do ride the bus to the movies. I do it myself, as when I took a Santa Monica bus into Santa Monica to see *Speed*, which is about a Santa Monica bus with a bomb on board that starts its journey in, where else, Santa Monica. Coming home by bus was a little tense.

Derek Garubo's "moviegoing habits are, to be perfectly honest, solely controlled by whatever dire degree of poverty I find myself in. I see about one movie in a theatre a month, and I rent approximately ten videos per month from Blockbuster Video." Ted Cantu, a twenty-seven-year-old graphic designer, tries "to avoid the Hollywood films—many of them are just simply unwatchable. The story lines are usually predictable and just plain dull. Not only that, it's expensive to patronize these films. It's better for the major studios to take money directly from my bank account and save me the torment." Richard Gonzalez is also concerned about the cost. "I look for bargain matinees and the two-for-one specials, anything that I can afford. I can go alone to watch a movie instead of dragging my whole family alongside of me to see a movie I've been raving about."

Nancy Lathrop stays in her suburb these days. "You give up certain things for monetary reasons. You can get into the twilight show. Ample parking. I think you give up the theatregoing experience, of which there is not much left." Scott Oppenheimer tends to go even later. He had been working the 3 P.M. to 11 P.M. shift and attended the Friday and Saturday midnight shows 75 percent of the time the year before he filled out the questionnaire. Needless to say, he had trouble staying awake during the films and even more difficulty with movies he tried to watch at those hours on home video.

Olufemi Samuel is a self-described "fanatic moviegoer—period. Sometimes, I try to stop myself from going to the theatres when I'm bored, so I opt for the shopping malls just to window shop and pass time. However, the ridiculous thing is that I always find myself in malls with theatres." Movies are twenty-four-year-old D'Arcy West's "main source of entertainment, and I go as often as someone will take me or I have extra money that week. I won't pay to go see bands or get into clubs, which is usually the same price as a movie, but I don't mind dropping ten dollars for a film."

Movies are a group experience for nineteen-year-old Leandro Vasquez. "From the very few that I have, my moviegoing habits consist of: a social fling between some friends and me, on some occasions at some pretty neat-looking theatres. I usually slouch in my chair with my hands in my pockets if I don't like what I'm watching, which is more than often. I also squirm around a lot. Whether it's the seats or the films would be hard for me to tell... I usually end up at some Cineplex, where my buddies have a large option on what to watch. It sucks, because I'm always watching some stupid film that everybody else thinks is good. Maybe I have no taste in films? Or is it the other way around?"

People probably do not ask Vasquez for his opinions, but they do ask Marion Levine. "People who don't even like spending time with me will always ask my opinion of Hollywood's latest. My father was in town recently, and we had a forced-familiarity kind of lunch where we each pretended not to hate each other's guts. Guess what his first question was? 'What's worth seeing?' And although we wildly disagree on basic things like the meaning of family and the principles of child rearing, he will always listen carefully when I tell him what I thought about a particular film."

Choice of theatres is important to Patrician Cortazar, especially when she is in Los Angeles, the home of the movie palace.

El Capitan is now shockingly beautiful. I had been out of the country for a couple of years and was taken there to see *Aladdin* (1992) and *Beauty and the Beast* (1991)—what a return home to Hollywood! Just for the new high-tech, ear-piercingly painful THX intro, it's almost worth going. If you've ever been deconditioned by bad and cramped theatres of Europe and miniscule boxes in New York, this place is a joy . . . but it seems that there are few films that could live up to being deserved of a presentation like that. . . .

In New York, the movie decides the location. All fun, wild films such as *Do the Right Thing, Boyz N the Hood, Angel Heart* (1987) are all seen in Times Square, because viewer participation is insured. Dramas, uptown at a large theatre such as *Tie Me Up, Tie Me Down* (1990) at the Ziegfield. Independent and art films at Carnegie Hall, Film Forum, Millenium, ABC No Rio and Angelika theatres. I hate the cubicles there; ratio-wise, the screens are smaller than my TV, and I will only go to them if it is an absolute must-see movie that is not playing anywhere else.

Aubrey Solomon, a writer-producer in Los Angeles, goes to "screenings at WGA (Writers Guild of America, West), screening rooms, at home. Only occasional visits to theatres during the year with paid admission (usually a family movie). Heavy theatre attendance during Academy screening times when admission's free [for Guild and Academy members]."

Ira Katz is an actor and "will usually choose to see a movie primarily because of the actors involved. If there is an actor whose work I admire or whom I've heard good things about, then that would be cause for me to pay seven or eight dollars to see the movie. . . . If the acting was terrible but the movie itself was fun, I would still be interested, but it might just be considered a video rental instead." Donna Crisci has a different interest: "I seriously collect film scores, and who did the music to a film can sometimes decide whether I see it or not. I won't avoid a film because I don't like a composer, but I have gone to a film I would not have otherwise seen because a favorite composer scored it. . . . This really does play a factor in my filmgoing habits."

Kenneth Hughes admits, "Kenny don't do movies twice. . . . It is just a thing of mine. I really don't like reading or seeing things twice very often," while Fabrice very often sees "films a few times, watching the film for different aspects. As I 'wanted' to direct film, I usually watch the film the first time from the director's point of view. Then as an actor; I usually watch the film a second time . . . to concentrate on the acting alone."

When Marguerite Petersen was a child, her parents took her and her brother to the movies on Friday nights. "That continued almost 'every' Friday night from my earliest memories until I was about ten. Then it simply stopped. I would imagine it was because of the expense." Now that she has grown up and has a family of her own, "Our family has made it a habit to watch at least two movies every Friday night. We have done this for over ten years now." Except now they rent them on video.

Changing Experiences

As moviegoing habits change, so too do movie experiences change. As Carlos Nino puts it, "The moviegoing experience has been an ever-evolving process for me. There is always something new. . . . Whether I focus my attention on the score, the actors, the images, or the dialogue, I am always trying to see what the movie is trying to do. Either as a subversion or as an agent of justice and liberty. . . . I have grown to notice the beauty in the subtlety of the elements. I love films."

As you might imagine, Nino is a film student, but as both film students and non-film students learn more about films, they appreciate the good qualities of films even more. Oscar Jimenez thinks that when he was a child, "I could not understand all the connotations, expressions, and even language, but now when I see an old film that I have not seen for a while and that I remember liking, I suddenly realize all the other kinds of humor in it I hadn't noticed because of age; for example, sexual meanings in jokes." With Patrick O'Leary's "own experience working in films, I have a changed reaction toward some films. I'm able to appreciate some films because of the choices made in filming."

Lilia Fuller's "moviegoing experience has changed in the sense that . . . now I am looking for more sophistication. In that sense, I truly miss some French and Italian contemporary movies that my friends get to see back in Europe, and I am stuck over here with garbage like *Showgirls* (1995)." Valerie Hornig does not have as much time to see films as she did when she was younger, but now when she does go, "I choose to attend films in the smaller, independent theatres and watch a smaller-produced effort [rather] than a more commercialized one. In the past, I would have primarily only gone to see the big, blockbuster type of movies with a smaller independent or foreign film thrown in here and there for flavor . . . nowadays, my habits are just the opposite. And you know what? I feel that I'm seeing a better grade of films, getting more than my money's worth, and I really feel good supporting smaller independent theatre houses."

Alejandro Munoz has gone full circle. Earlier in the text, he talked about going from an interest in Hollywood movie stars to lesser-known actors to directors. He then "began to explore the international style of Luis Bunuel, Federico Fellini, Ingmar Bergman, and most recently, Pedro Almodovar. . . . Yet when all this is said and done, I can't resist the old habit of mine of watching and once more being captivated by the exaggerated nature of Hollywood-style films, and so I find myself once again standing outside a long line every once in a while to catch the first screening of a movie like *Jurassic Park*." In the two years prior to filling out the questionnaire, Bill Pulliam and his wife "have become much more dedicated followers of films. We have begun tracking works in progress, finding filmographies of favorite actors/actresses, looking for obscure films, and following the movie mags. In the past, it was more a matter of checking the newspaper ads and the local video store and leaving it mostly at that. I think the . . . discovery of Jason Patric and the realization that we had entirely missed a seven-year-long career of a great actor got us interested in probing deeper and seeing more of the less well-known films."

As a teenager, Ervin Riggs "was more into gangster-type movies because I thought that was cool. Now, I'm more into mysteries, because I feel mystery films are like chess. It makes you sit and think of the next move." Now in her twenties, Wendi Cole's movie tastes also matured. "When I was younger, I used to go to the movies to meet guys and hang out with my friends. We would mostly go to see scary movies. The scarier, the better. Now I want to see more adult films. I really have no particular interest in seeing horror films. When I tried watching one of the old *Friday the 13th* movies, the absurdity of it made me stop wondering why sometimes my brain shuts down. I realize it didn't get much exercise in my youth."

When Edwin Castro "was younger I did not care what type of movies I saw, just seeing a movie on a giant screen was enough. This was because I could see a movie in a different place other than home and see it on a giant screen. . . . As I became an adult, I started to notice the quality of the movie, the acting, the plot, and how it carried these things out in the movie. I became picky with the movies I was paying to see. I feel I had more fun going to the movies when I was a kid." Castro is not alone. For many people, moviegoing was better when they were younger. Brian Calderon "could get lost in a movie. That hasn't happened in over ten years. I am always aware that I am watching a movie now. . . . I still enjoy films tremendously, but some of the magic is gone."

Maryanne Raphael started going to the movies in the late forties. "When I first went to movies, I lived inside each of the characters, especially my favorite one[s], and everything was so real. I felt all their emotions, laughed with them and cried with them, shared their fear and their joy. Today I am a lot more objective. It takes a lot more depth of character, a lot more dramatic story to get my attention and keep it. But that little child that fell in love with the movies so long ago is still inside my soul, waiting for a movie to call her out, so I can live the story and come out singing, or wiping my eyes, or trying to recapture a dance or a certain smile." Nostalgia for the early experience also affects Edward Pina. "Every time I go to the movies, I can always remember the first time I went with my dad. Standing next to him waiting in line to get in. Not knowing what I was in for, and I was in for a big surprise."

Lam Yun Wah also gained a love of movies as a child and finds the experience has changed:

When I was small, I was thrilled with the idea of going to the cinema. Because my parents didn't go to a lot of movies, I watched only about five movies a year. I used to LIVE for a movie, i.e., I would keep thinking about a movie at least two weeks before I went to see it. After that I would replay the whole movie many times in my heart. I kept a book listing all the movies I'd seen then. I loved the cinema auditorium; I loved to experience the way the lights dimmed and things like ads or trailers appeared on screen. As years went by, I watched more and more movies, until one day I discovered that I've learned how to criticize a movie. At the same time, to my horror I found that I've lost the ability to love movies. I noticed the subtlest details of a shot; I compare the work of a director with others; I talk to people as if I know a lot about films, but I can never love movies and cinema as I did when I was ten. This is sad, isn't it. Well, I am trying my best to recapture the excitement I used to feel. Sometimes, at rare moments it works. Mostly it is during an old movie, like [Louis] Lumière's shorts and some Chaplin—some old [Yasujiro] Ozu. These movies excite me as if it is the first time I am ever seeing them.

Others also have learned more about film and have come to appreciate films less. Eva Mahgrefthe has become "older and a more critical judge of acting quality. Because film is a medium I love, I generally go into each one with high hopes. As an actress myself, I am quickly put off when I am faced with a poor performance in others. . . . However, I don't believe I will ever lose the quality of hoping for the absolute best in every film I see." Kalani Mondoy feels he has "become much more selective as to specifically what type of movies I like or prefer to see. . . . Now, I don't wait for people to tell me what the film is about. I've become a sort of mild critic. I demand to be entertained rather than placated. I want to see excellence, but I don't demand perfection."

Anthony Miele is a film student, and it has made him more critical of films as well as his own preferences. "I have never been happy with my taste in film, that is to say that I have never understood why I am not moved by more of today's releases.... Most people say that I 'hate everything' because I am just that, a film major. I do not believe this to be true. I think that since I am majoring in film, it has helped me realize that, for instance, Jim Carrey movies are NOT funny films. It has also made me watch films with a different eye than most."

The reactions of Miele and the others show how *personal* feelings are about the experiences of moviegoing and changes in those experiences. Over the years, David Morales has "become a little more disillusioned by the thought of going to the movies, because I feel like I'm paying for something up front at the box office at the same time that I really don't know what I'm going to get. I end up thinking a lot of what I'm seeing wasn't worth the money or time or trouble. But if the movie is good, it's still the same kind of high that I got as a little excited and awed kid." It takes a "little push" to get Kenneth Hughes to go to a movie, even though he works in the industry as an actor and choreographer. "I really don't like sitting on my ass for two hours so much anymore." On the other hand, Sang Sang Taing's moviegoing has taught him to "relax and entertain myself more.... By going to see a movie, it relieves my stress and lets me escape from reality for a couple of hours or more." Richard Bogren's personal reason for the decline in his moviegoing was the birth of his kids, although he expects "that once there aren't concerts, plays, sporting events, and the like to take up my free time, I'll be going back to the theatre again."

There are both external and internal aspects of the change in Virginia Keene's moviegoing habits. "Age, education and all of the movie miles I've logged over the years have combined to refine my tastes and expand my horizons. Money and time are tighter, so moviegoing is a less casual event. I almost always go alone now. It has become my private time." Moviegoing is even more personal for Peggy Dilley. She likes

watching movies in various ways. I guess in the movie theatre, at a bar-gain matinee, by myself, with not too many people in the theatre, is my favorite way to watch them. I watch almost all movies alone or with just strangers in the theatre. I usually mention the movies I've seen to my friends, but we don't discuss them too deeply, because most of my friends aren't so into movies as I am. Consequently, movies have become a very personal experience for me that is difficult to talk about with people. Maybe I should have started talking about this long ago. Maybe it would seem less private and freaky.... Maybe I'd find out how common this disease I have is.

It's definitely related to my schizophrenia, probably a major contrib-uting factor. Going to a movie is a special event for me. It's sort of like going to the mountain to have a dialogue with a great being who tells me truths that I'm supposed to carve on stone tablets and put into action in my life. I get an ego rush, a sense of identification that changes from one movie to the next that is so subtle and internal it seems to be almost beyond words, at least so far.

I become the characters in the movies. I dress like them, behave like them, try them on for size, and then discard them when the next movie's impact overrides the fading memory of the old. The novelty wears off, the hypnosis, and I have to go get a shot of new adrenaline, finding a new person to become, whom I have never quite been before.

I believe sometimes that I'm getting special messages—just for me— from a movie, that a movie was made because of me, because of something I said or did that a Hollywood person saw, picked up, and decided to make a movie on. I started getting this way at a very early age. I spent a lot of childhood in a fantasy inside my head. I had a separate world built up of fragments from storybooks, movies, mythology, cartoons, TV, etc. I would escape into this world and dialogue with the one godlike voice instructing me in how to be a person. It took me a long time to realize it had many voices that often contradicted one another, and maybe it didn't only speak to me. I'm just starting to realize that maybe we are all this way, all connected up to this big something in some way. I thought only crazy people were this crazy. And I must be very special.

When Laurel Jo Martin's father finally relented and let her grandfather take her at age fourteen to see *Fiddler on the Roof*, going into the theatre "was like entering a shrine; it was like a rite of passage for me. . . . I don't feel like I'm entering a shrine anymore, but I still go to get something. I wish I had the time and money to go more often. Sometimes in the middle of a good movie, I'll be totally into it and my brain will pull me out of it. It's like I become aware of watching a movie, and I start looking at the people watching a movie. It only lasts a moment or two. It's sort of like being tapped on the shoulder. Maybe it's my father."

Many people share Martin's concern with the increased cost of going to the movies. Among them is Natalie Sibelman, a research secretary in her forties, "The moviegoing experience has changed for me mostly due to economics. In the past, I would see almost every new movie that came out. Now I am much more selective. Since the movies are now $7.50 for an adult, most movies I feel are not worth this price. I do try to go to the first showing of movies now, but still I am more selective about the movies I see." Terence Atkins is concerned with more than just the ticket price: "The amount I have to pay for snacks and tickets and throw in parking, it's expensive." And D'Arcy West asks, "Why does it cost $7.50 to sit in a theatre the size of my living room?" Lisa Evans, in her twenties, has a brother who "has a friend that manages a movie theatre in Orange [California], so whenever I am visiting my family, I usually go see a movie. This is basically the only way I will go, because I believe that movies are too expensive nowadays, and besides, there are very few movies that appeal to me and that I think are worth my time to even bother going."

Evans is not alone in finding that her moviegoing habits changed because of a decline in the quality of the movies themselves. Peter Albers has an "increasing inability to simply be entertained in the face of gratuitous violence, racism, misogyny, etc. I don't consider myself an overly politically correct sort, but *True Lies*' (1994) attitude towards women kept me from being entertained at all." Gary Demirdjian is more general: "To me, the movies that come out now are . . . usually pale imitations of movies that were already made in the past, with some slight twists." Richard Henrie agrees, "It seems to me that Hollywood can't come up with any new ideas. I understand that a lot of money and time goes into movies, but it seems that they are afraid to try any new ideas. With all of those so-called 'creative' writers, I know there are new and fresh ideas. But they just don't want to take the chance on making these films. So we as the public have to see the same old retreads."

At the ripe old age of twenty-seven, Tandy Summers says,

> I don't know if it's me getting older, having seen repeating trends, or movies not becoming as good, but in the last six years [she was writing in 1997] very few films have piqued my interest. It's sad to see my favorite stars getting older. I just feel the industry has gotten too politically correct and "playing it safe" in the last few years. But the main factor is the older I get, the more I see Hollywood retelling the same old stories. A majority of Hollywood's films are geared towards kids. Thankfully, the last few years have had adult movies. I guess I would have really hated it being an adult back in the Spielberg eighties. I doubt it though. Those were good movies. *Independence Day* is a clone and not half as good. But I guess it is to kids what *War of the Worlds* (1953) was to me when I was a kid. And maybe I'm biased, but I thought *War of the Worlds* was a lot better. In a lot of ways I just see Hollywood remaking itself decade after decade—the same stories and themes updated with the latest technology. And the latest special effects do not make them better. I think the acting levels of the seventies are far superior to today. Today's *Anaconda* (1997) is no *Jaws*.

Aly Kourouma adds sadly, "Now I expect less from a movie. When I was younger, I wanted a movie to entertain me, to educate me and teach me something. But now I know that this task is far beyond Hollywood's capabilities. So now when I go to the theatre, it's only to have fun—nothing else—and I avoid thoroughly all these movies pretending to teach you something. . . . After all, we have literature for that, right?"

Part of the change in the moviegoing experience is the difference in movie theatres. Armando Sanchez thinks this has been for the better. "Before, theatres started to get ruined by people and were left that way. It was insane to go to one unless you liked the smell of the dirty carpeting and vomited-on seats. But now, that has all changed. . . . Occasionally, the managers of the state-of-the-art theatres keep them clean for those special engagements they want us to attend and we all like to go to." Nancy Lathrop, who is now married to a projectionist, became "real sensitive to the quality of the presentation" when she worked at a revival theatre in Los Angeles that had classic carbon arc projectors and a good projectionist. She appreciates good projection and good sound and thinks a lot of the old "attention to detail is gone" now.

The development of the more elaborate stereo and noise reduction sound systems, particularly in the seventies, has led audiences to a greater apprecia- tion of film sound. Some go as far as Luis Garcia, who will "always check whether a movie has DTS [Digital Theatre Sound] and THX, or at least a stereo sur- round sound. If the movie does not have at least one of these features, then I do not go to watch it." Olufemi Samuel also appreciates the "tremendous sound effect. This gives me the ultimate thrill any time and any day. Also, like ice cream gives some people orgasm, so does the sound effects of the theatre give me an orgasm."

I do not go quite that far, since being a pro-writer moviegoer, I tend to prefer hearing the dialogue rather than the effects. The problem I have with the newer sound technologies is that often the final sound tracks on the film are mixed so that more emphasis is placed on the music and sound effects than on the dia- logue. Have you ever noticed that not *one single* sound trailer, for THX or any other system, has ever emphasized the spoken word? And if you do not see the film in a theatre, the improvement in sound may not be noticeable. Larry Richardson, a classics professor at Duke University, tends to see what few films he does on airplane flights, where the sound is so bad he does not bother to rent the headset at all.

For some members of the audience, movie theatres have not gotten better. Marguerite Petersen "no longer enjoys going to theatres to see movies. I like the big screen (TV just doesn't cut it for movies like *Star Wars*), but the theatres are too small, noisy, dirty, and cold. Not in actuality but as in austerity." Judith Amory has similar feelings.

Going to the movies used to be the ultimate impulse action. "Let's flick out," and you just went. There was never a worry about getting a seat (the theatres were so huge), and we didn't even pay much attention to starting times. Now, suddenly, with multiplexes, the theatres are much smaller, and if the movie is at all popular and if you want to go at a popular time, there is plenty of anxiety about whether your attempt to see it will be successful. I say "popular time," but in the last few years I have been turned away on Monday or Tuesday nights, even once on a Friday afternoon. Lines at the ticket counter are long, and sometimes I have come in ten minutes after the movie started, even though I was in line in plenty of time.

Who wants anxiety to be part of an experience that's supposed to be fun? More and more, I don't want to go unless I know for sure the movie won't be crowded. Instead I think, "I'll wait until it comes out on video." If it's something I really want to see in a theatre (perhaps because it's a movie where the visual effects are particularly important), I try to think of a time when few other people will be going.

Amory is in her fifties, but Marci Kozin is a college student in her twenties, and she feels the same nostalgia for the big screen movie palaces. "I wish I could go back in time and view a movie on the big screen when theatres were called Palaces, and the audience dressed in their best clothes, and being at the movies meant something special." Marilyn Heath is in her forties and remembers theatres so ornate as to deserve the title of "palace."

In downtown L.A. in the fifties and sixties, there were theatres that had been old vaudeville palaces with triple balconies, crystal fountains up to the ceiling, intricate Arabian or Renaissance designs lavished everywhere from the marble floors to the walls, curtains, and ceilings. My two favorites were the Los Angeles Theatre and the Newsreel Theatre. They were more elaborate than the Pantages [a movie palace in Hollywood]. They were also full of mystery. The Newsreel had a second theatre downstairs where gnarly old men smoked cigars, watched old newsreels, and argued politics in the dark. I opened a tall door I'd never noticed downstairs in the Los Angeles Theatre and found a huge ballroom with big chandeliers covered in cobwebs. The ladies bathroom had a golden room with mirrors all around that made you go on forever adjoining what much have been a nursery, the walls painted in jungle scenery and wooden circus animals big enough to climb around on. At twelve, I remember finding a stairway that led up from the women's bathroom to an alley. I sneaked my gang of cholo boyfriends in past a shocked lady, and though we were poor we saw *Help!* (1965) over and over that way for days. I saw *Goldfinger*

(1964) there with my best friend when I was ten. We floated out of the theatre, walking on air, not caring where we were going.

Melanie Nielsen, a college student in Michigan in her twenties, dislikes the "large, impersonal movie theatres with twenty screens and even more concession stands." She finds it "comforting that it is still practical [to have] the restoration and upkeep of Detroit's more notable theatres such as the State and the Detroit Institute of Arts."

Amory and Nielsen, in comparing the older theatres to the newer ones, are talking about the biggest change in film exhibition since 1948: the development of the multiscreen theatre, or the multiplex. Prior to 1948, virtually all American movie theatres were single-screen theatres, since the design of theatres had evolved from live theatre and vaudeville, and many early movie theatres had been previously used for those events. The pre–1948 theatres were in the downtown areas of cities and towns, with some theatres in the surrounding neighborhoods. In the post–World War II era, Americans began moving out of the cities and into the suburbs. The old theatre chains, divorced from the production companies after the 1948 Paramount Decision, were not allowed by the federal judges overseeing the case to substitute suburban theatres for urban ones, so newer theatre owners began to get into the business.[1] Movie theatres built by the newer chains followed the audiences in the sixties and seventies, moving into spaces in the suburban shopping malls. The theatres were often afterthoughts, since the real estate developers building the malls tended to look for big department stores rather than movie theatres to "anchor" the malls.

Perhaps the theatres should not have been afterthoughts, since the new malls were built—figuratively and sometimes literally—on the land that had been taken up by drive-in theatres. As the suburbs expanded, the real estate on which the drive-ins sat became too valuable and therefore too heavily taxed to support drive-ins.[2] More intense use of the land was needed, and it soon became clear to developers and theatre owners that it was more economical to build multiscreen theatres than single-screen theatres, drive-ins, or hardtops, as indoor theatres are nicknamed.

The first multiplex was built in Kansas City in 1963 by Stanley Durward, the head of what became American Multi-Cinema. He had a theatre in Kansas City in the fifties that had a 300–seat orchestra and a 300–seat balcony. When a picture did not do well, he had to close down the balcony, but he "figured that maybe I could run two lousy movies instead of one and fill up the house."[3] He did not do it then, but when he approached the developers of the Ward Parkway, a shopping center, the space they had available would not allow for a single

700–seat theatre, but would allow for a 400–seater and a 300–seater side by side. It opened in 1963 and was eventually replaced in 1991 by a twelve-plex.[4]

Durward was right about the economics of the multiplex. Instead of being dependent on one film, the theatre owner spreads his risk among several, at least one of which may make some money. There is also the other economic consideration, perhaps the most important: the concession stand serves several auditoriums rather than one, and most of the profit in running a theatre comes from the concession stand. More auditoriums per concession stand means more profit. Developers began to take another look at multiplexes as department stores began consolidating and proving less reliable anchors. Movie theatres turned out to work beautifully as anchors, since more than half the people who go to a movie in a mall do some shopping while they are there.[5]

Multiplexes have increased both in numbers of theatres, and in numbers of screens, as happened with the Parkway. In the nineties, multiplexes turned into megaplexes, with as many as thirty screens each. By the late nineties, the Ontario Mills Mall, forty miles east of Los Angeles, included two theatre complexes within a few hundred yards of each other—one with thirty screens, the other with twenty-two. All of which fits in with the distributors' shift into wider releases of films. If the distributor wants to put his films onto two thousand or more screens, it helps to have the screens to do it, however small those screens may be.[6]

But moviegoers do not necessarily love the multiplexes. Rudie Bravo says, "I hate, hate, HATE the multiplex! Nine times out of ten they're showing the same schlock in all thirty postage-stamp screens, not enough legroom for a midget, theatres. This doesn't prevent me from going to them. But given a choice . . ." Film historian and projectionist Rick Mitchell resents "paying first-run prices for an auditorium not much bigger than my living room, with a screen smaller than the twelve-foot wide one I have at home. I do not go to the Beverly Center Cineplex [the first major multiplex built in Los Angeles] for precisely that reason. (Actually I've been boycotting Odious [his name for the Odeon chain] Cineplex theatres for the last decade anyway.)" Which may have meant that Mitchell is unaware that after opening in 1982 with all shoebox-size auditoriums, a few years later the Beverly Center remodeled and added two larger screens. The tendency in the late eighties and nineties in multiplex construction was to build complexes with several large auditoriums as well as several small ones.

I rather liked the smaller rooms of the Beverly Center Cineplex, since they felt like private screening rooms, but I stopped going there when they started charging for parking. Peter Albers also has problems with the Beverly Center and others. "I am a theatre snob. I now refuse to go to the Beverly Center—probably the worst seating arrangement of any too-small-to-begin-with theatre I've ever seen."

When Richard Bogren saw the restored version of *Lawrence of Arabia* a few years ago on a BIG screen, he realized how he had "forgotten the impact and feel of the experience after so many years in smaller shopping mall venues."

There is one distinct advantage to the multiplex. In his impoverished student days, Jack Hollander

> developed the habit (illegal or not) of "theatre-hopping." I would carefully check the newspaper listings for the times of the films at a multiplex and arrange my schedule to see more than one film. I would even occasionally try to outguess a stringent policy at the theatre by buying a ticket for the film I would see *second* and go to the other film first (in case I was caught going into the second theatre, I could always show my ticket stub!). Nowadays, I rarely do this (who has the time?), but I can give advice to those who might be contemplating this life of crime. Be sure that you stay in the first theatre through the credits. Ushers use more surveillance when the film first ends and the majority of patrons exit the theatre. Use the restroom after you leave the first theatre—ushers don't pay much attention to people returning to a theatre from the john. This really doesn't work well unless you are going to the movies alone. Don't try to enter a second theatre for a heavily attended film—other than there not being seats, the ushers will be more vigilant and it's just plain not fair (to the other patrons—none of this is fair to the filmmakers!). When you enter the second theatre, find a seat quickly and try to avoid the aisle seats.
>
> "Theatre-hopping" enabled me to see some weird double (and occasional triple and quadruple) bills. The most memorable was when I went to the Wilshire Theatre in Santa Monica. In one afternoon, I saw *Ordinary People* followed by *The Elephant Man* (both 1980). For some reason, I was emotionally numb for the next few days. Which brings to mind the point—Just because you CAN see more than one film at a time doesn't mean that you SHOULD!

While I cannot say I have never theatre-hopped, I generally try to avoid it for the reason Hollander suggests: it is very unfair to the filmmakers, and I am usually trying to see movies that I want to support with my money. There are, of course, some movies I wish I had sneaked into after I saw them, but by then it is too late.

The chief advantage of the multiplex is that there is generally one near you. Debra de St. Jean goes to the Beverly Connection and the Beverly Center, across the street from each other, because of "their convenience of being close to home." Living in the suburbs, Nancy Lathrop goes to the nearby multiplex for convenience as well. "You give up the kind of the old elegance, the feeling of 100 percent of the moviegoing experience. I guess this narrows down to about 85 percent or less, depending how tacky the cineplex is. But they have the little cup holders, which is a real nice touch. I like the little cup holders."

The people who work in the multiplexes have to deal with the audiences in them, which can have its moments. Scott Renshaw, now in his twenties, recalls

with particular fondness an incident that occurred when the six-screen multiplex theatre was showing *A Nightmare on Elm Street* (the original, 1984). This film was very intense and often got the audience rather worked up. One evening there was an electrical storm, and at a particularly suspenseful moment during the film, there was a power failure. Now all the theatres had emergency lighting, but in the theatre where *Elm Street* was playing, those lights were not functioning for some reason. So at the moment the power was lost, from the bowels of this pitch black theatre came a horrible shriek. Seconds later, a young woman came bursting through the doors of the theatre in a state of tremendous distress, followed shortly thereafter by a male companion, who was trying hard not to break into hysterical laughter.

While some multiplexes do make an effort to show "art films" in one or sometimes even two of their *smaller* auditoriums, the multiplex is primarily an instrument of brute commerce. Art houses, however, are known for their showings of less obviously commercial foreign language or American independent films. Alix Parson grew up in Lexington, Kentucky, and by her teen years in the eighties, the downtown theatres were integrated, and one of the old picture palaces, the Kentucky, had become a combination art house and revival theatre. It was there that she enjoyed seeing *Repo Man* (1984) "and the experience of seeing it. I was in high school and saw it in a really old theatre with an enormous screen. The place was packed with alternative kids. All of these things, including a great film, made it a really fun, almost communal experience."

While Scott Renshaw was working at a multiplex in Bakersfield, Rudie Bravo was working in an art house run by "Landmark back east, when Landmark was still doing daily changes, and I've watched a lot of movies, and a lot more than once. (For instance, I've seen *Stop Making Sense* [1984] fifteen times in a theatre: every night it ran. I have also seen all of *Berlin Alexanderplatz* [1979], except for the beginning and end of each segment, when I was still letting people in or getting ready to let them out.)"

Lisa Moncure did not discover art films until she left North Carolina and lived in Telluride, Colorado.

At the time, I knew nothing of foreign films. There was only one movie house in Telluride, and they were almost always showing some (what seemed to me) obscure foreign movies. It took me a while to accept sub-titles. I worked as a volunteer at the film festival in the summer, because there was really nothing else to do. I remember driving home one night during the festival and saw this drunken man walking down the street. He seemed to be lost. So I stopped to see if he needed some help. Tellu-ride was a very small and safe town where one did this sort of thing. He let me know he was a German film director (emphasis on the word direc-tor). I am sure he was the person they were paying tribute to that year, because he seemed to have this attitude of "don't you know who I am?" I of course had no idea who he was and sent him on his way. I guess he was used to having young women throw themselves at him.

Moncure obviously learned from this experience with an obnoxious director and went on to become the Filmmaker Liaison for the American Film Institute's Los Angeles International Film Festival, in between acting in such films as the Yugoslavian *Pretty Village, Pretty Flame* (1995).

A campus offshoot of the art house was the university film society. In 1981, Michael Thomas

was a Freshman at Syracuse University and joined a student-run movie theatre, where I learned 16mm and 35mm projection. The campus also had three theatres that showed old classics, foreign films, and R-rated six-ties and seventies films I was not allowed to watch as a kid. . . . While at Syracuse, I was exposed to a wide variety of films. Up to this point in my life, most of the movies I had seen in theatres were new releases. I saw many of Hitchcock's film during this time. . . . These films were among the first I would see on the big screen that were produced before I was born. Though I had seen many classic films on television, I was finally getting a chance to watch them as the filmmakers intended for them to be seen.

If art houses specialize in independent and foreign films, revival houses spe-cialize in serving the nostalgia for the films of the past. Like Thomas at the film society, Patrick O'Leary, now in his early thirties, learned about older films at revival houses. "I spent a lot of time in my teens at revival theatres. Actors from another era, such as James Dean, Anna Magnani, and Charlie Chaplin, made an impression on me when I saw their films for the first time in a revival the-atre." In the sixties and seventies, Monica Dunlap was seeing "a minimum of two films a week in Manhattan theatres, often at the Thalia, Bleeker Street, and other revival houses." After living in Telluride, Lisa Moncure moved to New York and lived down the street from two old movie theatres, the Thalia and the Metropolitan, that were always showing great old movies. Of the many films that I saw there, three stand out in my mind. They are *Brief Encounter*, *The Philadelphia Story*, and *My Dinner with Andre* (1981). *Brief Encounter* has to be one of the most romantic stories I've ever seen. I remember floating out of the theatre after seeing it. It was so much more romantic than the films we see today, because they never acted on their desire for one another. It was so much better to see two people who genuinely enjoyed one another for their personalities and the friendship instead of just lustful desires. In *Philadelphia Story*, I just simply adored Hepburn. Not to say that I didn't enjoy Cary Grant and Jimmy Stewart, but Hepburn is a woman, so I identified more with her. I'd really like to see it again, because it's been almost twelve years since I've seen it. When I left the theatre that day, I remember thinking, why don't they make movies like that now?[7]

The audiences at a revival theatre can be just as striking as the films. Aubrey Solomon saw *Singin' in the Rain* "on a very rainy night in February 1971 at a revival house on Melrose Boulevard. The house was packed, hot, and humid and there was a double bill with *Meet Me In St. Louis* (1944). I had never seen either, but it turned out to be a completely memorable evening. Everyone in the audience, without exception, loved the movie. There was cheering and applause as if it were a live performance. There was so much appreciation of this movie, it spread around the theatre and really enhanced the viewing. Not that the movie needed it."

Just as the drive-ins were destroyed by the increase in the value of the land they sat on, the revival theatres have been threatened by the arrival of television and, especially, videocassettes. In the over thirty years I have lived in Los Angeles, I have seen many revival theatres come and go. There is now only one major revival theatre as such left in Los Angeles, the New Beverly, but at least some of the work of presenting older films has been taken over by the Los Angeles County Museum (LACMA) and the UCLA Film Archive's screening program. And as older films become valuable assets for potential video sales, more efforts are being made to restore older films—sometimes with good results, sometimes not.

Sam Frank is a film historian with a particular interest in Ronald Colman. In the seventies he decided not to watch Colman's *Lost Horizon* (1937) since

it has become stale [to Frank]. When I watched it again with footage added in 1977 at the Bing Theatre at LACMA, I was excited by the added scenes. When I saw it again after that in 1979 at the Chinese Theatre, the sagging middle section with all the restored footage nearly put me to sleep. Restoring *Lost Horizon* to its premiere length was more a curse than a blessing. The movie needed to be cut, but the tragedy was it had not been recut properly. Take the right ten minutes out of it, and you have a better movie. It wasn't overlong because of the added footage; it was overlong because the added footage was mostly irrelevant or unneeded or stopped the movie.

I appreciate his position. I loved Orson Welles's shaggy-dog story *Touch of Evil* when I saw it in its first run in 1958, when it ran 95 minutes. A lot of other people loved it as well, and it became a classic. In the eighties, a supposed "original cut" of 108 minutes was found in the vaults at Universal and given an art house release, being promoted as Orson Welles's original cut. It was not as good as the original: it was slower, duller, and not nearly as much fun. In 1998, following a fifty-eight-page memo Welles himself had composed after seeing the original 108–minute version, the great film editor Walter Murch cut a new version that runs 111 minutes. It was quicker and sharper, and with a sound track infinitely improved from the 108–minute version, but it was still not quite as much fun as the 95–minute version.[8]

Sometimes the restorations work completely. In 1989, Columbia restored David Lean's *Lawrence of Arabia* under Lean's supervision. *Lawrence* being one of my favorite movies, I went to see the restoration the day after it opened (I had a class to teach on the day it opened), and I and the rest of the audience were stunned, just like the audience Donna Crisci saw it with a short time later. "I went to Century City to see it. This is my favorite film. To see it so beautifully restored, to hear it in its full splendor, to observe how superior it still is to current films amazed me. The audience this time was Lawrence and filmmaking afficionadoes. When it was over, we all stood and gave the film an endless ovation, some crying. Honor where honor is due."

Of course, you have to be careful where you see the rerelease of old films. My late father-in-law was on an airplane once and rented the headset to see the film, but as the film ran he realized that the Charlie Chaplin film was, except for the music sound track, primarily silent. He hardly needed the headset at all. And as a Scotsman who had his share of the thrifty gene, he was not happy.

Experiencing Emotions

Moviegoing becomes a habit not just because of the entertainment and/or enlightenment movies give us, but primarily because of the emotions they evoke. Sometimes the emotions are fairly simple, particularly when we are young, but they grow more complex as we get older.

When Judith Amory went to movies in the forties as a child with her parents, nobody bothered to check the starting times of the films. "You just went in and stayed until you recognized the spot where you came in. Consequently, I was about nine or ten before I discovered that movies were *supposed* to make sense. Until then, I thought everyone was as confused as I was."

Carlos Aguilar appreciated films in his childhood "as a source of wonderment," but in adolescence, "they became a way to forget. Through junior and high school I cut class on a weekly basis to disappear into dark movie houses. As a filmgoer, I never used films to live the life of the people on the screen like many moviegoers. I love to study the characters, like an observer strolling through a park, an asylum, a forest, or a carnival."

Al Gonzalez saw a set of different emotions, his own and others, when he was seventeen and took his girlfriend to see *Ordinary People.*

At the end of the movie, after the credits had rolled and the theatre lights had come up, I noticed a graduate school-aged couple sitting a few rows in front of us. It was a small auditorium and only a few people had remained. This guy looked over at the girl and asked, "Are you ready to go?" only to find that she had been silently crying.

The young man began to smile and reached over to wipe her eyes with his thumb, laughing slightly as if he found this to be irresistible. She in turn smiled as if embarrassed for having been caught in such an emotional state but nonetheless responded by turning her head slightly in order to kiss his hand. With this same hand, he brought her face to his and kissed her. They gathered their things and were gone.

The entire moment, which had been caused by the effect the movie had on the girl, which in turn affected this guy, lasted less than a minute. What the movie did for me was one thing, but what it did for this couple had a secondary effect on me. At seventeen, the whole scenario seemed so cool to me. To look at one's date and feel closer to her. To wipe her eyes, brush back her hair, and kiss her with genuine affection. It all looked so wonderful. To be that much in love. And from that moment to this day I have always wanted to be able to experience a moment like that at the movies, because it seemed like such a rare moment in life. When you genuinely feel close to someone and are reminded of that.

Ironically enough, I too was there with my girlfriend. In the end I looked over at her and asked, "Are you ready to go?"

She simply replied, "Yep." And we were gone.

Teddi Lawrence finds movies "have always been the perfect place to cry, and as I am a crier its good to have an institution wherein it's acceptable (or at least unseen). I even cried during the preview to *Bad Girls* (1994) (twice). I didn't cry during the film, though; I thought it was a big pile of cow excrement, a big pile." Women are not the only ones who cry at movies. Oscar Berkovich says, "I know it doesn't sound proper or I might be even exaggerating when I mention that I broke down in tears, and you might even laugh, but the reality is that I too have emotions and feelings." We all do. I find that documentaries bring tears to my eyes as well as the endings of *Roman Holiday* (1953) and *Love in the Afternoon* (1957), but you already know about me and Audrey Hepburn.

Jill Mitchell and her father had an emotional reaction when they saw the American film *Sophie's Choice* (1982) in Budapest.

Unlike my mother, my dad never goes to the movies, and I feel sort of responsible to force him to see certain films. We saw that this film was playing, and I really wanted him to see this one. So we made our way in a taxi to a part of town off the beaten track. At the theatre, the large Eastern Bloc-looking woman gave us a ticket off the big roll she carried, in exchange for the equivalent of about ten cents apiece. During the film, I had to talk my dad through the German and Polish parts, and he was able to follow pretty well. Of course, the film had a huge emotional impact on us, and to be sharing the viewing of the film with people who had undoubtedly had similar experiences as Sophie did herself lent a very different quality to the movie. It felt like my dad and I, unexposed to any such atrocities, were the character of the naïve Southern writer, and we were sitting in the dark movie theatre surrounded by dozens of Sophies. It was still daylight as we left the theatre, and the reality of what took place in the movie hit us as we walked back into our day in Budapest. The experience of watching the film was with us for the rest of our trip; it gave us a personal reference to what had taken place forty-five years earlier on the same soil. [The film was set in Poland, not Hungary, but you see her point.]

In Mitchell's early adult life, she spent time in Europe and "going to American movies was a way to kick homesickness for a little while, a way to keep in touch with what was going on at home, and also a way to feel proud of my country.... As I started to travel around, going to movies took on more dimensions. Sharing the viewing with people in their own country is a nice way to blend in with the rest ... and to see what their reactions are to points in the movie which may be culturally different."

American films can have an emotional impact overseas, even when they are not in English. Karpis Termendzyan was a four-year-old in the then-Soviet republic of Armenia when he saw the 1958 Kirk Douglas adventure movie *The Vikings*. "I remember coming home from *The Vikings*, which was my first American film. I was retelling the story to the taxi diver, because I was so excited and my parents were amazed that how I understood the film because I was only four years old and the movie was in Russian (I didn't know Russian then, but then I learned it quickly by watching every film in Russian.)."

In 1979 or 1980, Nancy Lathrop saw *Gone With the Wind* in London. "Seeing it with a non-American crowd was interesting. . . . They were really paying attention. I remember intermission, when I spoke to people around me and they found out I was American. I ended up teaching this little mini-unit on the Civil War to people.... They were asking basic questions. You know, 'A carpetbagger, what is a carpetbagger?'" During the same trip, she saw *To Have and Have Not* (1944) in France, with French subtitles. When Lauren Bacall's famous "If you want anything, just whistle" line came on, the Americans in the audience gave it a big response, but the French were baffled. "Somehow it must have suffered in the translation ... it was dead. It was interesting to see the lines, the Bogartisms, and the things that were almost camp to us, in a very enjoyable and loving way were taken very seriously by the French."

Adam Ozturk found that the French appreciated John Cassavetes's *Husbands* (1970) as much as he did. A friend had taken him to the showing. "The theatre was packed, the energy was good, and on came the film. Cassavetes brings you into very personal portraits of his family and friends. *Husbands* strives off that. I laughed my lungs off and also understood something about my father. This was my definition of 'an experience,' because I felt a lot of different feelings and had interesting thoughts of marriage, men and women. I knew it was all right to be a shambles emotionally and to take off and see other things than the usual. As people were leaving the theatre, you could feel the appreciation for

Cassavetes. I loved every second. Then my friend and I went for a drink, discussing the film all night."

Virginia Keene explains how movies make a personal impact:

> When I think about my most memorable movie experiences, most of them are movies. Just movies. That first meeting: the immediate, intimately personal connection I've made with certain movies I know will be fast friends forever. These are the films that swept me away, or opened my mind, or changed my mind, or thrilled me. The experience depends on something as transient as a mood or as deep as a religious conviction. They aren't always great movies or even good ones, but they're the ones I cherish and return to again and again. I always know the moment I find one of those friends, and I always remember the first time I saw that movie and all the events surrounding it.

Marion Levine still looks forward today to that kind of experience, even though she works in the movie industry. "The fact that I hate 90 percent of what this town produces is totally beside the point—I keep going, true believer that I am, in the hope that I'll be moved, enthralled, educated, inspired, or changed by the plight of those screen stars with whom I still undyingly pledge my allegiance." David Ko agrees. "I want to see more dreams come true and get our movies out of the ditch and back into the dreaming stage. . . . Believe me when I say that movies influence our children more than any other medium except maybe television. I think movies influence us ever more because we are forced to sit there in the dark with out complete attention—focused on what the filmmaker is trying to say."

As influential as Levine and Ko suggest movies can be, audience members respond not only in ways the filmmakers intended, but also in ways filmmakers probably did not intend. Marion Levine says, "I learned everything I know from the movies. I learned how to drink myself into a suicidal stupor by watching Piper Laurie in *The Hustler* [1961] (age nine [that's Levine at nine, not Laurie]). When we got home after the show that Friday night and my mother poured me a glass of milk before bed, I lowered my lids to half mast and sipped that vitamin D-enriched homogenized like it was the driest martini on the planet." Similar to Levine's early education in the art of drinking, as I was growing up in Indiana, I tended to imitate the cowboys in movies by drinking my Royal Crown Cola from my parents' shot glasses.

Laura Rivas's first memorable movie learning experience was the 1978 version of *Superman*. "I was seven when I saw it. It taught me that if I have the opportunity of helping people, I could do it. . . . In the same afternoon I went home and I helped an old lady that used to live next to my house. I helped her with the groceries and I felt good."

Sometimes a movie can give you more than you expect, as happened with a teenaged Sam Frank when he saw *The Pawnbroker* (1965).

I had been told by classmates of mine who had snuck in to see it that it had a scene where a black prostitute was flashing her breasts at Rod Steiger. Previously, my exposure to female nudity was photos in skin magazines I nervously looked through at the local Thrifty.

Except for *Citizen Kane*, I was used to mainly linear movies, often with fantasy effects. *The Pawnbroker* was both a revelation and confusing as hell in the opening reel because of its montage flashback structure. I had known about the horrors of the concentration camps from watching *Judgment at Nuremberg* (1961) on the *ABC Sunday Night Movies* in 1963 (my parents encouraged me to stay up 'til 12:30 A.M. to watch all of it), but this was a brand of hideous inhumanity I had never known existed. For the first time watching a movie, I felt a mixed bag of nauseated emotions. I was utterly appalled, but riveted by the story of a man who couldn't bear to change the date page on his office calendar because it symbolically meant denying his past. It took a while for the movie's meaning to get through to me, but it did.

The nude scene that was supposed to be titillating was deliberately cross-edited with flashes of Steiger's wife being prostituted at the death camp so that instead of being aroused by it, I was distracted and focused on the pain of Steiger's horrific memory; exactly the visceral effect that was intended. The people who made this movie knew what they were doing even though it was hard to follow at times.

But, the scene that dropped my jaw and sent me into paralytic shock was when Steiger atones for the murder of his well-intended Latino assistant by crucifying one of his hands on the spike he uses for receipts. The religious symbolism of it went over me, but watching a man who has been emotionally dead for years inflict this kind of punishment on himself overwhelmed me. I couldn't move, I couldn't breathe, my jaw remained dropped as Steiger slowly removed his hand and walked into the street while the camera tracked up, out, and over him, conveying the idea that here is a basically decent man who blames himself for another man's death, toward whom he has been wrongly bigoted, and he has no one to turn to. I didn't know quite how to feel, quite what to think. I rode my bike home from the movie in a daze of unreality. It took me a few days to get back to reality.

We tend to think of the emotions films produce in us as an individual thing, personal to us. As Teddi Lawrence puts it, "The moviegoing experience, although it didn't cause me to be 'a loner,' made being 'a loner' enjoyable. I don't want to seek friendships, because I like to do things off the cuff and usually don't have time to do anything anyway. I always have a date on Friday night—it either comes from Vidiots or it goes to the AMC [theatres]." But Lawrence adds, "On the other hand, if I am socializing with friends or perspectives [perspective friends] we'll usually see a movie (so much for that argument)."

What happens, of course, is that we want to share the emotions with our friends, and sometimes those relationships and experiences become the focus of moviegoing. Lam Yun Wah says, "To me, going to the cinema is a private experience. I like watching movies alone. But in this society [Wah lives in Hong Kong], you sometimes have to watch movies with other people: girlfriends, other friends, family, etc. It becomes a sociable event there. You have to be 'responsible' to your companions—from choosing the movie to discussing whether you like it or not. I don't like it. Well, these films [he had listed such films as the *Star Wars* trilogy, *E.T.*, *Top Gun*, and *Jurassic Park*] were ones I watched with people I knew. I don't say I hate these films, I just tend to remember more about the people I went with than about the films." With David Ko, it was a childhood friend "who had a bladder problem. We didn't like to take him to comedies because every time a really funny part came on, he would pee in his pants on the chair. So we would then have to move to another set of chairs. We could tell how much he liked a movie by how many times we moved."

Laura Rivas enjoys going to the movies with friends. "I could feel the emotions . . . with your friends around you and other people. Sometimes me and my friends discuss the movies, and we argue because they like what the characters do, or what the movie tells you and I do not agree with that." D'Arcy West and her friend have good times poking fun at bad movies. She says her

best moviegoing experiences are all times when I've seen a really awful movie with a really great and funny friend. For example, my best friend and I might go have some sushi dinner and get really loopy from stuffing ourselves with good food, expensive food, and then see whatever movie is playing nearby that neither of us has seen yet, which is almost always something awful—*Candyman* (1992) or *The Hot Spot* (1990) come to mind. And it's usually the last show of the night, on a weekday, so the theatre's really empty. And the movie's so bad that we start laughing and giggling until we can't stop, and my friend starts coming up with alternative titles, such as *Crapman* for *Candyman*, or *Craplin* for *Chaplin* (1992).

And we're laughing so hard we usually end up having a better time than if the movie is good on any sort of true level.

What West and her giggling friend are part of is the way the presence of the others in the audience makes up the experience of moviegoing. This is most obvious when there is true audience participation with the film. Rudie Bravo saw films many times when she went to work for the Landmark chain, but "the repeat experience wasn't new to me when I began working in a theatre. I'd already seen *The Rocky Horror Picture Show* over two hundred times (as 'bra-and-slip Janet')." She was definitely not alone. One of Paula Lampshire's most memorable moviegoing experiences was her first time at *Rocky Horror*.

> I went to see it at the local theatre with my friends from college. We knew all the songs because we would sing them in drama class for fun. They taught me "The Time Warp". . . . So anyway, we were all there ready to watch the show when my friends proceeded to lift me above their heads like a sacrifice and started chanting the word "virgin," "virgin," "virgin." Boy, was I embarrassed. Well, then I resigned myself to the fact that everyone in the theatre knows that personal information about me now. It wasn't until later that evening that I found out that it meant I was a *Rocky Horror Picture Show* virgin because it was my first time seeing the show. Boy, was I relieved. So the movie began, we responded to the parts of the show that required it, and we went up on stage and danced to "The Time Warp." Overall it was a pretty fun night.

Angela West saw the film when she was eighteen and living in New York. Brian, a friend from Denver, was visiting her. He was a Tim Curry fan, and when they found out the film was playing,

> there was no way in stopping Brian from attending. One cold January night, with snow up to our ankles we took a subway across the city to this small theatre for the limited engagement of *Rocky Horror*. I'd never seen so many bizarre people in my life. Men in women's clothing, women in nothing but skimpy lingerie, and thousands of hair-dyed macabre makeup freaks waiting in line to buy a ticket. Shyly, we walked to the counter and bought a ticket. Feeling a little out of place, we somehow managed to muster up the confidence to go inside. We were greeted by a pink-and-purple-haired usher. Flashing a light for us to see our way into the theatre, she smiled, then laughed madly. I grabbed tight to Brian's hand. Once inside, the circus didn't stop. People were throwing popcorn at the screen

before the movie had even begun. Others were desecrating the place with water balloons. Brian and I sat hurriedly in an aisle seat, ready to leave at a moment's notice. Without further hesitation, a fat bald man came to the front of the theatre and tried to gain the attention of the mad, crazed house. Reluctantly, everyone calmed down to a mild roar. He immediately began to introduce the cast of characters doing the floor show that night. . . . I'd never seen such a collection of theatrical freaks in all my life. After much applause and rude comments from the audience, the movie finally began. The lights went out in a mysterious way, and the curtain slowly drew back as the crowd went mad.

I sat there mesmerized at the entire spectacle. Almost peeing in my pants at the excitement it brought with it. Suddenly, a pair of red lips began singing on the screen. To my amazement the audience was singing the song word for word. My friend Brian began to cut loose and blurt out a few rude comments. People around us laughed and patted him on the back. "That's a new one," they said. I asked Brian how many times he had seen this movie and he looked at me proudly, "Only one hundred and fifteen." I gasped at the number. How could anyone see a movie that many times? It was obvious that as the movie went along others had seen it many more times than Brian. Susan Sarandon was barely audible as people said her lines word for word and Barry Bostwick was less interesting than the smart-assed comments from the peanut gallery. I looked at the screen and noticed the people doing the floor show were amazingly identical to the actors on the screen. These non-paid actors must have spent hours rehearsing their parts. All for the love of splendor and grandeur. They were the major contributors to this more than second-rate film. As I sat in my seat, I began to realize the immense effects this single film had on a generation, my generation. They found themselves through a cheesy film musical and in some way their finding gave them a sense of accomplishment. A whole culture had been spurred from the words "Sweet transvestite in transsexual Transylvania." A culture of cross-dressing, homo-sexuality, and drug inducement. Not to say all these things were bad, only to say that in some strange way they made a statement that individuality is not only okay, but it's downright fun. Eventually, I stopped analyzing and put my hands on my hips just in time for the audience to shout, "Oh, shit, no hips."

Arnold Quinlan attended several screenings of *The Rocky Horror Picture Show.* "I did actually bring toast, rice, newspaper, and a water bottle. I saw the movie eight times but never got to the point of remembering all my lines."

Skylaire Alfvegren, who likes to dress up to go to the movies, is too young to have been part of the heyday of *Rocky Horror Picture Show,* but she made up for a while in high school in West Covina, a suburb on the east side of Los Angeles. "After one particularly successful drama production, I proposed that a group of us attend the local premier of *The Addams Family* dressed as close to what could be termed 'in costume' as possible. A gawky Filipino with a Darkman [comic book hero] complex, two giggly, stout Caucasian boys in pitifully applied pancake makeup, and me—resplendent in almost every piece of black clothing I owned. It was a decent night."

Ira Katz takes an actor's view of the audience participation at a film. "It's interesting that in the live theatre the audience affects the actor's performance and each individual's experience. In the movie theatre, the audience can't affect the actor's performance, but it does affect each person's experience to the performance. And it seems to me that the larger the movie theatre, the better the experience. . . ." Lizy Moromisato agrees "because when there is a bigger audience rooting for a particular character in the movie, laughing at a joke, in other words reacting to the movie along with you, one feels more involved with the movie." She dislikes the smaller auditoriums of the multiplexes for that reason. "Psychologically, I will not react to the movie as freely as I would if I were in a bigger theatre with more people around me."

Since Marilyn Heath's father's "passion for film knew no time limit, we saw movies in all-night cheap theatres with hobos asleep all around. One time they all woke up roaring and stamping, watching *The Hill* (1965), starring Sean Connery. *The Hill* had only male actors in it. It was about a hellish South African military prison [actually a British military prison in North Africa] that made the audience's blood boil. That was probably the most exciting movie audience interaction for me because a theatre full of shouting vehement vagabonds at 3 A.M. was soul-stirring." She was about twelve at the time.

Dorian Wood recalls the Los Angeles premiere run of John Waters's *Hairspray* (1988). "The theatre was packed. I remember that my mother was desperate to see this film, though I had never heard of a Waters (or even a Divine) movie. I'll never forget how much we laughed throughout the entire thing. And to top it all off, during the final credits when each character was introduced, the entire audience would hiss at the bad guys and cheer at the Ricki Lake and Divine characters. Despite the audience's dress code (straight out of Goodwill and Victoria's Secret), everyone felt comfortable with each other. It was a rare, special moment."

Lawrence Dotson recalls the opening night of one of the *Friday the 13th* movies. "My friends and I were in this huge movie house, and it was packed with people from our high school, other high schools, and a bunch of 'old people' in their twenties and thirties. The crowd was very rowdy. As the movie was coming toward the end, everyone in the film had been slaughtered except for the hero, the heroine, and a young black boy. He had several close calls with

Jason, but always managed to escape. On a few occasions, he saved the main characters from being killed. Every time this kid was in action, the audience erupted into the cheer 'Black Youth! Black Youth! Black Youth!' It was a gas."

Robin Magee remembers a double bill of *Ballroom Dancing* [I think she means *Strictly Ballroom* (1992)] and *Stop Making Sense* (1984) at the Michigan Theatre in Ann Arbor. "The audience got up and danced and sang through the show." The Ann Arbor audience Magee talks about was probably made up of college students, who can be very vociferous. Scott Renshaw recalls an audience in the late eighties in a campus auditorium at Stanford University.

> Every year they show *The Graduate* on the Sunday before commencement. I went to the showing my freshman year, never having seen it before but aware of its reputation. Now because it was an annual tradition, the seniors in the crowd were on their fourth showing, and turned it into an audience participation à la *The Rocky Horror Picture Show*. The responses . . . included shouting out "plastics" at the appropriate time, booing every mention of U.C. Berkeley, and, during the scene in which Benjamin drives to Berkeley on the top deck of the Bay bridge (the top deck is actually the westbound [away from Berkeley] direction), shouting "You're going the wrong way."

Not every form of audience participation is fun for others in the theatre. Daniel Barr took his girlfriend to see *My Beautiful Laundrette* (1985). "My girlfriend was napping on my lap due to several glasses of champagne she had been drinking earlier. Suddenly she sat up, saw the spinning laundry machine title sequence and then proceeded to vomit all over my lap." Rocio Vargas gets "so involved in the movie I am watching that I will talk back to the actors when danger approaches, or I will advise them regarding what is the best thing for them to do. Sometimes I even argue with them for the stupid thing they did or did not do, and on several occasions, I have embarrassed my peers by getting up from my seat in an effort to influence their actions."

Undoubtedly Vargas's behavior would have upset Nancy Lathrop. "I think what has kept me away from more films than anything else are wart-nosed audience members. People who think they are at home with their television sets and can talk. It just drives me nuts." She will often wait until the end of the run of a film to see it with a smaller audience, to avoid the "popcorn-smacking next to me. . . . Audiences drive me crazy. Maybe I'm just intolerant of stupidity. I'm just amazed at how poor their behavior is. On one level, just the fact that they would talk during a film is amazing to me. And then, of course, the things they say are even more amazing."

Derek Garubo gives a specific example. "I remember this hick couple saying to one another as the characters on screen were about to make love, obviously half naked and heavily kissing, 'I think she's gonna fuck'um, Earl!' And I might add at normal speaking level in a quiet theatre. To which Earl replied with a lovely snort—for something to spit later, I guess. Classy people, eh?"

Kevin Kennedy was "ecstatic" when a friend of his invited him to a screening at the Directors Guild theatre in Hollywood. "The place was so crowded that we had to sit close to the front, but it was great. Everything about the screening rooms at the DGA makes going to a movie fantastic. People do not talk while the film is running—that is a big plus!" Of course, the film he saw there was Clint Eastwood's *Unforgiven*, which *would* keep an industry audience quiet. Would *you* talk back to the film if you thought Eastwood might be in the room?

Audience reactions, while sometimes pleasurable—particularly with bad movies—are also at the heart of many bad experiences at the movies. Aubrey Solomon tends to go to industry and private screenings because audience behavior has taken a lot of the joy out of general moviegoing for him.

Moviegoing used to be something to look forward to. Big screens, respectful audiences, the best entertainment. Now, it's degenerated to, at best, something marginally pleasurable, more often an ordeal of putting up with unruly teens, parents with infants, and so many third-world immigrants translating the dialogue it's reminiscent of the Tower of Babel. No more are there ushers to quiet the natives, or projectionists to focus, frame or even make sure there's a picture on the screen. For that reason, I prefer *not* to see movies in theatres, which removes much of the fun of being in an audience. But until moviegoers are civil, intelligent, and semi-human, what's the point?

Judith Amory adds, "It's also my impression that people have become ruder in theatres, more likely to chat and disturb others. But I admit that I may just be getting older and more curmudgeonly. . . . At home, I can tell my husband to shut up if he talks during a movie (and after some backtalk, he probably will). In a theatre, one might get stabbed for that!" People talking "really pisses me off," says Brian Calderon, so much so that he "will and have gotten into fights because of people talking during the movie. I still enjoy films tremendously, but some of the magic is gone."

Glinn Leevitt has "wasted money sitting behind obnoxious people, large people, and the likes. Nothing annoys me more than this. While watching *Higher Learning*, I was behind a lady who kept hiccupping—for two hours! I think everyone around us enjoyed making fun of her more than the movie." Needless to say, since I see a lot of movies in theatres, I have run into all kinds of audiences who have diminished the moviegoing experience. Unlike Leevitt, I always seem to end up sitting in front of obnoxious people, or rather after I get there early enough to choose a seat not surrounded by people, some people come in and sit behind me. And usually start talking. Once it was an older couple at a foreign film, one of whose eyesight was failing and who required the other one to read the subtitles out loud.

The stupidest audience I ever saw a movie with was a presumably middle- to upper-class subscription audience at a Los Angeles Philharmonic concert. In October 1998, the Philharmonic conductor, Esa-Pekka Salonen, and arts *wunderkind* Peter Sellars adapted some music by Jean Sibelius for the orchestra to play as a live accompaniment to the 1928 silent film *The Wind*. The music was somewhat appropriate, but the audience began giggling at the beginning of the film, as sometimes happens at silent movie screenings. But the giggling continued, with the audience seemingly determined not only to purposely avoid getting into the film, but also to trivialize it as much as they could. Mostly I think this was an example of the cultural divide in Los Angeles. The Philharmonic subscription audience is made up of people from Hancock Park east out through Pasadena, the type of people who have always looked down on movies as inferior to the other arts. If the same film had played on the west side of Los Angeles, at say UCLA or LACMA, the audience there would have very easily gotten into it, as I've seen them do with other silent films.

For Therese Ribas, "Bad movies and bad company just don't mix," and counts as some of her worst experiences seeing films such as *The Crying Game* with her now ex-boyfriend. "I remember enjoying *The Crying Game* later, when I could view it in the comfort of my own home, instead of getting up every other five minutes to get my (ex-) boyfriend some refreshments. What a jerk!" Her worst experience was with an "ex-colleague" of hers. "What topped it off is that we almost got thrown out of the theatre, because my friend took her baby along and she would not stop crying. I was very embarrassed because to remedy the situation, she first attempted to breastfeed her child right there in public! When that didn't work, she had to take herself out of the theatre while people yelled at her and warned her to take that '****ing [sic] baby outta there!'"

Armando Sanchez also had trouble with children, presumably a little older, when he saw *Scream* (1996). "The film was great, but the audience was awful. Ladies and children just couldn't stop screaming, and most of the time for no apparent reason. I hated how primitive they were acting, and so I left." For Kevin Kennedy, the audience for another movie was even worse. "About fifteen years ago . . . some friends and I went to a ninety-nine-cent theatre, and a knife fight broke out in the front row. Shortly thereafter, the theatre was closed because they had problems like that often." Kenneth Hughes was at a family movie, between the two films of a double bill when he turned to face the man in the row behind him "as we were talking about the previous movie, and he stood on his chair and like thunder smashed his hard shoe on my face. . . . I still am at a loss as to why or what it meant. I guess it is divine wisdom and upon showing my worthiness it will reveal its 'wisdomness' to me." The only fight I ever saw break out in a theatre was between a couple of Westside L.A. yuppie scum who got into a fight over whose seat was whose in a theatre in Westwood. They were not very good at it.

Sometimes the theatre personnel do try to keep order, as Karpis Termendzyan discovered in 1995 when he went to see *Braveheart*.

> It had just opened at the theatres, and we [he and his friends] went to see it at the Universal Studios Cineplex. We bought tickets for a different movie because we wanted to see a couple of films. First we went to see the film that we had the ticket for . . . after that we went to see *Braveheart*. We were very excited because we love epic films like these. During the first fighting scene between the Scottish and English, we went crazy—screaming and shouting very loudly—because it was so violent and truly captured the blood and everything. The manager came and warned us to keep quiet or otherwise he'll be forced to remove us from the theatre. After that we were quiet for like twenty to twenty-five minutes, and then I got in an argument with one of my friends about the movie being based on true events. When the manager came again, he asked to see our tickets; because we didn't have the tickets for this film, we tried to change the subject by saying the sound was too loud, but he didn't buy it. Then I had a little fight with the staff, because I didn't want to leave and miss the ending, but after the security showed up I had to leave. My friends, too, and they were blaming me for everything.

You will be relieved to know that Termendzyan thinks that "now I am not like that anymore."

Scott Oppenheimer had a different problem at the same Universal Cineplex. "I saw a rat crawl across the baseboard, which runs two or three inches parallel to the bottom of the screen. So the light from the Woody Allen movie illuminated the rat. Once the rat was out of view, I then couldn't concentrate on the movies as I became very interested with the floor below my seat. That was very annoying. I called someone in management a few days later, and I was told the fields behind the theatres were a problem, especially with all the new construction, digging, and garbage containers in the back, etc. He sent me two passes."

Sang Sang Taing had trouble with the smell of American theatres when he was growing up in Los Angeles. "The worst things were the stinky smell at all the downtown theatres that I came across. . . . The smell of the theatre made me want to throw up (as a matter of fact, I did a couple of times). Because of this bad experience that I had from my childhood, I never dared to go near an American theatre." He finally started going to American theatres. He discovered the source of the smell. "I strongly don't like popcorn, so I asked my friends who are going to eat popcorn to sit a distance away from me. The main reason is I get really sick when I smell popcorn."

If bad audiences and theatres cause some of the unpleasant experiences people have at the movies, the rest of these problems come from bad movies, or at least movies people do not like. D'Arcy West's worst moviegoing experiences "have always been going to see a movie that I want to be good, *Reality Bites* (1994) or *Manhattan Murder Mystery* (1993), and going opening night and the theatre's stuffed and the room is too small—like it might as well be showing on an airplane screen—and everyone's talking through the whole movie, filling the air with pretentious comments to impress their dates, and the movie ends up being really lousy and disappointing. Another outstandingly horrible experience I had was seeing *Hook* in the dead of winter in San Francisco, and the heater was broken in the theatre. We bought hot dogs just to keep our hands warm. And, of course, the movie was truly terrible."

Sam Frank liked seeing horror movies when he was growing up in the late fifties and early sixties, when he "would cover my eyes with my hands when the horror scenes came up, then peek through my fingers at them anyway. Today's horror movies, like an appallingly gory stinker I saw last year called *The Addiction* (1995), make me cover my eyes to shield myself from disgusting splashes of gore for their own sake. I feel sickened instead of thrilled." He is not alone.

For many viewers, it is not that the bad movie is scary or gory, but that it is just plain bad. Jack Hollander was in the UCLA student band in 1976 and went with the band to the Liberty Bowl in Memphis. One of the activities band members had scheduled was a free screening of the then-new remake of *King Kong*. "Let's just say that the 'sophisticated' college audience didn't appreciate the subtle nuances of the film (oh, heck, when Jessica Lange gets blow-dried by the ape and says, 'Gosh, my friends won't believe this' neither did we—and yes, there were the inevitable 'blow-job' cracks from the more sophomoric among us). On our way out of the theatre, numerous cries of 'We got what we paid for' and 'I demand a refund' (I think that was my crack) were heard. I don't think I've ever attended a more reviled showing of a film than that."

Sometimes bad reactions to a movie are quieter. Lawrence Dotson was on his first date. "I took the girl of my dreams, at the time, to Westwood. We went to see *Chariots of Fire* (1981). The commercials looked good, and I thought I'd impress her by going to see a grownup movie (we were in the eighth grade). I must have fallen asleep one-third of the way through the movie! Needless to say, I didn't even get a goodnight kiss from the girl." Olufemi Samuel and his whole family had trouble staying awake through *The Hunt for Red October*.

I went to see this film with my family, because Sean Connery was my uncle's favorite James Bond. The first ten minutes I concluded that the movie was dry. Before I knew what was going on, my entire family was fast asleep except for my uncle. And my dad said that since I was the family's film mogul, he was pretty sure that I was enjoying the movie and that I would tell him about the movie later on. The truth was that I wasn't enjoying the film at all; I was just staying awake in order to save my reputation as a film genius. Five minutes later I looked at my uncle to see how he was doing, and he was dozing off in his seat. This was the last straw; I passed out right there on the spot, and when I woke up the next morning, I was home.

For some movies, leaving is the only answer. Valerie Hornig was in her early twenties when she saw *Monty Python's The Meaning of Life* (1983) and says that

up until that point, I was pretty open to almost anything in the form of cinematic efforts. Well, apparently I was not quite open enough. If this film's scene of an obese man vomiting until the furniture floated around him was considered entertaining, then I definitely missed the party. Although I had paid seven dollars for my ticket to this 'event,' I was more than happy to give up my seat before this film ended. I left, surrounded by the still-laughing faces of my fellow audience members. I had never before and have never since left a movie before its completion, but I have no regrets for my actions that afternoon in Manhattan Beach.

Glinn Leevitt walked out of *Twister*. On Mother's Day he "was dragged to see *Twister*. I had to sit in the front right of the theatre. Watching this type of movie in this spot make me sick. I had to leave and get a refund before I lost my Mother's Day lunch." One of the worst experiences Lilia Fuller had was seeing *Showgirls*. "It is not the subject matter that made me think so, but the tasteless presentation of somebody's screwed idea about the showgirls in Las Vegas. Such a low class is really difficult to achieve." Which brings us back to film director Preston Sturges's "a little sex."

If films connect with us through emotions, good and bad, then it is not surprising that they connect through one of our strongest emotions. We have already seen how the sexual element of movies and moviegoing connect with us as adolescents—no wonder, given the sexual intensities of puberty. Movies also work on our adult sexuality as well, and while the emotions involved may not be quite as intense as those in puberty—although some are—the emotions may be darker, lighter, or more complex.

Movies like *Casablanca* have always connected with our romantic side.

Marion Levine says of the film, "Seeing it as a teenager is a waste of time—it's meant to be savored by a middle-aged woman, preferably with a man at her side and a box of tissues in her lap, or vice versa." Wajeeh Khursheed, a man, replies, "I enjoy watching 'love stories'; it gives me an idea of how people in different parts of the world and in different times acted. I get feedback for my own relationships in case I am in that situation. *Casablanca* had scenes that were very similar to my lifestyle and situations that I have been in lately while dating a girl that comes from a very conservative family."

Sangbum Lee admits, "Often I am attending a film I do not really want to see, because my date wanted to see it, though sometimes I did enjoy that film, even though I did not think it was going to be my type of picture." David Ko, now in his twenties, is even more blunt. "I usually use love stories, such as *Betty Blue* (1986), *The Lover* (1992), and *Map of the Human Heart* (1993) as a form of foreplay on my dates. A movie is the best way to get cozy and comfortable with someone and possibly make a move or two. And the theatrical movies always get out late at night, and a casual line afterwards is: let's go to my place. Or we make out in the car. Hopefully I got past that stage in the movie already. For two hours I get to sit next to the cute girl I adore, smell her hair, hold her hand, and put my arm around her when she's scared."

Sometimes the date as foreplay does not work. Albert Nazaryan had a crush on an older girl and "convinced her friends to take me along with them the next time they went to see a movie. I recommended *Stakeout* (1987) because Siskel and Ebert both gave it thumbs up. We spent two hours watching a couple of rat-faced leading men doing completely unappealing things. I felt I had betrayed the girl I loved. I have been suspicious of critics ever since." Nor is foiled foreplay strictly a heterosexual phenomenon. You may recall that a younger Paul Sbrizzi liked the "buck naked" scientists in *The Andromeda Strain*. Sbrizzi and his date were going to see *The Doors* (1991) when his "date informed me just before the movie starts that he had spotted his boyfriend in the theatre."

A female friend and employee of a theatre complex invited Skylaire Alfvegren to a screening of *Go Fish* (1994), "a film I was somewhat eager to see for I had heard good things about it. The experience was memorable mostly because my friend kept running her hand up and down my thigh throughout the film. I found this amusing, and a welcome, if unsolicited, distraction from that boring . . . film." Later the same year, Alfvegren went to a screening of a Troma Films "newest future classic," *Teenage Catgirls in Heat*. There were seven other people at the screening. "I came prepared for the worst, and it still exceeded my expectations. I came dressed in teenage catgirl wear and was hit on by a fifty-year-old Israeli film producer upon my departure." That year was busy for Alfvegren, because she also saw a revival of *Last Tango in Paris* with her boyfriend, "and we were intrigued by the age difference between the main characters, as sixteen years separate us. We went in there giggling, and left the theatre silent and sat in the car for a good twenty minutes."

Michael Behling became a fan of Russ Meyer's *Beyond the Valley of the Dolls* (1970) "which exhibits Meyer's (and Roger Ebert's [the co-writer of the script]) amazing command of the semiotics of kitsch. Oh, also I think there were some amazing jugs happening in that film." Soft-core porn like Meyer's became one of the last attempts to save the drive-in theatres in the seventies, and there were even some drive-ins that got into hard-core. The problem was that in many cases the screens were visible from the surrounding areas, and complaints closed the theatres, or at least stopped the showing of porno films. One drive-in near my hometown of Bloomington had a particular problem. The approach to the theatre was along a road that had slight hills and valleys in it. Approaching the theatre in the fifties had been fun, since you could get a brief view of the film on the top of the hill, then not see it in the valley, then another clip at the top, and so on. With porno films, I am told by people who went to the theatre then, it was very frustrating because you always thought that the bits that happened in the valleys were probably more interesting than what you saw on the hills. Traffic accidents ensued.

In the early seventies, there was a brief period when porno films seemed to be gaining public acceptance, before videotape came along and took sex out of the theatres and back into the homes where it belonged. Angela West tells about her worst moviegoing experience at one of the few remaining porno theatres on Hollywood Boulevard.

A friend and I thought that exposing ourselves to Live Girls, Nude! Nude! Nude! [not the title of the film, but the generic listing on the marquee; why should they bother to change it every week?] may enrich us in some form. Boy, we were wrong. I knew what to expect going in, but in some way my expectation could never prepare me for the genuinely horrible experience. A sleazy, overweight Mexican . . . man took our money at the counter. He seemed pleased that we were willing to pay the admission price of three bucks. I suppose more frugal customers had tried to talk him down in the past. With our tickets in hand, we followed the ramp that led to a heavy red curtain. A little Spanish guy politely opened the curtain for me. Considering I was the only woman in the entire place, I suppose it was the gentleman's thing to do. Without further hesitation, we quickly took our seats in the back of the room. It was a cold room, dark and stained with the smell of sexual odors. [If you think the floors are sticky in regular theatres . . .] I was obviously sitting in a puddle of something. My brain didn't want to accept the truth, so I fed it a lie by rationalizing that some friendly theatre patron had spilled their drink and forgot to clean it up; of course, it didn't smell like 7–Up, but on to more pressing matters.

The movie started a little late, due to the lack of paying customers. After a long period of creative visualization, wishing I were somewhere else, the curtain finally rose and the drunk, smelly men began to cheer. Lesbians—the entire screen was filled with women eating women, women fucking women, women spanking women. I sank into my seat feeling the "7–Up" penetrating through the bottom of my jeans. I glanced around at the various men in the room. Most of them had hard-ons that wouldn't stop. Large bulges in their pants that seemed to grow as the movie progressed. Suddenly, I realized a large majority of them were glancing back at me. I immediately grabbed on to my male friend and looked to the screen casually.

As the movie's plot began to unfold—Brandy was a nurse at County General screwing Tova, an epileptic patient from Brazil—I noticed men getting up and going to the back of the movie theatre. Curious is my nature, so I got up under the disguise that I had to use the bathroom and walked to the back of the house. As I got closer to the dark shadows, I heard the distinct sound of a woosh, woosh. Then the groans of sexual ecstasy. Basically that was the end of my tolerance for this circus of sick, sexually disturbed men. I went to my friend and demanded that we leave immediately. He protested, saying that Tova had gone into a coma and Brandy thought the only way to get a response from her was oral sex. I grabbed his hand and yanked him from his seat. When I got home that night I must have taken three baths. Somehow, I couldn't erase the memory of that horrible place out of my mind. Nothing could wash the effects of Live Girls, Nude! Nude! Nude! from my conscience. It is a movie that I will remember forever.

I must admit that during the period of "porno chic" in the seventies, I saw a porno film or two every year just to keep informed, although most of them seemed to be more of a turn-off for me than a turn-on. One of the occupational hazards of teaching, especially film, in Los Angeles, is that you tend to run into your students when they are nude. In the early seventies, there was a woman student I'll call "Wendy" in my class. She was not a particularly good student, but she tried hard. One day Wendy asked me for a favor. Her child had been hurt while she was in school. Normally the police would have let her off with a warning, but she was a white woman living with a black man, and some members of the Los Angeles Police Department then frowned on that and wrote her up for child endangerment. She asked me if I would write a letter to the judge saying she was indeed a student at LACC. She allowed as how I did not have to say she was a *good* student, since she knew she wasn't. I wrote the letter for her and gave it to her the next day. The following Sunday night I decided to see my soft-core porn film for the year and went off to the Pussycat Theatre in Santa Monica. I did not even bother to check the starting times, so I got in in the middle of the first feature. The film was about a young, virginal woman who went to work in a large company, only to discover that the company workforce was having constant orgies. By the time I took my seat, the first orgy was in progress, and the woman went in to complain to her boss. He was sitting behind his desk with no shirt on, and next to him was a woman who had previously been established as his personal executive secretary. She was topless and obviously doing something to the boss under the table. The dialogue in the scene was between the woman and the boss, but I kept looking at the secretary. She looked like Wendy. She had the same dimple in the chin as Wendy. I had no idea if her breasts looked like Wendy's because I had never seen Wendy's. Maybe they were, maybe they were not. Then at the end of the scene, the secretary had one line. It was Wendy, who had a very distinctive voice.

I avoided saying anything to Wendy, since with not only the court case but also final exams coming up, I figured she had enough on her mind. At the beginning of the next semester (she passed my classes, writing one of the great free-association, if not accurate, final exams), she came in to see me to tell me she was dropping out of school because she had gotten a job working as a script supervisor. I brought up the fact that I had seen her in a movie in which she was at least partially nude. She asked, "Which one?" This was not her only film.

Since the era of porno chic, I generally avoid porno films, particularly as they have less and less story material and less and less characterization. Not that they ever had a lot of either. Sex is nice, but as a part of life, not just by itself. I tend to find films with real characterization much sexier. *Bull Durham* (1988), about two of America's favorite subjects, baseball and sex, is much sexier to me than porno films. Of course, that may have been nostalgia as well as lust on my part, since I was in my late forties by the time it came out. And *Bull Durham* plays the nostalgia card in a very eighties way. "Rock Around the Clock," which was an incendiary, sexy, urban anthem in 1955's *Blackboard Jungle*, and a semirebellious, semisexy, semiconservative anthem in 1973's *American Graffiti*, was now being used to represent nostalgia for small-town America and its values. Such as "a little sex."

Since I like other things as well as sex, one of my most memorable moviegoing experiences combined nearly everything I love. In the late seventies, my wife and daughter and I went to see a movie. Naturally, I got a bag of popcorn and a

Coke before the movie. Unlike Sang Sang Taing, I like the smell of popcorn. After the young woman at the refreshment stand put the popcorn and Coke on the counter, she bent backward slightly, raised her bare foot and flicked something off it.

How many times in your life do almost everything you love in the world come together at one time?

Eastwood

Now that we have begun to see the complexities of the relationships between movies and their audiences, we can apply much of what we have learned by looking at a star and filmmaker and his audiences. It is only appropriate that we take a star whose career has extended over the time period covered by this book. It is also a career made not by critics or studio publicity machines, but by his audiences.[1]

In the early fifties, before there were cinema courses at Los Angeles City College, a young ex-lumberjack from northern California named Clint Eastwood enrolled at LACC, taking courses in business administration.[2] In 1954, even though the old studio system was beginning to break up, some studios still had actors under contract, and Eastwood was given a six-month contract as an actor at Universal studios. He appeared in bit parts in a number of B pictures released in 1955, such as *Revenge of the Creature*, *Francis in the Navy*, and *Tarantula*. I saw all of these in Bloomington, but I have no recollection of Eastwood in any of them. Universal was not impressed either. He was let go from the studio in October of that year.

In 1959, Eastwood began a seven-year run on a Western television series called *Rawhide*. He was not the star but the second lead. During the 1964 summer hiatus for the series, Eastwood appeared in an Italian Western made in Spain, which eventually bore the title *A Fistful of Dollars*. When it was completed in the fall of 1964, the producers were not impressed with it, nor were film distributors in Rome and Naples. Because of financial considerations, the producers had to arrange at least a week's run in a theatre. Instead of showing it in the less sophisticated southern Italy, for some reason they opened it—without publicity—in Florence. According to legend, at the end of the week the theatre owner was making so much money he refused to return the print to the producers. The picture became a giant box office success in Italy.

A Fistful of Dollars did not open in the United States until 1967, since the film was an unauthorized remake of Akira Kurosawa's 1961 Japanese film

Yojimbo, and it took that long to clear the rights from Kurosawa. The American critics were not kind. Bosley Crowther of the *New York Times,* was just as clueless about it as he would be about *Bonnie and Clyde* later that year. Judith Crist at the *New York World Journal Tribune* called *A Fistful of Dollars* a "cheapjack production . . . misses both awfulness and mediocrity."[3] The picture eventually grossed $4.2 million, considerably less than that year's *The Graduate, Guess Who's Coming to Dinner,* and *Bonnie and Clyde,* but more than Otto Preminger's *Hurry Sundown.*[4] It was a hit, but it was new enough and strange enough not to be a blockbuster.

Some viewers have confused *A Fistful of Dollars* with its antecedent. Michael Behling says, "I'm not sure if I saw this. I saw a few Eastwood cowboy flicks and a few Kurosawa films with the same plots and get them all confused." The violence in *Fistful* was gorier and less poetic than in *Yojimbo* and could be seen as part of the increasingly violent imagery that began the sixties in *Psycho,* showed up in *Bonnie and Clyde,* and became even more vivid two years later in *The Wild Bunch.*

Cowboys in American films had always been laconic, but Eastwood, cutting out a lot of the dialogue in the script, said even less. Moe Gardener thought, "how nice it is not to have people always talking." Peggy Dilley had a different response to the so-called "spaghetti Westerns," including this one. "They bore me. I fall asleep. They grate on my nerves. Clint Eastwood does. I don't know why. Maybe they're too visual for me. Maybe too male. I need more verbal." Aubrey Solomon, on the other hand, was

probably one of Eastwood's earliest fans. I saw [*A Fistful of Dollars*] on a double bill with *For a Few Dollars More* [the 1965 sequel, released in the United States in mid-1967] in 1968 and very much enjoyed them, which is surprising considering my prejudice against English-dubbed movies. But these were among a small handful of dubbed movies that were successful in the U.S. Aside from the Italian swarthiness of most of the actors, I enjoyed the "different" look of the old West. Of course, there was enough violence and action to keep the movies going at a steady pace. Seen today, both [*A Fistful of Dollars* and *For a Few Dollars More*] seem a lot slower in pacing than at the time of release. *The Good, The Bad, and The Ugly* [1966, the third film in the unofficial trilogy, released in the United States in 1967] seems to hold up a lot better."

James Ford, who was about ten when *A Fistful of Dollars* first came out, remembers the experience. "Clint! One of my first drive-in experiences. My older brother took my younger brother and me. I couldn't get enough. Have seen it over and over, as I have most Clint Eastwood movies. Now more for nostalgia." Nostalgia is not the first concept that comes to mind when one thinks of Eastwood, but the impact of his work sticks in people's minds—a prerequisite for nostalgia. Hollywood is now haunted by its recent, as well as its distant, past.

Blair Woodard became "a huge fan of spaghetti Westerns," but he first saw *Fistful* on television, although he has "since rented it to be able to watch uninterrupted. I think the greatest accomplishment was the evolution of the antihero and a more gritty Western style." Like Woodard, I first saw *Fistful* on television, having missed it in the theatres. By the time I first saw it, I had seen so much of the style that it did not seem as fresh as it did to its first theatrical audiences. Having seen and loved *Yojimbo*, I found this rip-off amusing. Woodard and I were not alone in initially catching *Fistful* on television. Like many movies, it added fans as it was repeatedly shown on television, which in turn created fans for Eastwood and his subsequent films.

Michael Cohen is a "sucker for the laconic," and he "never missed a chance to catch a [director Sergio] Leone Western on TV, although I never had the desire to see them in a theatre. Eastwood offing those three goons for insulting his mule in *Fistful of Dollars* was one of Clint's best moments, but I think *The Good, the Bad, and the Ugly* was much better." Richard Henrie also liked *Fistful*, especially the "close-ups of these hardened faces of characters and the authenticity." Leone had perhaps learned a little too well John Ford's dictum about photographing the eyes, since the extreme close-ups of the eyes became one of his directorial signatures, particularly in the Eastwood trilogy. It is a style that takes advantage of Eastwood's squint. Javier Rodriguez first saw *A Fistful of Dollars* on television, "and I was so shocked at the Western. . . . the shootouts were really a turn-on for me. And the lonely towns made the film very real to me."

The images of the lonely towns came from Leone's wonderful use of empty space to suggest a human absence. They also came from a particularly low budget on *A Fistful of Dollars*. Leone could not afford the extras that showed up in increasing numbers in the trilogy as the budgets increased. Rick Mitchell noted the budgetary limitations of the film when he first saw it in 1967. "I don't remember being really impressed, not thinking it even compared to the B Westerns still being made by Universal and Columbia. Perhaps it was the dubbing, which kept putting me in mind of the sword-'n'-sandal 'epics' the Italians had previously been making." Shaun Hill-Kret, who only saw it later, also thought it was a "cheesy Western, but I loved it. I loved the character with no name and have rented it a dozen times. Anytime it comes on TV, I watch it. A fun movie."

Although I missed *A Fistful of Dollars* in theatres, I did see the second film, *For a Few Dollars More*, when it opened in the summer of 1967. I had more of a reaction to Eastwood's co-star, Lee Van Cleef, than I did to Eastwood. Eastwood had made no impression on me previously. On the other hand, I remembered

Van Cleef from *High Noon* (1952) and other Westerns of the fifties, and I was glad to see him in a big part. I was struck by Leone's visual look, which seemed to apply Antonioni's use of empty space, suggesting a moral as well as a human vacuum to a revisionist view of the Western. I was not particularly struck by the "authenticity" of the film, which seemed to me just as bogus, but dirtier, than the B Westerns I grew up with.

The acting of the supporting cast, and Leone's Italian-opera style seemed very over-the-top, and Eastwood was a model of refinement compared to everybody else in the film. It has also struck me, as I have watched the trilogy several times since, that while as a director Leone used Eastwood's stillness against the operatic abundance very effectively, he did not have a clue about Eastwood's humor. Eastwood brings a dry, laconic wit that is a wonderful counterpoint against the excesses of the film, and the director hardly seems aware of it. It is certainly not a wit that shows up in Leone's non-Eastwood Western, *Once Upon a Time in the West* (1968, released in the United States in 1969), which, while critically acclaimed, grossed only $2.1 million, half the gross for *A Fistful of Dollars*.[5] Leone never had another commercial hit in America after he stopped making pictures with Eastwood. No wonder he tended to disparage Eastwood and his talent in later interviews.[6]

Eastwood began to grow on American audiences. While *A Fistful of Dollars* grossed $4.2 million, *A Few Dollars More* grossed $4.3 million, and *The Good, the Bad, and the Ugly* brought in $6.03 million.[7] Donna Crisci did not see an Eastwood picture until *The Good, the Bad, and the Ugly* and then "didn't like that one that much. Now, however, I think Clint is really cool." Hollywood, which had continued to think of Eastwood as just a television actor, and not even a television *star*, took notice of the grosses of the trilogy. His first post–trilogy American film was 1968's *Hang 'Em High*, a Western with the hard edge of the Italian films (the film begins with him lynched and left for dead), but without Leone's stylistic excesses and more conventional American production values (it was shot mostly on a Western street set on MGM's old back lot, where I had driven the tour bus). *Hang 'Em High* grossed $6.71 million.[8] *Where Eagles Dare*, a World War II action film, came out the same year and grossed $7.15 million,[9] proving that Eastwood could do more than Westerns.

Not every Eastwood increased the gross of the previous film. In 1971, Eastwood starred in *The Beguiled*, which I saw at the American Film Institute. I admired not only the film, but also Eastwood's willingness to get into the dark side of the male psyche, unusual for a male action star. I began to think there was more there than just the dry wit. The American audience in general did not respond, partly, I suspect, because of the darkness of the film, but partly because Universal's advertising created awareness of it as a Clint Eastwood action picture. Audiences who turned up expecting that were disappointed and probably upset by what they saw, and the audiences who might have liked the picture were turned off by the ads. The film was so dark, however, that I doubt if it ever could attract a large audience.

While some critics began to appreciate Eastwood and his films, Pauline Kael, the sharpest and most interesting film critic writing at the time, did not. And never did. Her review of Eastwood's 1971 cop film, *Dirty Harry*, condemned the film as "fascist"[10] because it shows a police detective going beyond the rules to get a killer. This review set the critical book on Eastwood for nearly fifteen years. One can look at reviews of other Eastwood films by other critics after Kael's review and see the influence, not necessarily in what is said, but in how Eastwood is discussed. Kael's condemnation of *Dirty Harry* did not hurt it at the box office; if anything, the controversy increased attendance. The film was released in late 1971 and made most of its money in 1972. It grossed $16 million, over twice what any previous Eastwood film had brought in.[11] *Dirty Harry* was the fifth highest-grossing picture of 1972, making less than *The Godfather*, *Fiddler on the Roof*, *Diamonds Are Forever*, and Bogdanovich's *What's Up Doc?*, but more than Bogdanovich's *The Last Picture Show*, *Clockwork Orange*, *Cabaret*, and *Everything You Wanted to Know About Sex But Were Afraid to Ask*.

Kenneth Hughes reacted as much to Eastwood's character as to the film. "He was very cool and funny as heck. . . . He fixed the world and never got anything back." Julio Carmona saw *Dirty Harry* "when I was still fairly young. My father was a big Clint Eastwood fan, and we watched his movies whenever we could. I remember seeing a rugged character that didn't take any crap from anyone. I always liked Eastwood, maybe because of the characters he played or maybe because my father liked him." Angela West's father was also a fan. "My father always made me rent his movies at the video store. I always did it reluctantly, but when I got them home and started watching them, I was always involved. I felt myself becoming friends with Dirty Harry. Knowing him more than any other character on the screen. Feeling empathy for his screwed-up life. Always rooting for him to kick some crook's ass. He was bad and cool, and though I'd never admit it to my father, I loved watching the movie."

Arnold Quinlan's parents had a slightly different reaction. While watching the film on television, shortly after the famous "Do you feel lucky?" speech, "my parents sent me to bed because 'due to mature content this material isn't suitable for younger viewers.' This scenario happened more than once, and I guess it was all right to wait until I was older. I may have hated them for it at the time, or maybe I just thought it was unfair. I don't know. I saw the film later with many others and, well, Clint is my hero." The first time Shaun Hill-Kret saw *Dirty Harry*, "I thought Clint was totally cool. Now as I watch I see more of a message in the movie. I think this movie had a time, but it feels dated."

Javier Rodriguez saw *Dirty Harry* first on TV. "The gun part [the "Do you feel lucky?" scene, I assume, although guns do show up a lot in the film] was my favorite. Especially when he used it to scare the bad dudes off. Also when he would shoot someone and the person would fall thirty feet back. I thought that was so cool and well deserved." Alejandro Munoz remembers, "*Dirty Harry* was the first Clint Eastwood film I had ever watched, and it made me an instant fan of both him and guns. Now *there* is an interesting point: the idea that it was movies that persuaded me toward the acceptance of violence in my life. I am not lying when I state that after this movie I ached for a Smith and Wesson." Kurt Knecht saw *Dirty Harry* by accident when his local video store had mistakenly rented out the copy of *The Christmas Story* (1983) he had reserved for New Year's Eve. "I scanned the shelves of the store, but practically everything was gone except *Dirty Harry*. I reluctantly took the film home and was pleasantly surprised. The film was gritty and hard and tough. I felt good watching the bad guys get their comeuppance. It was the beginning of my vigilante justice phase (my 'good triumphs over evil' phase). This phase did not last long, and it toppled underneath Charles Bronson's *Death Wish* series [1974–1994]. Even the later *Dirty Harry* films weren't as good—probably because they were not as original as the first."

Desreta Jackson is a young black woman who did not like *Dirty Harry*. "I never understood what people found so great in Eastwood. He was just another cop that made his own rules. But when cops on the streets do it, we end up with stuff like the Rodney King trial." On the other hand, Eastwood's films have generally been very popular in the black community. When Eastwood was at a public showing of *Dirty Harry,* he was sitting next to a black man who did not recognize him. When at the end of the movie Harry throws down his badge, the man said, "Man, San Francisco lost one damn good cop."[12] Larry Cole, writing about Eastwood in the *Village Voice*, recalled his own experience of watching the film with a gang of Lower East Side street kids when it first came out, and he thought their approval of the film showed how the oppressed took on the values of the oppressors, but he later realized the kids liked the simple justice of the story.[13]

Bryan Cawthon thinks the "movie makes it difficult to care for our judicial system. If only cops had all the right answers like Clint. I don't understand how I can dislike this type of film and not be able to change the channel. I didn't want that serial killer to get away. I had to watch." Carlos Gabriel just "can't stand this guy!" Jack Hollander realizes "there are those who feel Eastwood gives a carefully mannered performance. . . . I, on the other hand, think that it's just bad acting. I didn't care for this film the first time I saw it, and subsequent viewings have done little to change my opinion (although later films have given me a chance to see a 'better' Clint Eastwood)."

Tandy Summers saw the sequels before she got around to seeing *Dirty Harry* at the age of twenty. "My first impressions were 'this was a film I didn't want to watch.' I only saw clips of it and never gave it a chance. I just thought the psycho was too crazy. I finally watched it one morning on TBS and was hooked. Since then I always catch it. It's become one of my favorite movies. I totally like the psycho and the bizarre music."

I saw *Dirty Harry* when it first came out and found it mildly amusing and suspenseful. I was more taken with the sequels, which, given the success of *Dirty Harry*, there were bound to be. As noted earlier in this text, the first sequel, *Magnum Force*, was one of the early studio films to open in wide release. It brought in rentals of $18.3 million, making it the fourth highest-grossing film of 1974, the year it made most of its money. It was outgrossed by *The Sting*, *The Exorcist*, and *Papillon* and made more than *Herbie Rides Again* (the first of three sequels to *The Love Bug*), *Blazing Saddles*, and *Serpico*. What was intriguing to me about *Magnum Force* was the way the plot seemed to answer the criticisms of *Dirty Harry* as a fascist film. In the new film, Harry was fighting true fascists within the police department. The next sequel, *The Enforcer* (1976), had the macho Harry Callahan paired off with a woman partner (Tyne Daly), which created its own amusements. It grossed $24 million in 1977, well behind *Star Wars*, *Rocky*, and even *Smokey and the Bandit*, but ahead of *The Spy Who Loved Me*, *Herbie Goes to Monte Carlo*, and *Annie Hall*.[14]

Michael Behling gets the Dirty Harry films "all confused with each other," while Wendi Cole says, "There were so many that they begin to blur for me after a while. The one I am speaking of [when asked to write about *Dirty Harry*] is the one with Tyne Daly in it. Even though this movie was serious, I thought Clint and Tyne were hilarious. I hated it when she died though. I was not thrilled about that at all."

One Wednesday afternoon in August 1976, I saw a double bill of Burt Reynolds's first directorial effort, *Gator,* and Eastwood's *The Outlaw Josey Wales.* According to my diary, I thought *Josey Wales* was "an off-beat Clint Eastwood flick. Slow-moving, but a very nice feeling to it." My recollection now is that I was more impressed with it than that, but that may be the way it grew on me. I know I certainly recognized at the time that it was both a summing up of his Leone Westerns (the grubbiness, the extremes of violence) and a turning away from it (this is no Man With No Name; everybody knows his name). The opening pastoral shots and the disruptions to the family suggested Henry King's opening of *Jesse James,* and the variety of connections with Josey's real family at the beginning and the surrogate family he collects over the course of the film gave Eastwood's character here human connections his characters in the Leone pictures did not. It also struck me that it was Eastwood's bicentennial film, in that the post-Civil War theme of reconstruction reflected the kind of reconstruction that was just beginning in post-Vietnam America.

Arnold Quinlan was more impressed with the film than I initially was. "The best, as far as I am concerned. I was lucky enough to see this one in a theatre. . . . Sad, funny, sad, exciting, sad, funny, exciting, definitely one of the best films he has ever done. My favorite scene is the bounty hunter that says, 'It's a living.' Josey comes back, 'Dying ain't much of a living, boy.' The bounty hunter leaves. He comes back. 'I had to,' he says. 'I know,' says Josey. He then blasts him out the doors again. Awesome!" As violent as it was, what struck me was the ending, in which, having dispatched the worst of the bad guys chasing him, Josey lets the more conflicted one live, as if to say there was too much violence in the world. Aside from *Billy Jack*, it is the only American film I know that leads up to a final fight and then works without it.

Shaun Hill-Kret was not quite as taken with *Josey Wales*. "Good, honest, two hours worth of excitement. Did nothing for me emotionally, but always fun to watch." Aubrey Solomon also had a mixed impression. He saw the film at a prerelease screening at USC. "I admired Eastwood's directorial skill and thought it was his most ambitious film to date. I remember the beautiful Panavision photography and composition but little else. I know everybody's talking about it as a masterpiece now, but it didn't strike me at the time." The critics were also less than impressed. True, Kevin Thomas did write a nice review in the *Los Angeles Times*, and *The Outlaw Josey Wales* did show up on *Time*'s year-end list of the ten best,[15] but *Variety* described it as "Formula Eastwood slaughter film for regular market," while Rex Reed in the *New York Daily News* wrote, "Seems to last two days. . . . [Eastwood] is accompanied by a stock company of ferocious hams. Either they are terrible actors, or it just looks like overacting when you move your eyebrows on the same screen as Eastwood."[16] In looking through the reviews of the picture in the clipping files at the library of the Academy of Motion Picture Arts and Sciences, I could not find a single review, even the good ones, that seemed to get what the film was about.

Perhaps the worst review of *The Outlaw Josey Wales* was in the *New York Times*. The reviewer seemed mostly concerned about all the spitting in the movie. Being a Yankee newspaper, the *Times* complained the film was more sympathetic to the southern characters than to the northern ones, adding, "There is something cynical about this primitive one-sidedness in what is not only a historical context, but happens to be our own historical context." As for Eastwood, the review said he "doesn't act, he spits."[17] The man who wrote the review, Richard Eder, later won the 1987 Pulitzer Prize for his book reviews. I will leave it to you to decide what that tells us about the connections, or lack of them, between the east coast intellectual establishment and the mainstreams of American life. *The Outlaw Josey Wales* grossed $10.6 million in 1976,[18] the following year added another $2.2 million,[19] and by 1982 had added another $700,000.[20] In 1976 it was the thirteenth highest-grossing film, outgrossed by *One Flew*

Over the Cuckoo's Nest, All the President's Men, and just slightly by *Taxi Driver*, although *Josey Wales*'s final total five years later was higher than the latter's. *Josey Wales* grossed more in 1976 than *Barry Lyndon*, Burt Reynolds's *Gator*, and Hitchcock's *Family Plot*.[21]

For James Ford, *The Outlaw Josey Wales* is the "Clintessential Western," his favorite, although "I have suggested this film so many times to friends who are critical of Eastwood. It usually doesn't work." I have not found that to be the case. I first tried it in my classes at LACC in 1984, and like certain other films, it works particularly well in the context of a film history course. I even tried the film the quarter I taught at UCLA in 1986. The class "got it" in the context of the course as well as my LACC students had, although Eastwood was only beginning to get any critical respectability by then. The classes at both schools saw how Eastwood has borrowed from other directors, how the representation of violence has changed, and how the themes of home and community put the film in the center of traditional American films.

Eastwood's American films were also making an impact overseas. Michael Sampson grew up in the Central American country of Belize, watching mostly American Westerns as a child. "Of course, I thought that most of America had gunfights going on. . . . Of all the movies I had watched as a child, I remember Clint Eastwood the most. I really don't know why. . . . The Clint Eastwood films may have stuck in my mind probably because of the level of violence that was depicted seemed acceptable."

Meanwhile, back in America, the other establishment media continued to be clueless about Eastwood. Richard Schickel and Jay Cocks, film critics for *Time*, had begun to think in 1977 that Eastwood might be worth a cover story in the magazine, since *Josey Wales* had been on their ten-best list for 1976. They presented the idea to the editors, which made the editors "squeamish," according to Schickel,[22] who later wrote, "They knew what 'thinking people' thought of Clint." What finally came out in the magazine was a story that was as much about, and more favorable to, Burt Reynolds, as it was about Eastwood.

Having thrashed such intelligent people as Bosley Crowther, Judith Crist, Sergio Leone, Pauline Kael, Rex Reed and Richard Eder, as well as the media establishment in general, for being clueless about one or more elements of Clint Eastwood, I now have to admit my own cluelessness. In 1978, against the advice of most of his staff,[23] Eastwood made a comedy with an orangutan. The reviews for *Every Which Way but Loose* were generally awful. In the *New York Daily New,* Rex Reed called it "the latest Clint Eastwood disgrace. . . . Anyone who sees it has suffered enough brain damage already."[24] I saw it and thought it was a mediocre redneck comedy. It grossed $48 million. More than twice *any* of his previous films.[25] And I have no idea why. My only consolation is that nobody else seems to know either. And it was not just this film. Two years later,

Eastwood did a sequel called *Any Which Way You Can*, which grossed $39.5 million, making it the sixth highest-grossing picture of 1981, after *Raiders of the Lost Ark*, *Superman II*, and *Stripes*. It made nearly three times as much that year as *Raging Bull* and more than four times as much as De Palma's *Blow Out*.[26]

I can only think of two comments that may explain why the orangutan films were so successful. One of the dimmest people I knew at the time said he had liked one of the orangutan pictures—I forget which one—because he knew people who were as stupid as those in the movie. Perhaps the film appealed to a lot of people who felt that at least they were smarter than the people in *this* film. This is a reason, by the way, why a lot of stupid movies get to be hits: audiences can feel good about themselves by feeling superior to the characters in the movies and the movies themselves.

The other comment came from William Goldman in his book *Adventures in the Screen Trade*. "Eastwood has to beat up on people. When he doesn't, as in *The Beguiled*, or the more recent and very sweet *Bronco Billy* (1980), a film he also directed, the audience is considerably smaller. *Bronco Billy*, for example, attracted less than a third of the audience than the Eastwood film that preceded it, *Any Which Way You Can*. Clint Eastwood is really only Clint Eastwood when he's the toughest guy on the block." [27]

This may explain why Peggy Dilley found Eastwood "too male" and said, "The only Clint Eastwood movies I've liked have been the ones he was in with Sondra Locke. She made up for what he lacked and made intolerable movies kind of funny." It may also explain why James Ford differs: "Just about everything Clint Eastwood has ever done I like. Only *The Gauntlet* (1977) leaps to mind as an exception." *The Gauntlet* costars Sondra Locke as Gus Mally, a hooker who is a witness in a trial and Eastwood as the detective trying to keep her alive. The reviews as usual were terrible, commenting on how unreal the violence of the film was, making it like a cartoon. But the reviews also missed the point that it *was* a cartoon: a Roadrunner cartoon, with Locke as the Roadrunner and Eastwood as Wyle E. Coyote. Which is probably why James Ford did not like it: Locke beats up on Eastwood as much as the Roadrunner destroys Wyle E. Coyote.

I began to notice a curious thing about Eastwood's films and his audiences. I saw *The Gauntlet* at a matinee in Marina Del Rey, a yuppie suburb of Los Angeles, and the guys in the crowd tended to look not like redneck bikers, but like white-collar workers. The guys cheered whenever Eastwood manhandled Locke but were quiet when Locke manhandled Eastwood. There was enough of the former, and enough violence in general, that the film grossed $17.5 million, less than *Grease* and *National Lampoon's Animal House*, but more than *The Turning Point* and *An Unmarried Woman*.[28] Still, there was Locke's toughness. . . .

In the fall of 1983, we began to see the trailer for the fourth Dirty Harry film,

Sudden Impact. The trailer told nothing of what the film was about, but focused on a scene early in the picture in which Harry has the drop on a crook in a café and suggests to him, "Go ahead. Make my day." The audience loved the trailer, because it suggested that Dirty "Do you feel lucky?" Harry was back in business. The critics generally hated the picture, but by now I was adept at reading between the lines of the reviews, and it looked as though something interesting was going on. Harry was dealing with a woman who was just as much a "vigilante" as he was, and while the reviews generally did not give away the ending, it sounded as though the "fascist" Harry did not blow her away at the end. I saw the picture, and I was right: there was a lot more going on here than any review I had seen.

About a week after I saw the picture, I got a call from my sister-in-law, the noted feminist art historian Ann Sutherland Harris. She was asking me for suggestions for Christmas releases she could take her then-six-year-old son to. I mentioned a couple of family films, and then because I love to tease Ann, I suggested there was a new picture she might like as a feminist. It was about a rape victim who gets revenge on those who did it. Ann fell into my trap and asked me if it was a new European film. No, it was the new Clint Eastwood film. You may not remember the sort of snort that intellectuals gave in those days when you mentioned Eastwood, but Ann gave it. Then, with no conscious thought on my part, out of my mouth popped, "You know, Ann, on the basis of this film, you may have to consider Eastwood a feminist filmmaker." Another snort. Then she said, "Well, maybe you should write an article for *Ms.* magazine."

I didn't write it for *Ms.* When an article in the *Los Angeles Times* on women's roles in current films failed to mention Sondra Locke in *Sudden Impact*, I wrote up a piece on the different interesting women in Eastwood's films and sent it to the *Times.* In what became the third paragraph in the story, I wrote "Eastwood may be not only one of the best but most important and influential (because of the size of his audience) feminist filmmaker working in America today."[29] I knew, of course, that there was no way the *Los Angeles Times* was going to publish anything so preposterous, which would inflame the West Side "whine-and-cheese" liberals who patronized the department stores that advertised heavily in the *Times.*

The article appeared in the *Times* on March 11, 1984, and the letters and replies continued for four weeks after that. My wife has been a research associate for a number of scientists at UCLA and was with Paul D. Boyer when he did the work that eventually won him the Nobel Prize in 1997. I had never before seen her fall out of her chair laughing, but she did when she read the opening line of Nancy Simons's letter: "Obviously, Tom Stempel would not know a 'strong' woman unless she shot, knifed, castrated or emotionally abused him." I myself was particularly partial to Clair Peterson's opening line: "All the world knows those who teach film never—*never*—have a sense of humor."[30] The smartest counterargument came two weeks after those two letters from a longer piece by Nancy Webber, an instructor of film appreciation at Los Angeles Harbor College, who analyzed why Eastwood's films do not present traditional feminism.[31] Her points were well taken, even though I used the "feminist" label as an entry to talk about an artistic element in Eastwood's films that few writers had picked up on.[32]

I was unaware that a few months prior to my story, Norman Mailer had written a positive piece about Eastwood for *Parade* magazine.[33] He had not written anything as inflammatory as my line about feminism, but the fact that one of the icons of the literary establishment was taking Eastwood seriously began to shift the critical book on him. What my article did was give writers who previously had no way to "legitimately" write about Eastwood a way to do so. Roger Ebert did two print interviews and one television interview with Eastwood in which the issue was highlighted. Molly Haskell did a short piece on Eastwood for *Playgirl* magazine that said it was "still stretching it a bit to call Eastwood a 'feminist' director," but still took him at least somewhat seriously.[34] My favorite was a *New York Times Magazine* cover story in 1985 entitled "Clint Eastwood, Seriously," primarily because (a) it was the *New York Times*, and (b) it made no reference to Richard Eder's review of *The Outlaw Josey Wales* nine years before, while saying, "Perhaps his best film, *The Outlaw Josey Wales*—all outrage, and, most of all, fury against killing, brutality and war—was made in 1976." The article did include the following: "Someone writes that he is a feminist film director."[35]

By the late eighties, the idea had become so much a part of the critical book on Eastwood that writers just assumed it was part of what we had always thought about him. In 1993, Paul Smith, writing an intelligent, in-depth book on how Eastwood developed the images that he did in the public mind, only picked up on references from about 1990.[36] It did not surprise me when Eastwood's biographer, Richard Schickel, wrote in 1996 that I had "advanced this idea at a moment when, seemingly, its time had come."[37] Schickel appears to be just as astonished as I am that its time had come, but it obviously resonated with people writing about Eastwood. It *may* even have made some difference to any civilians watching Eastwood's movies.

If at the beginning of 1992 anyone had suggested that at the end of the year, the two leading contenders for the Academy Award for Best Picture of the Year would be a low-budget British film about an Irish Republican Army terrorist's relationship with a transsexual and a Clint Eastwood Western, he or she would have never been allowed to eat lunch in Hollywood again. We saw earlier how Miramax promoted *The Crying Game* into position, but with Eastwood's *Unforgiven*, it was the film rather than the promotion.[38] The first trailer for the film suggested merely another Clint Eastwood violent revenge Western. The trailer worked as most good trailers have worked, as we saw with the *Star Wars* trailers: the film delivered more than the trailer promised. With the *Star Wars* films, there were characters and scenes not hinted at in the trailers. With *Unforgiven*, the film was deeper and richer than anything the trailer suggested.

When Peter Albers first saw Clint Eastwood, "I lumped him in with cement heads like Charles Bronson, or Arnie [Schwarzenegger], and even when he started making films like *Bird* (1988), I still wasn't convinced. But when I saw *Unforgiven*, I realized he was something different. I thought *Unforgiven* was special because it carried through on its own premise so well—the title, for example, by the end of the movie not only makes sense, but perfectly describes the state of all the main characters, no one 'forgiven.' I was also impressed at how well and how believably he demonstrated in that climactic shootout what he had earlier explained to the kid—that it's easy to shoot a can in the back-yard, but when the shit hits the fan, you see who's truly the most unforgiven."

Brian Hall "first started liking Clint Eastwood when I saw *The Good, the Bad, and the Ugly.* And seeing *Unforgiven* was a different experience. This was not your typical bang-bang, shoot-'em-up Western like I was expecting. This was a film about paying the consequences for taking a life. With all the sense-less violence in films these days, this film was very sobering." Kenneth Hughes thought, "Thank God the man hung on after those damn monkey movies for his rebirth." As Aubrey Solomon, who had been an early Eastwood fan, watched the film, "I knew there was something very special about it. I was amazed at its darkness on the theatre screen. It was quite a masterful job for Eastwood, even though his directing was way beyond his acting. It was nice to know that his career was still going strong and he would finally get the acclaim as a filmmaker he deserved."

Terrence Atkins had a more conventional fanlike response. "Any time you put Clint Eastwood on the back of a horse and a gun in his hand, you've got a movie." Lawrence Dotson had been a fan for a while.

> I remember when my grandpa was visiting us one summer. I knew that he loved Westerns, so we rented all the Clint Eastwood movies that the video store carried and had ourselves a mini festival! I loved my grandpa a lot because he spoiled me rotten, so I have very fond memories of watch-ing movies like *A Fistful of Dollars, The Outlaw Josey Wales* and even the classic *Dirty Harry*, which isn't a Western in the general sense. . . . Clint also made a big impression on me in *Unforgiven*. It was cool how his character changed from bad to worse to the Clint I know and love in a Western. It was as if he had given up his old character, and created a new one that wasn't so quick to draw on a desperado.

For Michael Thomas, *Unforgiven* "brought back all the fond memories I had of the spaghetti Westerns I had seen as a kid," the kind of nostalgia James Ford mentioned earlier. Blair Woodard, who had liked *A Fistful of Dollars* and *Dirty Harry* for its "evolution of the antihero," found that carried over to *Unforgiven*. "I think Eastwood has been able to do a lot to change the stereotype of both the Western and the detective drama. To give the characters many flaws but who live by their own set of standards and justice."

Arnold Quinlan, whose favorite Eastwood film is *The Outlaw Josey Wales*, found *Unforgiven* less to his liking, but "when you have a favorite, you have a favorite." I can see his point. *The Outlaw Josey Wales* is still my favorite Eastwood movie, and although I think *Unforgiven* is a better, richer, deeper movie, when you have a favorite. . . .

Peggy Dilley just "hated [*Unforgiven*]. OK, there was beautiful scenery and they tried to say something important about justice, I guess, but it had Clint Eastwood. Too visual. Too boring. Some people like that, I guess. I don't understand why. Is it just politics? Conservatives win?" Dennis Wilkes "hates Westerns but enjoyed this film. I also liked the racial issue used by casting a black man as Clint's best friend." Mario Franco saw it "in a movie theatre with a handful of guy friends; the movie made me feel that as much as we restrain who we really are, we eventually have to be ourselves." Carlos Nino saw the picture, but still "can't stand this guy" any better than he could in *Dirty Harry*.

Richard Henrie thought *Unforgiven* was good, which was "funny because I have this thing about certain actors, i.e., Clint Eastwood, Sylvester Stallone, and Arnold Schwarzenegger. Those guys will be in their seventies and eighties and still making their types of film.... This film, *Unforgiven,* poked fun at the aging gunfighter who could not shoot straight or even get on his horse. I'm glad Clint Eastwood recognized this and put it in his film." Ira Katz "didn't think it was an antiviolence film, even though it had been described as such. I wondered how this man could do all this killing and then leave to go home with his children. It also never made sense to me that he couldn't shoot at all when he was sober, but after some drinks he was a crack shot."

Al Gonzalez generally does not like Westerns, but "I enjoyed this film very much. In the first place, it had a great cast. The cinematography was beautiful, and the story was simple but compelling enough. Usually a Western has to have a great script for me to like it, such as *High Noon* or *Red River* (1948)." I, of course, grew up on Westerns and loved those with good scripts, such as the ones Gonzalez mentions, and of course, *Jesse James*. If *The Outlaw Josey Wales* is Eastwood's *Jesse James*, *Unforgiven* is his *The Gunfighter* (1950). *The Gunfighter* was produced and co-written by Nunnally Johnson, the writer-producer of *Jesse James*, and as it looks at a gunfighter who is trying to quit, it reexamines the myths of the old West that *Jesse James* promoted. *The Gunfighter* is the first of the revisionist Westerns, which include *High Noon, A Fistful of Dollars*, and *Unforgiven*. It is not surprising that *The Gunfighter* came out just at the beginning of the decline of the studio era, when Hollywood was beginning to reexamine itself. Of course, *Unforgiven* is more explicit than *The Gunfighter*, both in terms of violence and showing the effect that violence has on people. It is also more explicit in other terms. A 1950 film would not begin with a prostitute making fun of a cowboy's sexual equipment.

Al Gonzalez also "noticed that [*Unforgiven*] is a film that men tend to enjoy whether they like Westerns or not, while women tend not to care much for it." James Ford knew this was true, even before he saw the film. On opening day at the Mann Chinese in Hollywood, "I was there for the 11 A.M. matinee bargain four-dollar show. Alone. My girlfriend didn't appreciate Clint like I did, and there was no use trying to explain. So there I was, expecting another typical Clint Eastwood Western. When those credits rolled at the end of the movie, I knew I'd seen something extraordinary. Clint delivered Clint. In fact, he out-Clinted himself . . . Cinematography, direction, writing, acting, editing, the music. . . . it all came together in *Unforgiven*." On the other hand, Eva Mahgrefthe "had never seen a Clint Eastwood film before *Unforgiven*, except for the occasional Sunday afternoon gun battles as my father watched them on television. It showed me the power of the Western and the lure of the Eastwood mystique. Gene Hackman's performance was a strong one as well. Some of the violence was troubling, and I would not see it again. However, I do agree that it was a well-made film." Another woman, who works in the industry, thought, "this movie was sadistic and pretentious, actually exploiting violence while pretending to make some philosophical statement about it. It was particularly hateful in its treatment of women, although that was acceptable apparently because the killer's sidekick who had equal access to women as whores was a black man. It was alienating to me to watch the Hollywood establishment treat Eastwood as a cultural hero because of it."

Hollywood did reward Eastwood for *Unforgiven*, giving the film four Academy Awards, including one for Eastwood for Best Director. The picture was the fifteenth highest-grossing picture of 1992, with film rentals of $36 million. It was outgrossed by *Home Alone 2: Lost in New York, Aladdin*, and *Fried Green Tomatoes*. It brought in more than *White Men Can't Jump, Under Siege*, and *Honey, I Blew Up the Kid*.[39] The following year, it added $8 million in rentals, which moved it ahead of *Fried Green Tomatoes* in total rentals.[40] Marcus Franklin thought that while it was "good for a Western, *The Bridges of Madison County* (1995) is a stronger film for Eastwood."

Shaun Hill-Kret thought *Unforgiven* was "long and too stylized. I feel like this movie was stuffy and kept me emotionally unattached. For once, Clint stopped being fun and felt too dramatic." For Robin Magee, *Unforgiven* "was the beginning of my Clint Eastwood fixation. I was impressed by his sense of humor. The second time I saw this movie, the violence really got to me." Bill Pulliam "thought it was very good. Particular aspects of it I remembered were the slow, painful deaths of characters (instead of nice and clean 'bang you're dead'), the fact that women were a driving force rather than a backdrop, and the sets. We had just moved to Colorado, so I found the nineteenth-century Western architecture particularly interesting. Some friends of ours summed up the moral as 'never laugh at a cowboy's pecker.'"

I happened to be in Colorado myself the year after the film came out. My wife and I were visiting our daughter, her husband, and our new granddaughter in Denver that summer. One day, looking for a movie to go to, I was wandering through the upscale Cherry Creek shopping center. Next to the Mann Eight-Plex, was a Warner Brothers Studio Store, which had opened the year before. I was surprised. By 1993 Disney had a long tradition of commercializing its films, but Warner Brothers? The first time I visited the store, the front window was filled with framed blowups of four photographs. One was Paul Newman, another Montgomery Clift, and the third Marlon Brando. The fourth was Clint Eastwood. But it was a picture of him from the Metro-Goldwyn-Mayer release *Where Eagles Dare*.

I went into the store and looked around. There were the obvious Warner Brothers cartoon items. An assortment of Looney Tunes collector's mugs, with Bugs Bunny and Daffy Duck. An old-fashioned restaurant sugar container featuring Sylvester and Tweety with mallets on opposite sides and the line "One lump or two?" There were the nostalgia pieces one would expect from Warner Brothers. Coffee mugs with Errol Flynn or Bette Davis, both from obscure 1937 films. A T-shirt with Bette Davis in *Cabin in the Cotton* (1932) saying her famous line, "I'd love to kiss you, but I just washed my hair." Notepaper and T-shirts with "You dirty rat," the famous James Cagney line he never said. Of course, there were items from *Casablanca*. A T-shirt with Bogart and "I stick my neck out for nobody." And a little throw pillow with "I was misinformed."

But aside from the picture in the front window, there was nothing else in the store connected with Eastwood—Warners' biggest star for the past twenty years. No "Do you feel lucky punk?" T-shirts or coffee mugs. No "Go ahead. Make my day" throw pillows. No imitation .44 Magnums, "the most powerful handgun in the world." Or real ones, for that matter. And when I visited the store a few days later, the pictures of Newman, Clift, Brando, and Eastwood had been removed from the window and placed on the back wall. And replaced by animated Batman and Superman T-shirts and sweatshirts.

Why no Eastwood material? Partly the store was working by commercializing on nostalgia, and while we have seen some audience members feel nostalgic for the Eastwood spaghetti Westerns, he is not a figure who generally inspires the easy sentimentality of nostalgia. He is too contemporary, even in his Westerns, and has too complex a relationship with his audiences, as we have seen by the variety of reactions to his films, to lend himself to the easy commercialization of the studio store. Or maybe Warners was just afraid his blue-collar fans would actually show up in what was intended as an upscale store.

Shortly after I visited the Warners store in Denver, one opened up in the Santa Monica Place mall. I have dropped in from time to time, usually on my way to a movie in Santa Monica. Still no Eastwood material. And there is less and less older material. No more Bette Davis and Errol Flynn material. Not even *Casablanca* material. Mostly just items from the studio's animation past, which lend themselves to commercialization.

In November 1998, I went into the Santa Monica store, and as a film historian, I was struck by a major disconnect. A few years before, Time-Warner had taken over Ted Turner's companies. Since Turner had previously taken over the library of pictures made by Metro-Goldwyn-Mayer, the old MGM films were now owned by Warners. In November 1998, Warners released a restored version of the MGM classic *The Wizard of Oz*. The Warners store was now filled with stuff from a film made by one of its traditional rivals. Nostalgia, not to mention a sense of history, had become mere commerce. The studio of Errol Flynn, Bette Davis, Humphrey Bogart, and Clint Eastwood had become the merchandiser of the ruby slippers.[41]

Time passes, things change.

A Concluding Thought or Two

One of the great myths of the last half of the twentieth century was that the media are as influential and persuasive as they think they are. Yes, movies can influence people's behavior. We have seen evidence of that in many places in this book: the people who wouldn't take a shower after *Psycho*, the people who had trouble with the ocean and other bodies of water after *Jaws*. A classic example of movies influencing behavior not previously mentioned in this book stems from the 1934 hit *It Happened One Night*. In one scene Clark Gable is getting undressed and takes off his shirt to reveal he is not wearing an undershirt. According to legend, undershirt sales for men plummeted.

However, the following year Gable appeared in *Mutiny on the Bounty* wearing early nineteenth-century English naval breeches and a ponytail. The picture was an even bigger hit than *It Happened One Night*, but I have seen no indications that American men started wearing breeches and ponytails. (And before you say that is not a fair comparison, since *It Happened One Night* is a contemporary film and *Mutiny on the Bounty* is a historical film, remember that Donna Crisci put sparkles on her eyelids after seeing *Cleopatra*.) In this book we have seen people unmoved by *Psycho*. Most noticeably we saw in examples of how unsuccessful trailers and film promotion in general can be. Films (especially promotional films) influence only if they resonate in some way with their audiences.

Look at it on a macro level: From the late forties to the late eighties, films and other media in Eastern Europe were completely controlled by Communists. This was followed by the collapse of the Communist empires.[1] In America in the fifties, the media were primarily conservative, and that was followed by the upheavals of the sixties. In the seventies, the media were more liberal, and that was followed by the Reagan years of the eighties. On a micro level, think of all the movie trailers and product commercials you have ever seen. How many of them have caused you to buy the product or see the television show or the film? If advertising was all that sure-fire, we would *all* be driving Edsels and drinking New Coke.

What all this suggests is that the selling side of the media is not as effective as legend would have it. I have studied documentary film for nearly thirty years, including propaganda films, and it is apparent that propaganda films generally do not change people's opinions.[2] What they can do, and what the media in general can do, is two things. First, films and the media can make people aware of something they had not been aware of before. This is a primary function of move trailers. Whether viewers take action is up to them. Second, films and media can reinforce opinions that people already have, which is why trailers and ads are repeated. Again, whether this leads to action is up to the viewer. It follows that the study of media influence, particularly in the area of imitative violence, needs to focus more on the psychology of how an *individual* reacts than on any generalizations about the media as a whole.

This need to focus on the individual's reaction to the media is something to keep in mind in view of the 1999 shootings in Littleton, Colorado and the lawsuit that evolved out of *Natural Born Killers*. When the Littleton shootings occurred, the immediate reaction of the media was that the two boys who did the shooting *must have* seen the 1995 film *The Basketball Diaries*, since the shootings were similar to the dream sequence in the film and the film had been seen by the fourteen-year-old boy who went on a shooting spree a year and a half before Littleton in Paducah, Kentucky. However, I have not been able to find any evidence that the two Colorado shooters ever saw the film, and the references to the film soon dropped out of the media discussion.

In the ongoing (as of June 2000) case of *Natural Born Killers*, one of the persons wounded in a crime spree by a couple who had seen the film filed suit against director Oliver Stone and Time-Warner, claiming the film had incited the crimes. The case was initially dismissed in January 1997 on grounds that the film and filmmakers were protected by the First Amendment. However, in March 1999, the U.S. Supreme Court allowed the case to continue. The fact that no one has ever won a case of this kind and that the criminals took acid as well as watching the film may make it difficult for the plaintiffs to win their case.[3]

Why the myth of the persuasiveness of the media? Obviously, the media would like you to believe they are so influential because it reinforces the already gigantic egos of those who work in the media. Advertising people would hate to have to admit what success they *do* have is mostly a matter of pure luck. People in positions of power in other areas buy into the myth because they are afraid it might be true; they have been suspicious of the movies from the beginning. Kevin Brownlow's elegant *Behind the Mask of Innocence: Sex, Violence, Crime: Films of Social Conscience in the Silent Era*[4] quotes politicians, educators, and religious leaders of the first decade and a half of the twentieth century about film. Their comments could be put verbatim into the mouth of any person of similar stature today.

The reason people in power fear the movies is that they know, in their heart of hearts, how little influence they themselves have. Is there a politician who does not *know* how many people do *not* support him? Is there a religious leader who does not *know* how ungodly his flock really is? As an educator, at the end of each semester, as I read the final exams, I suffer what I call the "My God, how much I've taught them and how little of it they have learned Blues." We are all afraid that something may be more influential that we are. Thus, there are always going to be public attacks on the media by people in positions of power, now and forever. (And fortunately, sanity in the public discussion eventually prevails—sometimes sooner, sometimes later. Less than two months after Littleton, Representative Henry Hyde's (R-Ill.) Children's Defense Act, which aimed at banning children under seventeen from violent films altogether, was defeated by a wide majority—even conservative Republicans voted against it.[5])

What is surprising is that academics studying the media have fallen for the idea of the power of the media as well. The left-wing film historians, such as the estimable David Bordwell and Kristin Thompson,[6] assume that the capitalists running the movie business can persuade the audiences to see anything the bosses want them to. Not true, as we have seen. The right-wing observers, such as Michael Medved in *Hollywood vs. America*, assume that the liberals in Hollywood are forcing non-American values on the audience, although Medved is at a loss to explain in his book why after all those liberal films of the seventies, the country turned to conservatives in the eighties. Perhaps this is because, as I have suggested here, people take what they want from the media and lead their own lives.

Neal Gabler, in his 1998 book *Life the Movie: How Entertainment Conquered Reality*,[7] suggests that movies and other media have overtaken real life. He needs to get out of New York and into the rest of the country. In the last few years, I have visited such states as Colorado, Wyoming, Georgia, Kentucky, Indiana, Connecticut, and yes, even New York State. It has been truly humbling to me as film historian living in Los Angeles, but also pleasing to me as a human being, to see how outside of the media capitals of New York and Los Angeles, the American people have a truly solid sense of proportion about the media. They know the media give them information and entertainment. Well, sometimes the movies give them entertainment. Sometimes they provoke us into action, but most of time they do not.

It also seems to me that if you are looking at the question of influence, you should more legitimately look in the other direction. Hollywood seems to be more influenced by its audiences than vice versa.[8] We saw how the success of De Mille's *Samson and Delilah* in the fifties persuaded Hollywood to make biblical pictures, a trend that died out in the sixties when audiences stopped going to them. There was an increase in violence in films after the surprising success of *Psycho*. The success of *The Sound of Music* caused Hollywood to make a series of similar movies. The failure of those films along with the success of such youth pictures as *The Graduate* and *Easy Rider* persuaded Hollywood to aim for younger audiences. And if some of the people at Fox in 1977 had been right and their other sci-fi picture of the year, *Damnation Alley*, had been the hit instead of *Star Wars*, you can bet the son of my wife's friend would be playing with George Peppard action figures today.

Audiences have more influence on Hollywood than the other way around, because Hollywood has more at stake in the relationships between audiences and movies. For audiences, what they choose to see is a minor part of their real life. For someone in the film industry, the choices those audiences make are a matter of, if not life and death, then at least of his or her career. The documentary filmmaker, Frederick Wiseman, when asked about the social influence of films, sagely noted, "Most filmmakers think their film is the only event in the lives of the audience."[9] Of course, it is not. One of the supposedly most influential radio commentators of the nineties said of the media in the discussion of the Littleton shootings, "People in the media think that they're front and center in peoples' lives and as such, when anything happens, they have to have played a role in it. Most people are just going around living their lives."[10] This is probably the only occasion you will ever find Frederick Wiseman, Rush Limbaugh, and me agreeing on anything, but this time Limbaugh is right.

And sometimes, when there is a movie they want to see, people will go. . . .

Appendix

This is the last version of the questionnaire that provided the responses you have read in this book.

MOVIEGOERS!!!!!!!!

This is a request for information and attitudes for a new book about Hollywood and the movies tentatively to be called *Talking Back to the Screen*. One of the subjects of the book will be how audiences feel about movies and the moviegoing experience of the last forty years. You may be quoted directly, so your writing out your answers and returning them indicate your willingness to be quoted in print. You may use a pseudonym if you like.

Please include the following information: **NAME, ADDRESS, PHONE, AP-PROXIMATE AGE,** and **OCCUPATION.**

What are your moviegoing habits? How often? Where do you see them (in theatres, on TV, on video, etc)? How many per year in theatres? How many per year on cassette?

How many on free or cable TV?

What were your first moviegoing experiences?

What are your most memorable moviegoing experiences? Your best? Your worst?

What are your recollections of the first times seeing these films: *Gone with the Wind, The Wizard of Oz, Citizen Kane, Casablanca, Sunset Boulevard, Singin' in the Rain, On the Waterfront, The Ten Commandments, North by Northwest, Psycho, Dr. Stangelove, Dr. Zhivago, The Sound of Music, A Fistful of Dollars, Bonnie and Clyde, The Graduate, Easy Rider, Dirty Harry, The Godfather, The Godfather Part II, The Exorcist, Jaws, The Outlaw Josey Wales, Star Wars, The*

Empire Strikes Back, Return of the Jedi, Raiders of the Lost Ark, E.T., Top Gun, The Godfather Part III, Unforgiven, Jurassic Park, Forrest Gump, Twister, Independence Day?

What are your recollections of seeing these films later? In theatres? On TV or video? Did your view of these films change?

What trailers (previews of coming attractions) do you remember the best?

How has the moviegoing experience changed for your over the years?

Notes

Introduction

1. Bruce Austin, *The Film Audience: An International Bibliography of Research* (Metuchen, N.J.: Scarecrow Press, 1983). As the title implies, this is a survey of the research done on film audiences. Austin's introduction (pages xvii–xxxiv) is a good general overview of the kinds of research that have been carried out and why more of it has not been done. Austin followed this up with *Immediate Seating: A Look at Movie Audiences* (Belmont, Ca.: Wadsworth Publishing Company, 1989), which offers a more detailed examination of research and research techniques, such as market approaches, theories of moviegoing, and contexts of moviegoing. Austin is very much the social scientist, complete with charts and statistical studies. If you want to find out how many "virgins," i.e. first-time viewers, there were in weekend showings of *The Rocky Horror Picture Show* in New Jersey in 1979, his pages 84 to 87 will tell you. This 1989 book is an updating of Leo Handel's earlier classic *Hollywood Looks at its Audience: a report of film audience research* (Urbana: University of Illinois Press, 1950).

A more recent look at audience research approaches is Denis McQuail, *Audience Analysis* (Thousand Oaks, Ca.: Sage Publications, 1997), which reaffirms that most research done in the area falls into the social science category. McQuail describes the three traditional approaches to audience research as Structural, Behavioral, and Cultural (21). The first two methods rely on surveys and statistical measurement in the traditional social science manner, while the Cultural approach goes for more qualitative research as it tries to understand the context in which audiences watch and the uses audiences make of what they watch. If forced to put myself in one of the categories, I would most likely fit in the Cultural category. My approach will also fit in with what McQuail notes (69–75) is traditionally called the "uses and gratifications" approach, which began with studies of radio audiences in the forties and was revived by media scholars in the seventies. The approach suggests, as I do later in this book, that audiences take what they want from the media, rather than being slaves to it.

2. Our British cousins have done a little more research in this area than have we Americans. Margaret O'Brien and Allen Eyeles's *Enter the Dream-House: Memories of Cinemas in South London from the Twenties to the Sixties* (London: British Film Insti-

tute, 1993) is an entertaining collection of interviews with people who attended cinemas at a particular time and place, but there is little attempt at a general look at moviegoing. I have not yet had a chance to read Annette Kuhn and Sarah Street's *Journal of Popular British Cinema 2: 1999 Audiences and Reception in Britain* (London: Flicks, 1999), but a review of it in *Sight and Sound* (May 1999, 28–29) suggests that it does spend time talking to audiences about their reactions, although in limited ways. The best of the British books I have found is Martin Barker and Kate Brooks's *Knowing Audiences: Judge Dredd, its Friends, Fans and Foes* (Luton: University of Luton Press, 1998), which unfortunately I only came across after I had completed this book. Barker and Brooks conducted surveys and discussion groups with potential audience members before and after they saw the film *Judge Dredd* (1995) and from the responses developed theories about the complexities of movie audiences that parallel much of what I discovered and go beyond it in some areas. They generally avoid the historical approach that I am using.

3. David Rosenberg, ed., *The Movie That Changed My Life* (New York: Viking, 1991).

4. Janet Staiger, *Interpreting Films: Studies in the Historical Reception of American Cinema* (Princeton: Princeton University Press, 1992).

5. For a recent excellent examination of how the media seem to get most things wrong, read Barry Glassner's *The Culture of Fear* (New York: Basic Books, 1999).

6. Staiger, 211.

7. I know the Internet is a notoriously unreliable source of *information* (check any movie web site if you don't believe me), but here I was asking for *opinions*, and I do not think people lied any more or any less on the Internet than they did elsewhere in their replies.

8. Bruce Austin found that research in the fifties showed that half of the audiences in drive-ins were there in family groups. Austin, *Immediate Seating*, 89.

9. Quoted in the Yale Class Book 1963, 11.

1. Childhoods

1. Quinlan has obviously absorbed a lot of movies, since the two lines beginning "You're tearing me apart" are from *Rebel Without a Cause*. He's put those in deliberately.

2. James Horwitz, *They Went Thataway* (New York: E.P. Dutton, 1976), 141. Horwitz has some good descriptions of what it was like to attend the Saturday matinee shows as a kid. He also tracked down many of the surviving B Western stars and talked to them.

3. Ibid., 192–93, 202.

4. The article is reprinted in James Agee, *Agee on Film* (Boston: Beacon Press, 1964), 2–19, unfortunately without the photographs that accompanied the original article.

5. Ibid., 2.

6. Deems Taylor, Marcelene Peterson, and Bryant Hale, *A Pictorial History of the Movies* (New York: Simon and Schuster, 1950). The 1995 documentary *A Personal Journey with Martin Scorsese Through American Movies* (British Film Institute) reveals that Scorsese grew up on the same book as well.

7. For the best history of motion picture exhibition, which includes a history of popcorn at the movies, see Douglas Gomery's *Shared Pleasures* (Madison: University of Wisconsin Press, 1992).

2. Hollywood's Fifties

1. This history of the development of *Sunset Boulevard* was first written based on Maurice Zolotov, *Billy Wilder in Hollywood* (New York: Putnam's, 1977), 156–71. A more recent and more thoroughly researched book, Ed Sikov's *On Sunset Boulevard* (New York: Hyperion, 1998) covers the same material in more depth on pages 281–89. Sikov points out that while Brackett is credited on the screenplay, he preferred the more lighthearted approach and was paid by Paramount only for producing the film, not for his writing on it (290).

2. Comden and Green's version of the writing of *Singin' in the Rain* is found in their introduction to the published screenplay (New York: Viking, 1972), 1–10. This quote is from page 5. Production details of the film can be found in Hugh Fordin, *The World of Entertainment* (New York: Avon, 1975), 347–62.

3. Fordin, 331 and 362.

4. John Houseman, *Front and Center* (New York: Touchstone, 1979), 372.

5. Leslie Halliwell, *Halliwell's Filmgoer's and Video Viewers Companion*, 9th Edition (New York: Perennial Library, 1990), 927–28, was particularly useful in putting together this list.

6. Richard Griffith and Arthur Mayer, *The Movies* (New York: Simon and Schuster, 1957), 387.

7. Aubrey Solomon, *Twentieth Century-Fox: A Corporate and Financial History* (Metuchen, N.J.: Scarecrow Press), 218, 227, 240, and 251.

8. Charles Champlin, *The Flicks* (Pasadena: Ward Ritchie Press, 1977), 23.

9. Gomery, 83.

10. Ibid., 239–40.

11. Movie theatre projectors in those days normally ran one twenty minute reel and then changed to another projector for the next reel; the platter system, where an entire film could be built up on one large horizontal platter and run without changeovers, did not become standard until twenty years later.

12. Not to mention sloppy production techniques: it was rumored that one system had the camera lenses placed at the distance between gorilla eyes and not human eyes; gorillas would have enjoyed the movies if they could have kept the glasses on, but humans got headaches.

13. The most detailed and scholarly account of the wide-screen systems of the fifties and beyond is John Belton's *Widescreen Cinema* (Cambridge: Harvard University Press, 1992). The main chapter on Cinerama is 85–112.

14. "All-Time Top Film Grossers," *Variety*, January 9, 1963, 13. I have used this list as the source of the rentals for the other fifties films unless otherwise indicated.

15. In descending order, they are *Ben-Hur*, *The Ten Commandments*, *The Robe*, *Samson and Delilah*, and *Quo Vadis*. See note 14 above for source.

16. Paul R. Mandell, "Parting the Red Sea and Other Miracles," *American Cinematographer*, April 1983, 125.

17. Belton, 113. The development and promotion of CinemaScope is on pages 113–57.

18. Dunne quoting Zanuck in Tom Stempel, "Oral History of Philip Dunne," unpublished, American Film Institute, 1970–1971, 145.

19. Zanuck memos dated July 25 and December 29, 1952, printed in Rudy Behlmer, *Memo From Darryl F. Zanuck* (New York: Grove Press, 1993), 221–22. Behlmer's selection of the surviving Zanuck memos gives a particularly good view of Zanuck's interest in and understanding of audiences, what they want, and what they don't want. You can see why Zanuck was a major force in the American motion picture business from the late twenties to the early seventies.

20. "Dunne Oral History," 150.

21. Philip Dunne, *Take Two: A Life in Movies and Politics* (New York: McGraw–Hill, 1980; Paperback reprint: New York: Limelight Editions, 1992), 255–56.

22. Solomon, 248–49.

23. Kevin Brownlow, *The Parade's Gone By* (New York: Knopf, 1968), 411.

24. Cost of the 1926 version from Brownlow, 411; the cost of the 1959 version from Andrew Dowdy, *"Movies Are Better Than Ever,"* (New York: Morrow, 1973), 178.

25. This is the figure listed in "All-Time Top Film Grossers," *Variety*, January 9, 1963, 13. A revised figure of $36,992,088 is listed in "All-Time Film Rental Champs," *Variety*, February 21, 1990, 187.

26. Michael Medved, *Hollywood Vs. America* (New York: Harper Perennial, 1992), 47–48. Medved's description of the screening for the critics and their reactions (45–48) is particularly illuminating.

27. Dowdy, 181.

28. *Variety*, February 21, 1990, 216.

29. Mandell, 46.

30. When I checked with Peggy some time later if it was okay to use that information, she replied, "Sure. Why not? It's the truth."

31. Mandell, 127.

32. "Par [Paramount] issues digital 'Commandments,'" *Daily Variety*, March 14, 1997.

3. Sex and Seriousness

1. See Alley Acker, *Reel Women* (New York: Continuum, 1991), 113–16.

2. Ford remembers having the crush on Bardot for "a couple of years" before *Cat Ballou* came along, but it was released the same year as *Dear Brigitte*. And he remembers being five or six when he saw *Dear Brigitte*, but he was likely older, given the age range he listed in the answer to the questionnaire. See how sex can screw up your memory?

3. I even put this bit of conventional wisdom in my book *FrameWork: A History of Screenwriting in the American Film* (New York: Continuum, 1988), 155–56.

4. Peter Biskind, in his book about movies of the fifties, *Seeing is Believing* (New York: Pantheon, 1983), page 4, points out the sources of these two views, although he

makes a case that what I have referred to as the white male view is the right-wing as opposed to the left-wing view. He may be right; however, that seems a little doctrinaire to me.

5. Produced by Judy Chaikin.

6. John Cogley, *Report on Blacklisting, Volume 1*, The Fund for the Republic, 1956, quoted in Nora Sayre, *Running Time: Films of the Cold War* (New York: Dial Press, 1982), 80.

7. Coles Trapnell to the author, October 17, 1990.

8. From Sage's report on *To You I Call*, November 24, 1950. The Sage files are in the Louis B. Mayer Library of the American Film Institute in Hollywood.

9. Elia Kazan, *A Life* (New York: Knopf, 1988), 520.

4. Opening the Sixties

1. I.A.L. Diamond, Wilder's co-writer on *The Apartment*, gave this explanation of the origin of the film in William Froug's *The Screenwriter Looks at the Screenwriter* (New York: MacMillan, 1972), 164. The real-life affair was between agent Jennings Lang and star Joan Bennett. It came to light when Lang was shot by Bennett's husband, producer Walter Wanger.

2. The 2000 television movie remake of *On the Beach* moved the time period ahead to 2004.

3. Donald Chase, "My Favorite Year 1959," *Film Comment*, September–October 1994, 66, 68. Chase suggests, as the first part of this chapter implies, that 1959 was one of Hollywood's better years.

4. For the genesis of *Psycho*, see Stephen Rebello, *Alfred Hitchcock and the Making of Psycho* (New York: Dembner Books, 1990; paperback: New York: Harper Perennial, 1991), 15–23 particularly on Hitchcock's attitudes.

5. Ibid., 162–63.

6. Ibid., 163.

7. Ibid., 134–35. Richard J. Anobile's Film Classics Library book of the film (New York: Avon, 1974), which is made up of shots from each scene of the film, with the dialogue printed underneath, includes the shot with the skull, 256.

8. It may have been more than just Janet Leigh that provoked the reaction. The art direction of both films was by Robert Clatworthy. Rebello, 69.

9. Pauline Kael refers to this in her essay "Bonnie and Clyde," which originally appeared in *The New Yorker* in 1967 and is reprinted in *Kiss Kiss Bang Bang* (Boston: Atlantic–Little Brown, 1968), 47–63. See specifically pages 47 and 49.

10. Vincent LoBrutto, *Stanley Kubrick: A Biography* (New York: Da Capo Press, 1999), 228–29.

11. "All-Time Boxoffice Champs," *Variety*, January 7, 1970, 25.

12. Medved, *Hollywood Vs. America*, 277.

5. Television and Movies

1. Sam Frank, *Sex in the Movies* (Secaucus, N.J.: Citadel Press, 1986).

6. Closing the Sixties

1. Curtis Lee Hanson, *Cinema*, Summer 1967, 3.

2. Bosley Crowther, "*Bonnie and Clyde*," *The New York Times*, August 14, 1967.

3. The rental figures are all from *Variety*, January 7, 1970, 25, except for the *Doctor Dolittle* figure, which is from David Pirie, *Anatomy of the Movies* (London: Windward, 1981), 306.

4. Medved, *Hollywood vs. America*, 276–78.

5. The *Times* was so chagrined by the fact that Crowther was so far off the public reaction that in the 1970 *New York Times Guide to Movies on TV* (Chicago: Triangle Books), while the entries for other films were condensed versions of the original reviews, the entry for *Bonnie and Clyde* said things like "beautifully made . . . the hypnotically evocative direction of Arthur Penn. . . . This striking color film should either appall you as a violence for art's sake or hook you completely as an artful romanticized cocoon spun and finally shattered by the violence within." (36)

6. David Newman and Robert Benton, "Lightning in a Bottle," their essay on their work on the film, appears in *Bonnie and Clyde* (New York: Ungar, 1972), 13–30.

7. Pauline Kael, "Crime and Poetry," in *Bonnie and Clyde*, op. cit., 195. This is a reprint of her original October 1967 *New Yorker* article, "*Bonnie and Clyde*."

8. Ibid., 197–98.

9. Newman and Benton, op. cit.

10. Kael, op. cit., 195.

11. Jerome Agel, *The Making of Kubrick's 2001* (New York: Signet, 1970). The letters section is on pages 171–92, and the letters quoted in this chapter are all from that source.

12. Robert O'Brien, the president of MGM who had encouraged and promoted Kubrick's project, was pushed out as president within a year of the release of *2001*. O'Brien had developed a reputation, deserved, of being more supportive of star directors like Kubrick and David Lean than Hollywood generally thought wise.

13. *Variety*, January 7, 1970, 15.

7. Dark and Golden

1. As the character played by Sidney Pollack in *The Player* says, "The rumors are always true." See Robert Evans, *The Kid Stays in the Picture* (New York: Hyperion, 1994), 215–31, for an entertaining, if self-serving, view of the production of the film, written by the head of the studio at the time. Or, for more objective versions of the story, see Michael Sragow, "Annals of Moviemaking: Godfatherhood," *The New Yorker*, March 24, 1997, 44–52; or Harlan Lebo, *The Godfather Legacy* (New York: Fireside, Simon & Schuster, 1997); or Peter Biskind, "Making Crime Pay," *Premiere*, August 1997, 80–86, 107–09. Biskind's material also shows up in his 1998 book, *Easy Riders, Raging Bulls* (New York: Simon and Schuster, 1998), an excellent look at the filmmakers of the seventies.

2. For what I mean by the technical sloppiness of Brando's performance, look at it shot by shot—for example, his screwing up his face when he looks at Sonny's body, and Brando's traditional mumbling with the cotton in his cheeks.

3. Stempel, *FrameWork*, see pages 183 and 191. Biskind's *Easy Riders, Raging Bulls* goes into the idea in much more depth than I did.

4. *Movieline*, August 1993. The section on the seventies runs from pages 42 to 66.

5. Quoted in Nat Segaloff, *Hurricane Billy: The Stormy Life and Films of William Friedkin* (New York: William Morrow, 1990), 145.

6. Although there were those at the time who noted that the move to second-run houses also coincided with Nixon's resignation, which may have meant that the film lost part of its intensity for at least American audiences; the "devil" had resigned, so we did not have to go to see fictionalized versions of the story.

7. *Hurricane Billy*, 147.

8. Black and Dark

1. Gomery's *Shared Pleasures* has a terrific section on the segregation and ultimate integration of American movie theaters, 155–70.

2. See Donald Bogle, *Toms, Coons, Mulattoes, Mammies, & Bucks: An Interpretive History of Blacks in American Film* (New York: Continuum, New Expanded Edition 1989, originally published 1973) and Thomas Cripps, *Slow Fade to Black: The Negro in American Film, 1900–1942* (New York: Oxford University Press, 1977) for histories of blacks in mainstream films as well as "race movies," as the low-budget alternatives were called.

3. Pleasant Gehman, "The End of the World," *Los Angeles Reader*, March 17, 1995, 20.

4. Douglas P. Shuit and Robert W. Welkos, "3 Injured as Gunfire Erupts Inside Theatre," *Los Angeles Times*, November 8, 1996, B1, B3.

5. "1 Killed, 2 Wounded in Shooting Outside Theater," *Los Angeles Times*, November 11, 1996, B3.

6. When I was doing revisions on the first draft of this section, I spent an afternoon with the always-helpful staff of the Academy's Herrick Library trying to track down this story. We could not find any reference to it in books or articles on the film. Maybe it is just an urban legend, but it is so delicious that I would like to think it is true.

7. A lot of the subplots of the novel had been dropped for the film.

8. "All-Time Film Rental Champs," *Variety*, January 7, 1976, 20.

9. See for example, Jack Ellis, *A History of Film* (Boston: Allyn and Bacon, 4th edition, 1995), 182–85, for lines such as this: "They [films noir] were clearly popular, perhaps appealing to something in audiences that distrusted the official rhetoric and opinion espoused by the dominant political forces" (184–85). I suppose in fairness to Ellis, I should mention that the next line is, "If not among the big hits, for the most part, the noir films continued as a steady stream."

10. "All-Time Film Rental Champs," *Variety*, February 25, 1991. The films of the fifties are on A-138, A-140, A-142, and A-145, and the films of the forties are on A-145 and A-146.

11. Arthur Knight, *The Liveliest Art* (New York: New American Library, 1957), 245–46.

12. Gerald Mast, *A Short History of the Movies* (New York: Pegasus, 1971).

13. Such as *Kiss The Blood Off My Hands* (1948), *Act of Violence* (1949), *Night and the*

City (1950), and *Thieves' Highway* (1949) just to take a semi-random list. See Alain Silver and Elizabeth Ward, *Film Noir: An Encyclopedic Reference to the American Style* (Woodstock, New York: Overlook Press, 1979), the best source of information about film noir.

9. *Star Wars*

1. The information on these screenings, including the quotes, is from Dale Pollock's *Skywalking: The Life and Films of George Lucas* (New York: Harmony Books, 1983), 179–83.

2. "All-Time Film Rental Champs," *Variety*, January 4, 1978, 25.

3. "Big Rental Films of 1978," *Variety*, January 3, 1979, 17; "Big Rental Films of 1979; *Variety*, January 9, 1980, 21.

4. "Box Office News," *Variety*, May 17–23, 1999, 30.

5. "All-Time Film Rental Champs," *Variety*, January 14, 1981, 28.

6. "All-Time Film Rental Champs," *Variety*, January 11, 1984, 16.

7. Claudia Eller, "*Star Wars* Triad an Unstoppable Global Force," *Los Angeles Times*, March 11, 1997, D1.

8. Howard Roffman, vice president of Lucas Licensing, quoted in Stuart Silverstein, Greg Hernandez, and Diane Seo, "*Star Wars* Glows at Center of Marketing Constellation," *Los Angeles Times*, May 1, 1999, C2.

9. Richard Natale, "'Eyes' Sees Its Way to Top Spot," *Los Angeles Times*, July 19, 1999, F7.

10. Film Education

1. The script was *The Frontiersman*, which was never made, but a former student who worked at a large agency later told me that the script was given to young writers to show them how to write a screenplay.

2. Quoted in Tom Stempel, "An Oral History of Nunnally Johnson," unpublished, UCLA, 1968–1969, 204.

3. My interviews with Nunnally and his co-workers became the basis for my first book, *Screenwriter: The Life and Times of Nunnally Johnson* (San Diego: A.S. Barnes, 1980).

4. For a sharp, funny look at the egos involved in industry screenings, see Bill Higgins, "Who's on the Sit List?" *Variety*, May 10–16, 1999, 1, 6, and 48.

5. One of the advantages of teaching film history at LACC is that so much early film history was made in the area around the college. Lois Weber's studio was right around the corner, and Griffith's studio was only six blocks away. You can stand on the campus, look northeast, and see the hills behind the town of Piedmont in *Birth of a Nation*.

6. Pauline Kael, Herman J. Mankiewicz & Orson Welles, *The Citizen Kane Book* (Boston: Atlantic Monthly Press, Little Brown and Company, 1971). The book includes Kael's famous essay "Raising Kane," one of the shooting scripts for the film, and the cutting continuity, or transcript, of the completed film.

11. Directors

1. Andrew Sarris, *The American Cinema* (New York, E.P. Dutton, 1968).

2. Bruce Austin notes that most audience studies show that it is the subject matter that makes audiences go to movies, not the behind-the-camera personnel. Austin, *Film Audience*, xxviii.

3. Robert E. Kapsis, *Hitchcock: The Making of a Reputation* (Chicago: University of Chicago Press, 1992).

4. "Big Rental Films of 1976," *Variety*, January 5, 1977, 14.

5. "All-Time Top Film Grossers," *Variety*, January 9, 1962, 61.

6. Elia Kazan, *A Life* (New York: Knopf, 1988). Kazan goes into great detail over his frustrations as a studio director in his autobiography.

7. "All-Time Box Office Champs," *Variety*, January 5, 1972, 11.

8. "Big Rental Films of 1969," *Variety*, January 7, 1970, 15.

9. "Big Rental Films of 1972," *Variety*, January 3, 1973, 7. The film was released in late 1971, so it shows up on the chart for 1972.

10. "Big Rental Films of 1973," *Variety*, January 9, 1974, 19.

11. For some of the reasons why this was so, see David Weedle's depressing biography of Peckinpah, *If They Move . . .Kill 'em* (New York: Grove Press, 1994).

12. "Big Rental Films of 1983," *Variety*, January 11, 1984, 80.

13. "Top Rental Films For 1992," *Variety*, January 11, 1993, 22.

14. See, for example, Kevin Brownlow's *David Lean: A Biography* (London: Richard Cohen Books, 1996) for some wonderful stories of exactly how disconnected a great director can get from the real world. Or for that matter, any autobiography by any director.

15. Peter Cowie, *Coppola* (New York: Da Capo: Updated Edition, 1994), 80.

16. "Big Rental Films of 1976," *Variety*, January 5, 1977, 14.

17. "Big Rental Films of 1981," *Variety*, January 5, 1982, 15.

18. "All-Time Film Rental Champs," *Variety*, May 9–16, 1994, 40, 44.

19. "B. O. Performance of Films in 1995," *Variety*, January 8–14, 1996, 38.

20. It was not just the projection system. The sound was recorded so badly the dialogue was unintelligible and Altman refused to rerecord it. See Biskind, *Easy Riders, Raging Bulls*, 107–08.

21. "Big Buck Pix vs. Rentals," *Variety*, January 13, 1982, 18. The chart shows that *Popeye* cost $20 million and brought in domestic (U.S. and Canada) rentals of $24.5 million. Overseas grosses would be enough to make the film a slight moneymaker. As for the critical reaction, consider Leonard Maltin's rating of the film as a BOMB in his *1997 Movie and Video Guide* (New York: Plume, 1996), 1050. Maltin calls it "an astonishingly boring movie."

22. See Andrew Yule, *Picture Shows: The Life and Films of Peter Bogdanovich* (New York: Limelight Editions, 1992), as well as Biskind, op. cit.

23. Biskind, 337.

24. "Big Buck Pix vs. Rentals," *Variety*, January 13, 1982, 18.

25. Biskind, 337.

26. For the complete, horrifying story, read Steven Bach's *Final Cut* (New York: Morrow, 1985).

27. "1990's Top Rentals," *Variety*, January 7, 1991, 88.

28. "1980–1984 Big Buck Scorecard," *Variety*, January 16, 1985, 58.

29. Susan Dworkin, *Double De Palma* (New York: Newmarket Press, 1984).

30. Julie Salamon, *The Devil's Candy* (Boston: Houghton Mifflin, 1991).

31. Ibid. 32.

12. Spielberg

1. In February 1999, what was billed as the "definitive director's cut" of *Close Encounters* played a two-day run at the Cinerama Dome in Hollywood. I did not see it. The rumor was that Spielberg had basically replaced all the good scenes he had cut out of the original.

2. Joseph McBride, *Steven Spielberg: A Biography* (New York: Simon and Schuster, 1997), 270–71.

3. "All-Time Film Rental Champs," *Variety*, January 19, 1980, 24.

4. "Big Buck Pix vs. Rentals," *Variety*, January 13, 1982, 18.

5. Ibid. The film had a domestic gross of $23.4 million.

6. McBride, 309.

7. Quoted in Ibid., 310.

8. "Big Buck Pix vs. Rentals," *Variety*, January 13, 1982, 44.

9. "All-Time Film Rental Champs," *Variety*, January 16, 1985, 28.

10. "Top 100 All-Time Film Rental Champs," *Variety*, January 15, 1981, 84.

11. McBride, 332.

12. "All-Time Film Rental Champs," *Variety*, January 16, 1985, 28.

13. "All-Time Film Rental Champs," *Variety*, May 9–15, 1994, 44.

14. "All-Time Film Rental Champs," *Variety*, May 9–15, 1994, 48.

15. Donna Rosenthal, "Did Cultures Clash Over 'Schindler's'?" *Los Angeles Times*, January 22, 1994, F1.

16. Kevin Weston, "Kids Weren't Laughing at Holocaust, Just Movie," *Los Angeles Times*, February 28, 1994, F3.

17. Jeffrey K. Watanabe, "Education Key to Seeing, Understanding the Film," *Los Angeles Times*, February 28, 1994, F3.

18. Michael Granberry, "Prosecutors Cite Film's Theme in Theatre Shooting," *Los Angeles Times*, February 8, 1994, A22.

19. "Top 250 of 1997," *Variety*, January 26–February 1, 1998, 17. By this time, *Variety* had shifted in its year-end reports from rentals to raw box office figures.

20. See, for example, Amy Wallace, "'Ryan' Ends Vets' Years of Silence," *Los Angeles Times*, August 6, 1998, A1, A21. Also see Jeff Kornbluth and Linda Sunshine, *'Now You Know': Reactions After Seeing* Saving Private Ryan, (New York: Newmarket Press, 1999), which is a collection of comments on the film taken from the chat room set up by America Online.

21. I saw a print of the reissue of the film for Academy consideration shortly after

the Awards that was in full color. This may just have been a mistake in the lab that nobody at DreamWorks caught, or it may have been somebody at the company listening to complaints about the desaturation. The videotape of the film seems to be somewhere in between the two prints.

22. Quoted in John Walker, ed., *Halliwell's Filmgoer's Companion* (New York: Harper Perennial, 12th Edition, 1997), 154.

13. Studios and VCRs

1. See Biskind, *Easy Riders, Raging Bulls* for the best overview of the directors' behavior of the period, but also Yule, Weedle, and Segaloff for specific examples. Biskind also brings up the payback in the eighties, specifically 413–15.

2. For a view of Phillips, read her *You'll Never Eat Lunch in This Town Again* (New York: Random House, 1991), but since she is an ex-druggie, you will have to read between the lines to figure out what a horror she must have been for the people trying to deal with her. For a view of Peters, read Nancy Griffin and Kim Masters, *Hit & Run: How Jon Peters and Peter Guber Took Sony for a Ride in Hollywood* (New York: Simon and Schuster, 1996). For a view of Simpson, from which the material in this chapter is taken, read Charles Fleming, *High Concept: Don Simpson and the Hollywood Culture of Excess* (New York: Doubleday, 1998), but you will want to take a long, hot shower after you finish.

3. Fleming, 24, although there are certain problems both with the story and Fleming's retelling of it. First, Simpson was born in 1943, which would have made him eight or nine when the film came out. Second, Fleming miscalculates and thinks Simpson was only three when the film came out. Third, Simpson told so many different variations on this story that none of them may be true.

4. Fleming, 19.

5. "Big Rental Films of '86," *Variety*, January 14, 1987, 25.

6. Fleming, 72.

7. Faye Brookman, "With big bux at stake, they do their homework," *Variety*, June 13, 1990, 45.

8. Quoted in "Hangin' With the Rhino," *LA Weekly*, June 18–June 24, 1993, 37, in a review of *The Tailhook Report: The Official Inquiry Into the Events of Tailhook '91* (New York, St. Martin's Press).

9. Leonard Klady, "That Championship Season: *Titanic* Fuels 9.9% B. O. Spike," *Variety*, January 11–17, 1999, 9.

10. Paul Sweeting, "Homevid revs [revenues] hit a record high," *Variety*, January 11–17, 1999, 20. Sweeting gives only the dollar figure for video rentals, which he gets from the Video Software Dealer's Association VidTrac data collection system. He notes that VideoScan, which tracks sales of cassettes, shows that in the 70 to 80 percent of the sales market they cover, there were a total of 274 million cassettes sold, but he does not give a dollar figure—not surprising since prices may vary. I calculated the $6.85 billion number by figuring an average retail sales price of $20 per cassette, then adding a quarter of that figure to account for what VideoScan does not cover. It has since been pointed out to me that if the VideoScan figures, which appear to be primarily retail sales, include

sales to video stores, which are at higher prices, then the total sales number will be higher.

11. I had thought the video store was the greatest, but I mentioned this one time to three people I was talking to, and the group's older man of the world told me AA meetings were best. The younger couple with us giggled and said they had met at AA. I bow to this trio's wisdom and experience.

12. Chuck Ross, "The Great Script Tease," *Film Comment*, November–December 1982, 15–19. All the material on his actions and Hollywood's reactions are from the article and from Richard Corliss's sidebar to it.

14. Promoting Habits

1. Justin Wyatt, *High Concept: Movies and Marketing in Hollywood* (Austin: University of Texas Press, 1994), 111–12.

2. "Variety Box Office," *Variety*, January 4–10, 1999, 11.

3. These figures are from the Motion Picture Producers Association annual reports, which are covered in *Variety* annually.

4. Leonard Klady, "Tyranny of TV still governs movie choices," *Variety*, June 27–July 3, 1994, 1, 102. This was true even of more adult films such as *Four Weddings and a Funeral*, where only 27 percent of the respondents said they heard about it on television, while only 20 percent heard about it via newspapers. Fifty-seven percent of respondents heard about *Naked Gun 33 1/3* on television, while only 10 percent heard about it in newspapers.

5. Quoted in Patrick Goldstein, "Naked Trailers," *Los Angeles Times Sunday Calendar*, August 25, 1991, 4.

6. Wyatt, *High Concept*.

7. Goldstein, "Naked Trailers," 5.

8. Faye Brookman, "Trailers: the big business of drawing crowds," *Variety*, June 13, 1990, 48.

9. Goldstein, "Naked Trailers," 4.

10. Biskind, *Easy Riders, Raging Bulls*, 337.

11. Claudia Eller, "Lucas Empire Strikes Gold Again," *Los Angeles Times*, May 21, 1999, C6. Robert Welkos, in "High Cost of Luring Audience," *Los Angeles Times*, September 3, 1999, F16, has a chart showing how much more other films spent on television advertising. *Star Wars Episode I* was outspent by *Notting Hill*, *The Mummy*, *Instinct*, *Love Letter* (which opened opposite Lucas's film), and *Eyes Wide Shut*.

12. Patrick Goldstein, "Reel Masters of the Two-Minute Drill," *Los Angeles Times*, August 27, 1991, F6.

13. Jeffrey Wells, "Film Clips," *Los Angeles Times Sunday Calendar*, August 1, 1993, 32–34.

14. Goldstein, "Naked Trailers," 22.

15. Richard Natale, "Indie Films No Longer Penny-Ante Affair," *Los Angeles Times*, April 14, 1995, F4.

16. Claudia Eller, "Miramax's 'Patient' Approach, *Los Angeles Times*, March 21, 1997, D4.

17. Ibid.

18. Nina J. Easton, "Good News/Bad News of the New Black Cinema," *Los Angeles Times Sunday Calendar*, June 16, 1991, 6.

19. Ibid.

20. Claudia Eller, "Taking the 'Menace' Out of Ad, Poster," *Los Angeles Times*, July 22, 1993, F1, F3.

21. Goldstein, "Naked Trailers," 5.

22. Ibid.

23. "Whatever," *Los Angeles Times Sunday Calendar*, May 17, 1998, 23.

24. Faye Brookman, "With big bux at stake, they do their homework," *Variety*, June 13, 1990, 45.

25. Wyatt, 145.

26. Deborah Caulfield, "*Annie*: The Bucks Roll in Tomorrow, Wanna Bet a Dollar That Tomorrow Green Will Shine," *Los Angeles Times Sunday Calendar*, May 16, 1982, 1, 3, 4.

27. "Big Rental Films of 1982," *Variety*, January 12, 1983, 13.

28. Dale Pollock, "*The Right Stuff*: The Tale of A $28 Million Movie That Never Got Into Orbit," *Los Angeles Times Sunday Calendar*, February 12, 1984, 28–29.

29. "Big Rental Films of 1983," *Variety*, January 11, 1984, 13.

30. William Goldman, *Adventures in the Screen Trade* (New York: Warner Books, 1983), 39.

31. Nikki Finke, "Film Ads: Would They Lie to You?" *Los Angeles Times*, December 9, 1988, VI–14.

32. Claudia Puig and Richard Natale, "A Scary Time at Box Office," *Los Angeles Times*, October 20, 1995, F1, F28.

33. Klady, "Tyranny," 102.

34. I am not sure if I read this somewhere, or heard it from somebody in the industry. If Wasserman wants to deny he said it, I'll be glad to change the attribution, but it seems to me to be a great truth about the movie business.

35. See Austin, *Immediate Seating*, 95ff for the story, including Short's reactions to his researchers' finding.

36. Jib Fowles, a media scholar, looked at the research on how influential television is, and what he discovered is that for every study that shows television has an influence, there is an equal and opposite study that shows it does not. His conclusion is that television viewers take what they want from television, which parallels Champlin's line about the "consent of the entertained." In the preface to the revised edition, Fowles describes the horrified reactions of other media scholars to the original edition: how dare he suggest that people can pretty much take television or leave it? Which would imply that ordinary people are just as sophisticated about the media, if not more so, than the media scholars. Jib Fowles, *Why Viewers Watch* (Newbury Park: Sage Publications, Revised Edition, 1992).

15. Changing Experiences

1. Gomery, *Shared Pleasures*, 89. For a good short description of the development of the multiplexes, see Gomery, 93–114.

2. For a complete history of drive-in movies, see Kerry Segrave, *Drive-In Theatres:*

A History from Their Inception in 1933 (Jefferson, North Carolina: McFarland and Company, 1992).

3. "First multiplex: an accident of design," *Variety*, March 8, 1993, 43.

4. Ibid., 50; also John Quinn, "From Tent Shows to a Nationwide Chain," *Variety*, March 8, 1993, 46.

5. Bob Howard, "Mining the Silver Screen," *Los Angeles Times*, November 19, 1997, D8.

6. On the other hand, the megaplex may only be a passing fad. In 1999 American Multi-Cinema announced its future locations would be in the twenty-screen range rather than the twenty-four-to thirty-screen range, because it found some of its thirty-screen theatres were too big for the markets they were serving. Martin Peers and Andrew Hindes, "AMC scales back plexes in reversal," *Variety*, May 24–30, 1999, 10.

7. As for *My Dinner with Andre*, Moncure says Andre's discussion in the film of people wanting to leave New York and never doing it "helped me to decide to move" from New York to Los Angeles.

8. For a nicely detailed analysis of Murch's work on the 1998 version, see Michael Sragow, "Retouching Evil," *Los Angeles New Times*, September 10–16, 1998, 13–21.

17. Eastwood

1. Pat McGilligan, in his *Clint: The Life and Legend* (London: HarperCollins Publishers, 1999), makes a case for Eastwood having created his stardom by the manipulations of his public relations team. I think Eastwood has done an excellent job of *managing* his stardom through publicity, but if audiences had not responded to his films, there would be no stardom to manage. After all, he was trying *and failing* to become a star through publicity before the Italian Westerns caught audiences' attention.

2. Richard Schickel, *Clint Eastwood* (New York: Knopf, 1996), 59. The biographical details on Eastwood in this chapter are from this book, unless otherwise indicated. Schickel indicates that Eastwood also studied drama at LACC, but McGilligan's check of the college's records shows he did not. Schickel's biography of Eastwood is a more-or-less authorized version, done with Eastwood's help. It is a positive view of Eastwood, with a few dark threads. McGilligan's, which has not as of this writing (late 1999) been published in the United States, is a more negative view, with a few light threads. The books—both of them enormously valuable—should be read together.

3. Both Crowther and Crist are quoted at greater length in Schickel, 178–79.

4. "All-Time Film Rental Champs," *Variety*, January 5, 1977, 16, 52.

5. "Big Rental Films of 1969," *Variety*, January 7, 1970, 15.

6. See Schickel, particularly 148–50.

7. "All-Time Film Rental Champs," *Variety*, January 5, 1977, 52, 48.

8. Ibid., 48.

9. Ibid.

10. The review originally appeared in the January 15, 1972, *New Yorker*, and is reprinted in her *Deeper into Movies* (New York: Bantam, 1974), 484–89, in what Schickel says is a slightly longer version (Schickel, 525).

11. "Big Rental Films of 1972," *Variety*, January 3, 1973, 7. Comparing *Dirty Harry* to Eastwood's previous films comes from Boris Zmijewsky and Lee Pfeiffer, *The Films of Clint Eastwood* (Secaucus, New Jersey: Citadel Press, 1982), 223. The list on this page is of domestic grosses of all of Eastwood's films, from the *Variety* annual of 1981. This list shows *Dirty Harry* with a gross of $17.9 million, so it added to its original grosses with reissues. The list also shows the 1969 film *Paint Your Wagon* as having domestic rentals of $14 million, which I find to be rather dubious, since "Big Rental Films of 1969," *Variety*, January 7, 1970, 15, shows rentals of only $2.2 million, and "Big Rental Films of 1970," *Variety*, January 6, 1971, 11, shows no additional rentals over $ 1 million.

12. Larry Cole, "Clint's Not Cute When He's Angry," *Village Voice*, April 24, 1976, 125.

13. Ibid., 124.

14. "Big Rental Films of 1977," *Variety*, January 4, 1978, 21.

15. Schickel, 336.

16. Both Murph.'s and Reed's reviews are excerpted in Zmijewsky and Pfeiffer, op cit., 190. One of the amusing elements of their book is their inclusion of quotes from the worst reviews of the films as well as the best ones.

17. Richard Eder, "*The Outlaw Josey Wales*," *New York Times*, August 5, 1976.

18. "Big Rental Films of 1976," *Variety*, January 5, 1977, 14.

19. "All-Time Film Rental Champs," *Variety*, January 4, 1978, 82.

20. "All-Time Film Rental Champs," *Variety*, January 13, 1982, 56.

21. "Big Rental Films of 1976," *Variety*, January 5, 1977, 14.

22. Schickel, 8–9. The rest of the details are from these pages.

23. McGilligan, 293.

24. Zmijewsky and Pfeiffer, 208.

25. Ibid., 223.

26. "Big Rental Films of 1981," *Variety*, January 13, 1982, 15.

27. Goldman, *Adventures in the Screen Trade*, 27. McGilligan, 300–01, suggests the country music soundtrack may have helped the box office as well, but I am not entirely persuaded that a music track can help a picture that does not work in some other way as well.

28. "Big Rental Films of 1978," *Variety*, January 3, 1979, 15.

29. Tom Stempel, "Let's Hear It For Eastwood's 'Strong' Women," *Los Angeles Times Sunday Calendar*, March 11, 1984, 5.

30. Both letters, *Los Angeles Times Sunday Calendar*, March 18, 1984, 99.

31. Nancy Webber, "What Eastwood Preaches Isn't Feminism," *Los Angeles Times Sunday Calendar*, April 1, 1984, 24.

32. Richard Thompson and Tim Hunter, in their "Clint Eastwood, Auteur," *Film Comment*, January/February 1978, 24–32, do mention the strong women in his films, but only in passing.

33. Norman Mailer, "All the Pirates and People," *Parade*, October 23, 1983.

34. Molly Haskell, "Clint Eastwood," *Playgirl*, November 1985, 12–14.

35. John Vincour, "Clint Eastwood, Seriously," *New York Times Magazine*, February 24, 1985, 15–21, 24–30. The comment about *Josey Wales* is on 16, the reference to him

as a "feminist" is on 18. It was typical, by the way, that I was not mentioned by name. All the references I have found have either said "someone" or "the *Los Angeles Times.*" It was not until Richard Schickel's 1996 biography that I was mentioned by name.

36. Paul Smith, *Clint Eastwood: A Cultural Production* (Minneapolis: University of Minnesota Press, 1993). This is a fascinating look at how public perceptions of a star are made, not only by his films, but by the writing about him. He does not get into first-hand audience accounts as I do, but he looks with depth and perception at what has been written about Eastwood and how he is viewed.

37. Schickel, 386–87.

38. McGilligan disagrees and he goes into detail about the attempts by Eastwood and Warners to manipulate opinion (470–72). But as we saw in chapter 14, manipulation will not work unless the film creates some resonance with audiences, which *Unforgiven* did.

39. "Top Rental Films For 1992," *Variety*, January 11, 1993, 22.

40. "All-Time B. O. Rental Champions," *Variety*, February 21–27, 1994, 22.

41. And with limited success. The studio stores are having financial problems. Richard Morgan, "Retail rut hits studio store glut," *Variety*, March 22–28, 1999, 7, 8.

A Concluding Thought or Two

1. Jib Fowles, in *Why Viewers Watch*, quotes from research by Harvard social scientist Raymond Bauer into Russian attitudes about the media, which shows that Russians took what they needed from the Soviet media and did not believe the rest of it (62). Why do we think we are that different from the Russians?

2. For a brief descriptions of one of the classic examples of this, see Thomas Bohn, *An Historical and Descriptive Analysis of the "Why We Fight" Series* (New York: Arno Press, 1977), particularly pp. 112–15, where he discusses the research the Army did to see what the reactions of the soldiers were in World War II to Frank Capra's propaganda series, *Why We Fight*. Basically the films did not change anybody's opinions. One exception to this is found in the research the government did in the thirties on two government-sponsored documentaries, *The Plow That Broke the Plains* (1936) and *The River* (1937), which showed they did shift opinions. Austin, *Immediate Seating*, 104.

3. For a summary of the case, see Josh Young, "Devil's Advocate," *Entertainment Weekly*, August 6, 1999, 27.

4. Kevin Brownlow, *Behind the Mask of Innocence: Sex, Violence, Crime: Films of Social Conscience in the Silent Era* (New York: Alfred A. Knopf, 1990).

5. Christopher Stern, "Hollywood Escapes Latest Vote on Violence," *Variety*, June 21–27, 1999, 8.

6. In their *Film History: An Introduction* (New York: McGraw-Hill, 1994), and in Janet Staiger's *The Classical Hollywood Cinema: Film Style & Mode of Production to 1960* (New York: Columbia University Press, 1985).

7. Neal Gabler, *Life the Movie: How Entertainment Conquered Reality* (New York: Alfred A. Knopf, 1998).

8. Even a social scientist liked Denis McQuail can admit that "it is plausible to

suppose that the media need their audience more than audiences need their media." McQuail, 14.

   9. Frederick Wiseman, at the Los Angeles International Film Exposition, 1976.

   10. Quoted in Eric Harrison, "Hollywood: Ground Zero: The entertainment industry looks inward and speaks out on its products and their relationship to real-life violence," *Los Angeles Times*, May 1, 1999, 12.

Index